Missions OF Love

Volume 7

Ema Toyama

Character

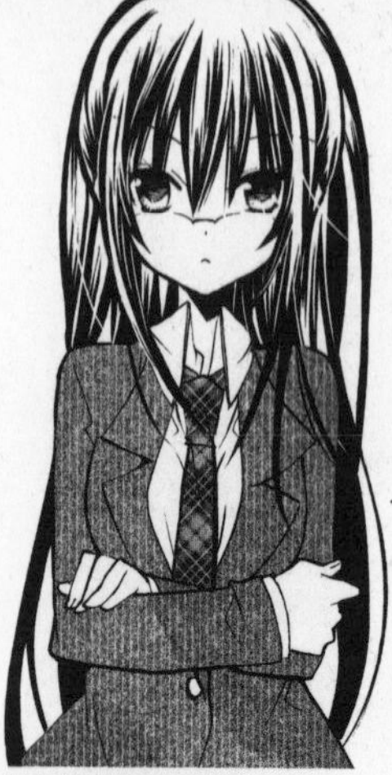

Favorite fragrance: yuzu.

Yukina Himuro

A third-year junior high student who strikes terror in the hearts of all around her with her piercing gaze, feared as the "Absolute Zero Snow Woman." Only Akira knows that she is also the popular cell phone novelist Yupina.

Shigure Kitami

The ever-popular, yet black-hearted, student body president. He made a game of charming all the girls and making them confess their love to him, then writing it all down in his student notebook, but Yukina discovered his secret!

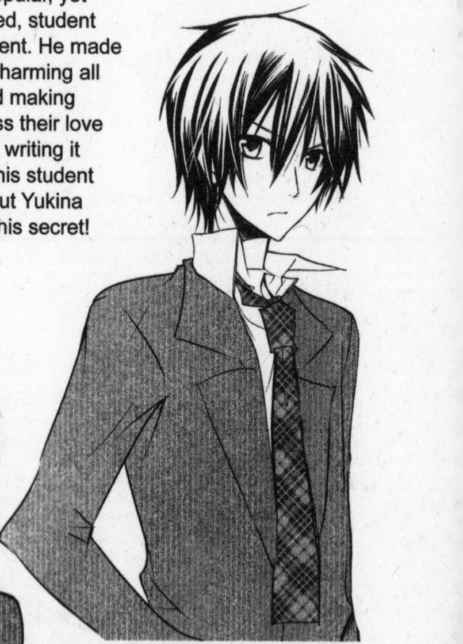

Favorite fragrance: bergamot.

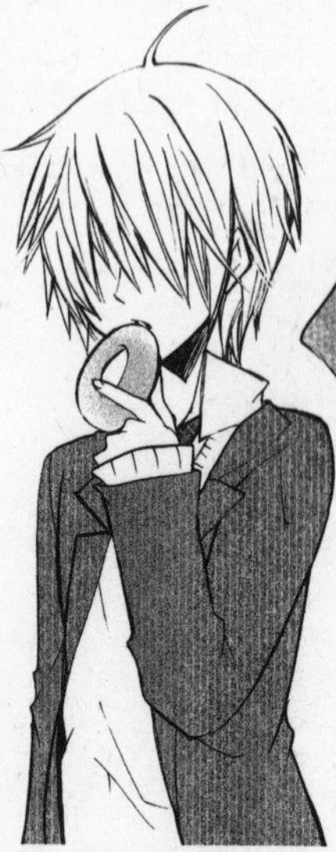

Favorite fragrance: peppermint.

Akira Shimotsuki

Yukina's cousin and fellow student. He loves to eat. As Yukina's confidant, he can always be found nearby, watching over her. There's a good-looking face hiding behind that hair.

ne!

It is time for love.
Secret cell phone novelist vs. the most popular boy in school.
A mission of love for absolute servitude.

Story

Yukina has been blackmailing Shigure into helping her experience romance, but with Akira confessing his love and Mami coming back to school, their relationship takes a step back for every step forward. Shigure's announcement that he will cure Yukina's weakness brings them closer together, but things take an unexpected turn when Mami tells Shigure how she really feels about him.

Mami Mizuno

A childhood friend of Shigure's. A sickly girl, she had been taking time off from school, but now she has returned. The teachers love her, and she's very popular with the boys. She's a beautiful young girl who always wears a smile, but....

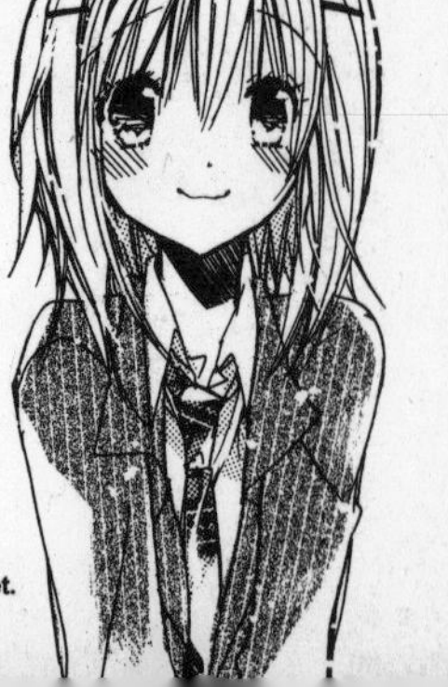

Favorite fragrance: orange sweet.

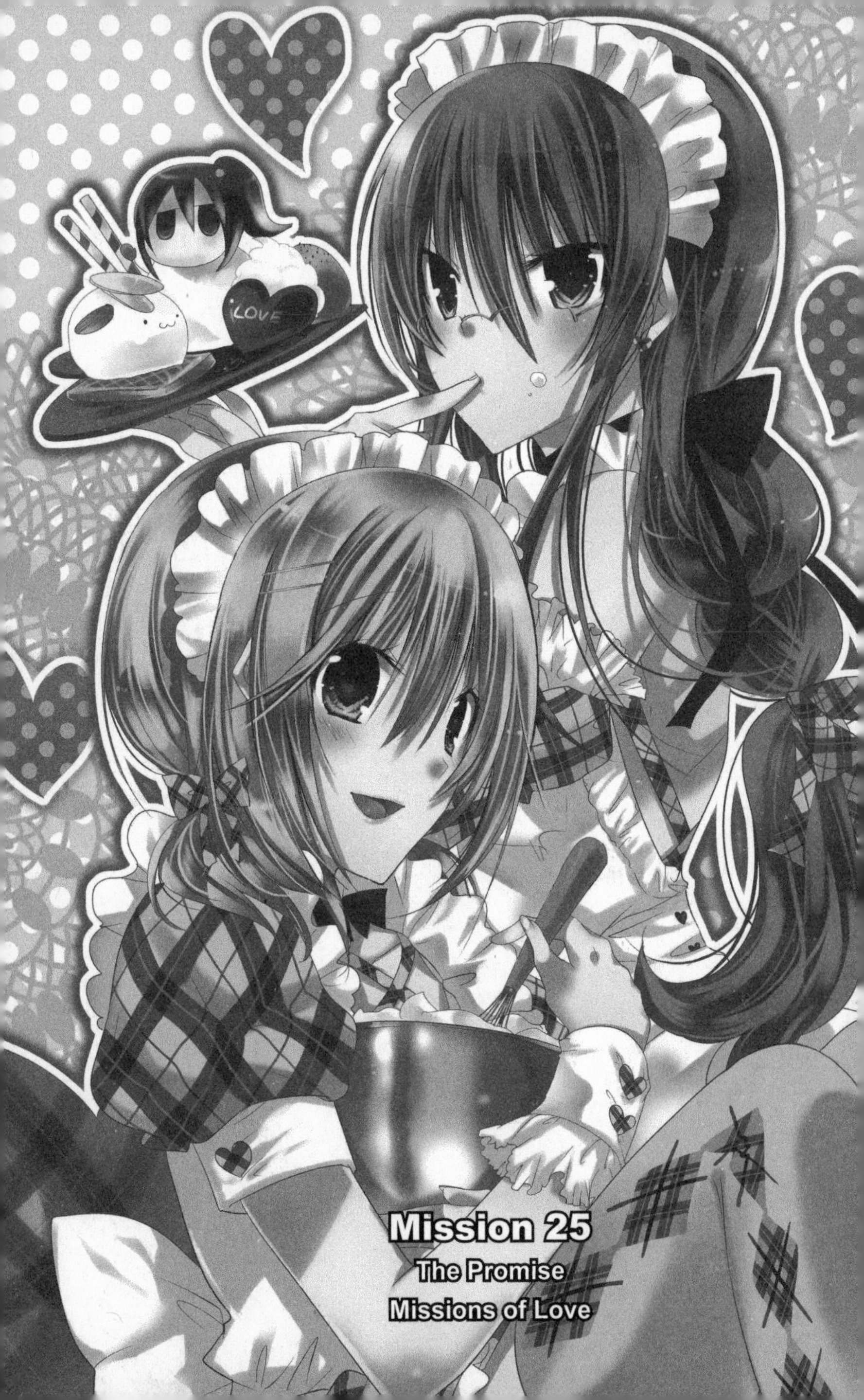
LOVE

Mission 25
The Promise
Missions of Love

Missions of Love

It is time for love.
Secret cell phone
novelist vs. the most
popular boy in school.
A mission of love for
absolute servitude.

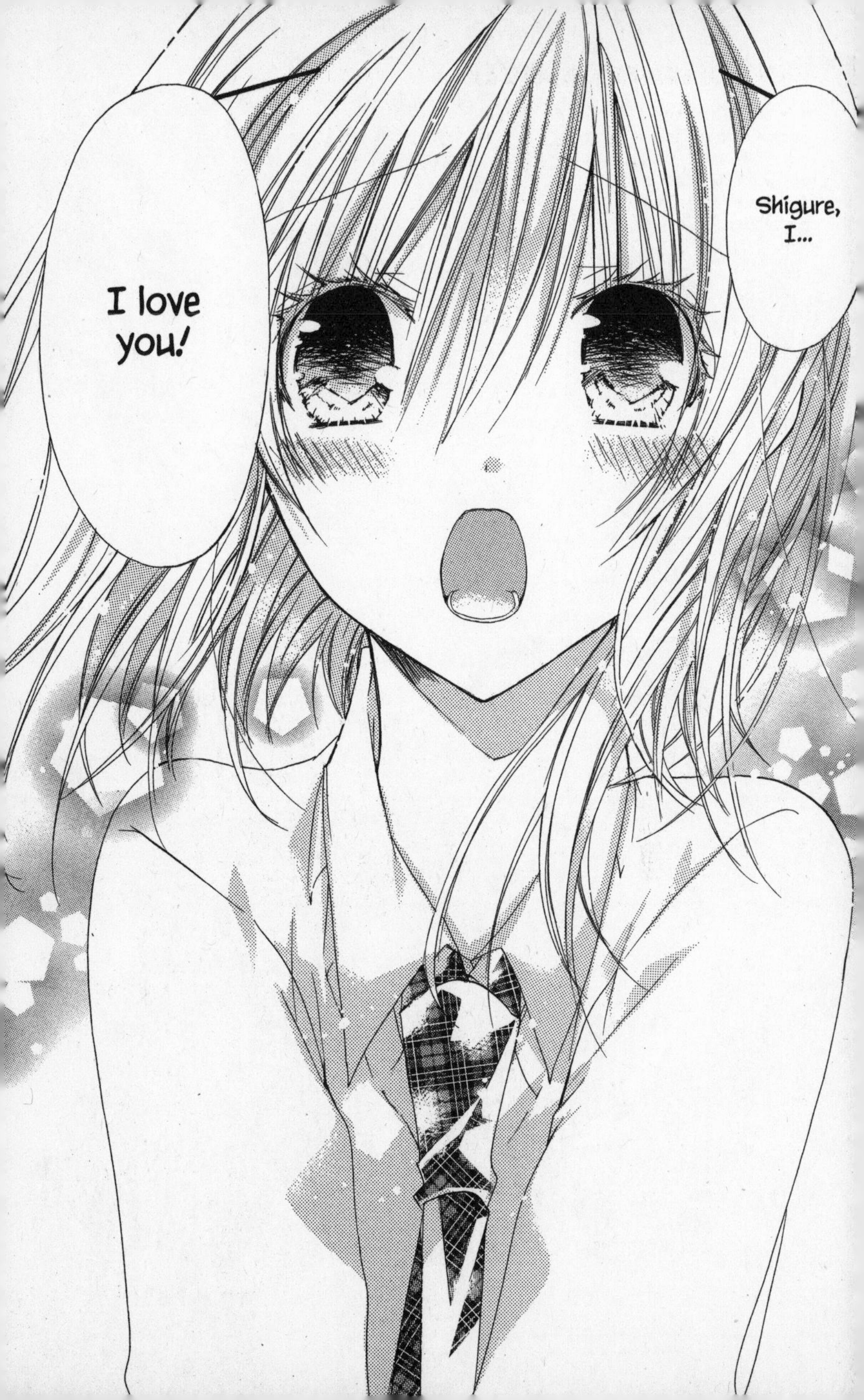
Shigure, I...
I love you!

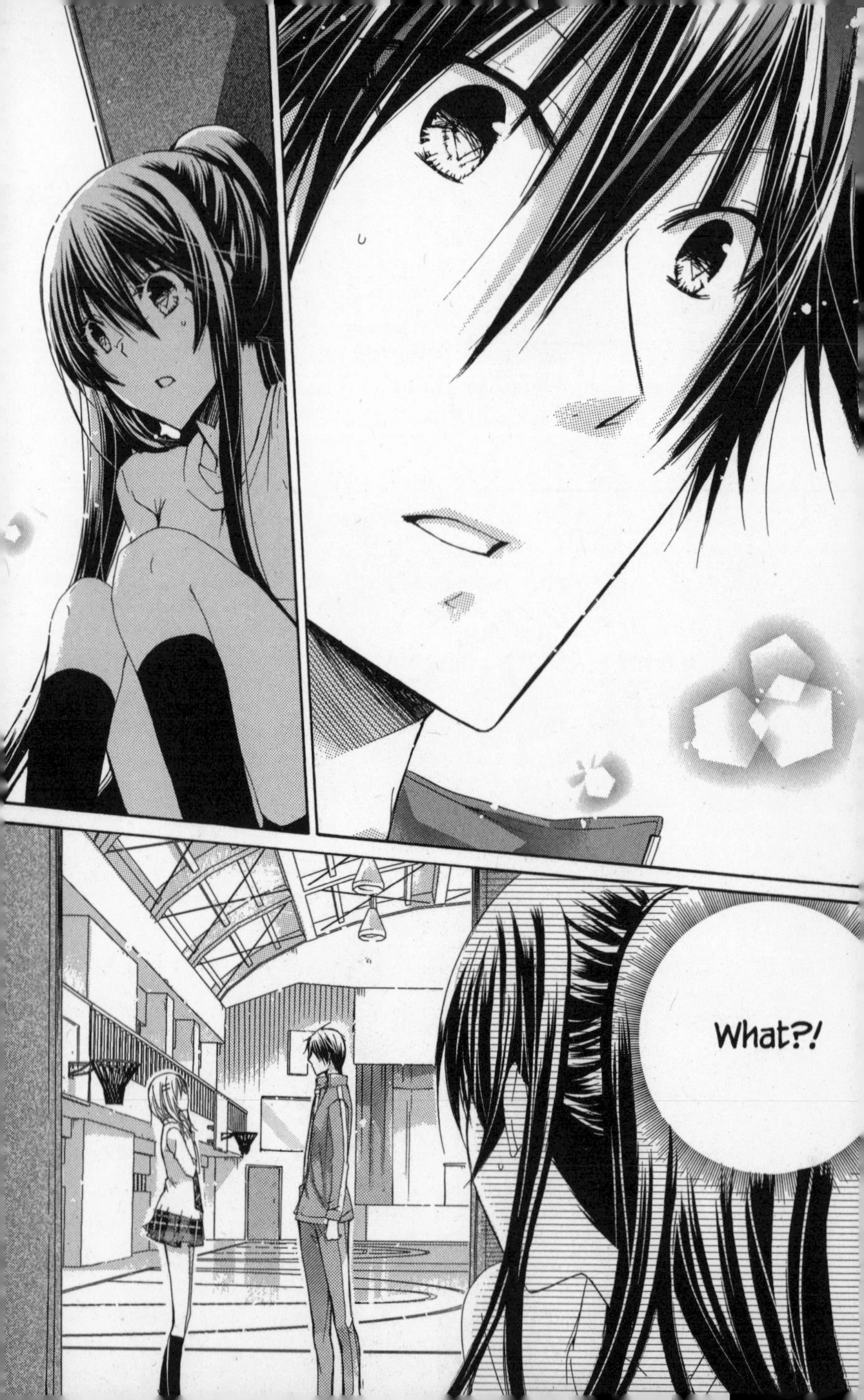
What?!

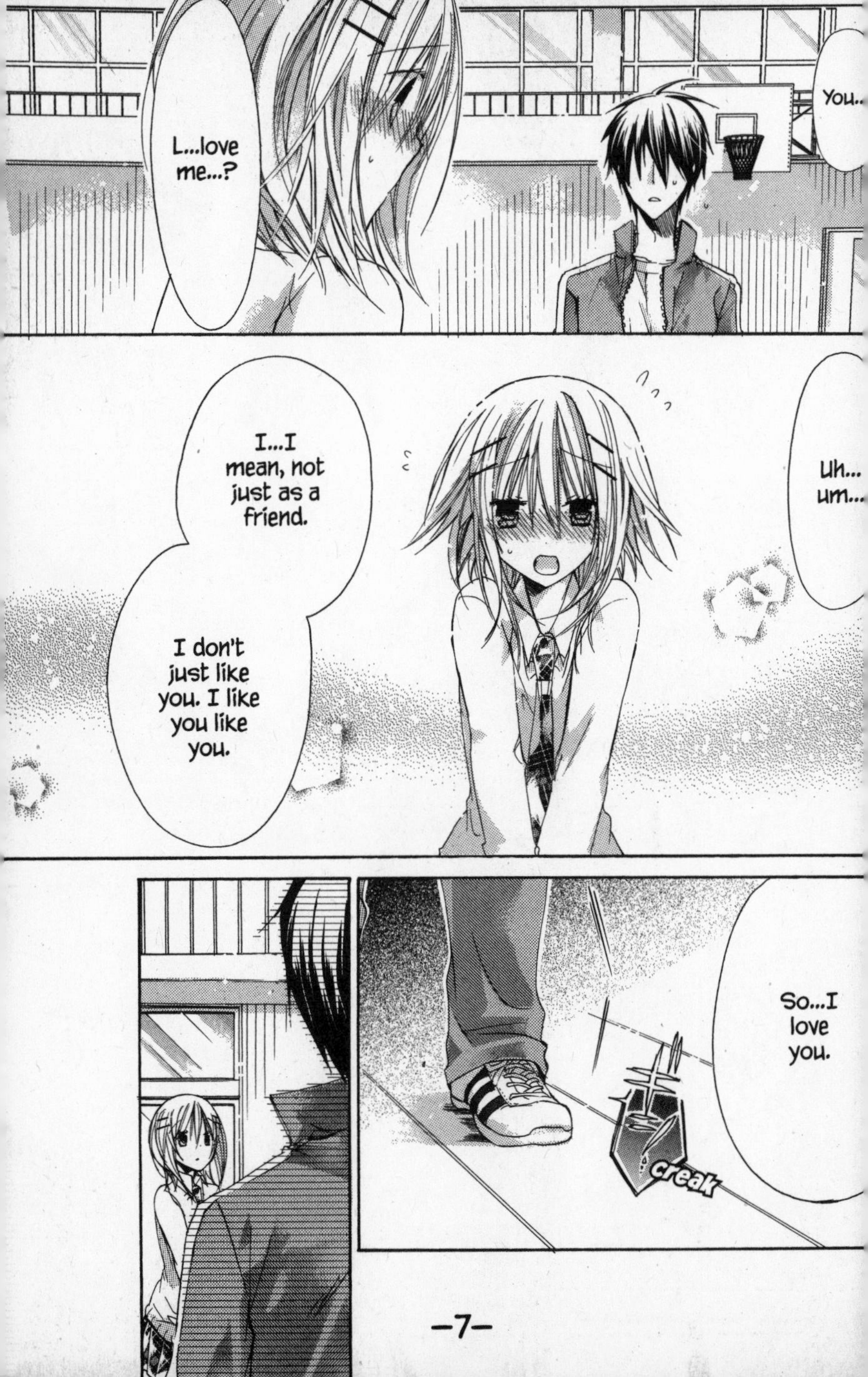
You...
L...love me...?
Uh... um...
I...I mean, not just as a friend.
I don't just like you. I like you like you.
So...I love you.
creak

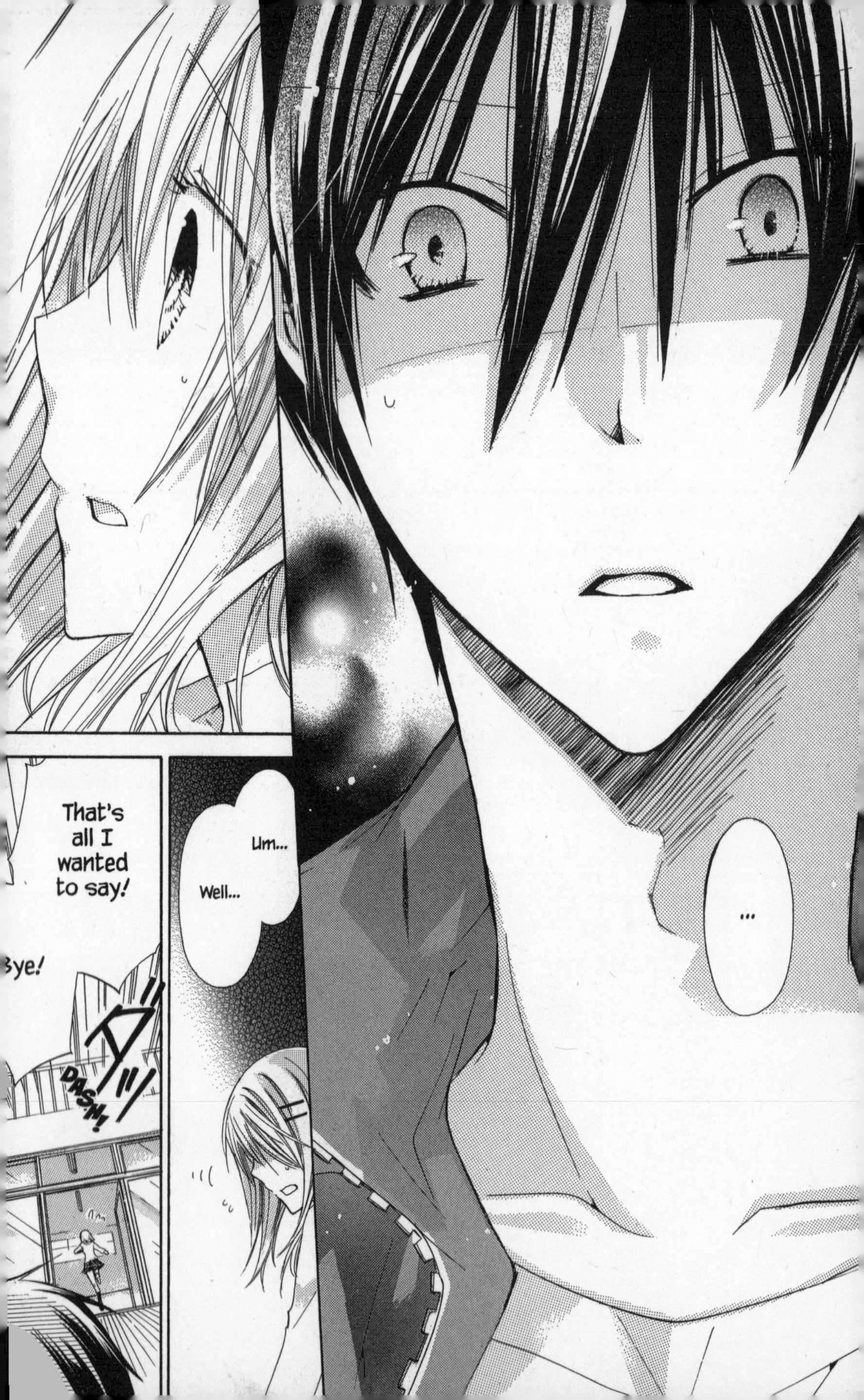
...
Um...
Well...
That's all I wanted to say!
Bye!
DASH!

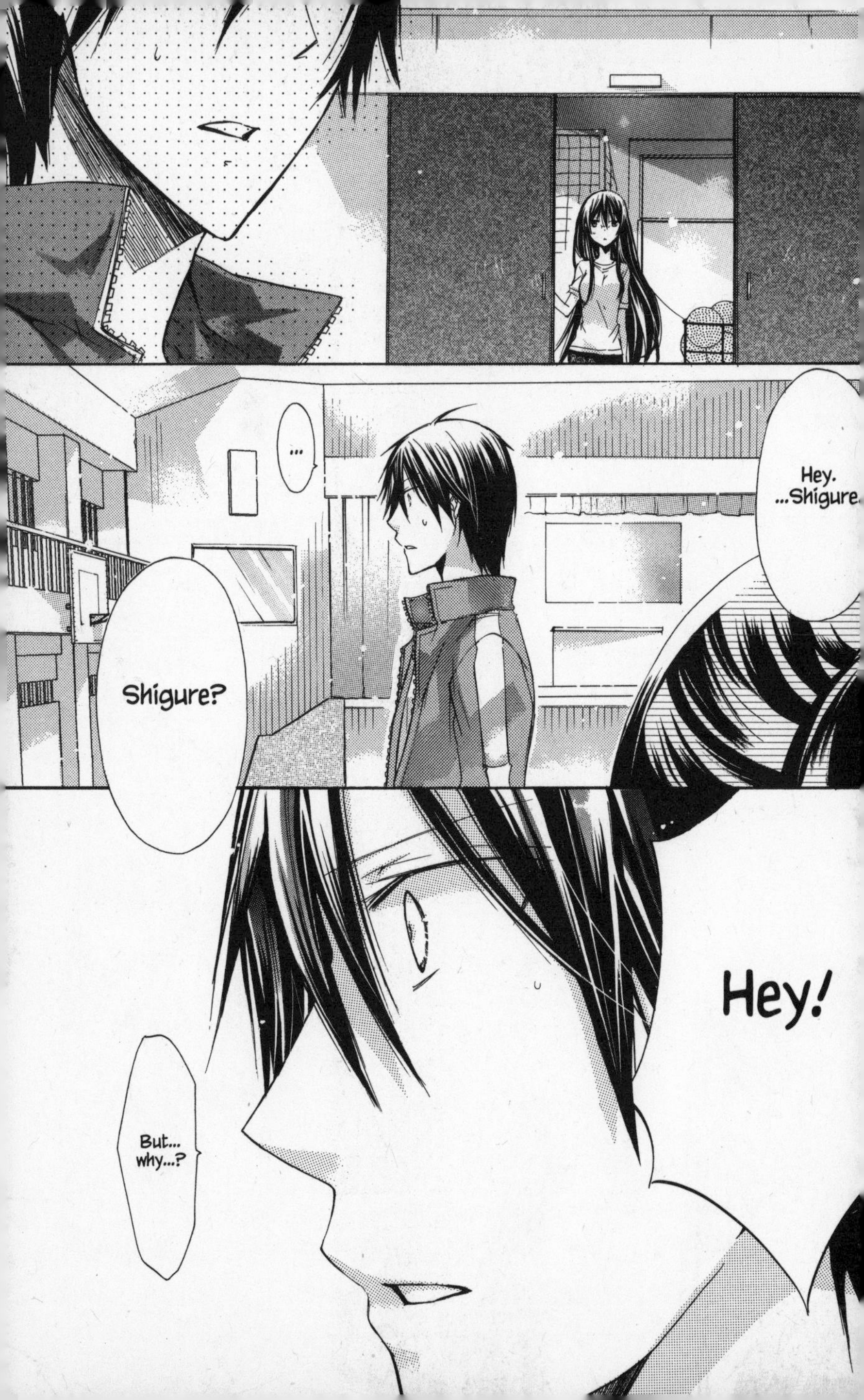
Hey.
...Shigure.
...
Shigure?
Hey!
But...
why...?

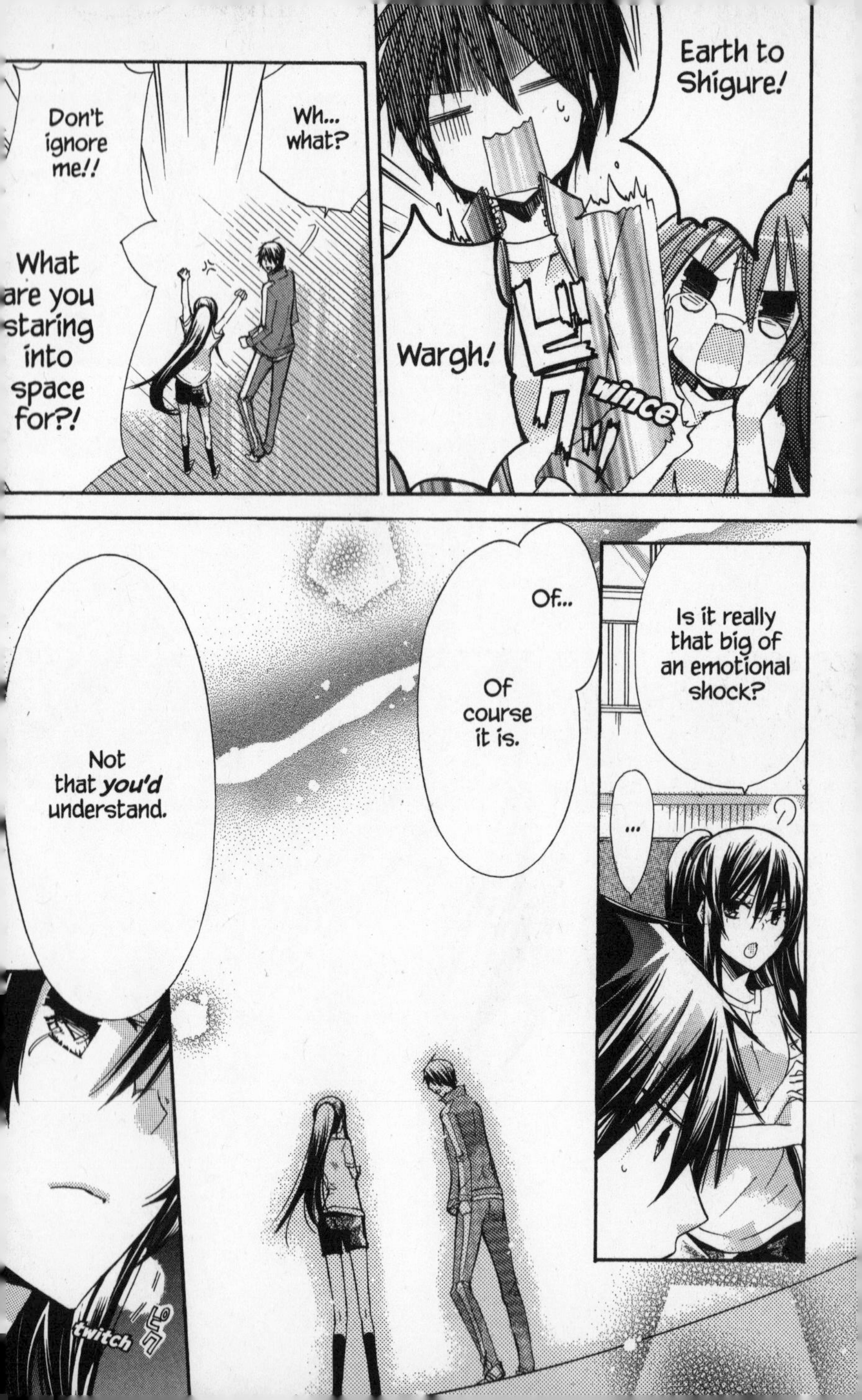
Earth to Shigure!
Wargh!
wince
Wh... what?
Don't ignore me!!
What are you staring into space for?!
Is it really that big of an emotional shock?
...
Of...
Of course it is.
Not that *you'd* understand.
twitch

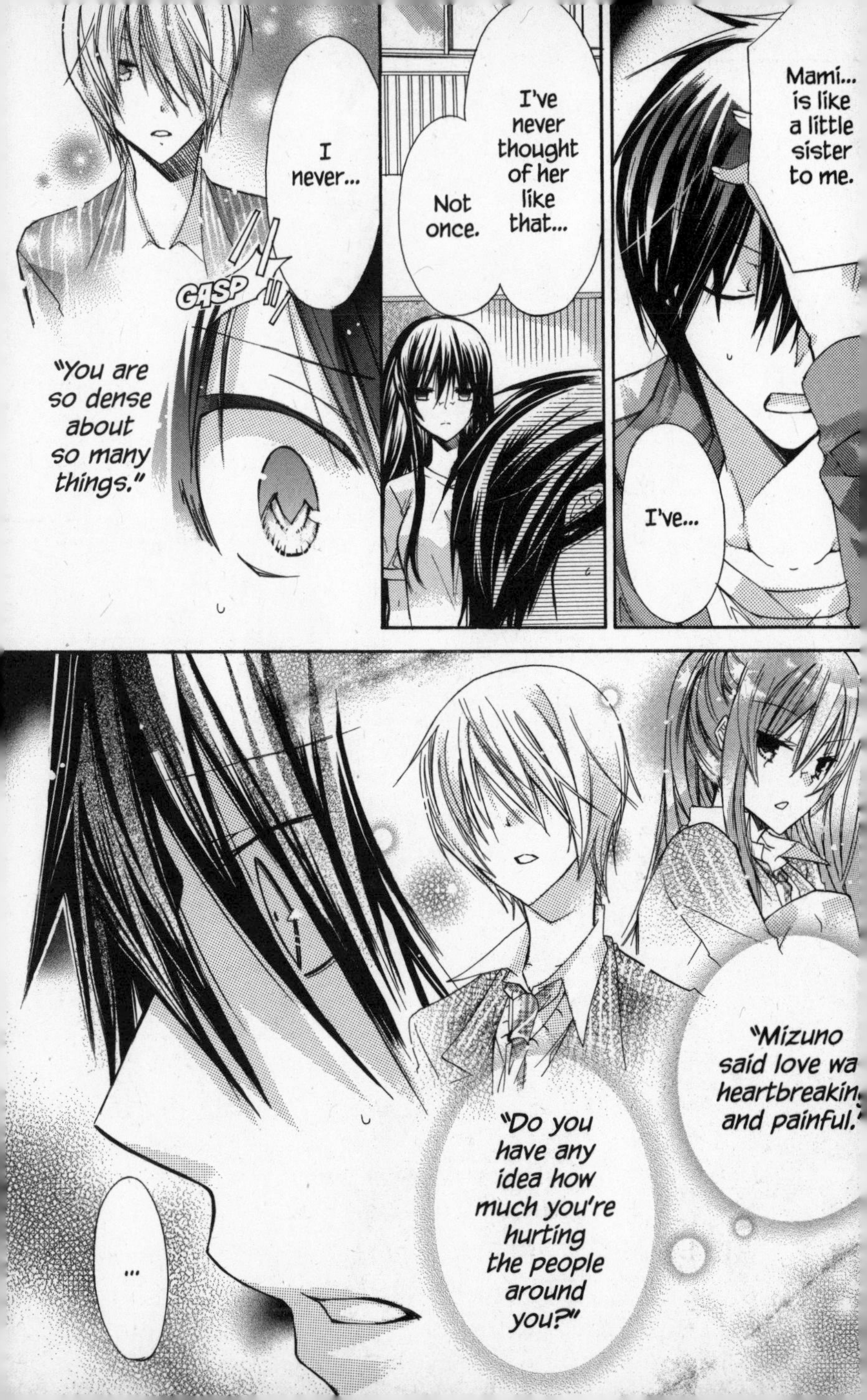
Mami... is like a little sister to me.
I've...
I've never thought of her like that...
Not once.
I never...
GASP
"You are so dense about so many things."
"Mizuno said love wa heartbreakin and painful."
"Do you have any idea how much you're hurting the people around you?"
...

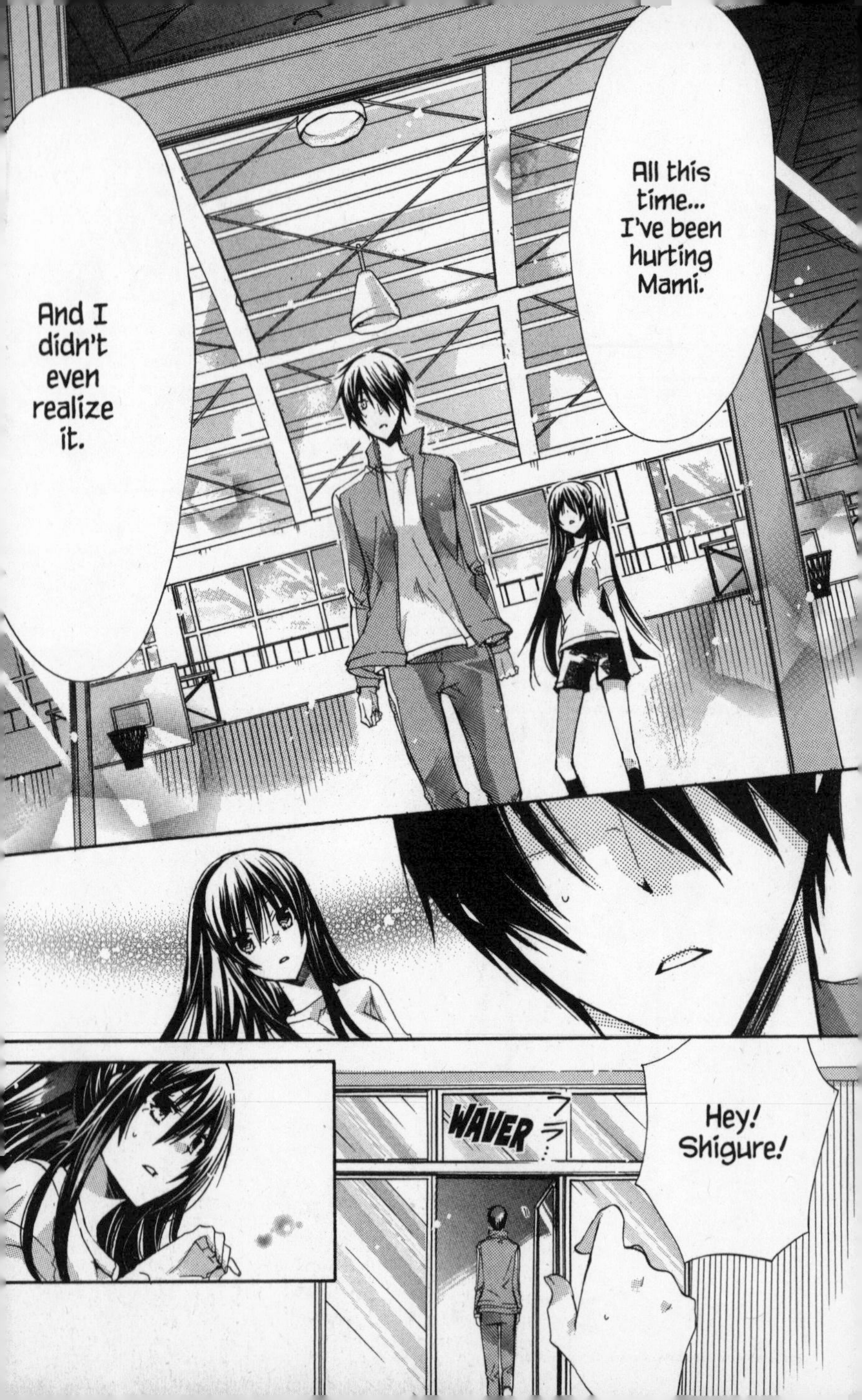
All this time... I've been hurting Mami.
And I didn't even realize it.
Hey! Shigure!
WAVER

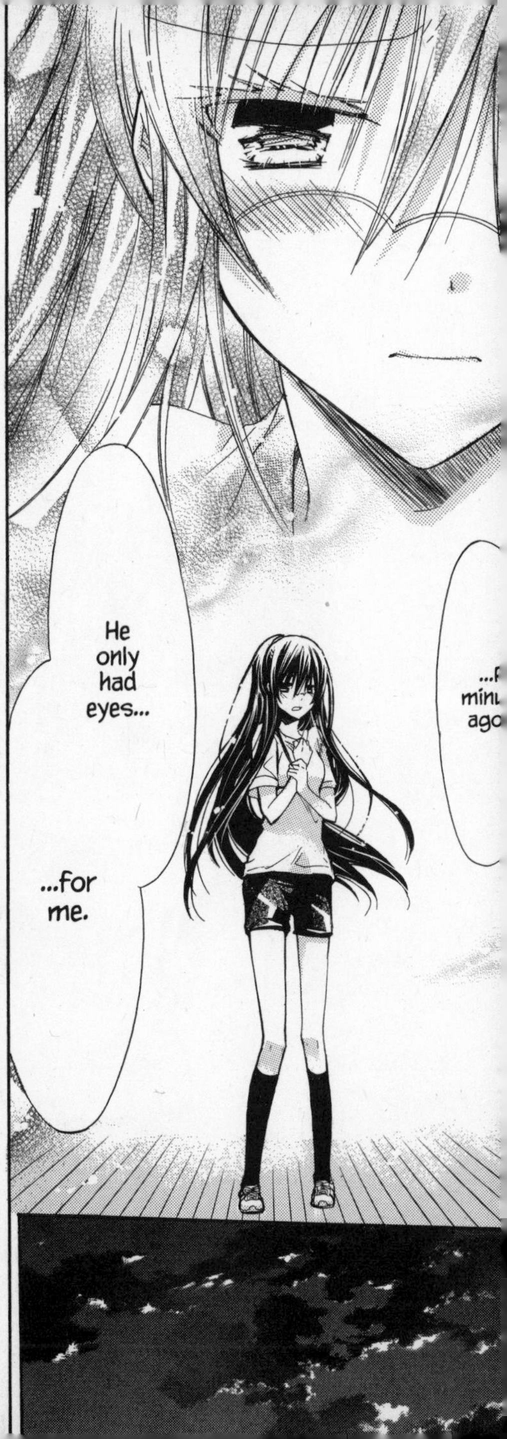
ago
He only had eyes...
...for me.

Previously

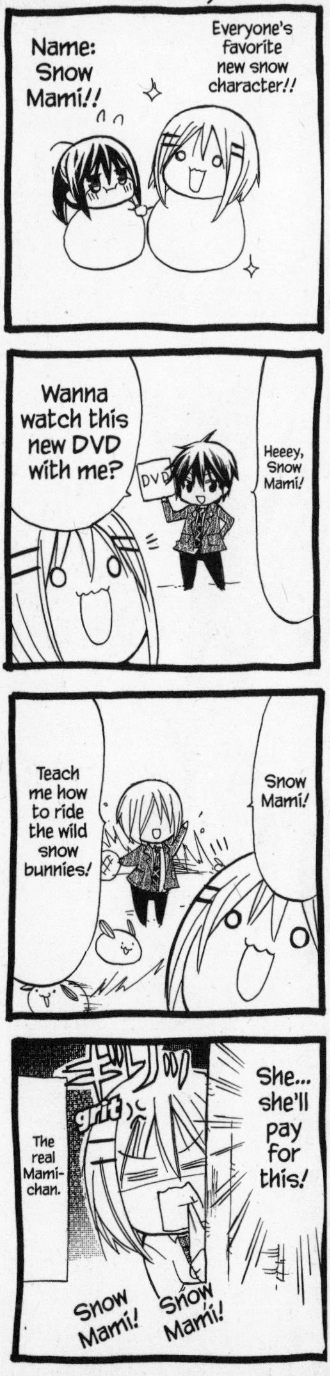
Everyone's favorite new snow character!!
Name: Snow Mami!!
Heeey, Snow Mami!
Wanna watch this new DVD with me?
DVD
Snow Mami!
Teach me how to ride the wild snow bunnies!
She... she'll pay for this!
grit
The real Mami-chan.
Snow Mami!
Snow Mami!

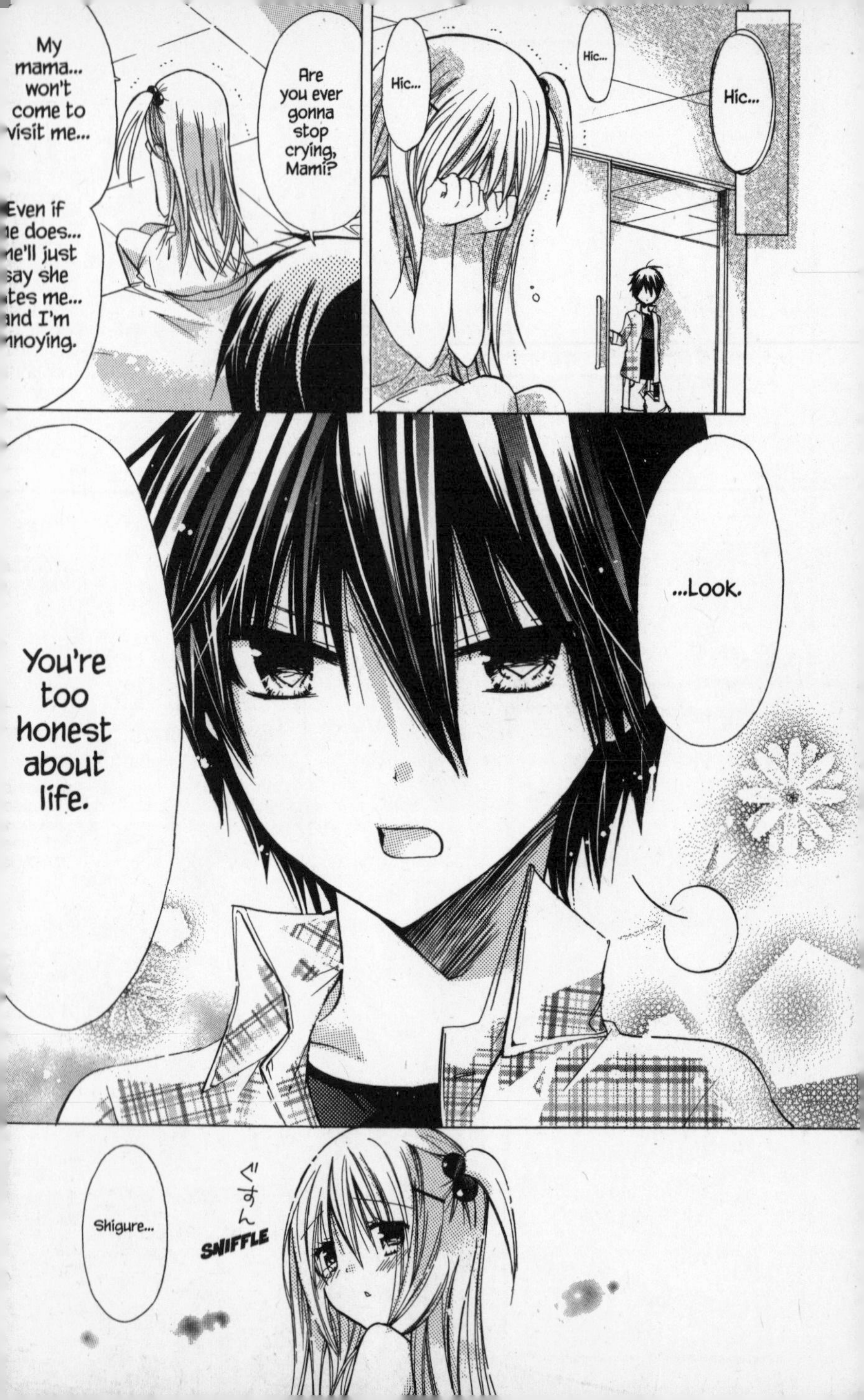
Hic...
Hic...
Hic...
Are you ever gonna stop crying, Mami?
My mama... won't come to visit me...
Even if
e does...
e'll just
ay she
tes me...
nd I'm
noying.
...Look.
You're too honest about life.
ぐすん
SNIFFLE
Shigure...

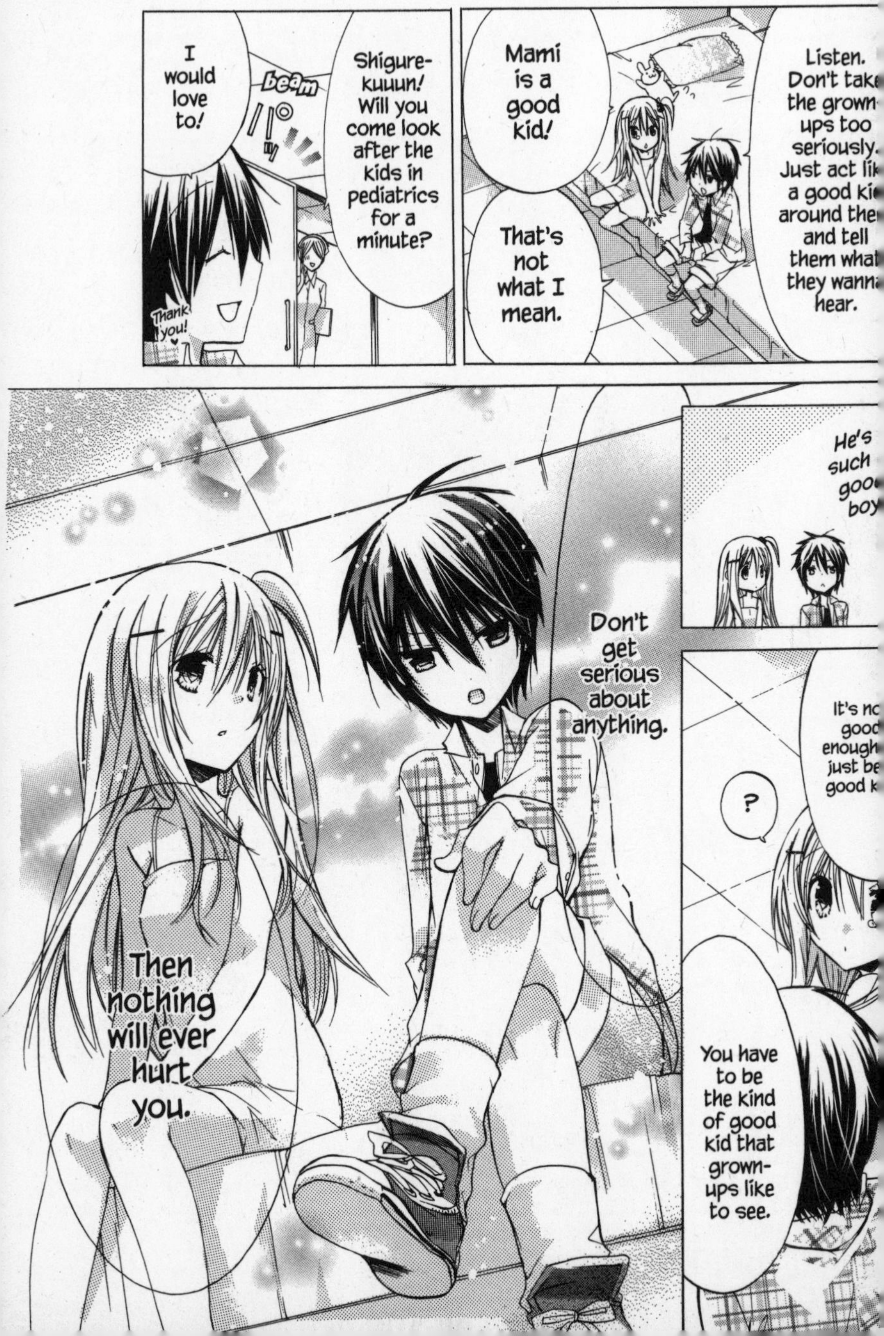
Listen. Don't tak the grown-ups too seriously. Just act li a good ki around the and tell them wha they wann hear.
Mami is a good kid!
That's not what I mean.
Shigure-kuuun! Will you come look after the kids in pediatrics for a minute?
beam
I would love to!
Thank you! ♥
He's such goo boy
It's no good enough just be good k
?
You have to be the kind of good kid that grown-ups like to see.
Don't get serious about anything.
Then nothing will ever hurt you.

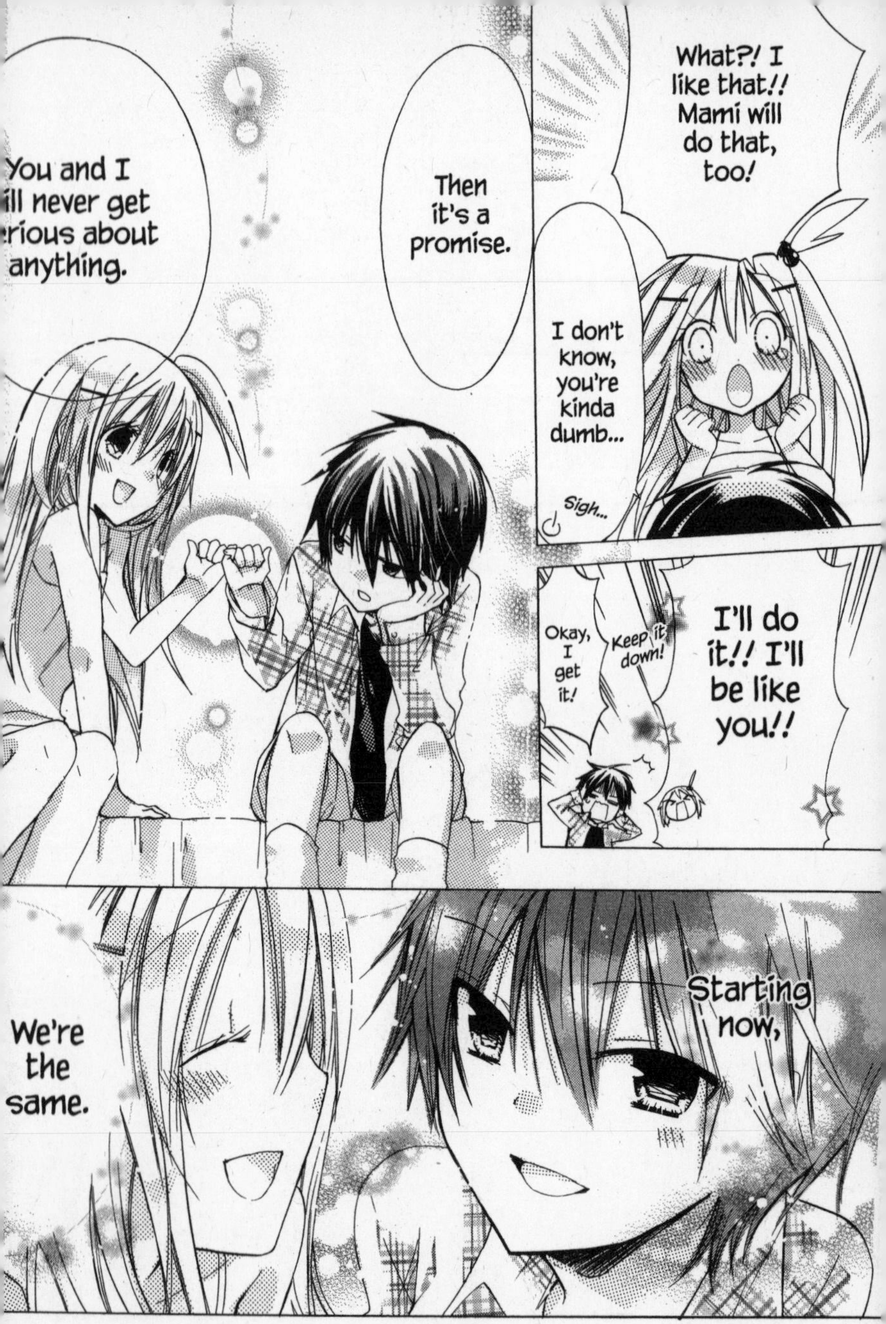

What?! I like that!! Mami will do that, too!
I don't know, you're kinda dumb...
Sigh...
I'll do it!! I'll be like you!!
Keep it down!
Okay, I get it!
Then it's a promise.
You and I ill never get rious about anything.
Starting now,
We're the same.

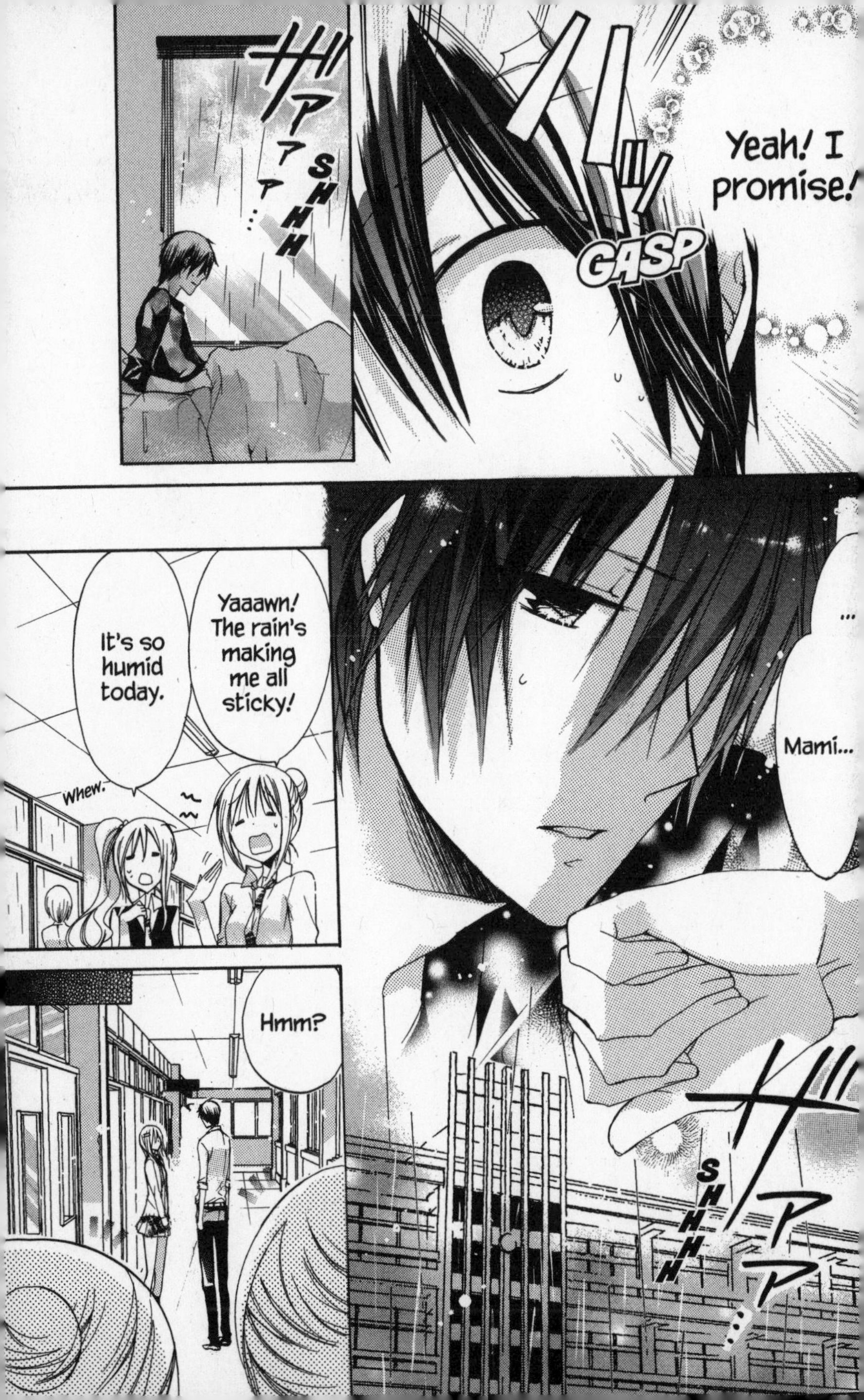
Yeah! I promise!
GASP
ザァァァ…
SHHHH
...
Mami...
ザァァ…
SHHHH
Yaaawn! The rain's making me all sticky!
It's so humid today.
Whew.
Hmm?

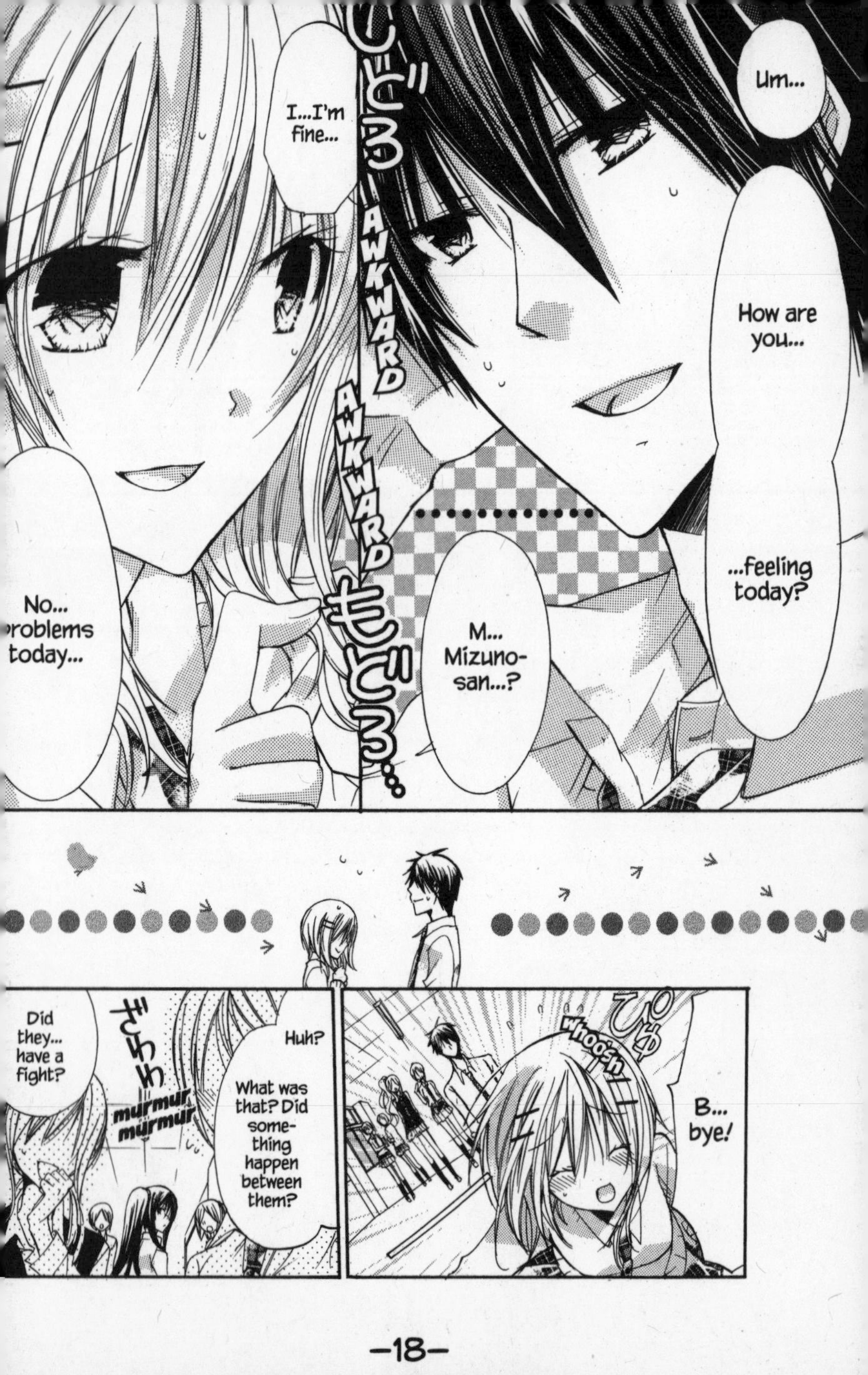
Um...
How are you...
...feeling today?
M... Mizuno-san...?
AWKWARD AWKWARD
I...I'm fine...
No... problems today...
whoosh
B... bye!
Huh?
What was that? Did something happen between them?
murmur murmur
Did they... have a fight?

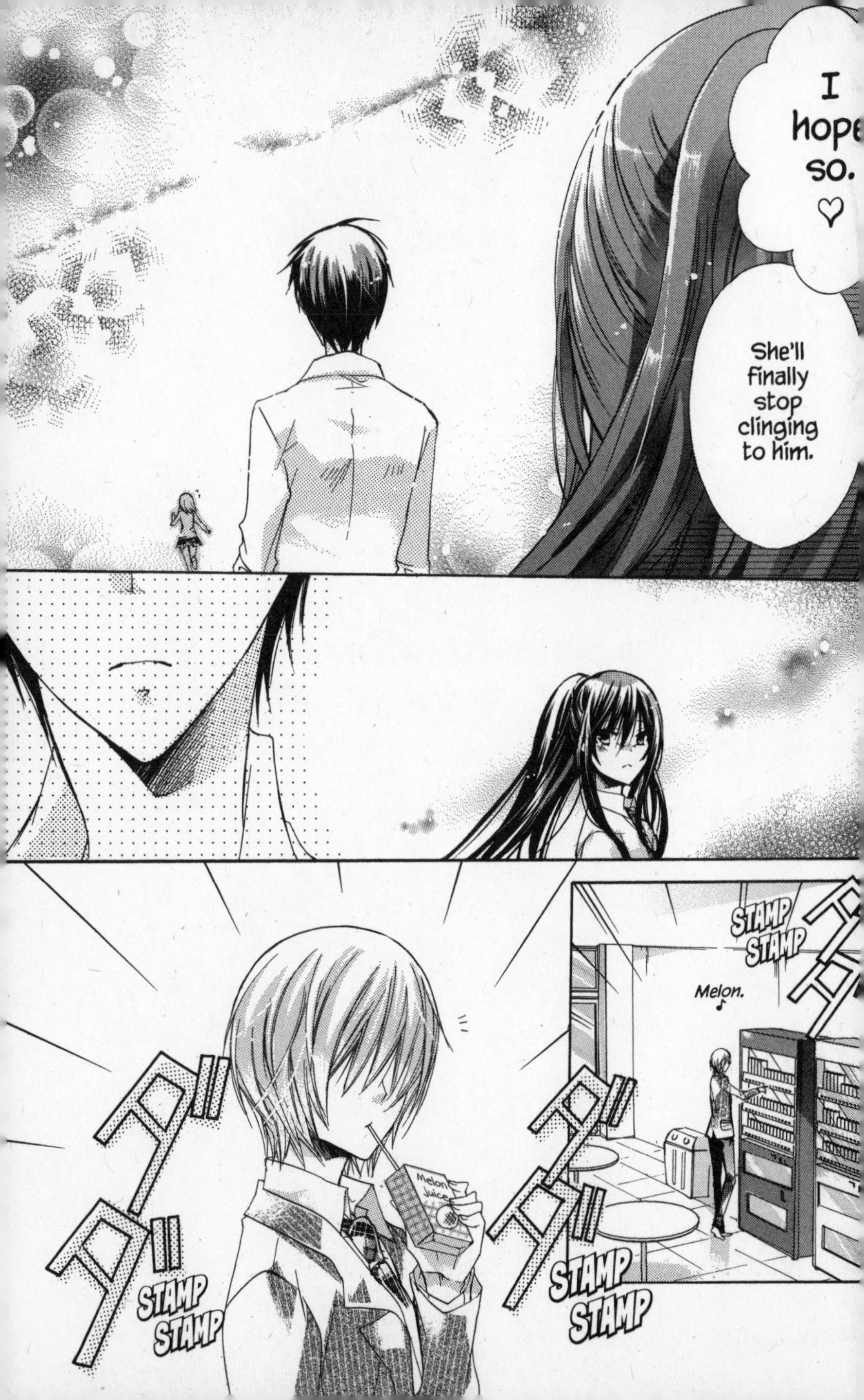
I hope so. ♡
She'll finally stop clinging to him.
STAMP STAMP
Melon. ♪
STAMP STAMP
Melon Juice
STAMP STAMP

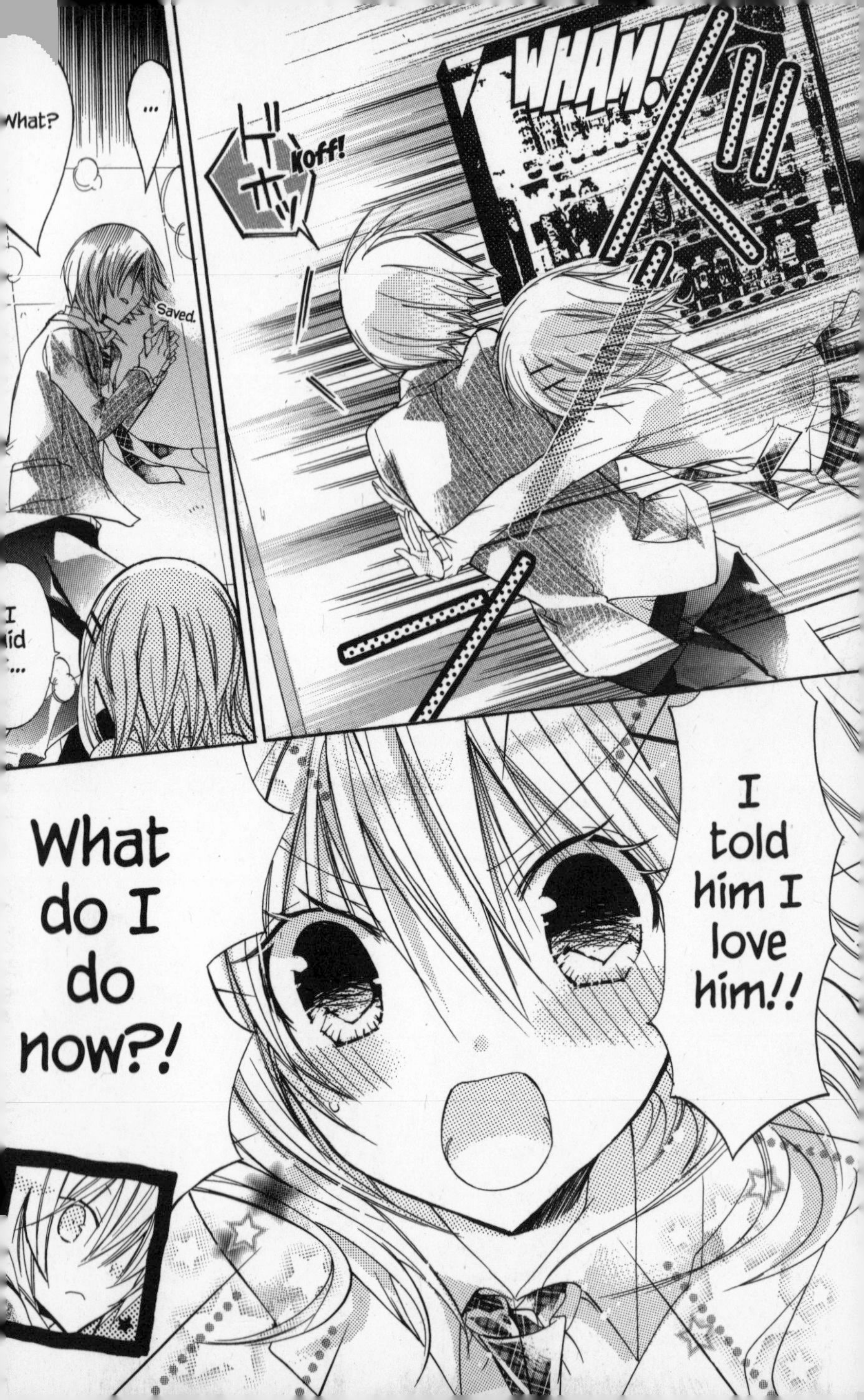
WHAM!
ゲホッ
Koff!
...
What?
Saved.
I
id
....
I told him I love him!!
What do I do now?!

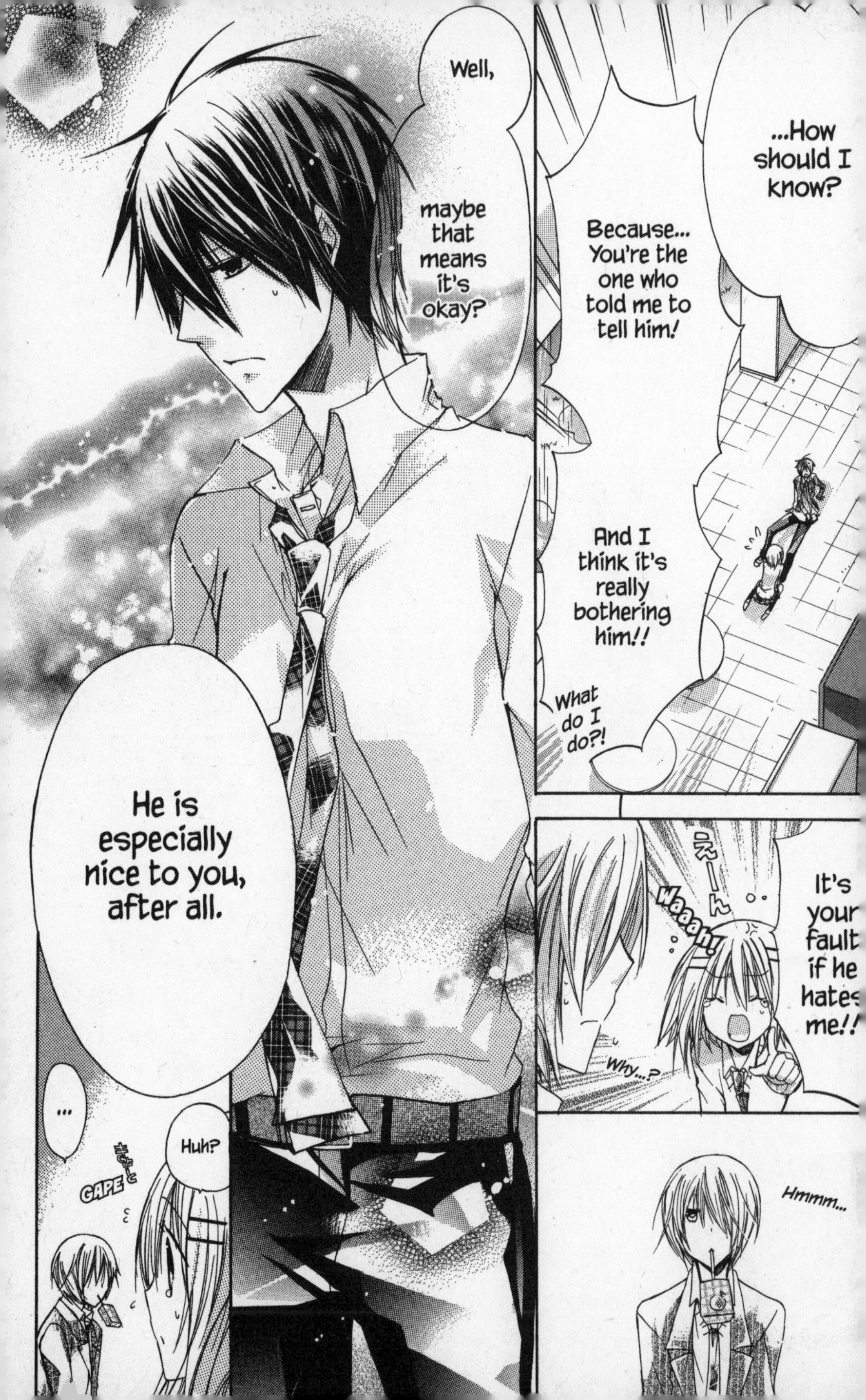
...How should I know?
Because... You're the one who told me to tell him!
And I think it's really bothering him!!
What do I do?!
It's your fault if he hates me!!
Waaah!
Why...?
Hmmm...
Well,
maybe that means it's okay?
He is especially nice to you, after all.
...
Huh?
GAPE

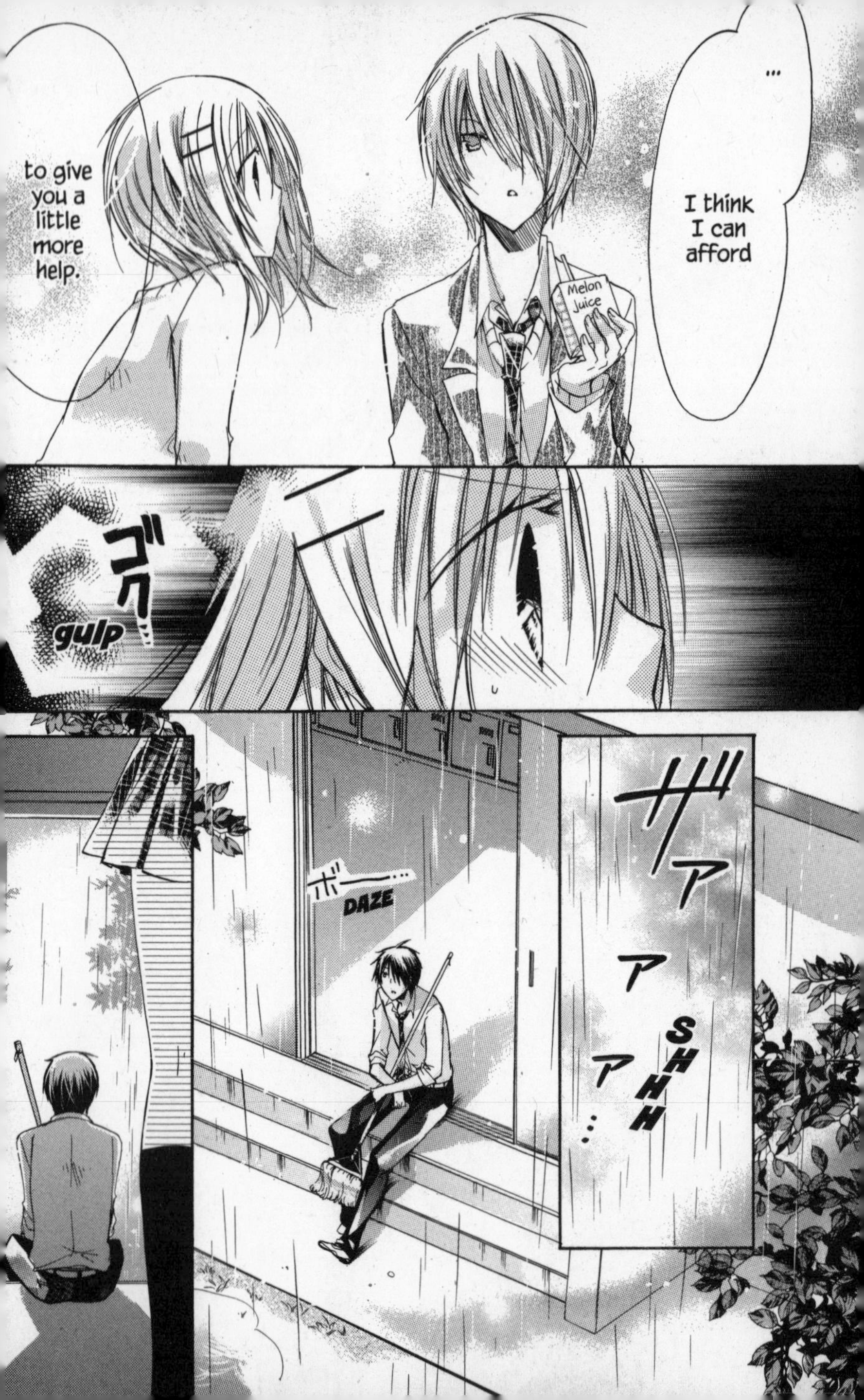
...
I think I can afford
to give you a little more help.
Melon Juice
ゴク…
gulp
ザァァァ…
SHHHH
ボー…
DAZE

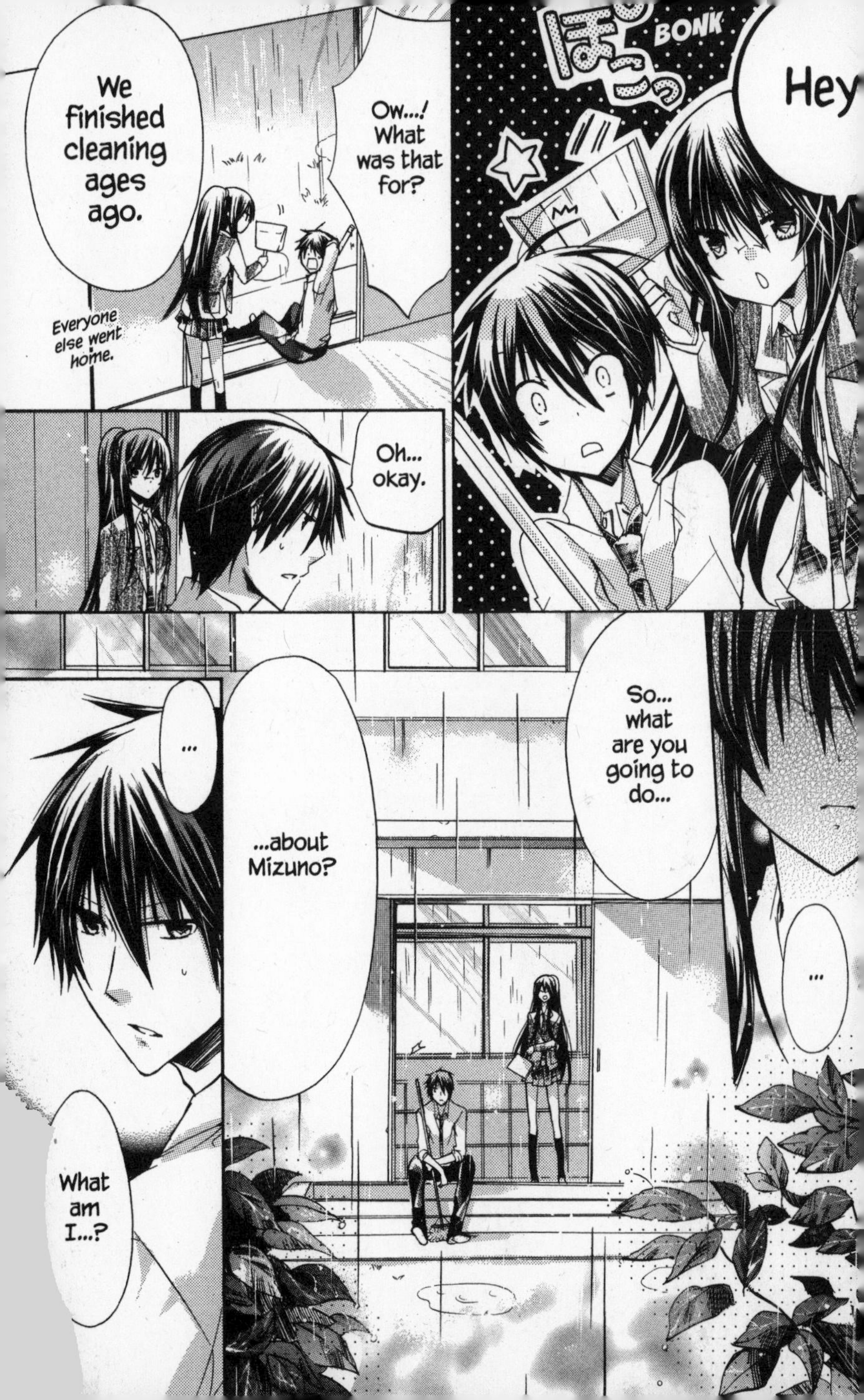
ぽこっ
BONK
Hey
Ow...! What was that for?
We finished cleaning ages ago.
Everyone else went home.
Oh... okay.
So... what are you going to do...
...
...about Mizuno?
...
What am I...?

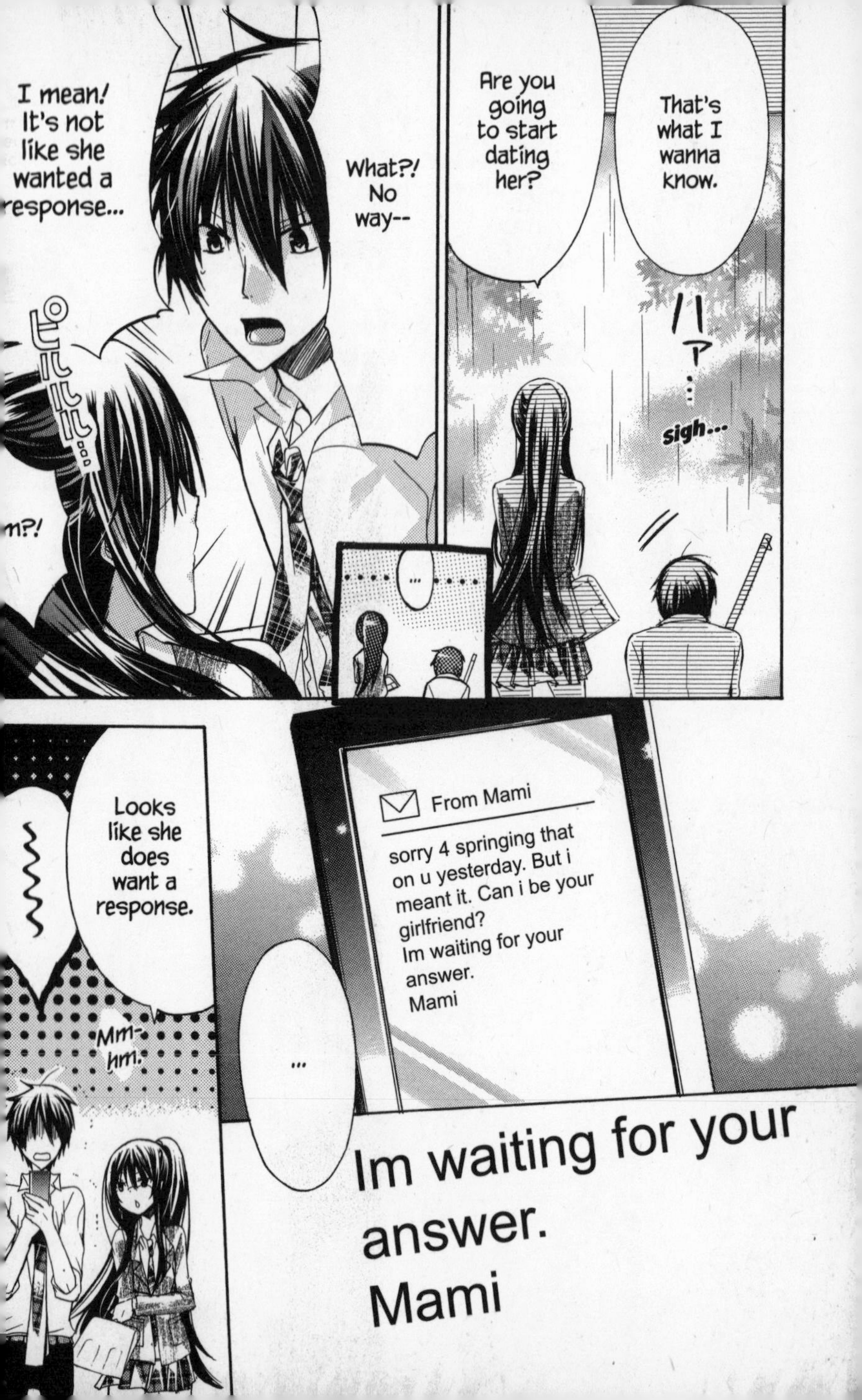
That's what I wanna know.
Are you going to start dating her?
ハア…
sigh...
...
What?! No way--
I mean! It's not like she wanted a response...
ピルルル…
m?!
From Mami
sorry 4 springing that on u yesterday. But i meant it. Can i be your girlfriend?
Im waiting for your answer.
Mami
...
Im waiting for your answer.
Mami
Looks like she does want a response.
Mm-hm.

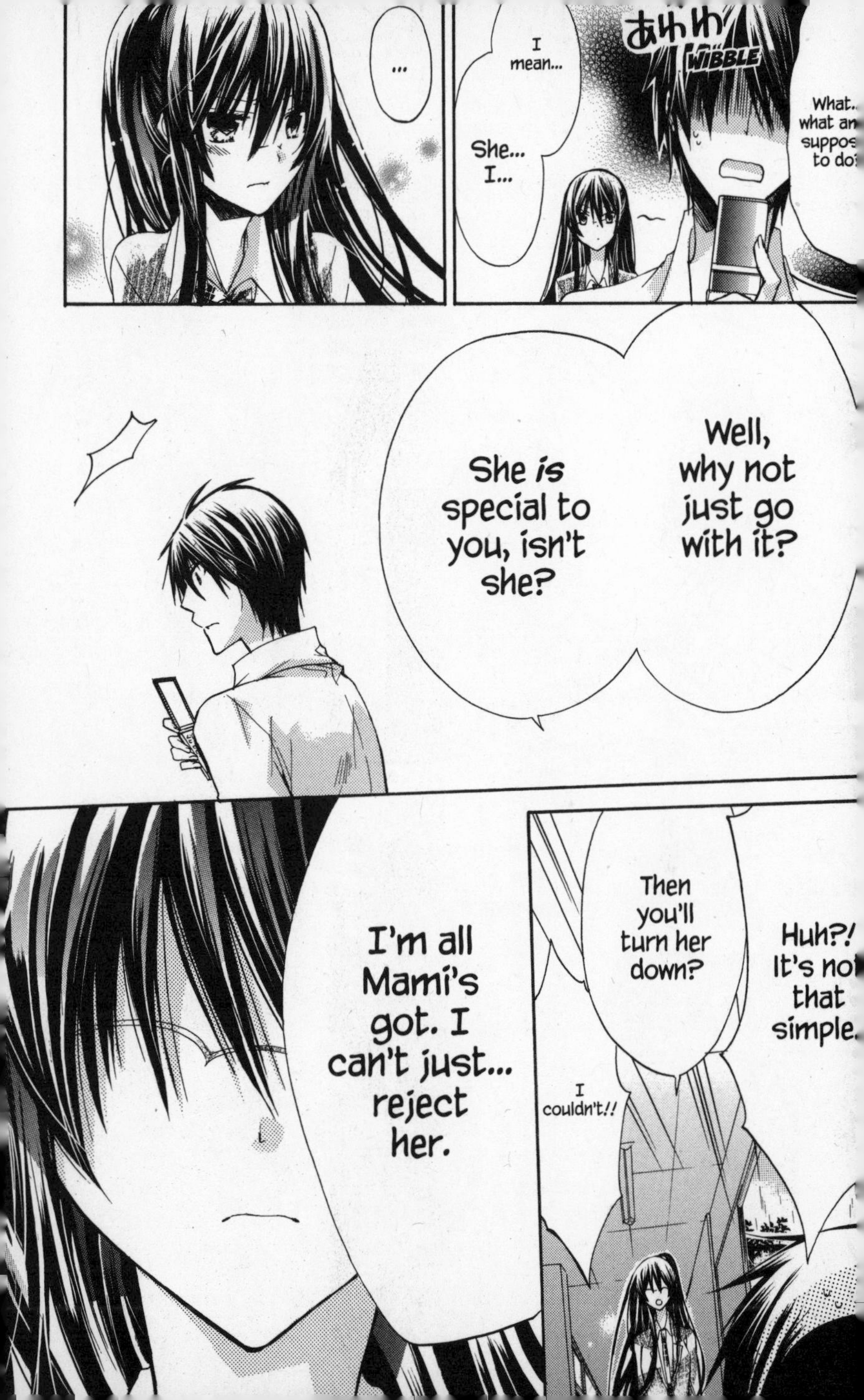
あわわ
WIBBLE
What..
what an
suppos
to do
I mean...
She... I...
...
Well, why not just go with it?
She *is* special to you, isn't she?
Huh?! It's no that simple.
Then you'll turn her down?
I couldn't!!
I'm all Mami's got. I can't just... reject her.

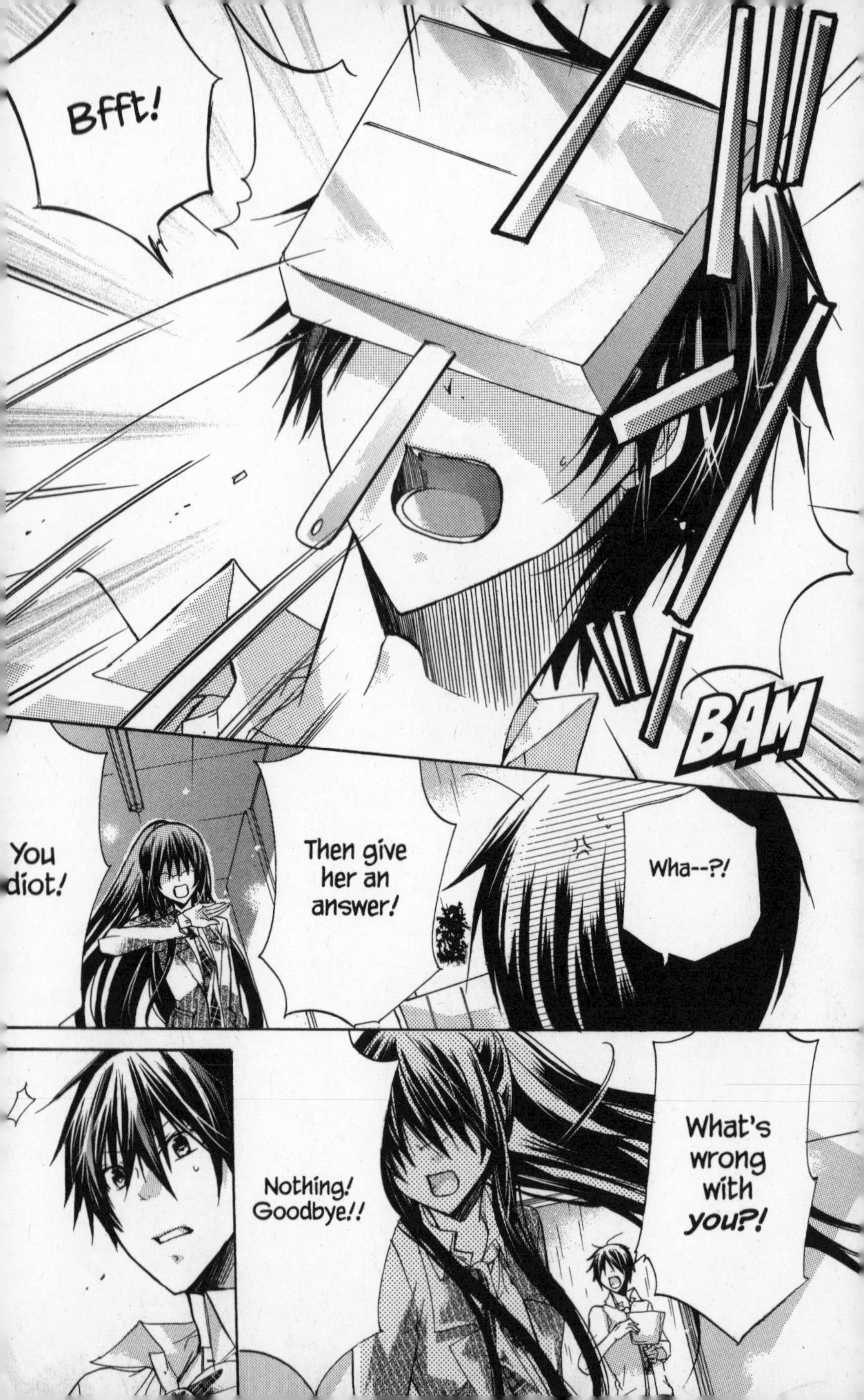
Bfft!
BAM
Wha--?!
Then give her an answer!
You diot!
What's wrong with you?!
Nothing! Goodbye!!

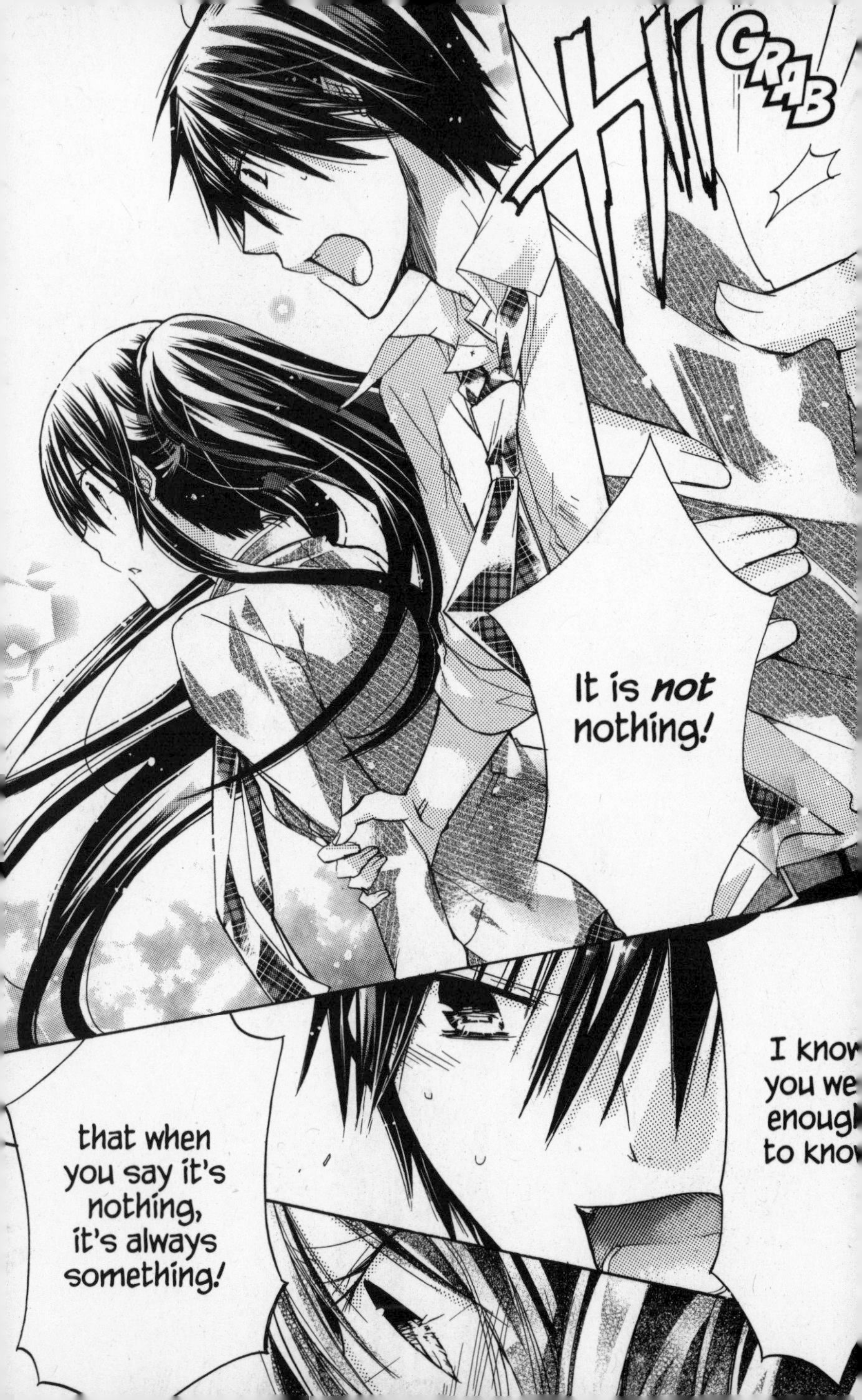
GRAB
It is *not* nothing!
I know you we enoug to kno
that when you say it's nothing, it's always something!

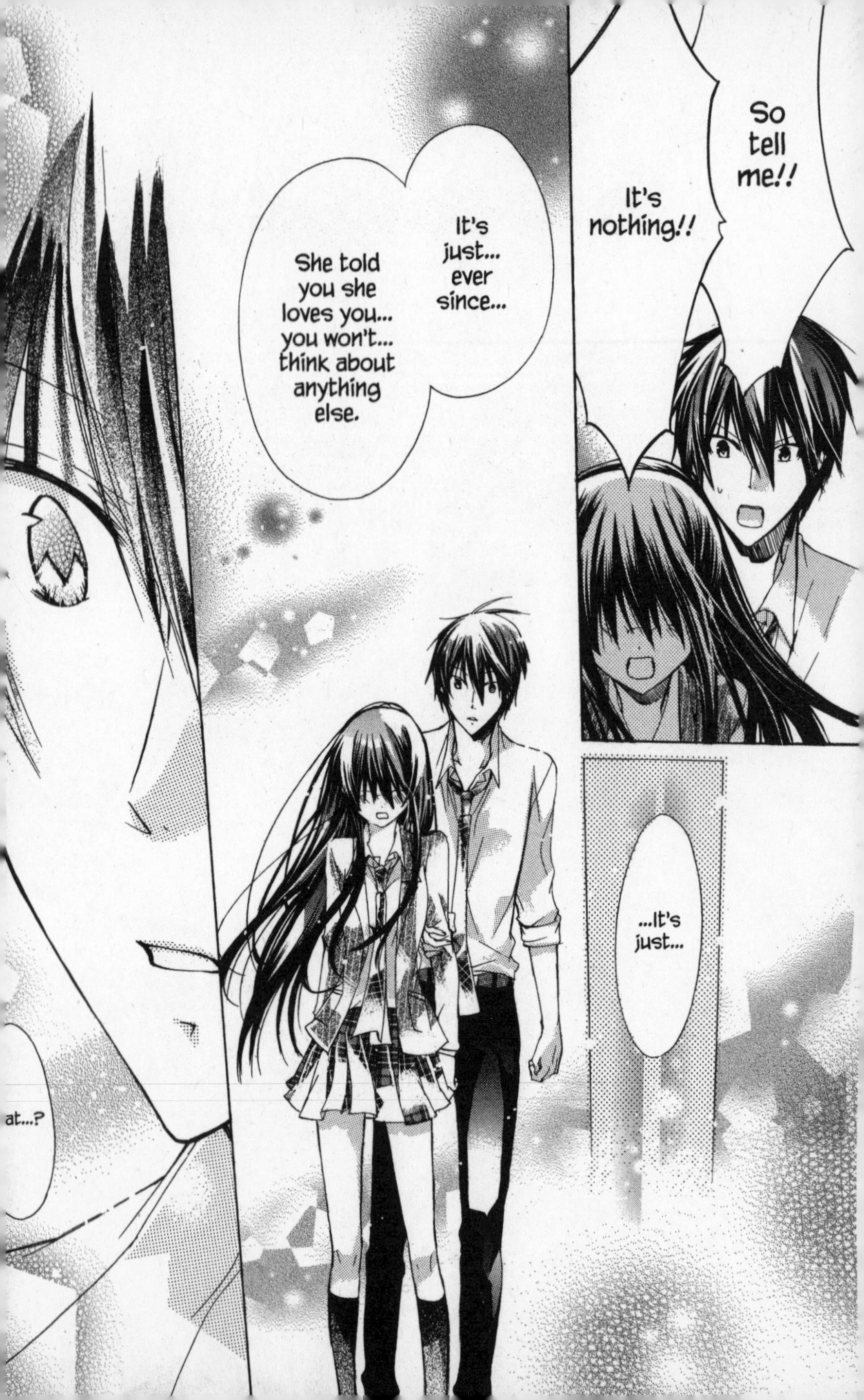
So tell me!!
It's nothing!!
...It's just...
It's just... ever since...
She told you she loves you... you won't... think about anything else.
at...?

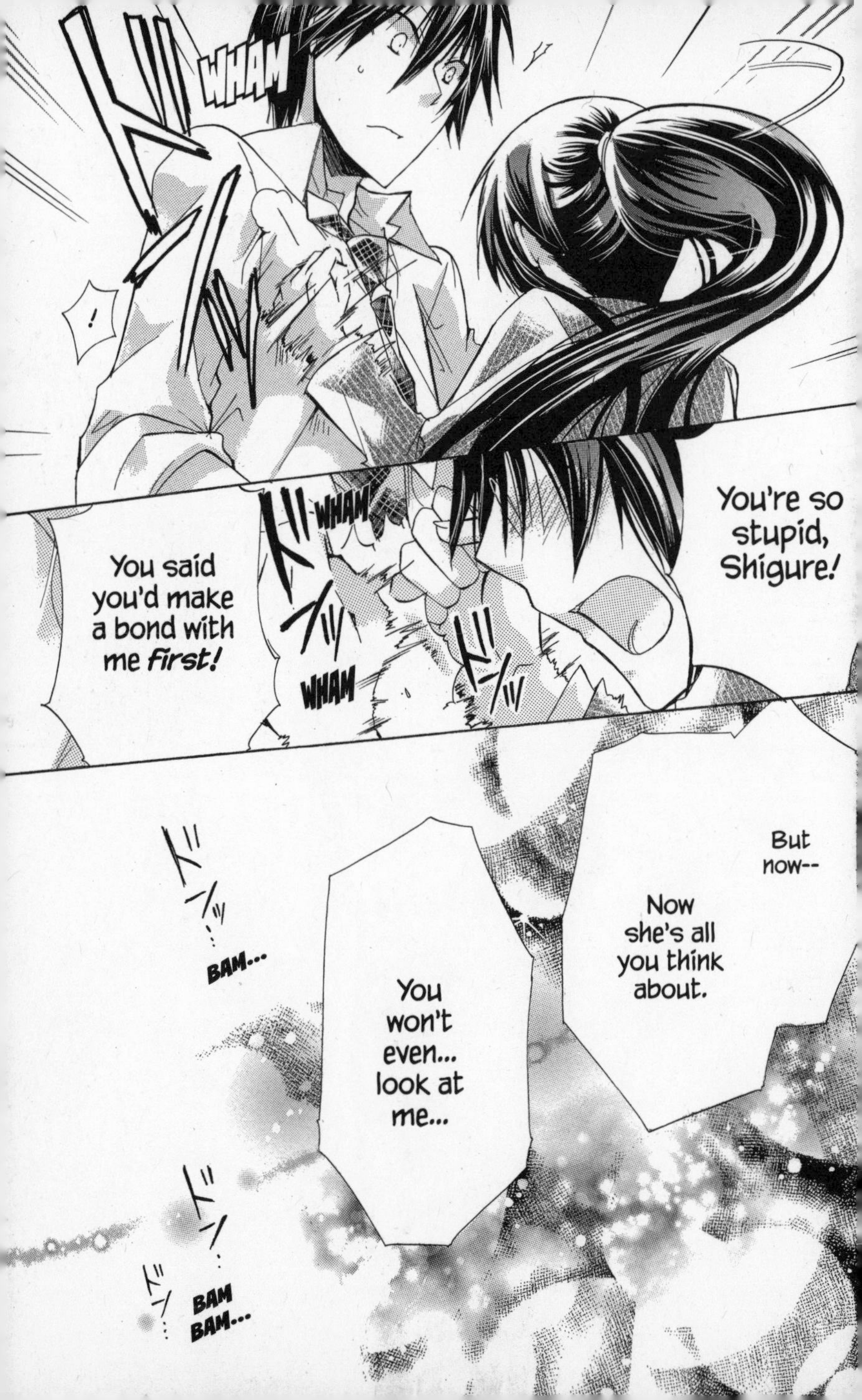
WHAM
!
You're so stupid, Shigure!
WHAM
You said you'd make a bond with me *first!*
WHAM
But now--
Now she's all you think about.
You won't even... look at me...
BAM...
BAM BAM...

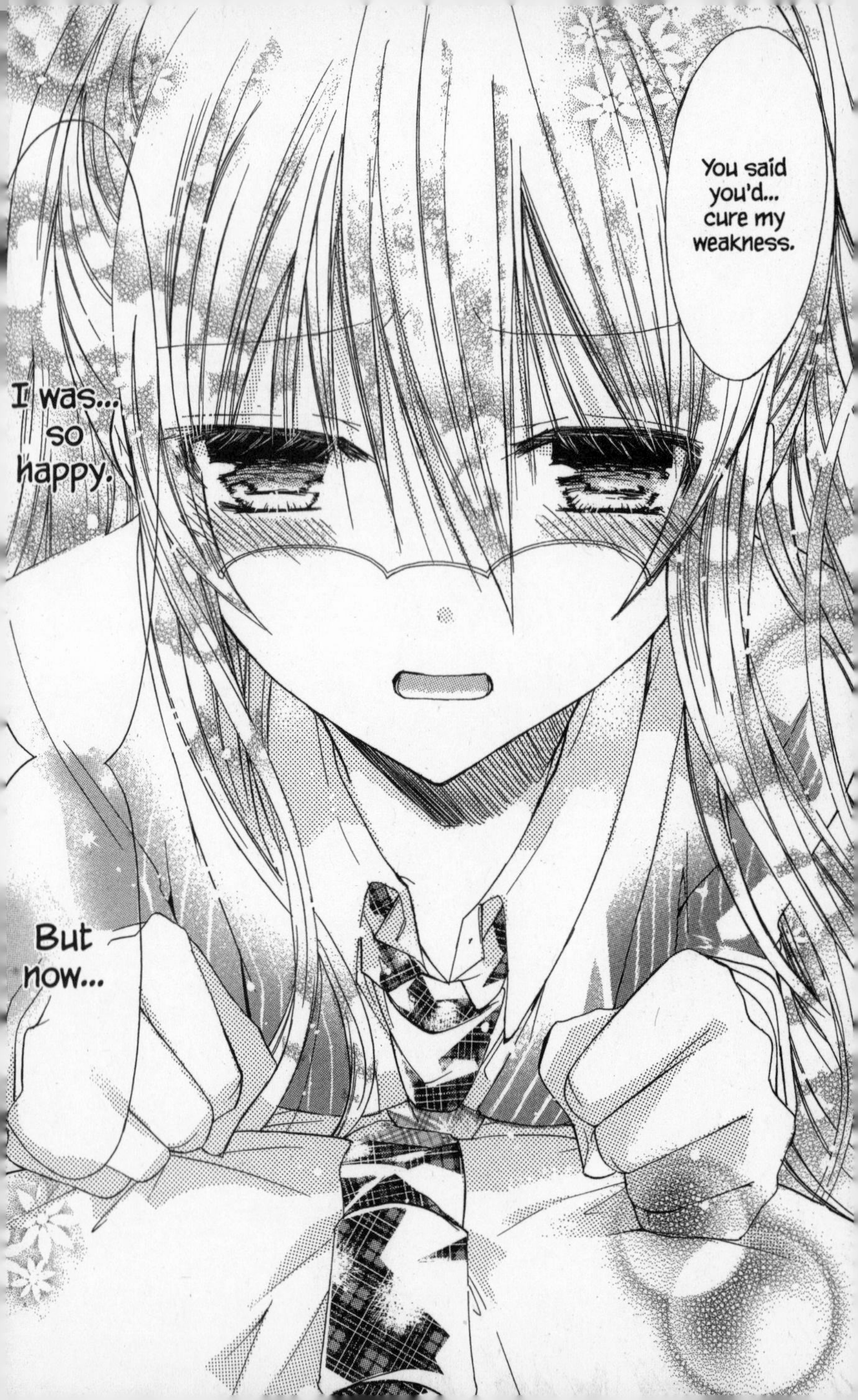
You said you'd... cure my weakness.
I was... so happy.
But now...

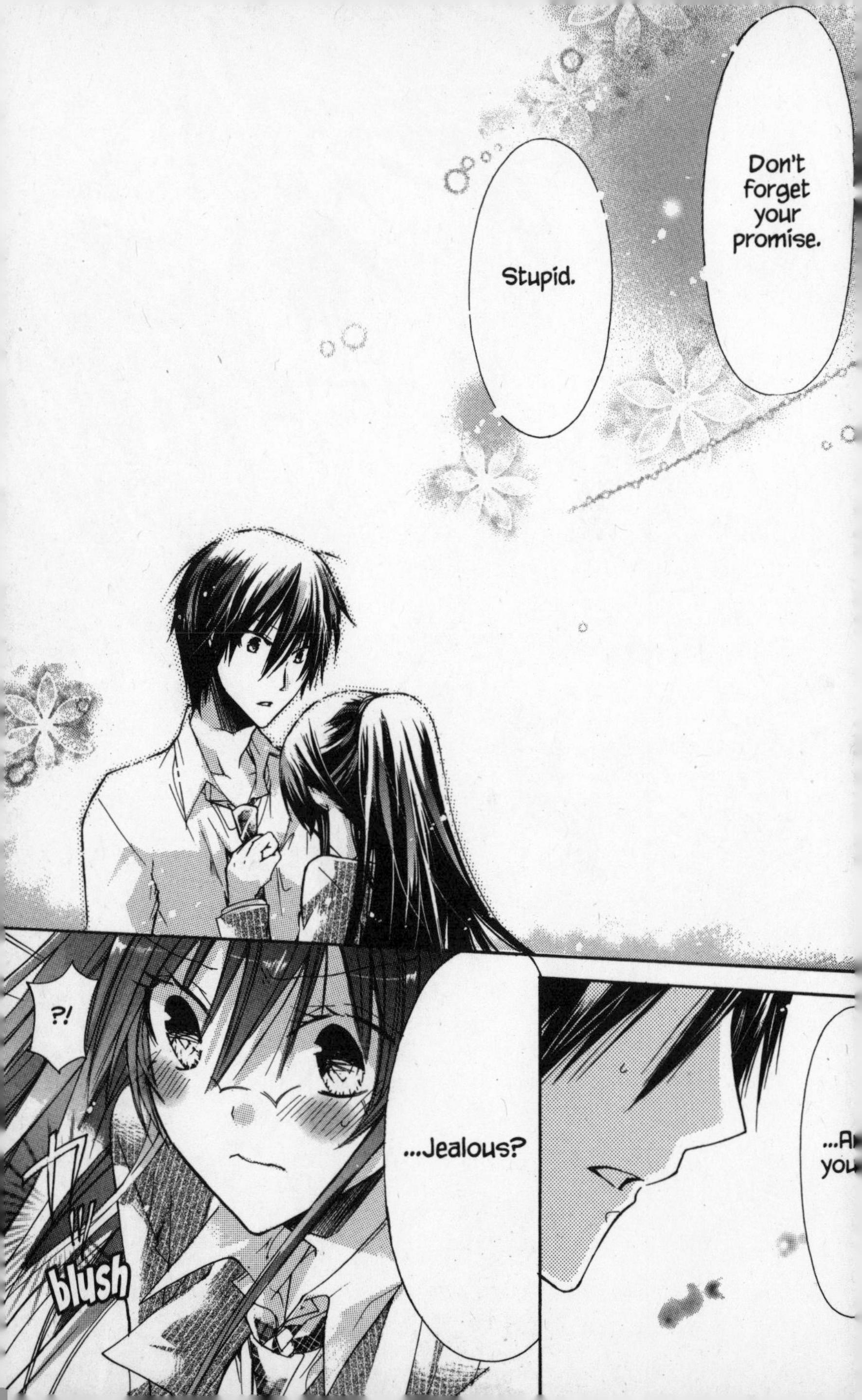

Don't forget your promise.
Stupid.
...A you
...Jealous?
?!
blush

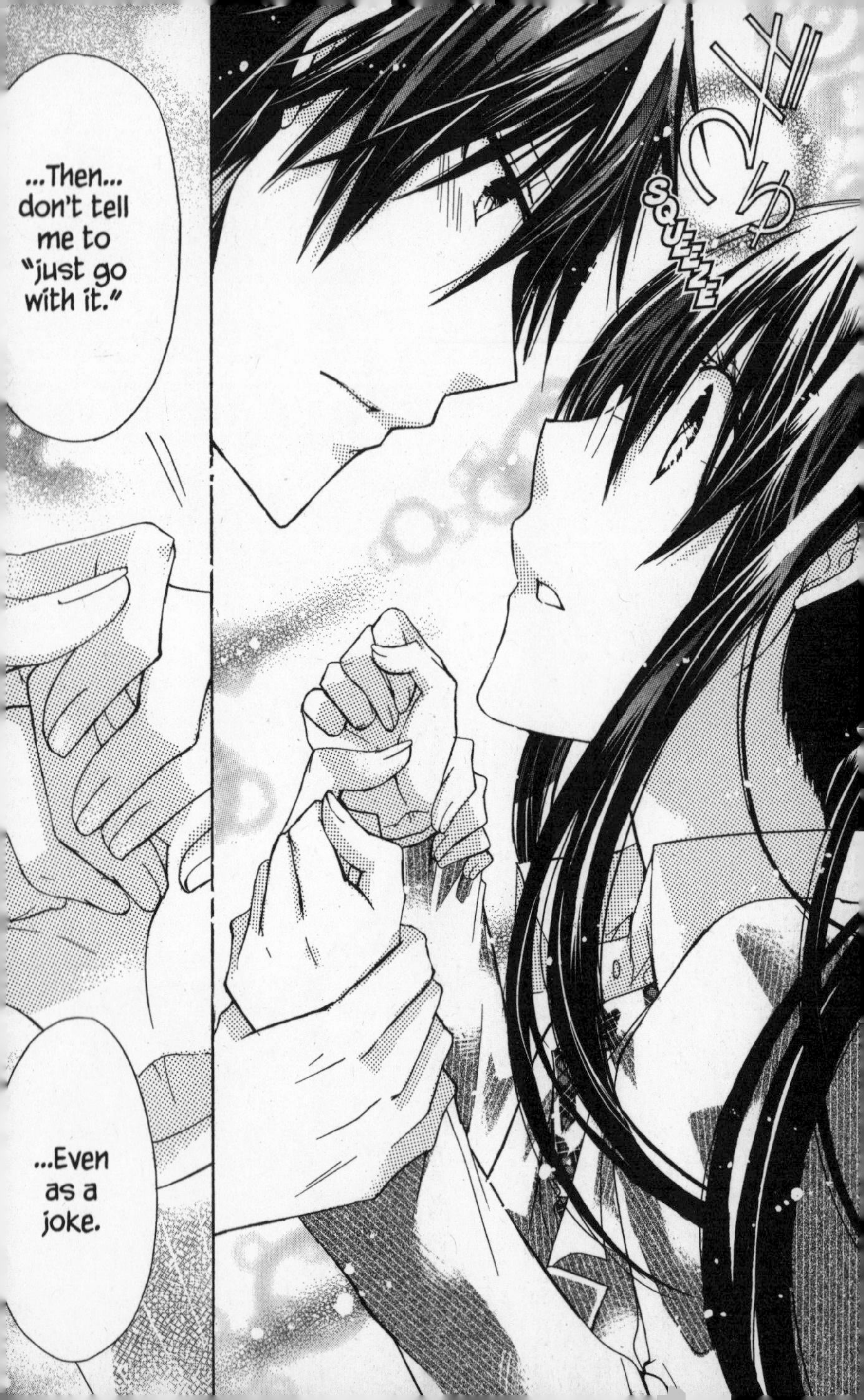
SQUEEZE
...Then... don't tell me to "just go with it."
...Even as a joke.

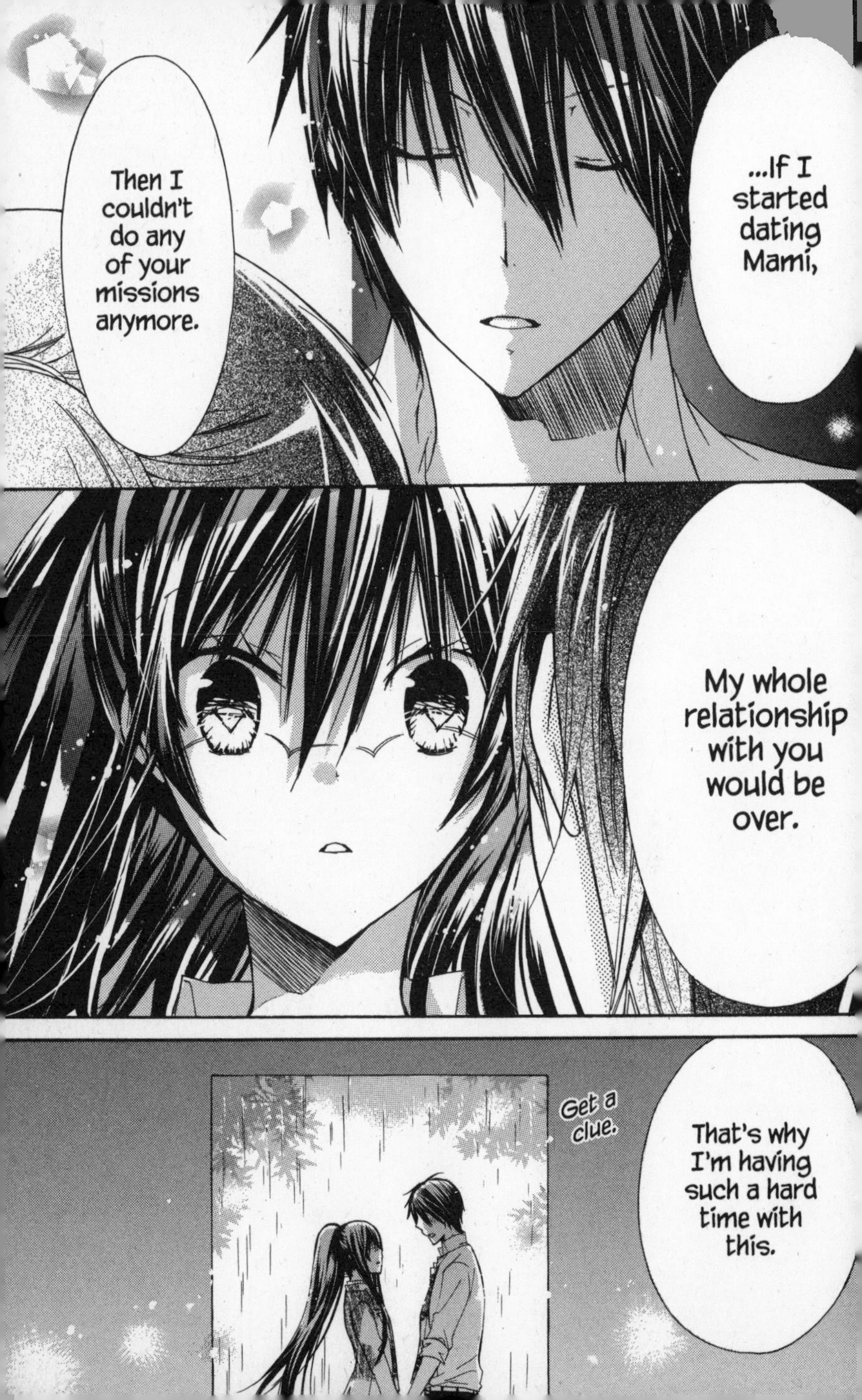
...If I started dating Mami,
Then I couldn't do any of your missions anymore.
My whole relationship with you would be over.
That's why I'm having such a hard time with this.
Get a clue.

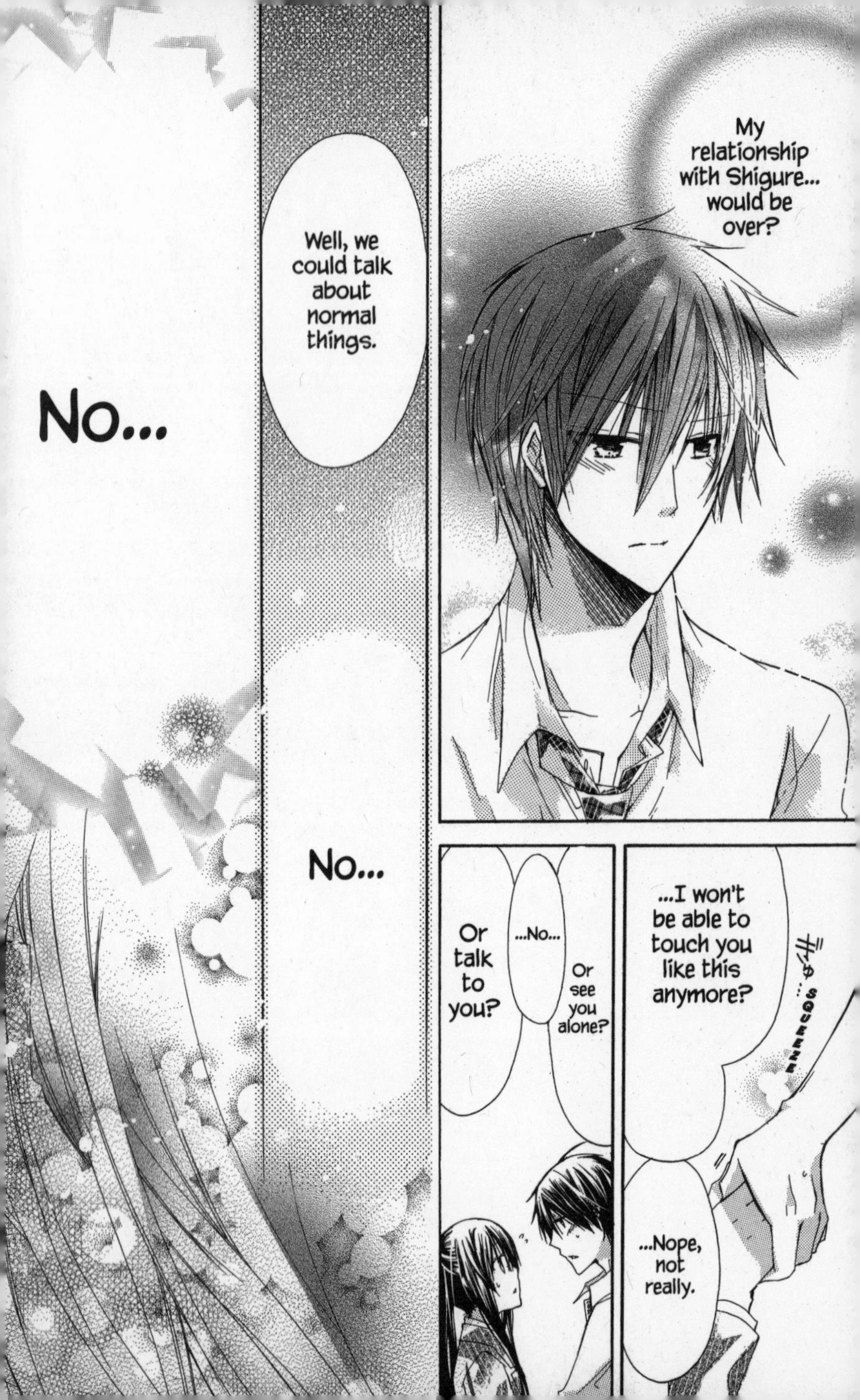
My relationship with Shigure... would be over?
...I won't be able to touch you like this anymore?
SQUEEZE
...Nope, not really.
...No...
Or see you alone?
Or talk to you?
Well, we could talk about normal things.
No...
No...

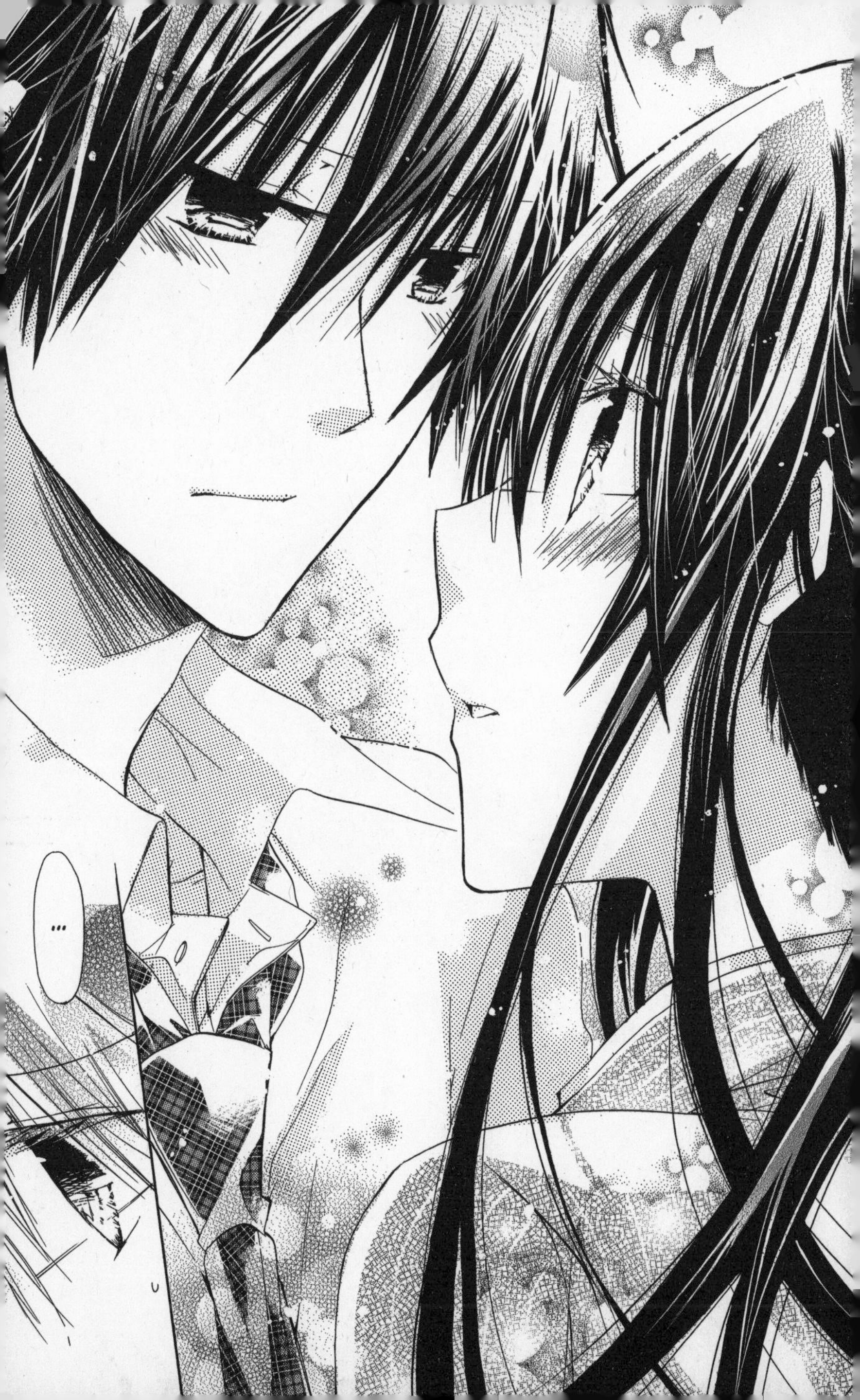
...

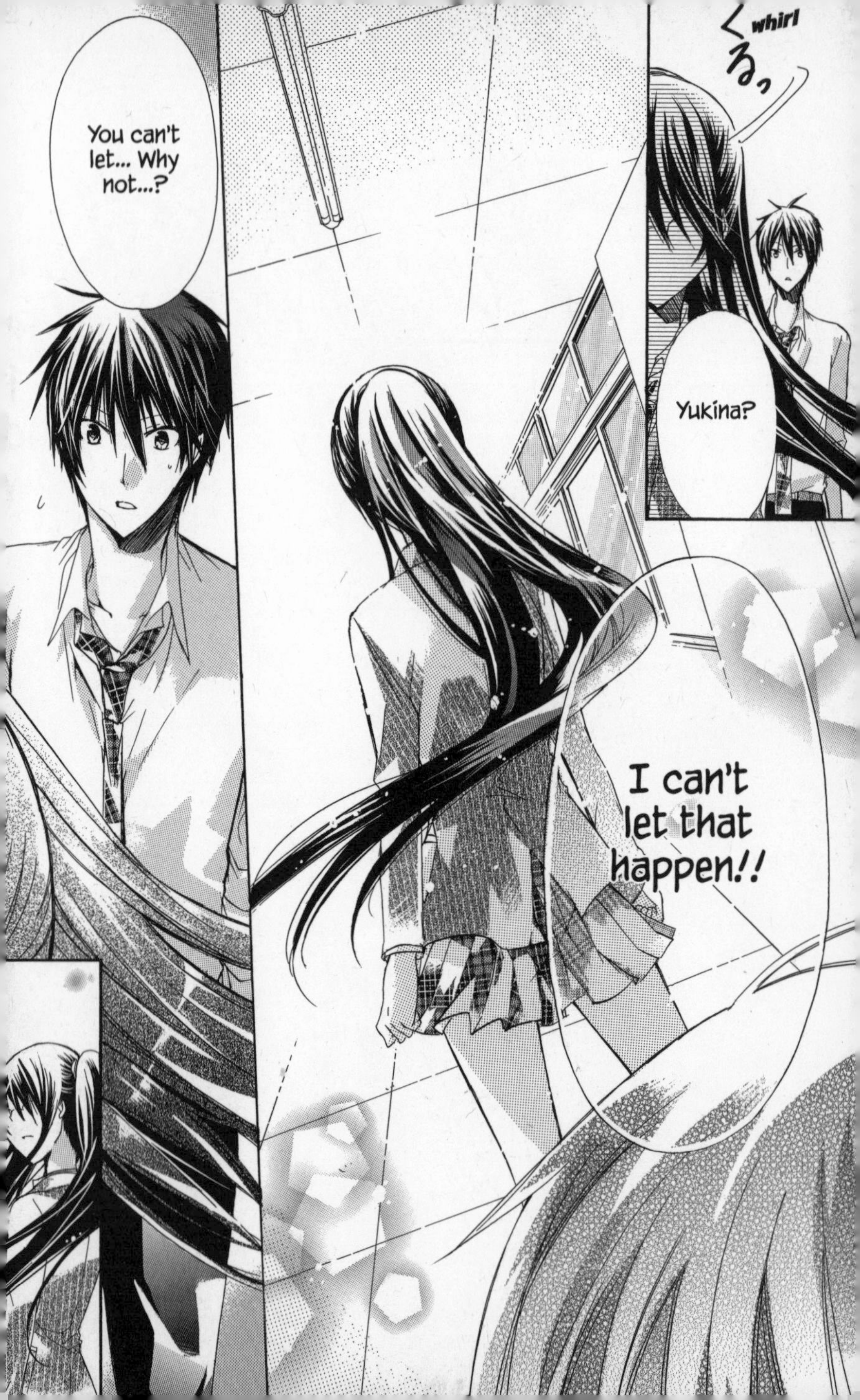
くるっ
whirl
Yukina?
I can't let that happen!!
You can't let... Why not...?

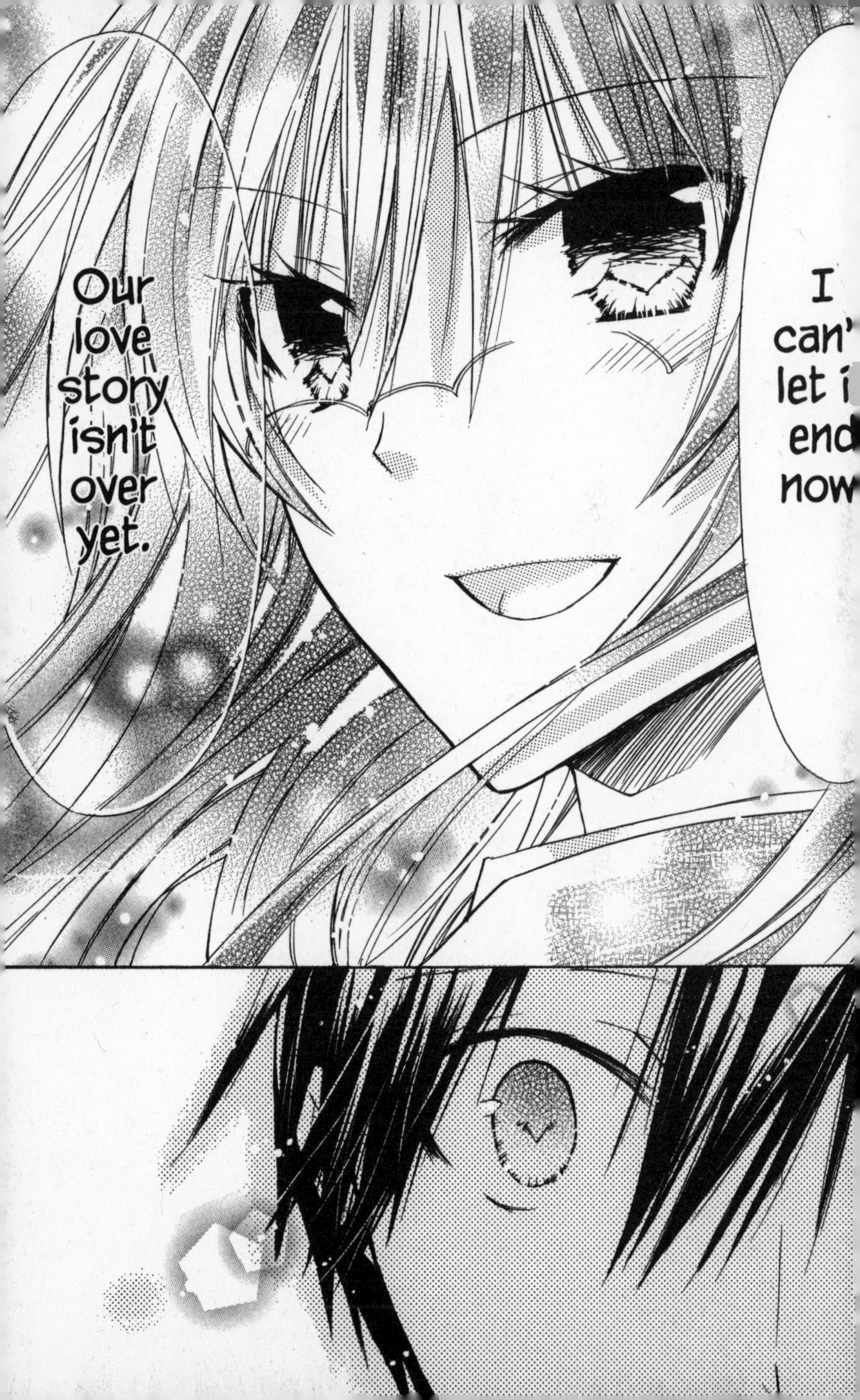
I can' let i end now
Our love story isn't over yet.

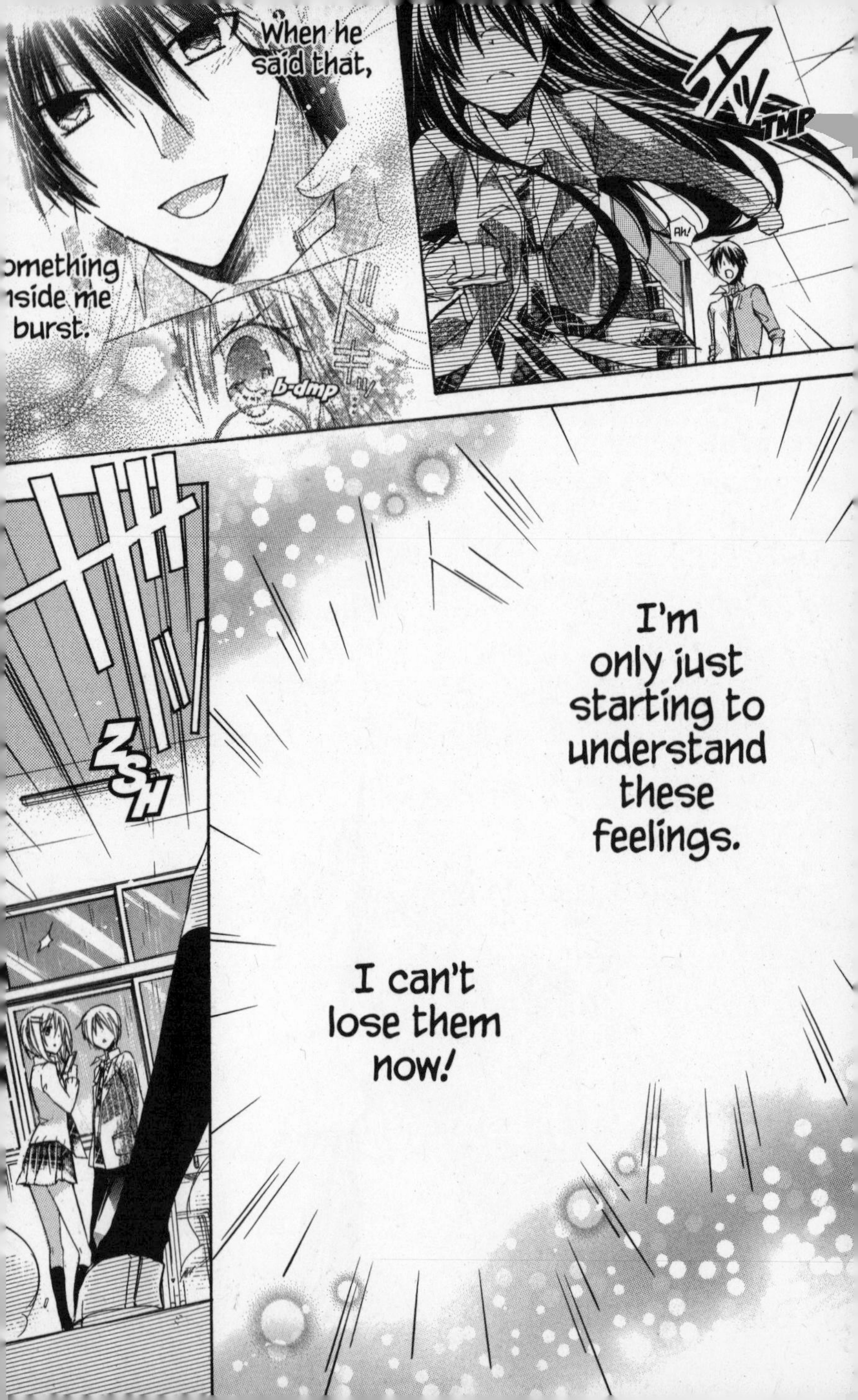
TMP
Ah!
When he said that,
omething nside me burst.
b-dmp
I'm only just starting to understand these feelings.
I can't lose them now!
ZSH

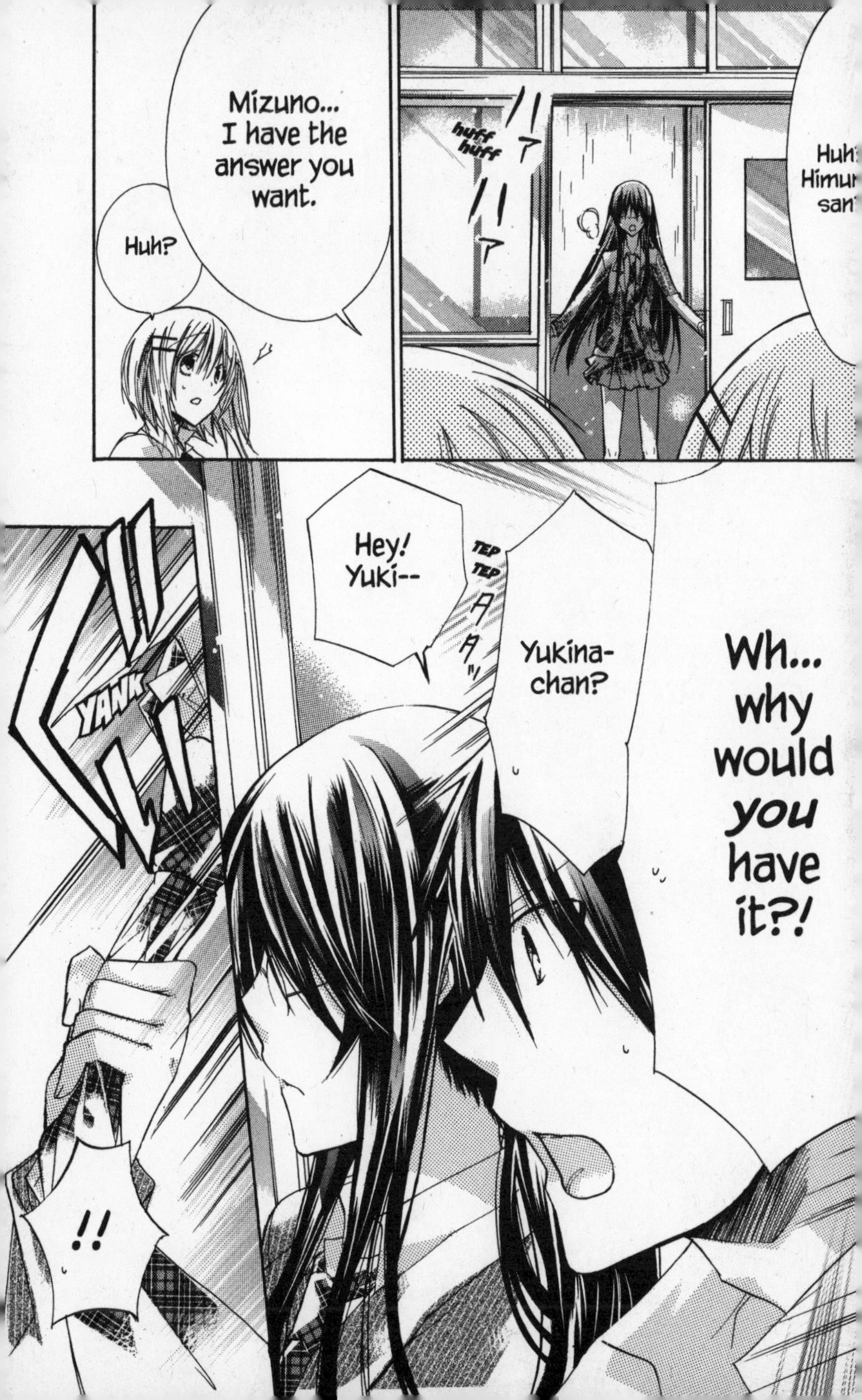

Huh Himu san
huff huff
Mizuno... I have the answer you want.
Huh?
Wh... why would you have it?!
Yukina-chan?
TEP TEP
Hey! Yuki--
YANK
!!

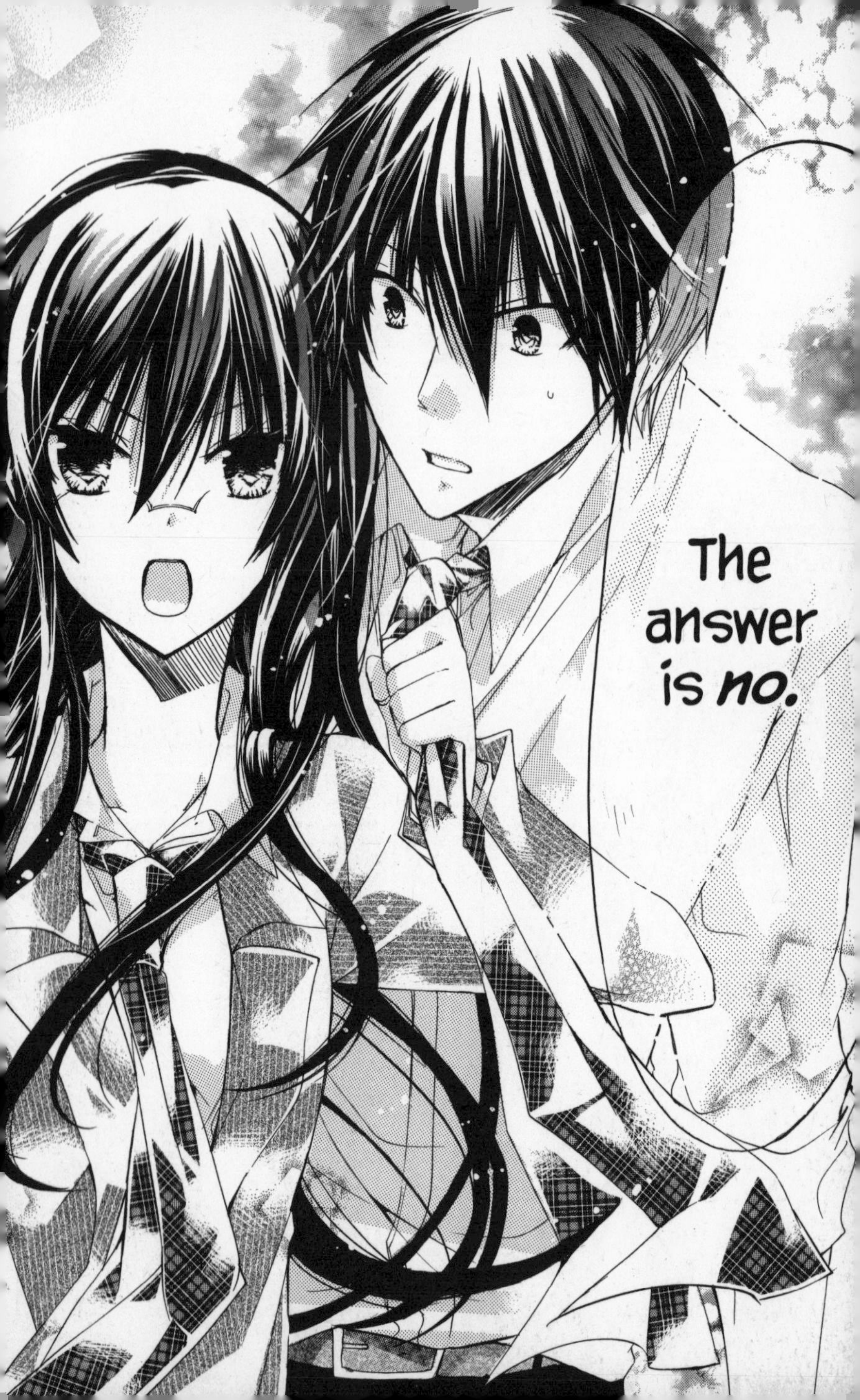
The answer is *no.*

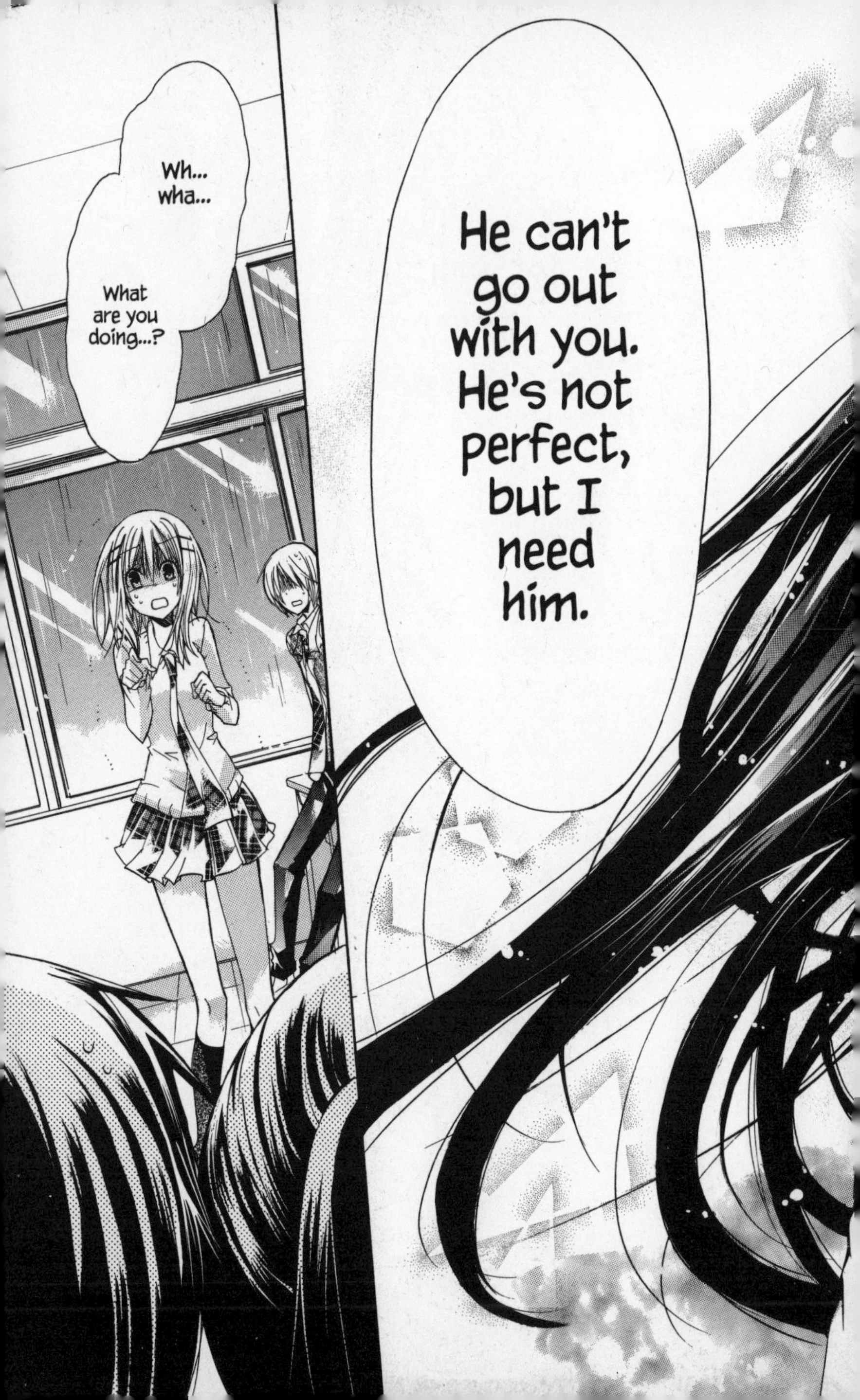
He can't go out with you. He's not perfect, but I need him.
Wh... wha...
What are you doing...?

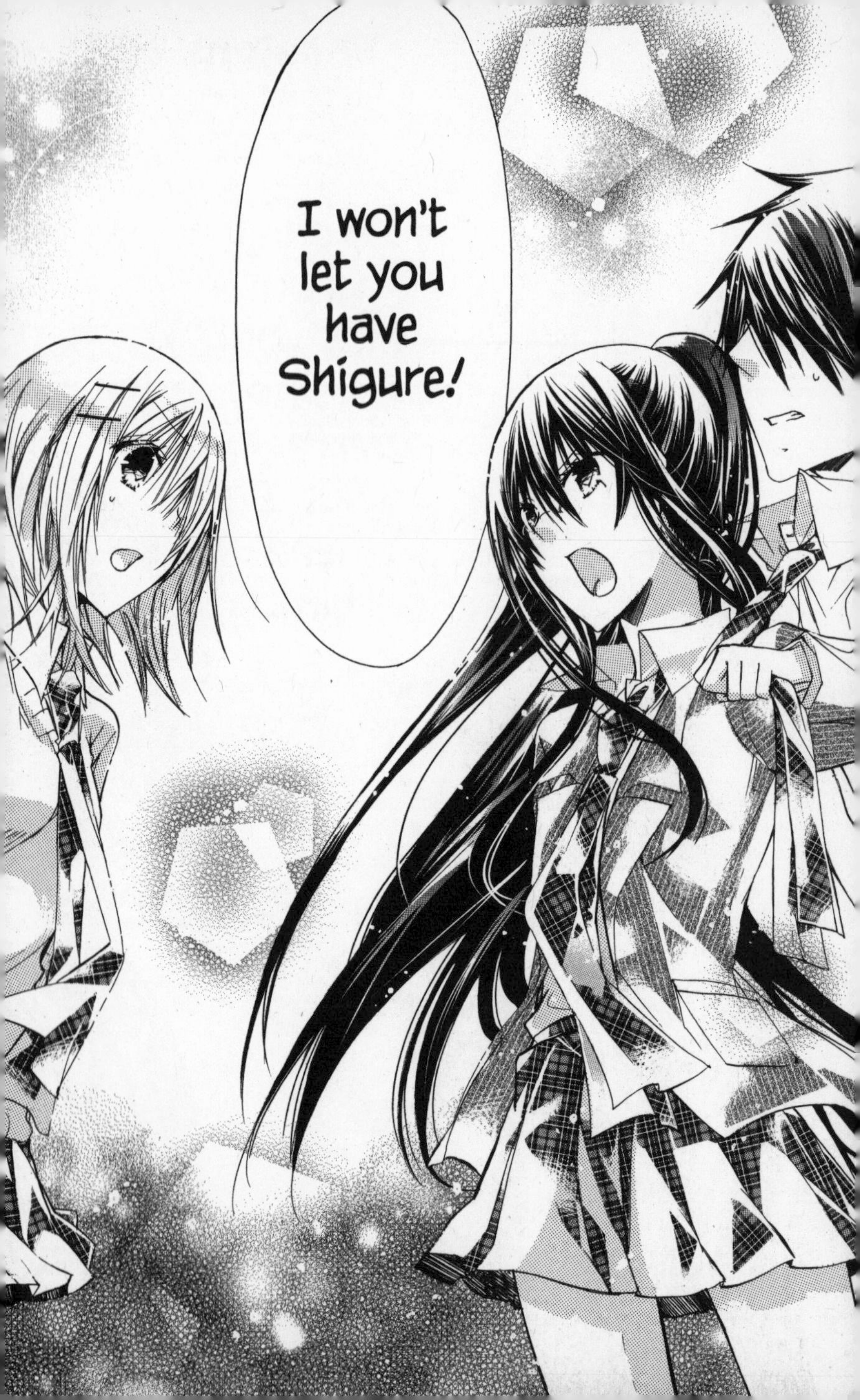
I won't let you have Shigure!

Missions of Lov

**It is time for love.
Secret cell phone
novelist vs. the most
popular boy in school.
A mission of love for
absolute servitude.**

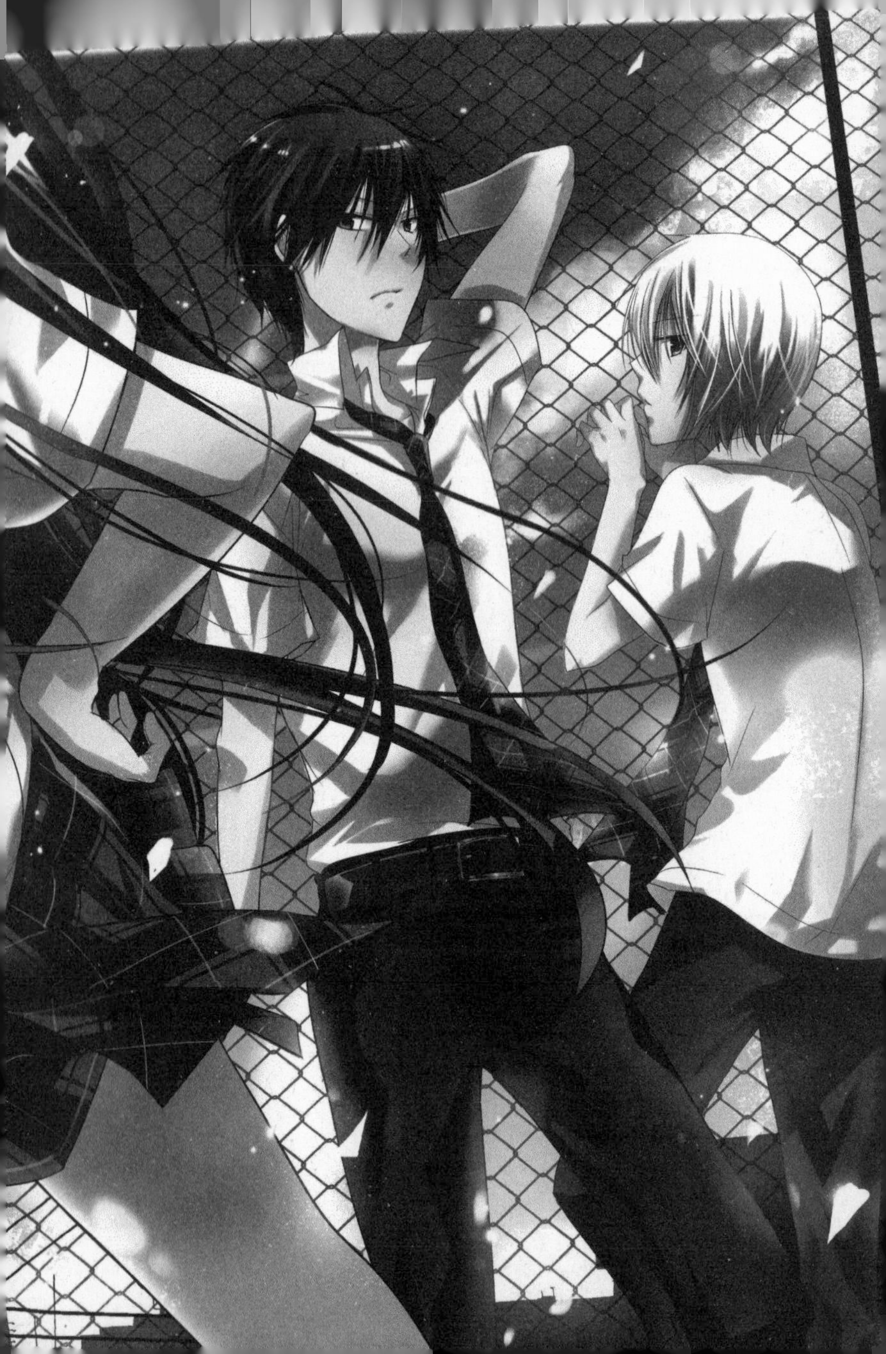

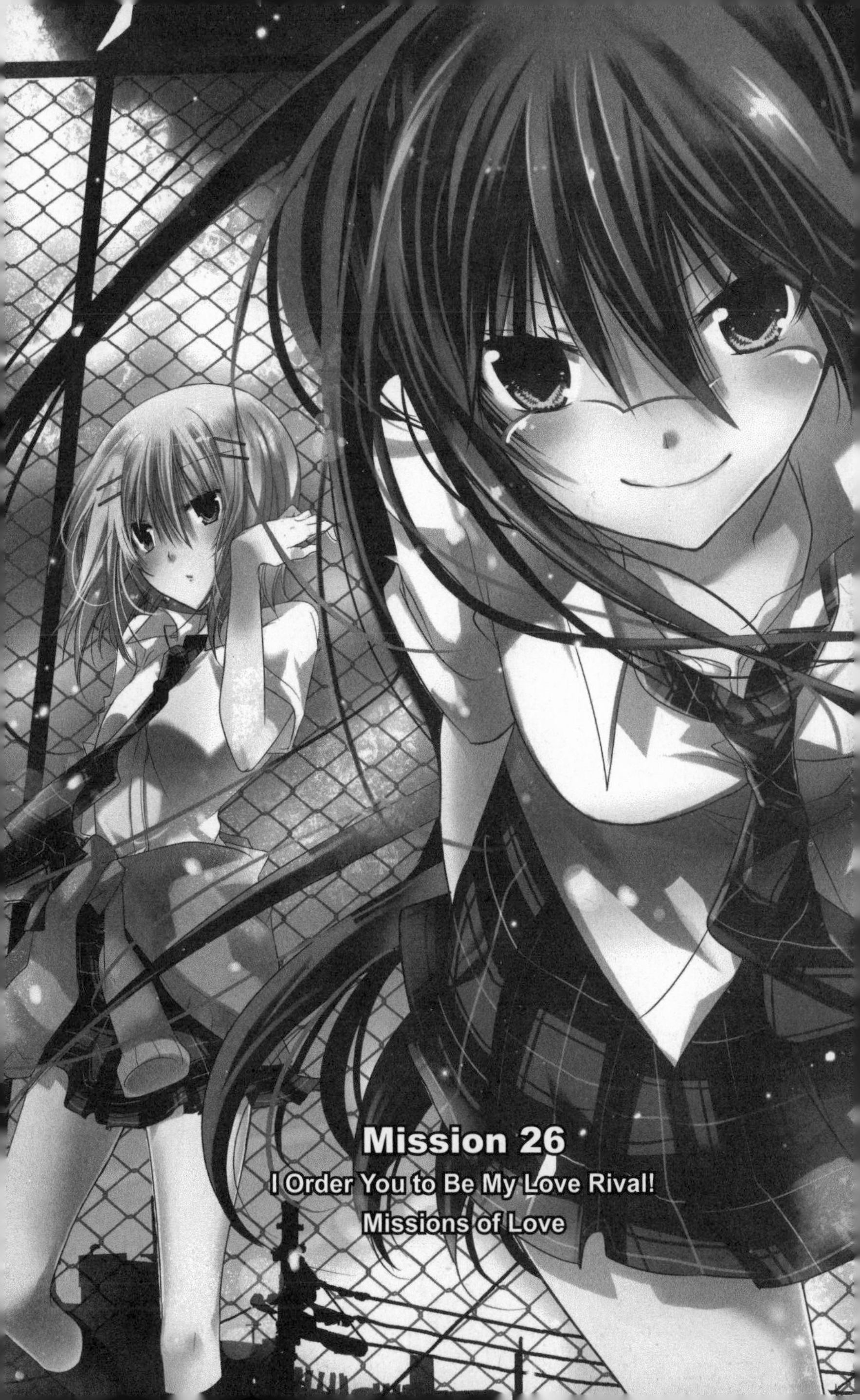

Mission 26

I Order You to Be My Love Rival!

Missions of Love

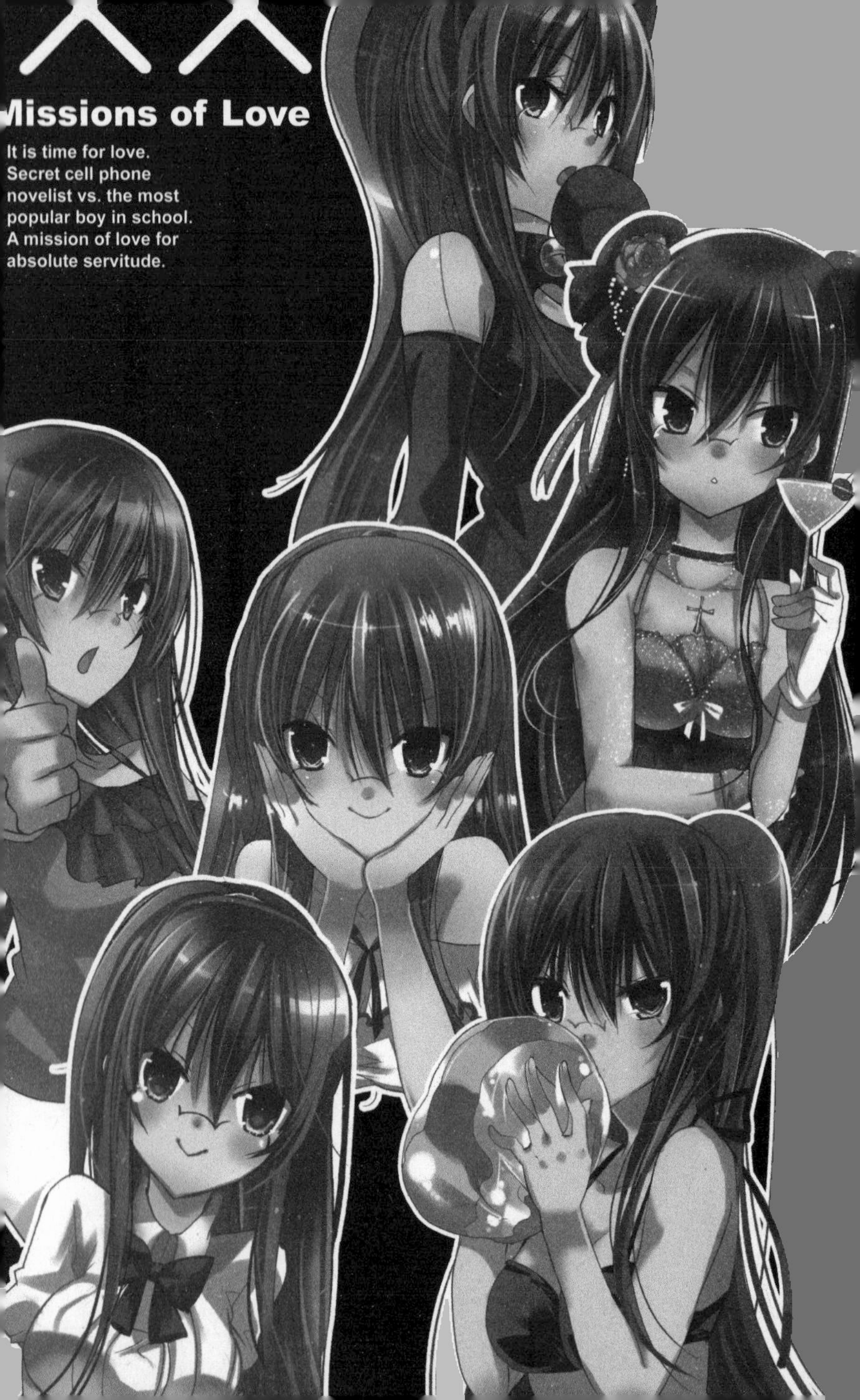
Missions of Love
It is time for love.
Secret cell phone
novelist vs. the most
popular boy in school.
A mission of love for
absolute servitude.

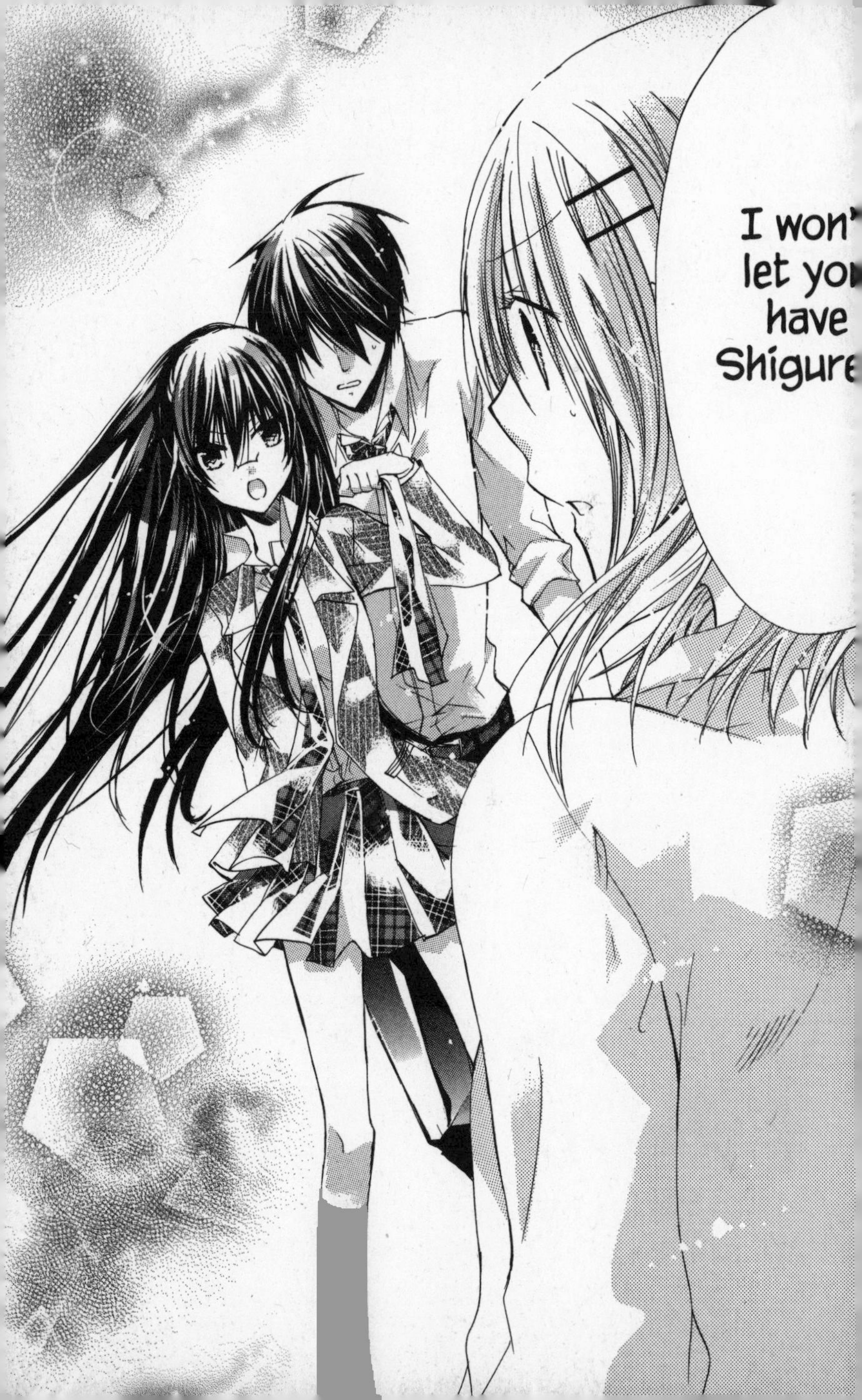
I won't let you have Shigure

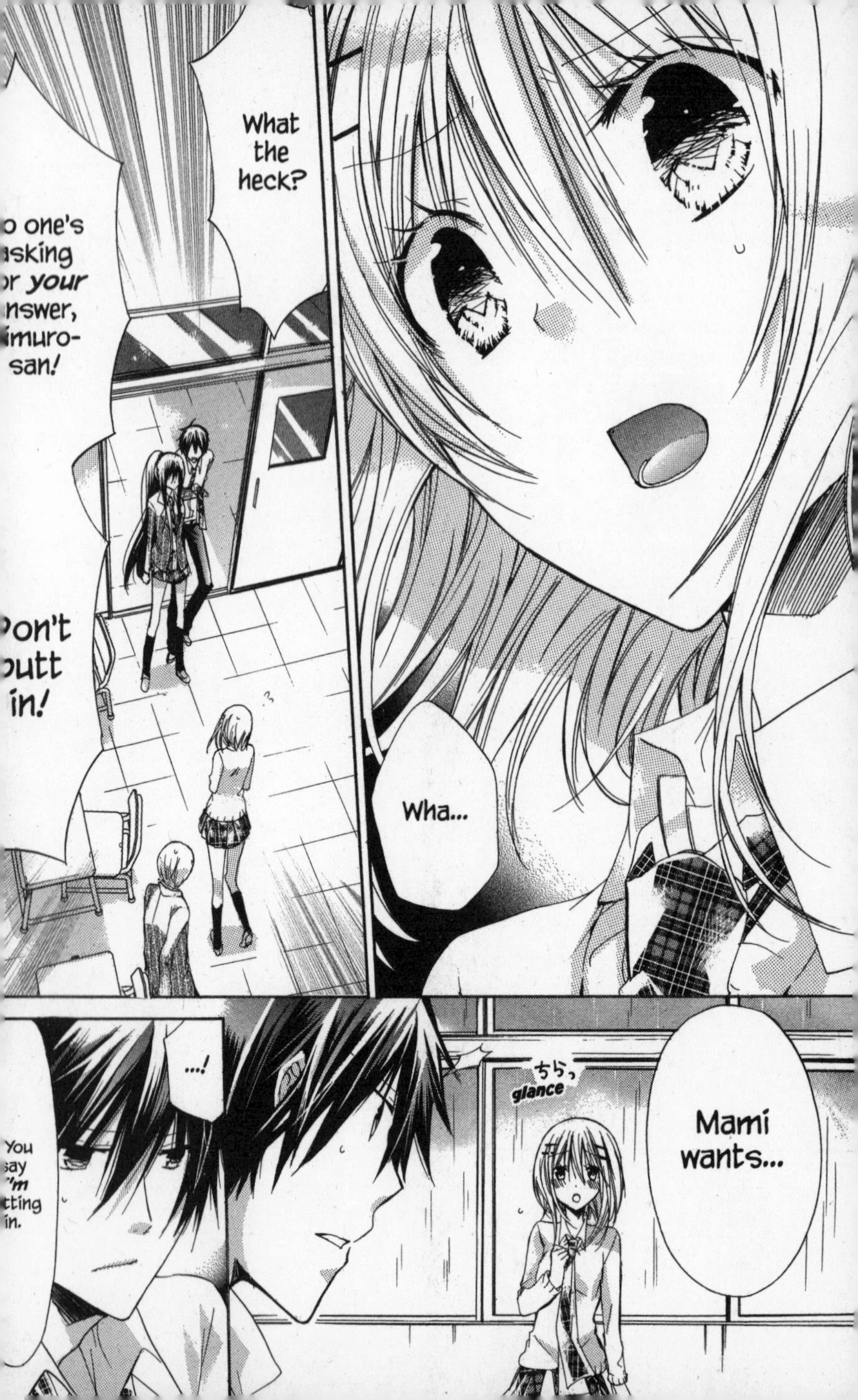

Wha...
What the heck?
o one's sking r *your* nswer, imuro-san!
on't utt in!
Mami wants...
ちらっ
glance
...!
You say 'm tting in.

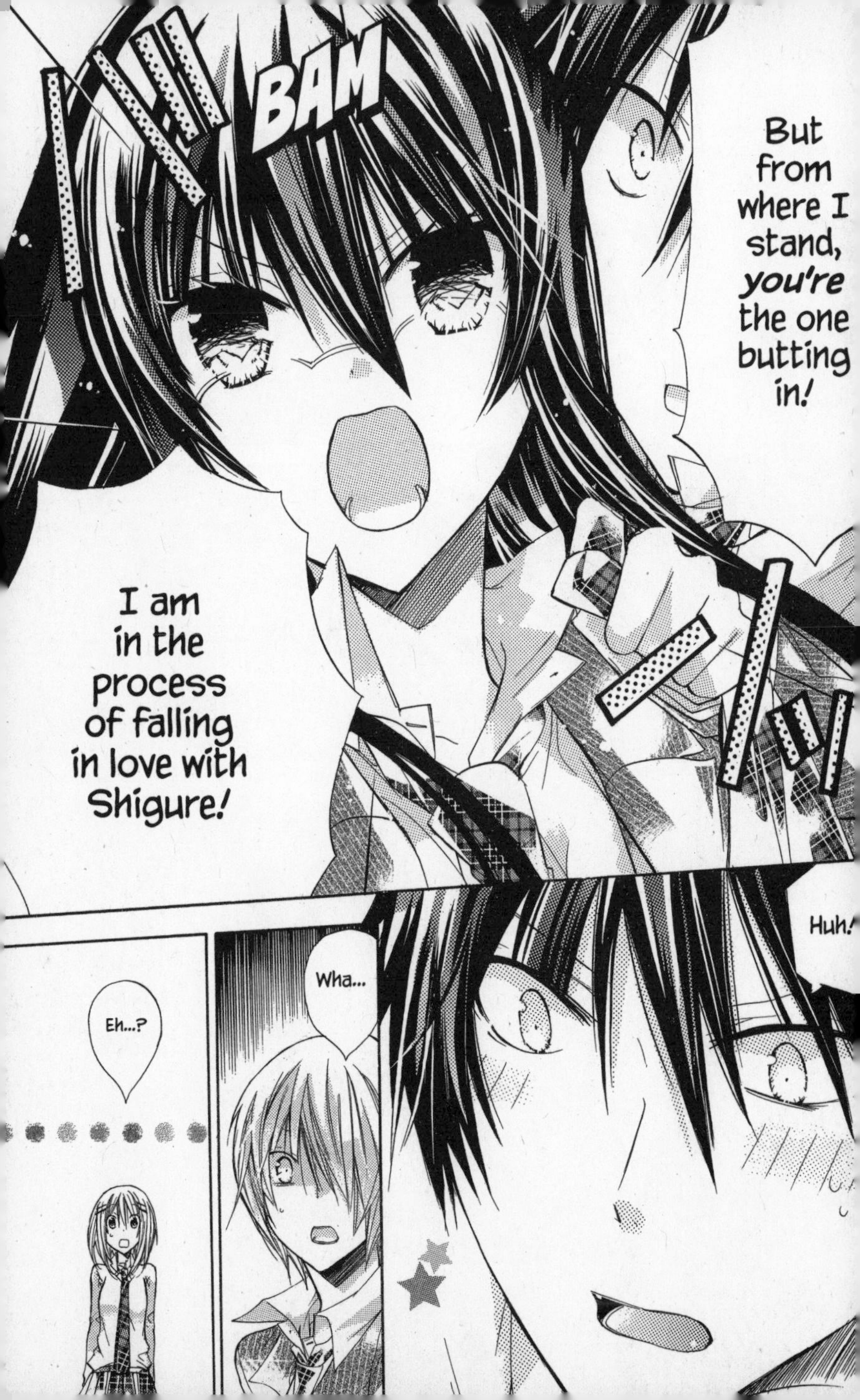
But from where I stand, *you're* the one butting in!
BAM
I am in the process of falling in love with Shigure!
Huh!
Wha...
Eh...?

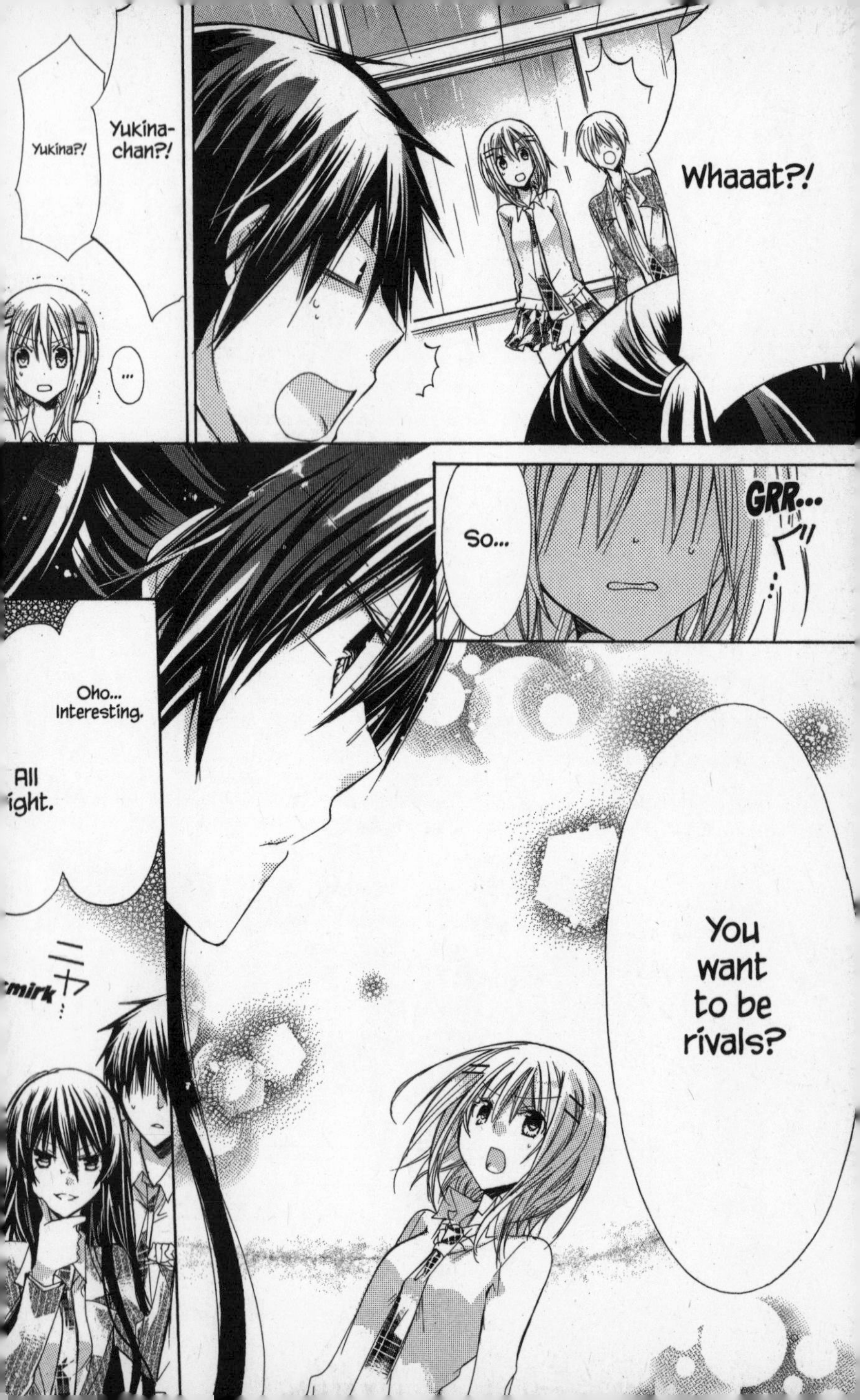
Whaaat?!
Yukina-chan?!
Yukina?!
...
GRR...
So...
You want to be rivals?
Oho... Interesting.
All ight.
ニヤ

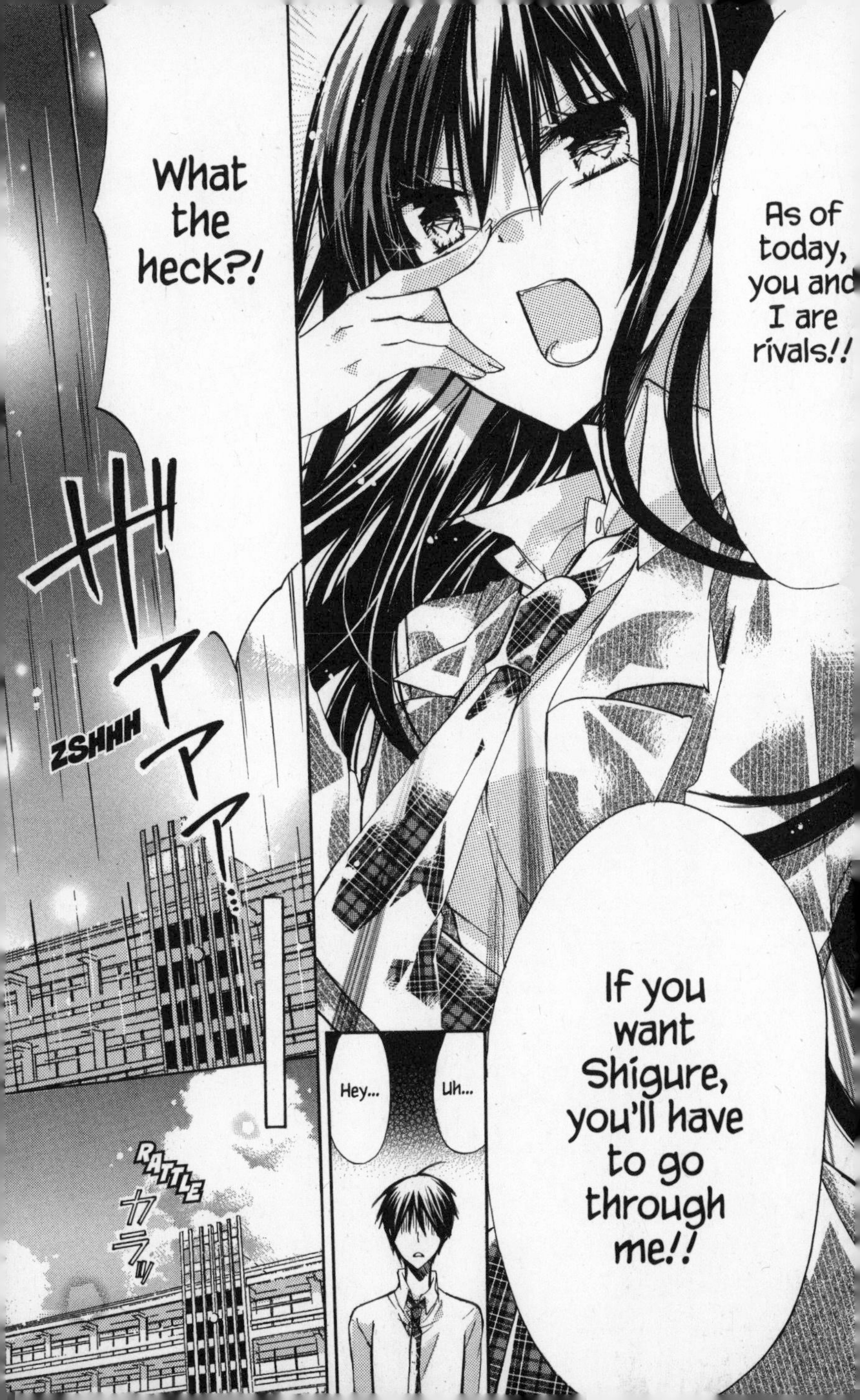
As of today, you and I are rivals!!
If you want Shigure, you'll have to go through me!!
Uh...
Hey...
What the heck?!
ZSHHH
RATTLE

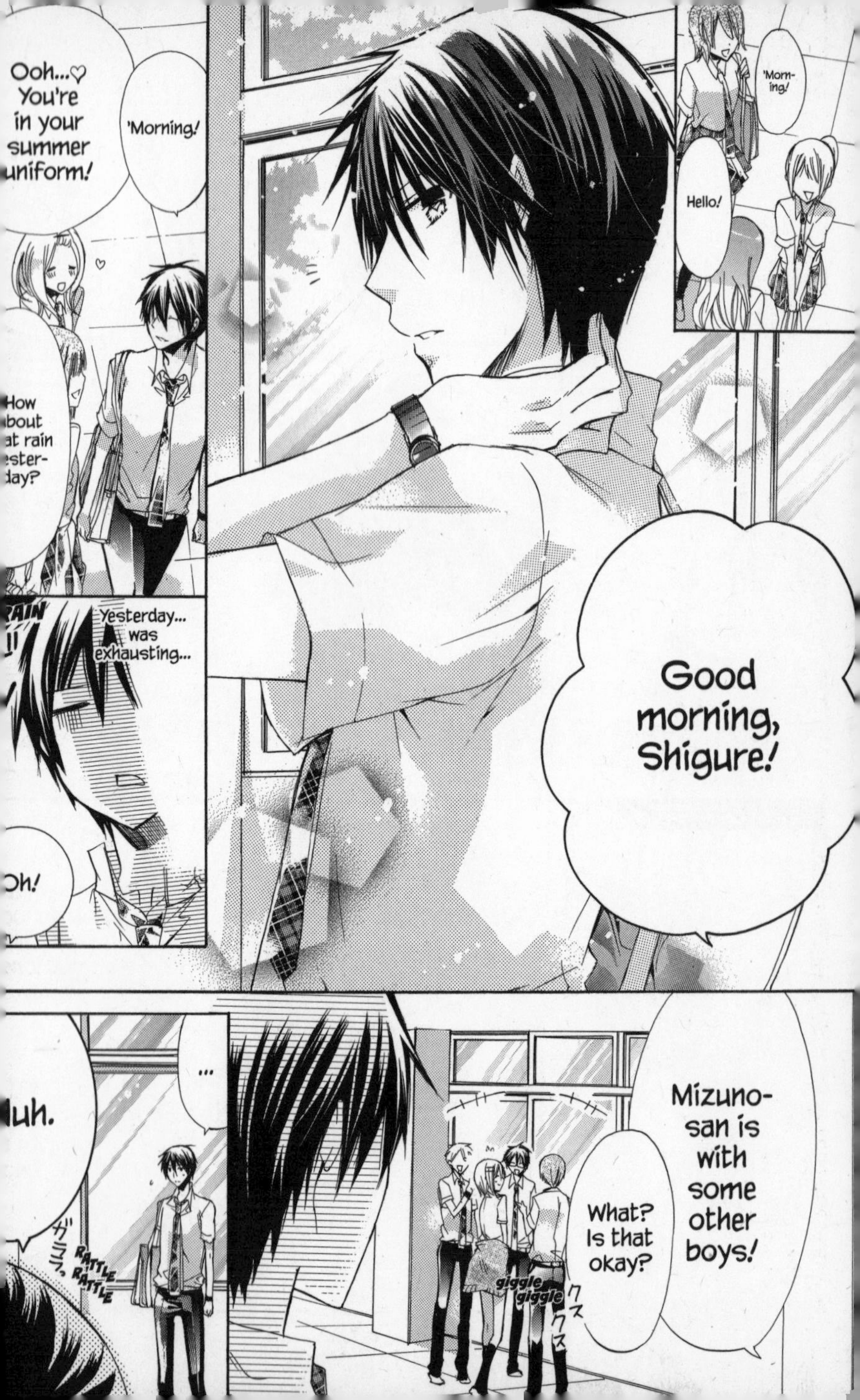
'Morning!
Hello!
Good morning, Shigure!
'Morning!
Ooh...♡ You're in your summer uniform!
How bout at rain ester-day?
Yesterday... was exhausting...
RAIN
Oh!
Mizuno-san is with some other boys!
What? Is that okay?
giggle giggle
クスクス
...
luh.
RATTLE RATTLE
ガラ

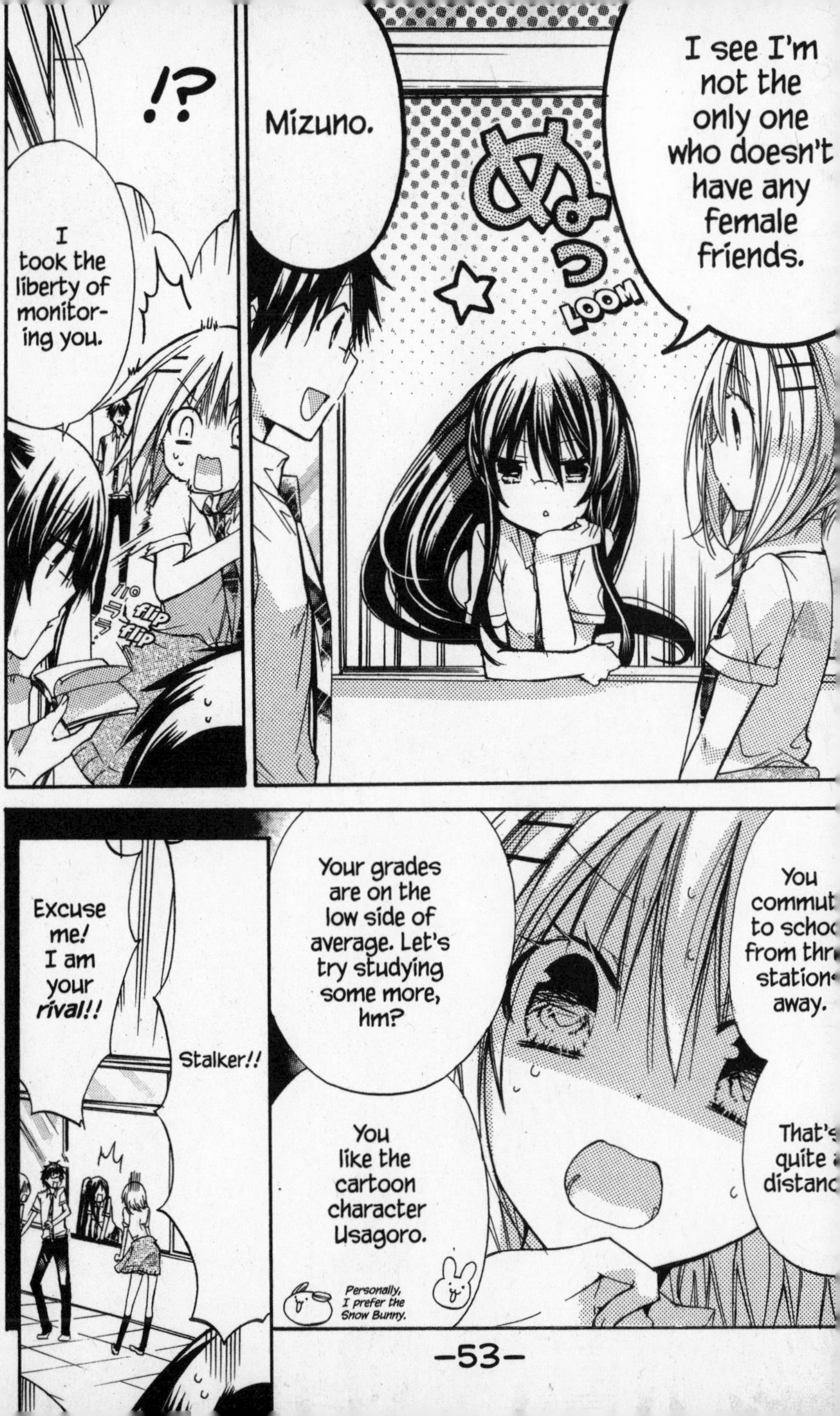

I see I'm not the only one who doesn't have any female friends.
Mizuno.
LOOM
!?
I took the liberty of monitor-ing you.
flip flip
You commut to schoo from thr station away.
That's quite distanc
Your grades are on the low side of average. Let's try studying some more, hm?
You like the cartoon character Usagoro.
Personally, I prefer the Snow Bunny.
Excuse me! I am your *rival!!*
Stalker!!

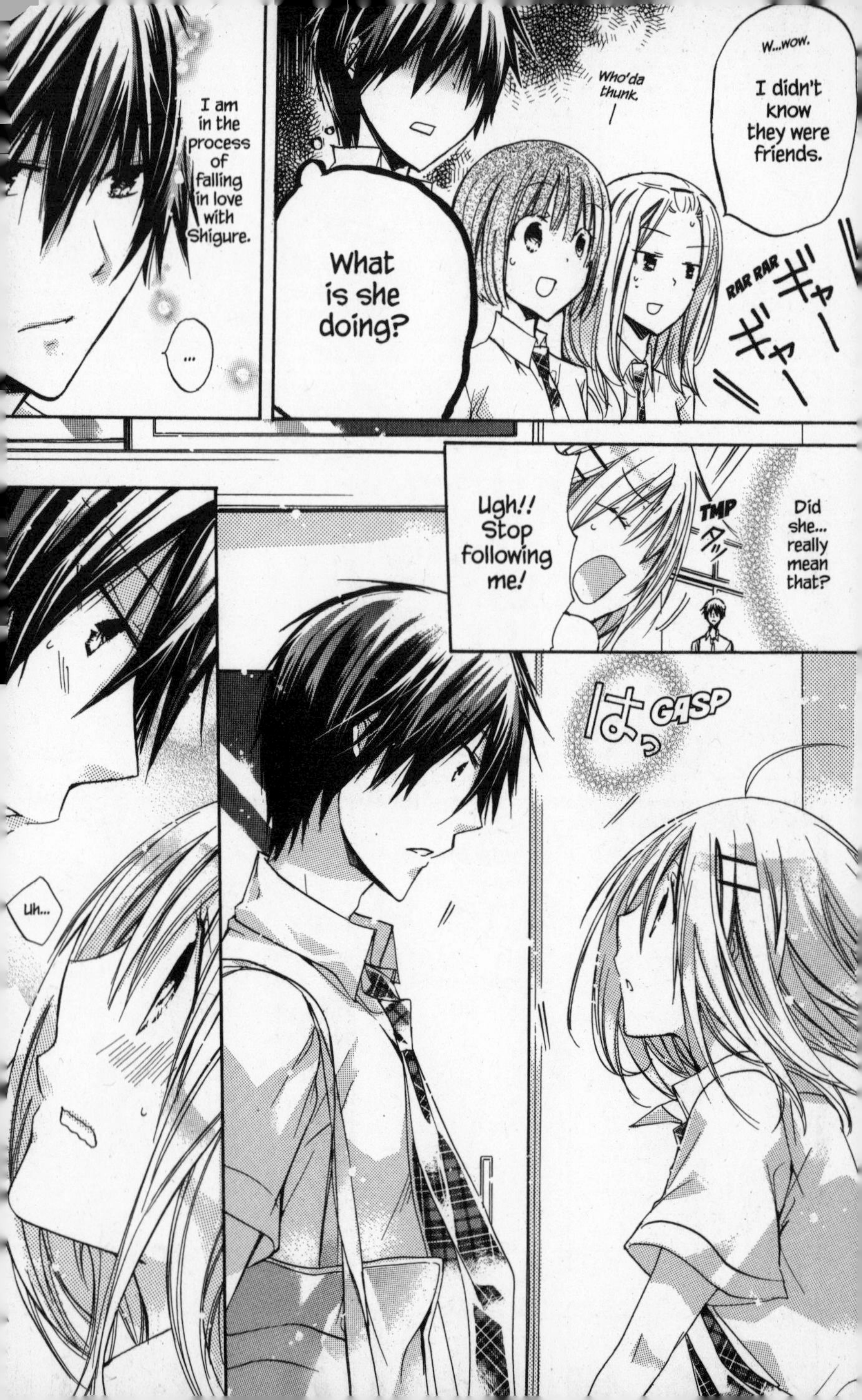
W...wow.
I didn't know they were friends.
Who'da thunk.
RAR RAR ギャーギャー
What is she doing?
I am in the process of falling in love with Shigure.
...
Did she... really mean that?
TMP タッ
Ugh!! Stop following me!
はっ GASP
Uh...

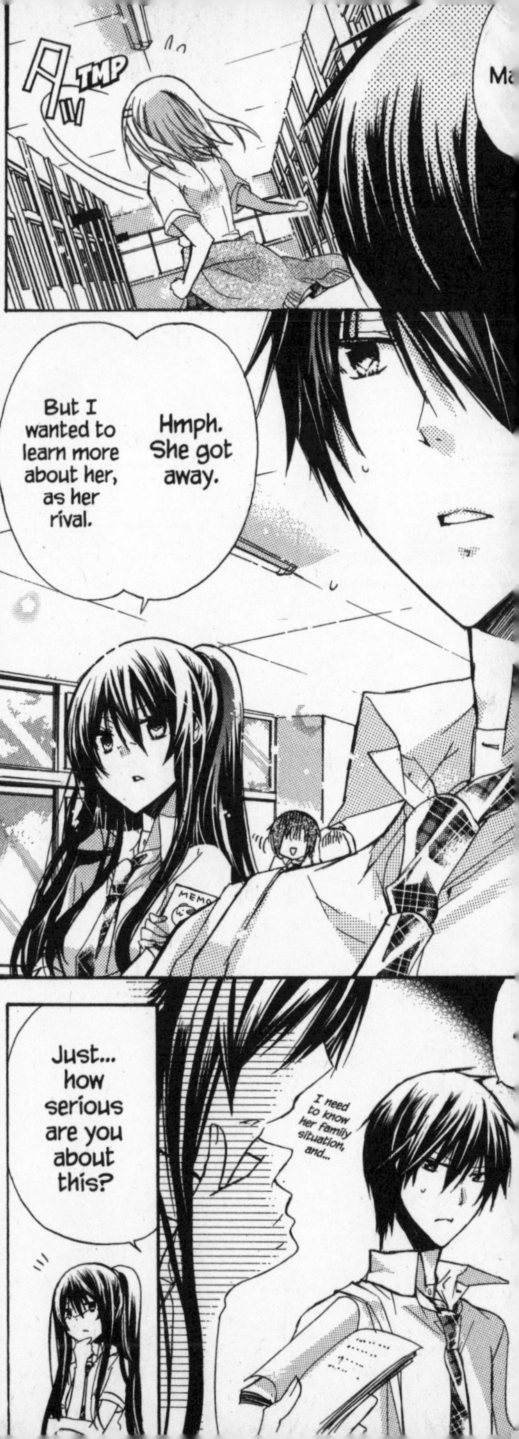
TMP
Hmph. She got away.
But I wanted to learn more about her, as her rival.
I need to know her family situation, and...
Just... how serious are you about this?

Mami and Snow Mami 1

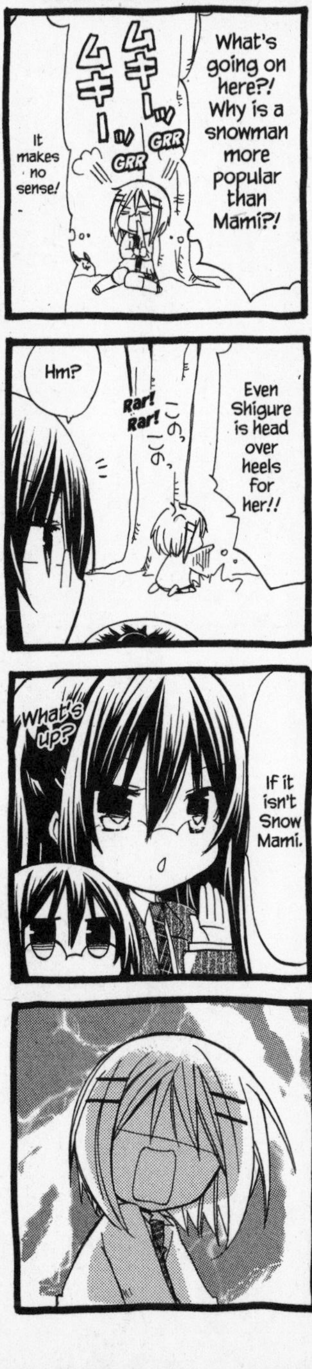
ムキーッ ムキーッ
GRR GRR
What's going on here?! Why is a snowman more popular than Mami?!
It makes no sense!
Even Shigure is head over heels for her!!
Rar! Rar!
Hm?
If it isn't Snow Mami.
What's up?

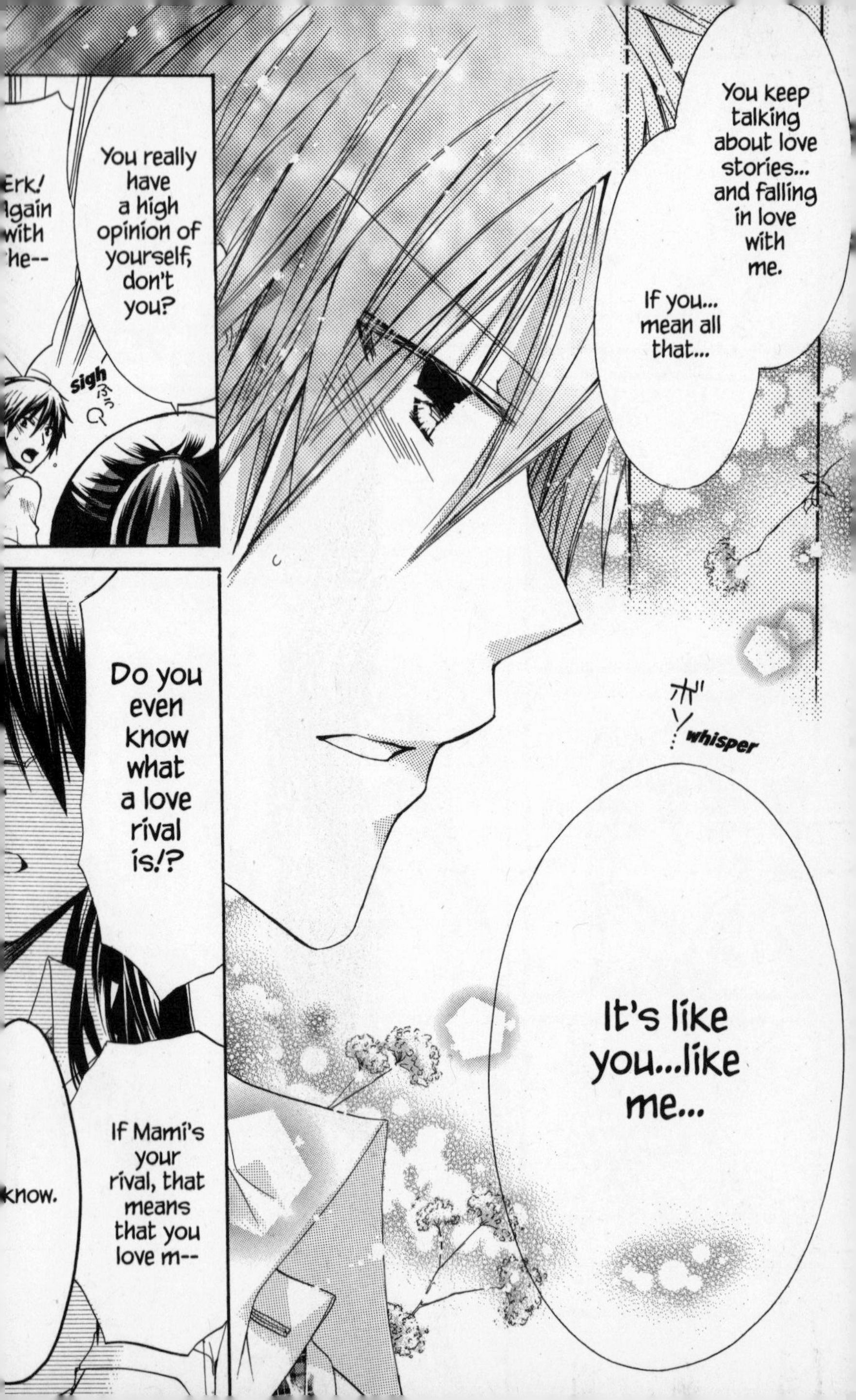
You keep talking about love stories... and falling in love with me.
If you... mean all that...
whisper
It's like you...like me...
You really have a high opinion of yourself, don't you?
sigh
Erk! Again with the--
Do you even know what a love rival is!?
If Mami's your rival, that means that you love m--
know.

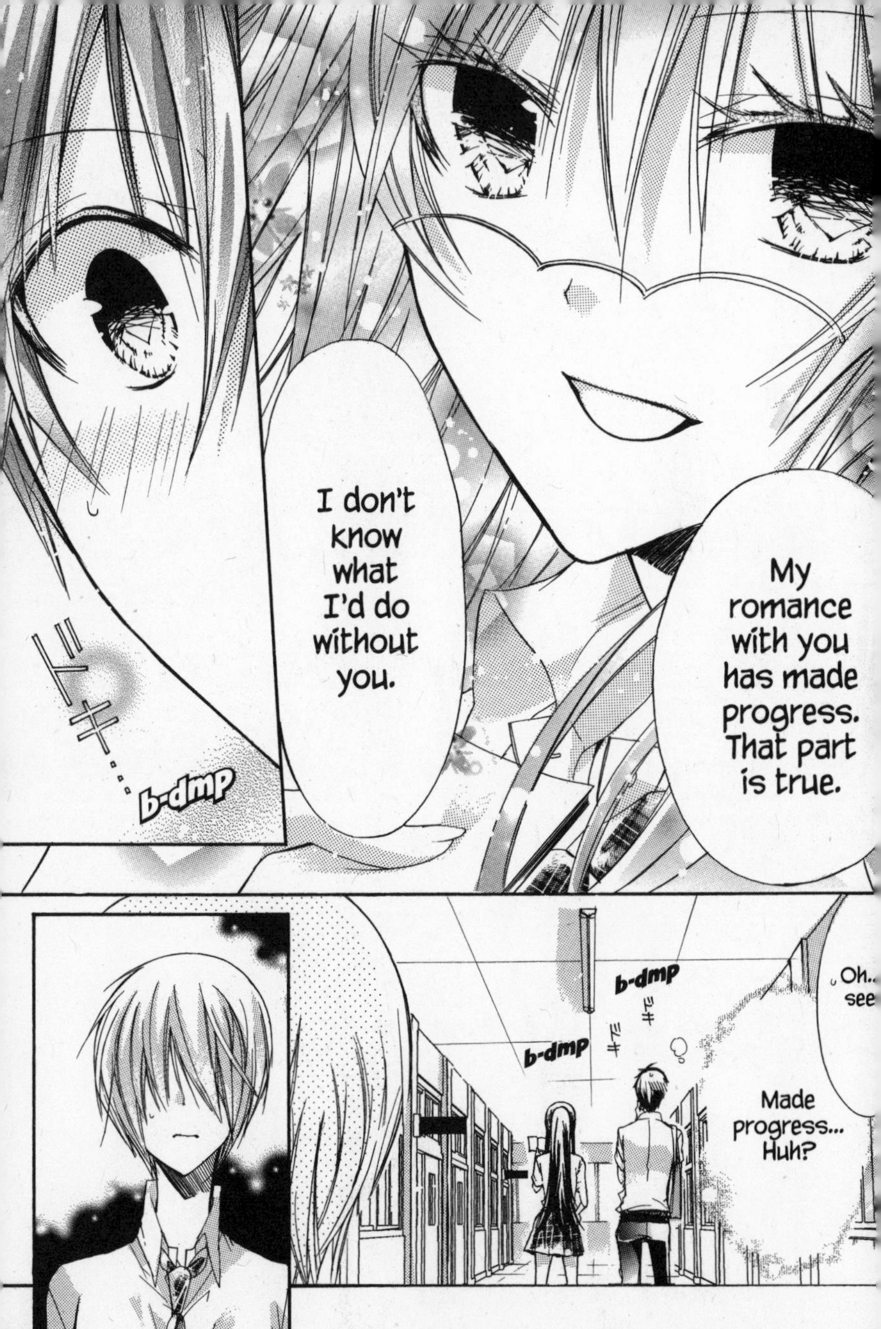
My romance with you has made progress. That part is true.
I don't know what I'd do without you.
ドキ...
b-dmp
Oh...
see
Made progress... Huh?
b-dmp
ドキ
b-dmp
ドキ

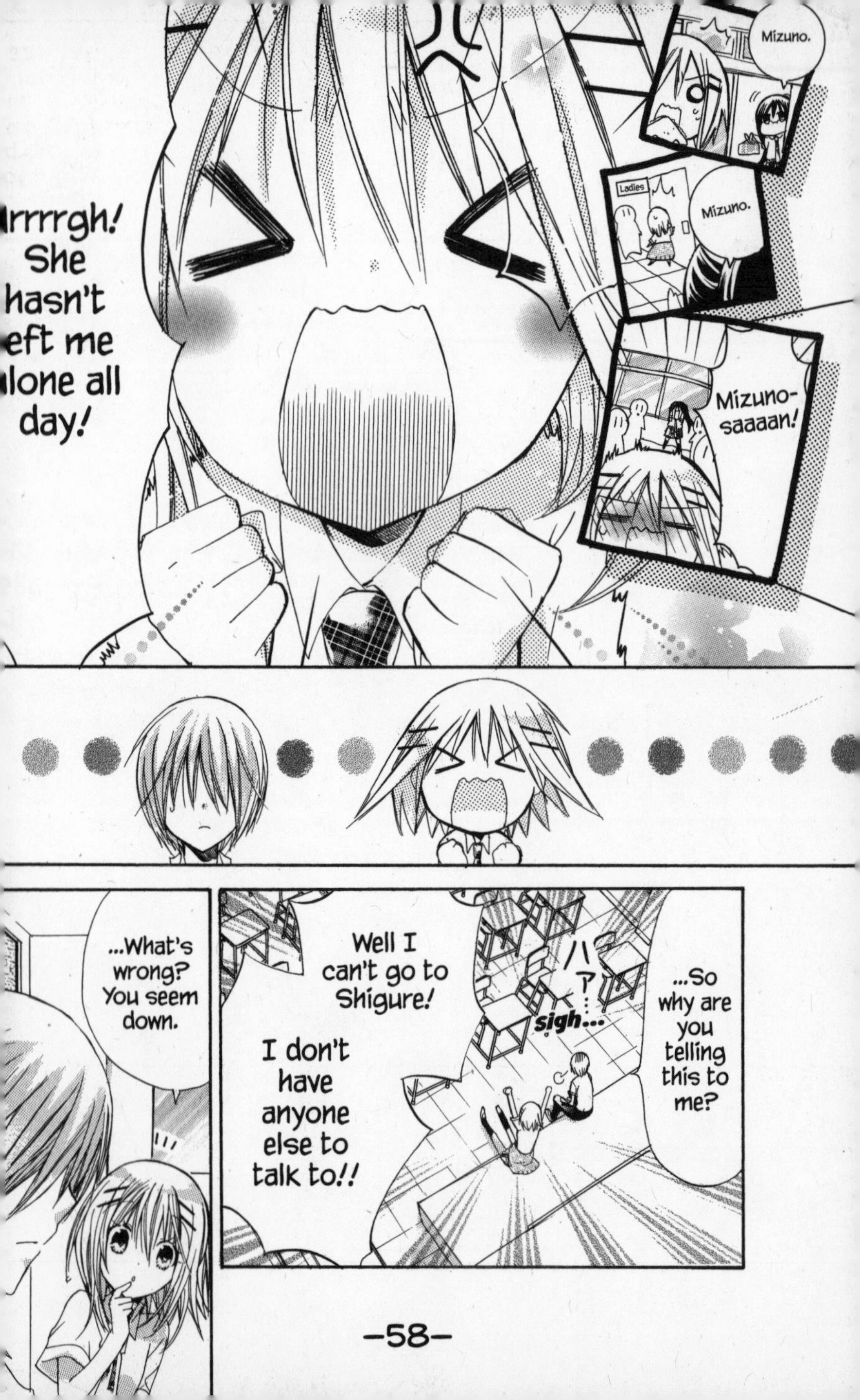
Mizuno.
Mizuno.
Ladies
Mizuno-saaaan!
rrrrgh! She hasn't eft me lone all day!
...So why are you telling this to me?
ハア… sigh...
Well I can't go to Shigure!
I don't have anyone else to talk to!!
...What's wrong? You seem down.

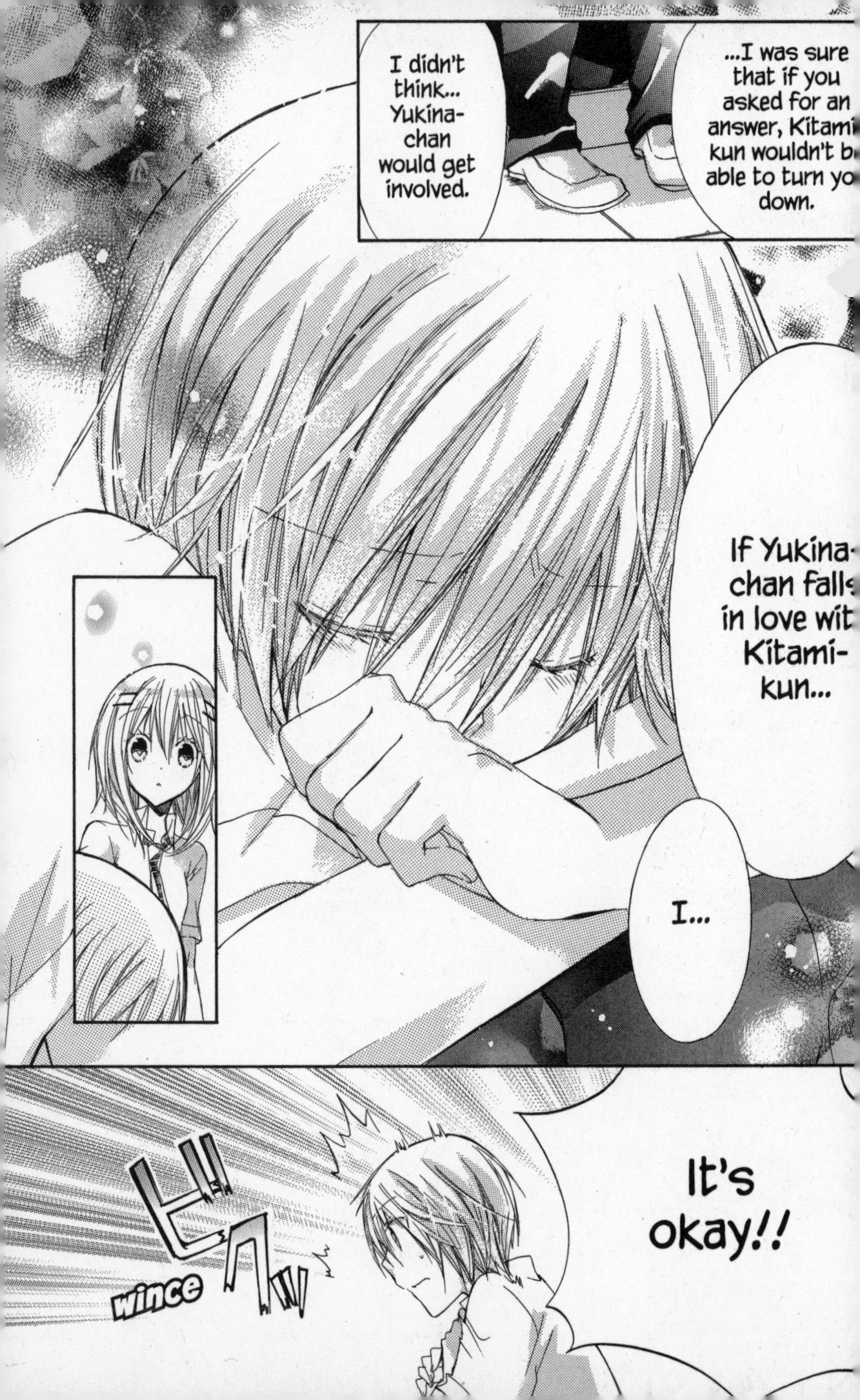
...I was sure that if you asked for an answer, Kitami kun wouldn't b able to turn yo down.
I didn't think... Yukina-chan would get involved.
If Yukina-chan fall in love wit Kitami-kun...
I...
It's okay!!
wince

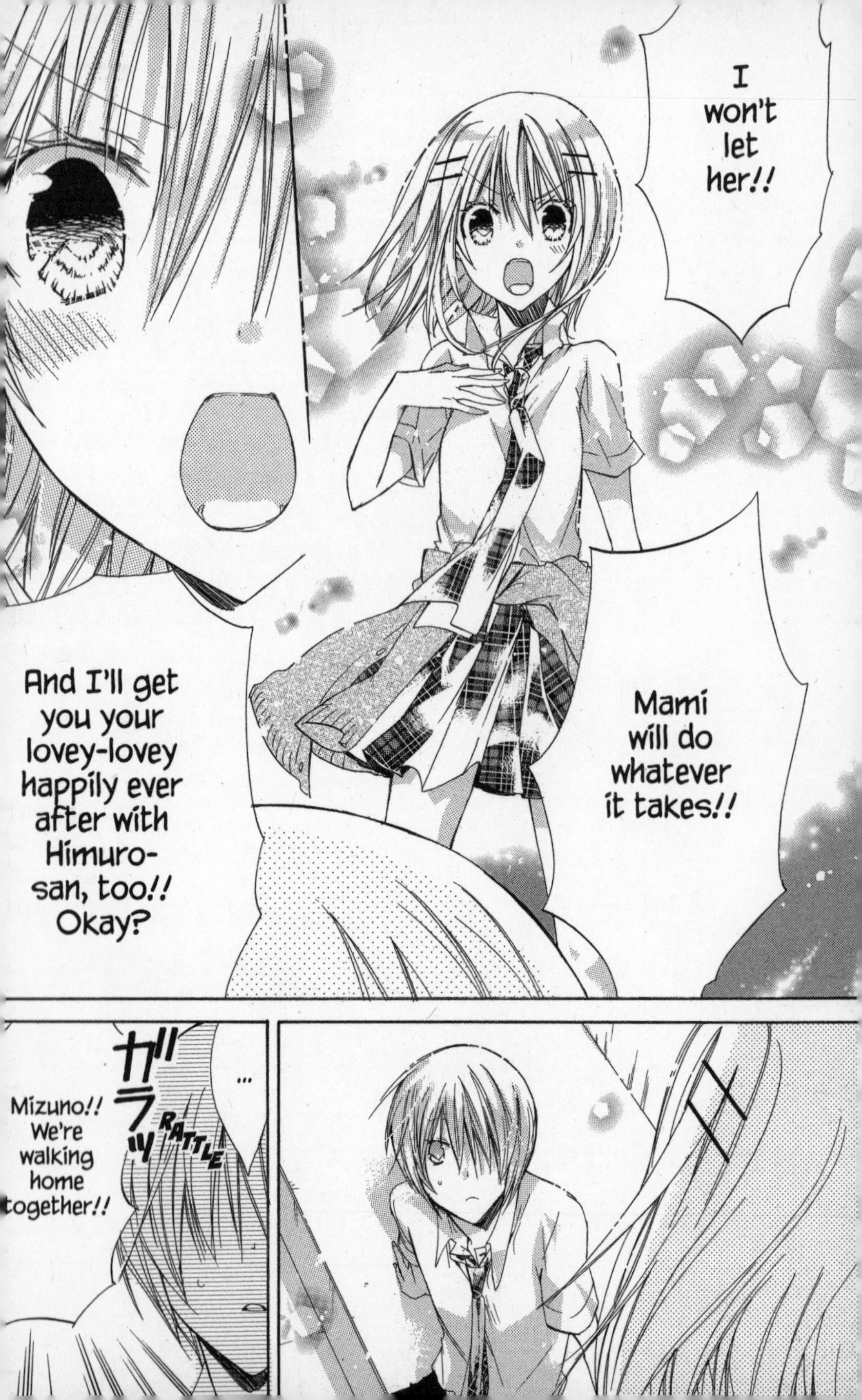

I won't let her!!
Mami will do whatever it takes!!
And I'll get you your lovey-lovey happily ever after with Himuro-san, too!! Okay?
...
ガラッ
RATTLE
Mizuno!! We're walking home together!!

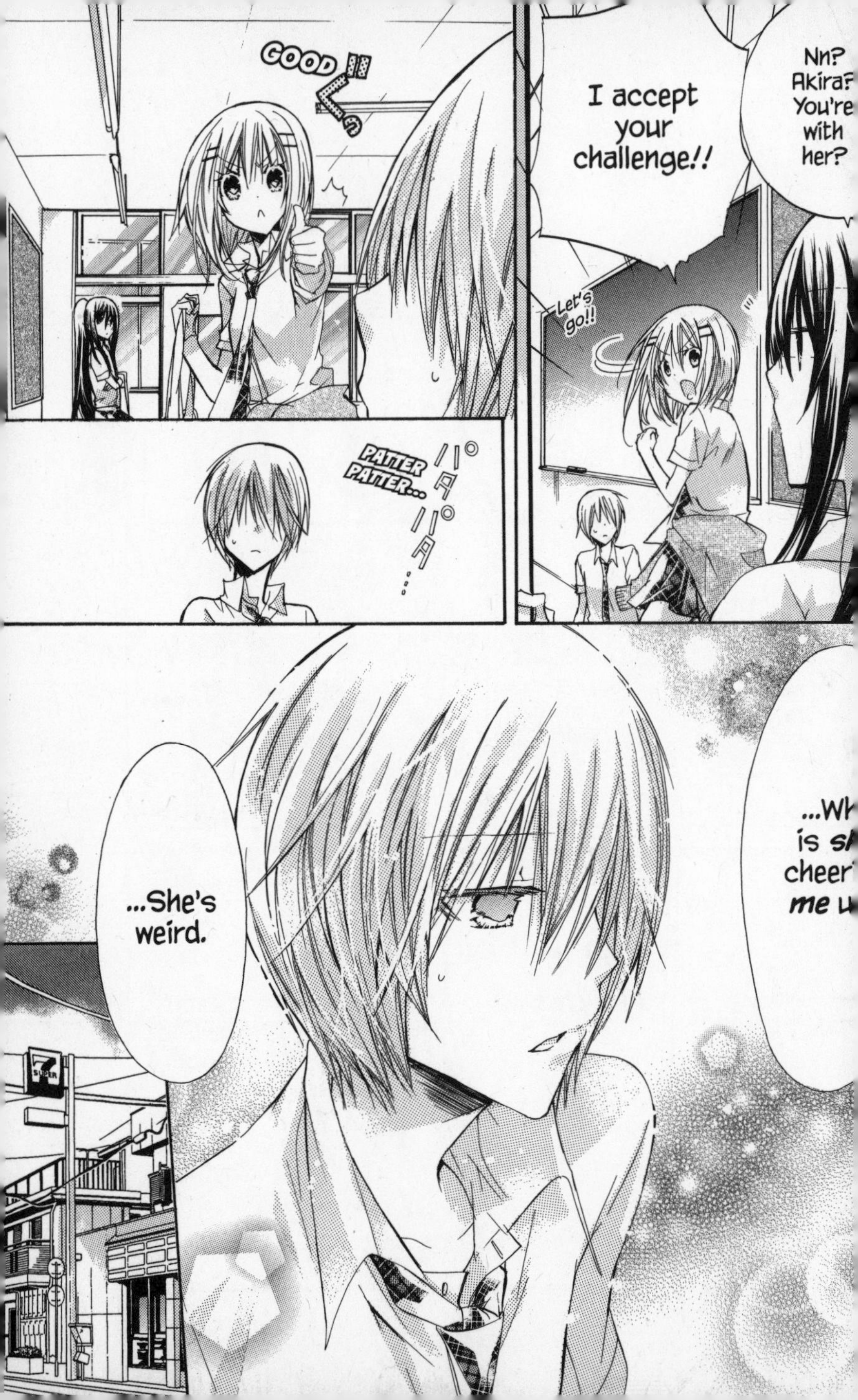

Nn? Akira? You're with her?
I accept your challenge!!
Let's go!!
GOOD!!
PATTER PATTER...
パタパタ...
...Wh is s cheer me u
...She's weird.

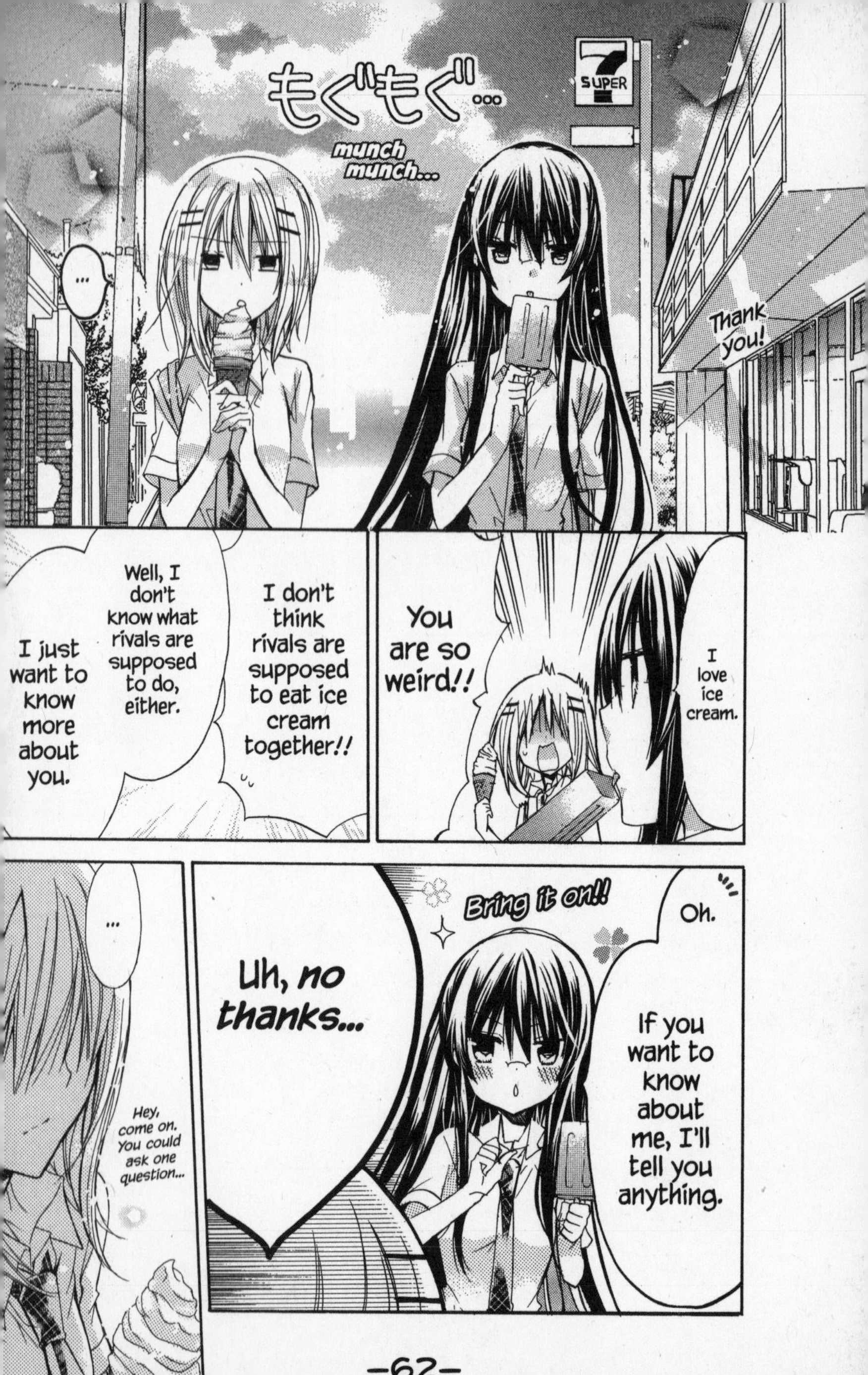
Thank you!
もぐもぐ…
munch munch...
...
I love ice cream.
You are so weird!!
I don't think rivals are supposed to eat ice cream together!!
Well, I don't know what rivals are supposed to do, either.
I just want to know more about you.
Oh.
If you want to know about me, I'll tell you anything.
Bring it on!!
Uh, *no* thanks...
...
Hey, come on. You could ask one question...

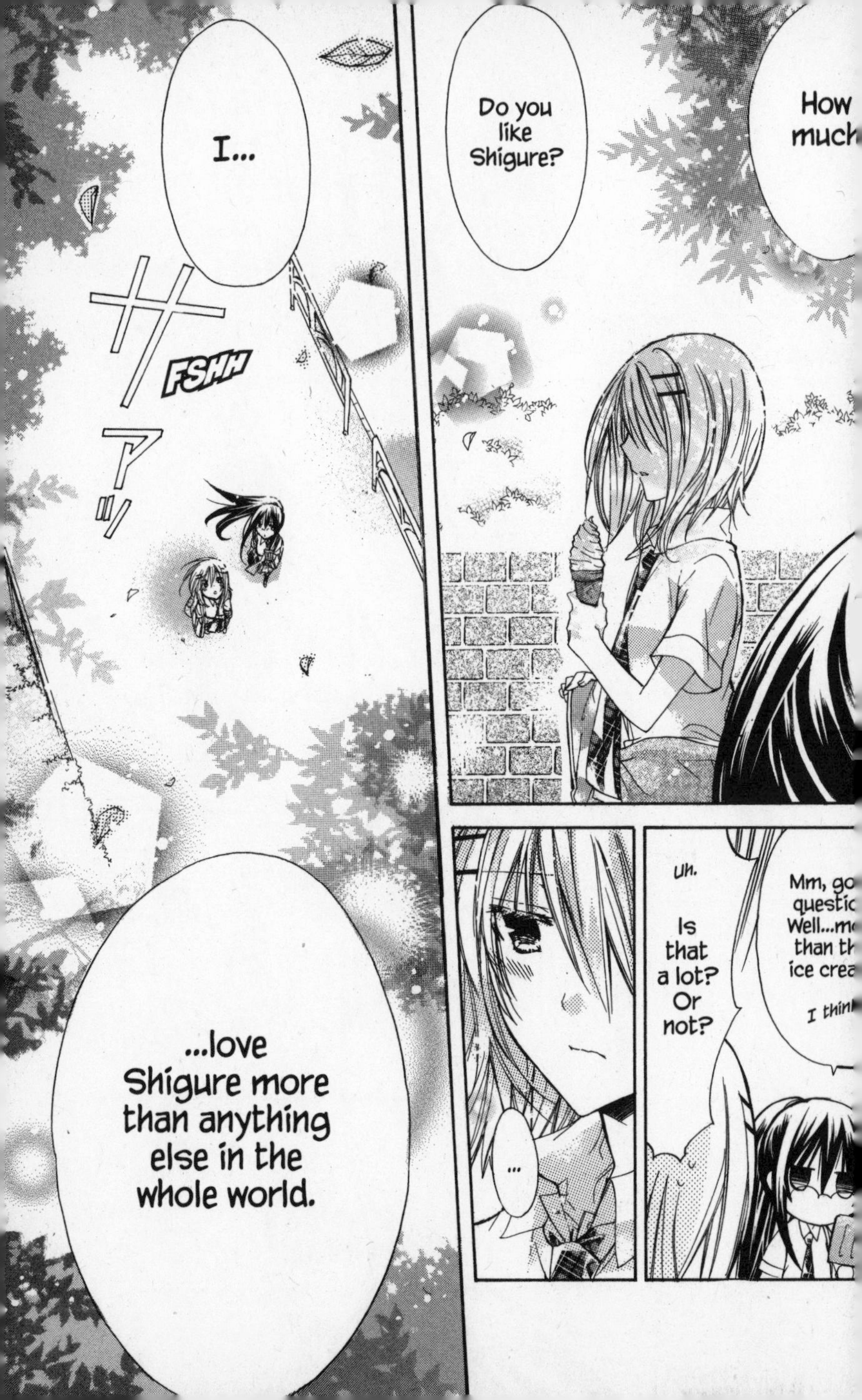
How much
Do you like Shigure?
Mm, go questic Well...m than th ice crea
I think
Uh.
Is that a lot? Or not?
...
I...
FSHH
...love Shigure more than anything else in the whole world.

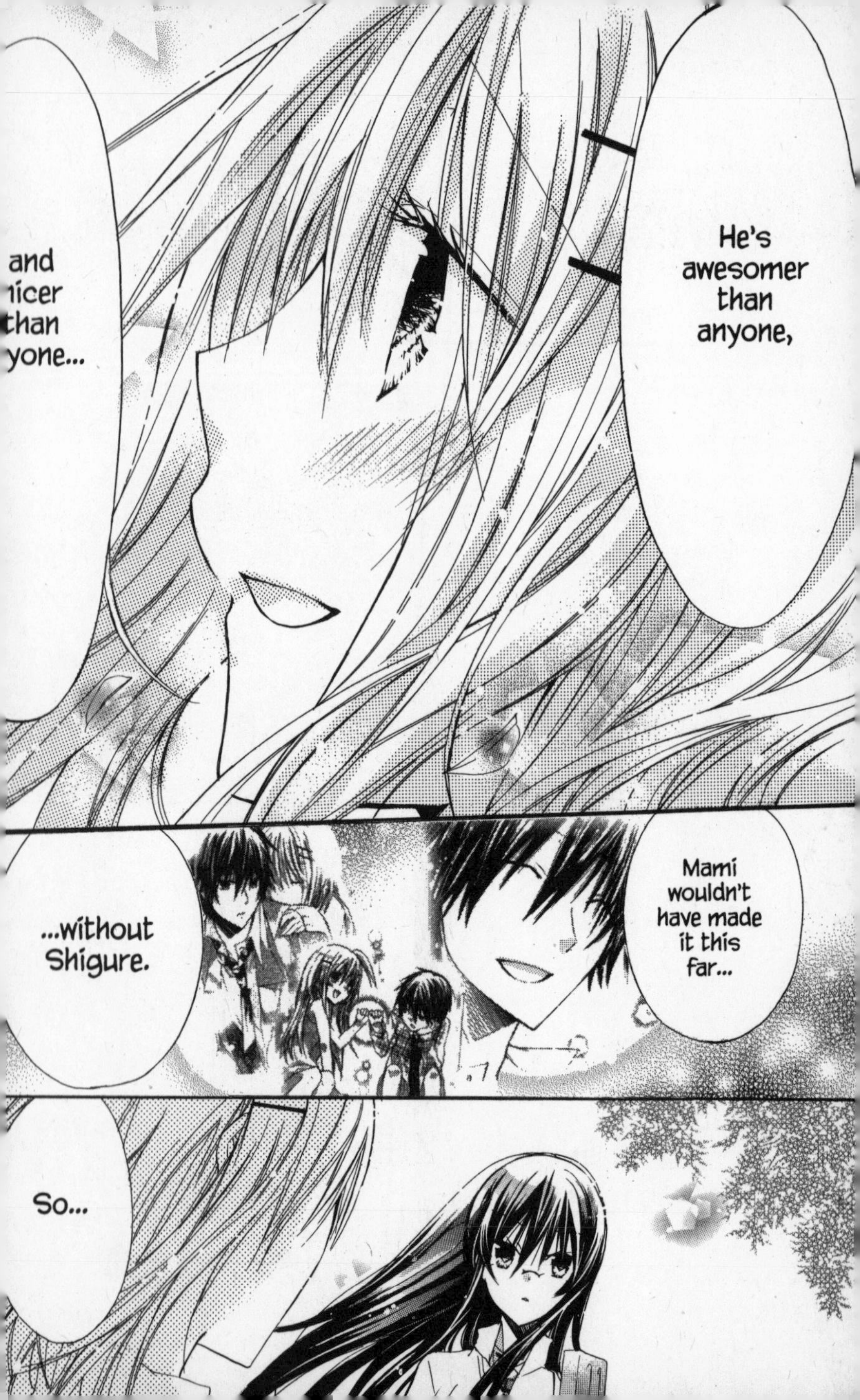
He's awesomer than anyone,
and icer than yone...
Mami wouldn't have made it this far...
...without Shigure.
So...

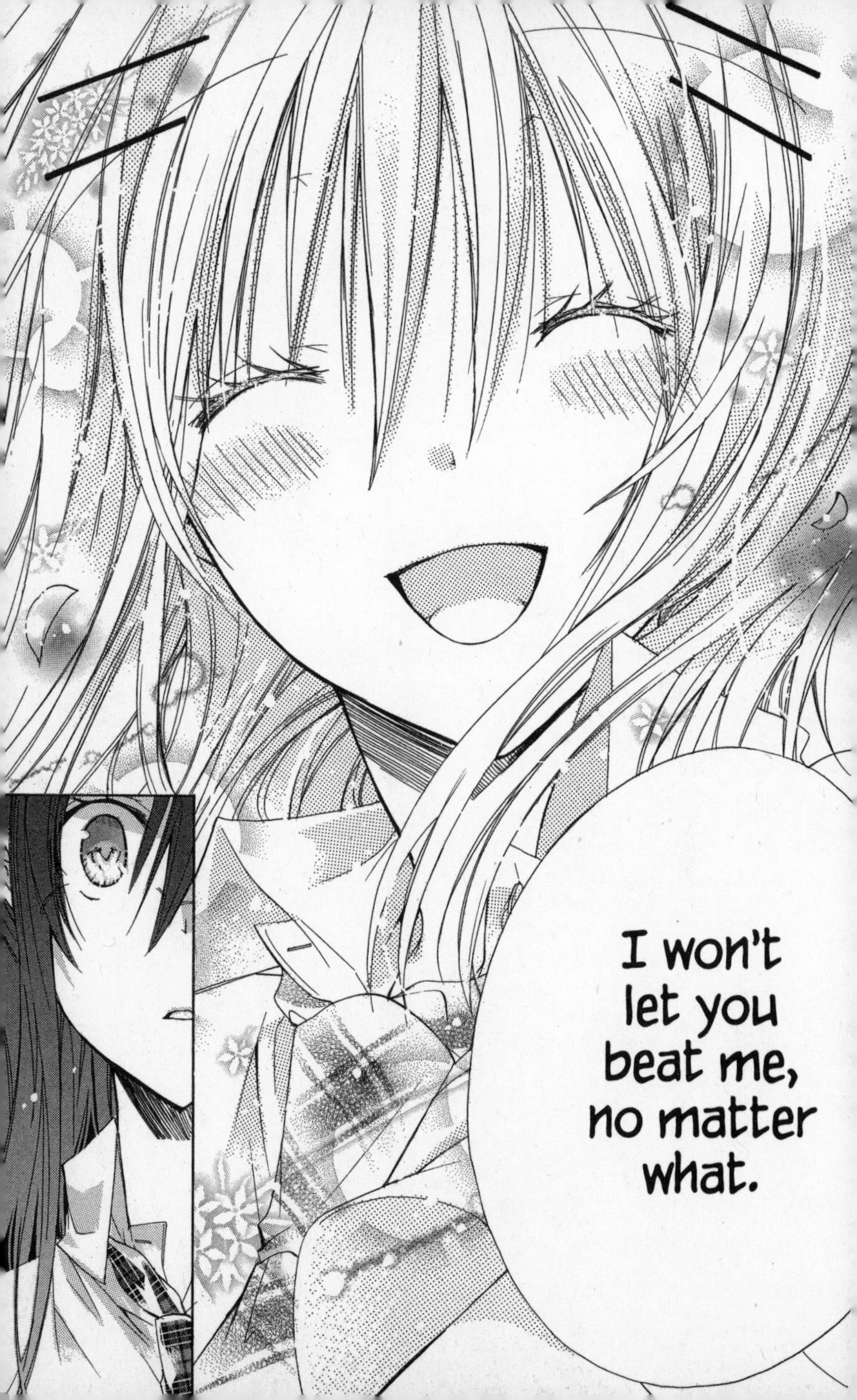
I won't let you beat me, no matter what.

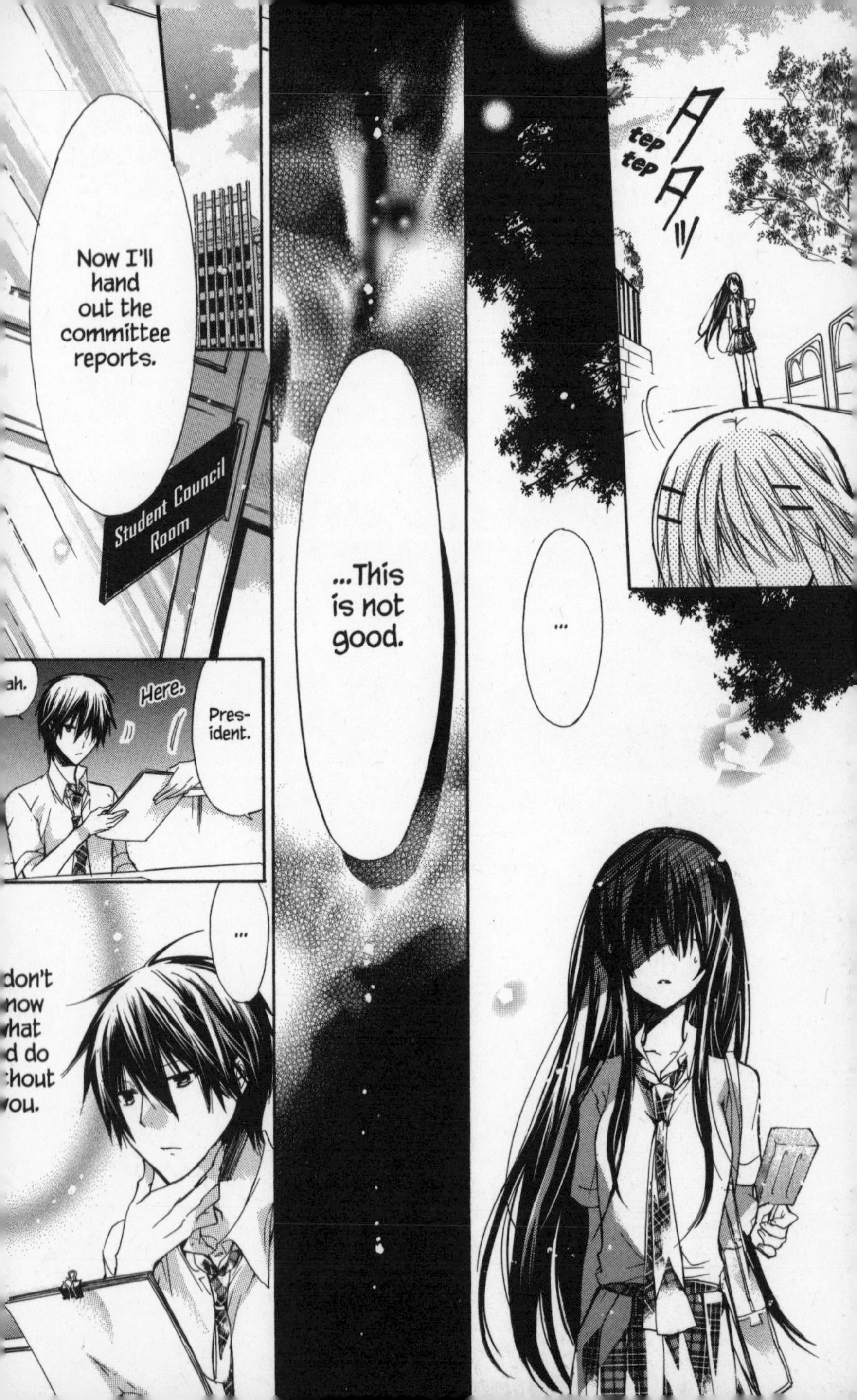

tep tep
タタッ
...
...This is not good.
Now I'll hand out the committee reports.
Student Council Room
Pres- ident.
Here.
ah.
...
don't
now
hat
d do
thout
ou.

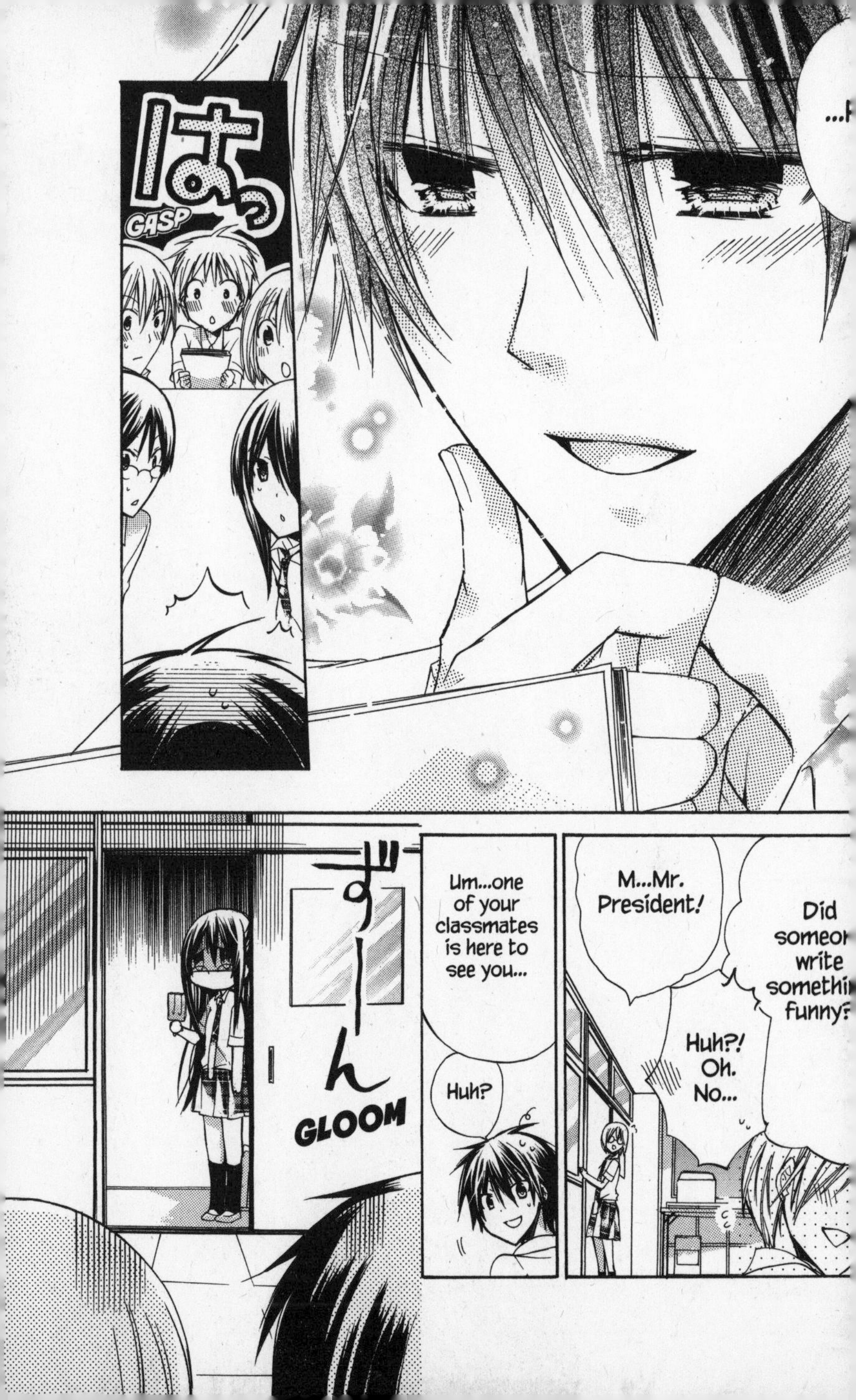

はっ
GASP
Did someo write somethi funny?
M...Mr. President!
Huh?! Oh. No...
Um...one of your classmates is here to see you...
Huh?
ずーん
GLOOM

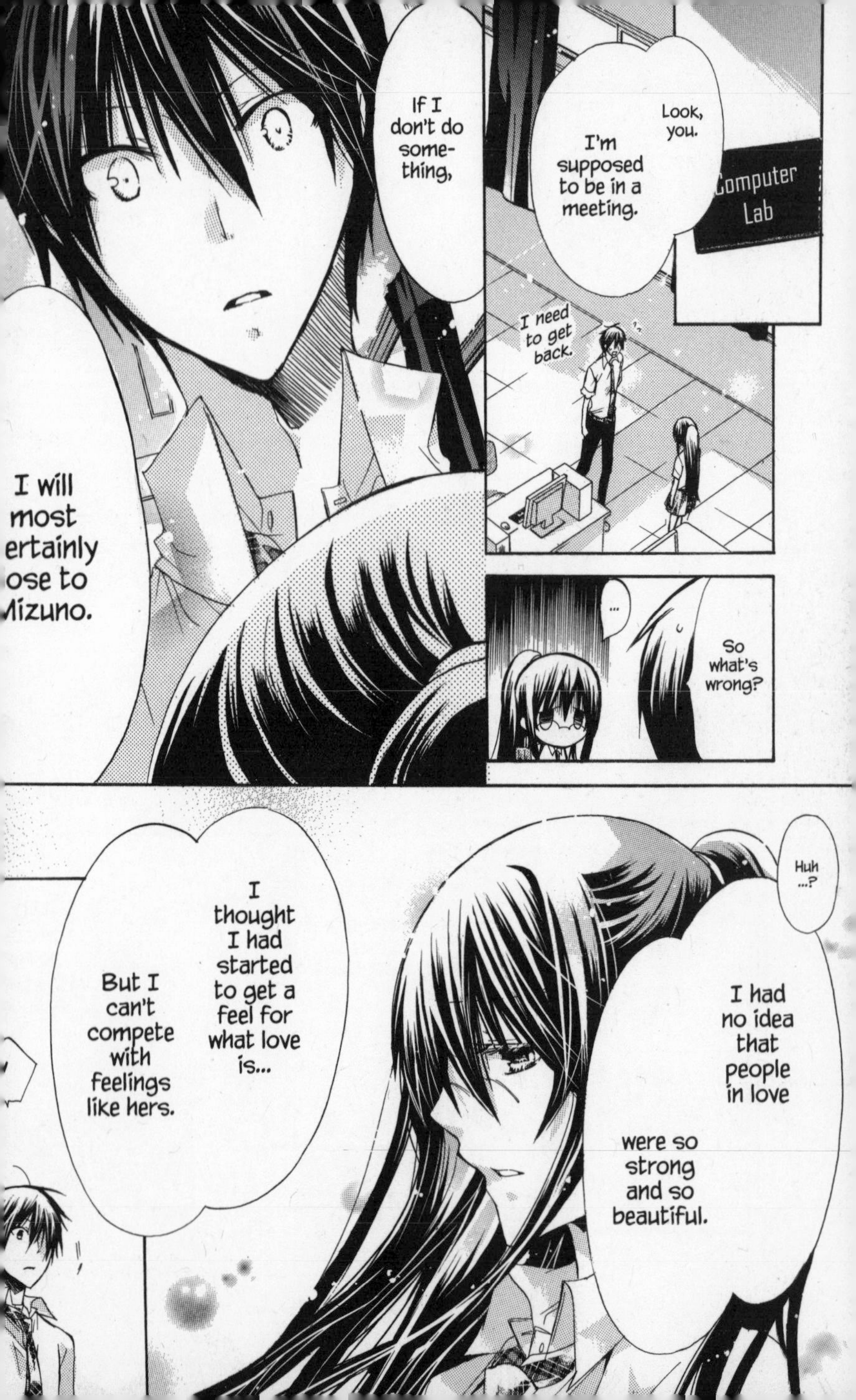
Look, you.
I'm supposed to be in a meeting.
Computer Lab
I need to get back.
So what's wrong?
...
If I don't do some-thing,
I will most ertainly ose to izuno.
Huh ...?
I had no idea that people in love
were so strong and so beautiful.
I thought I had started to get a feel for what love is...
But I can't compete with feelings like hers.

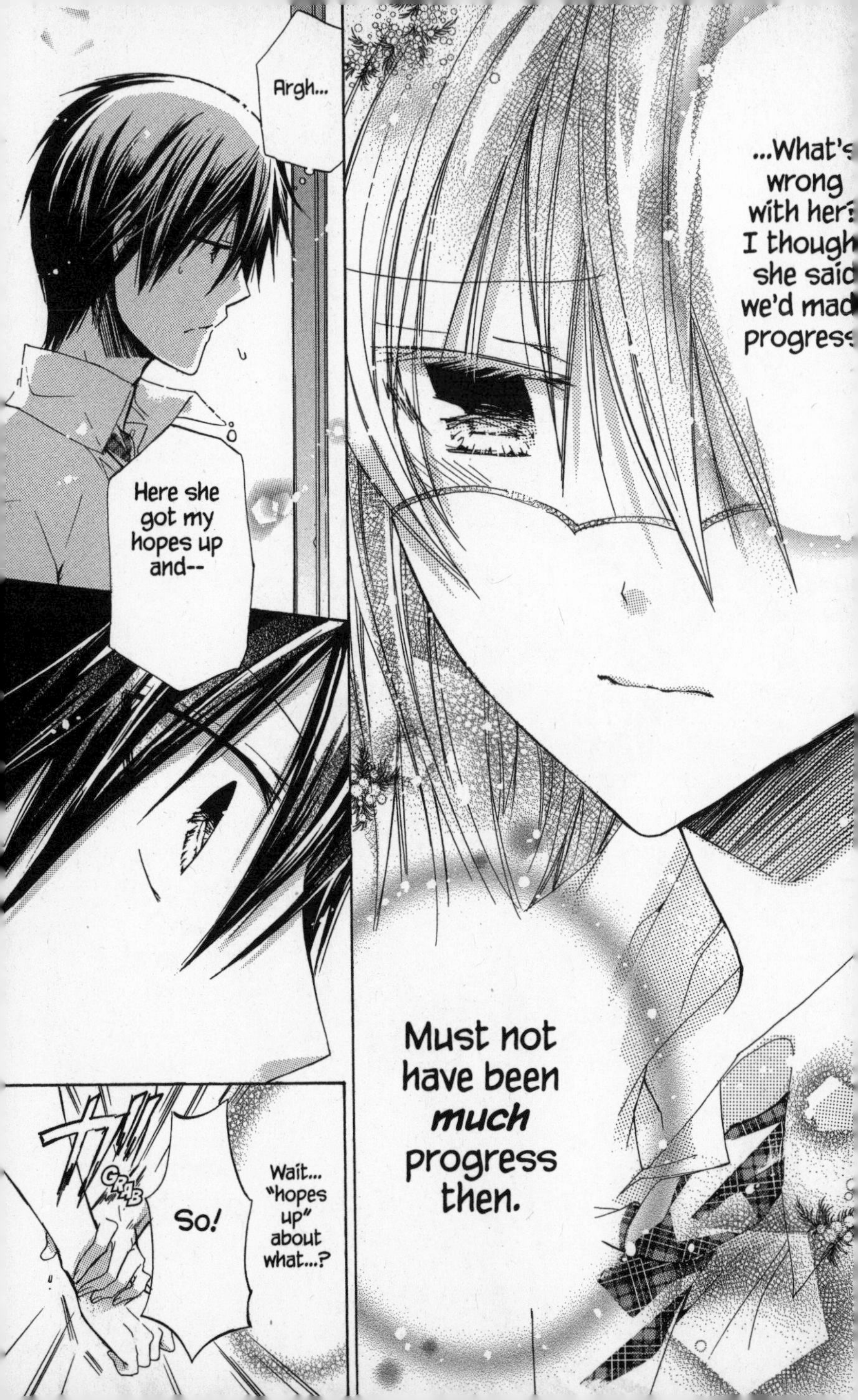
...What's wrong with her? I though she said we'd mad progress
Must not have been *much* progress then.
Argh...
Here she got my hopes up and--
Wait... "hopes up" about what...?
So!
GRAB

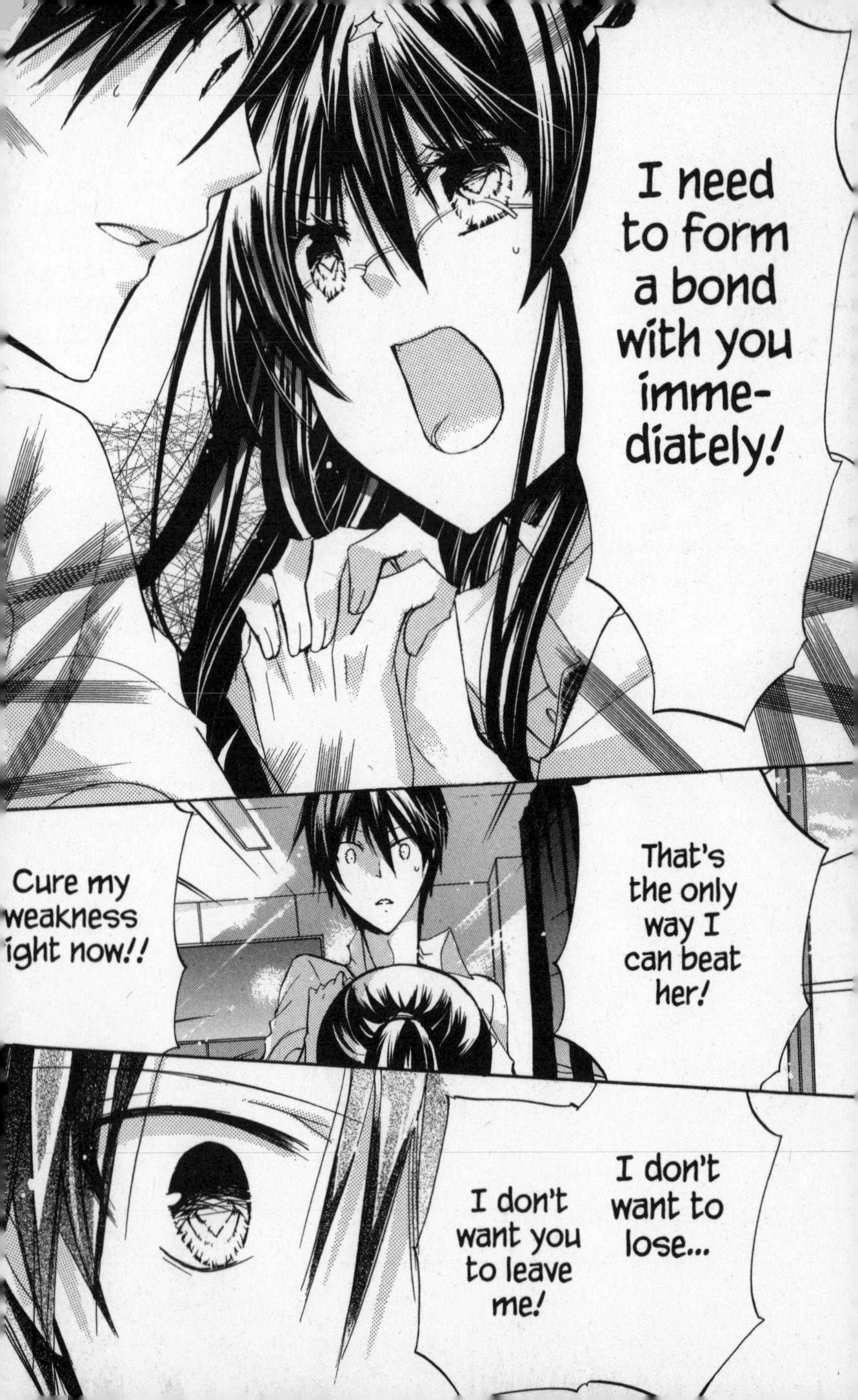
I need to form a bond with you imme-diately!
That's the only way I can beat her!
Cure my weakness ight now!!
I don't want to lose...
I don't want you to leave me!

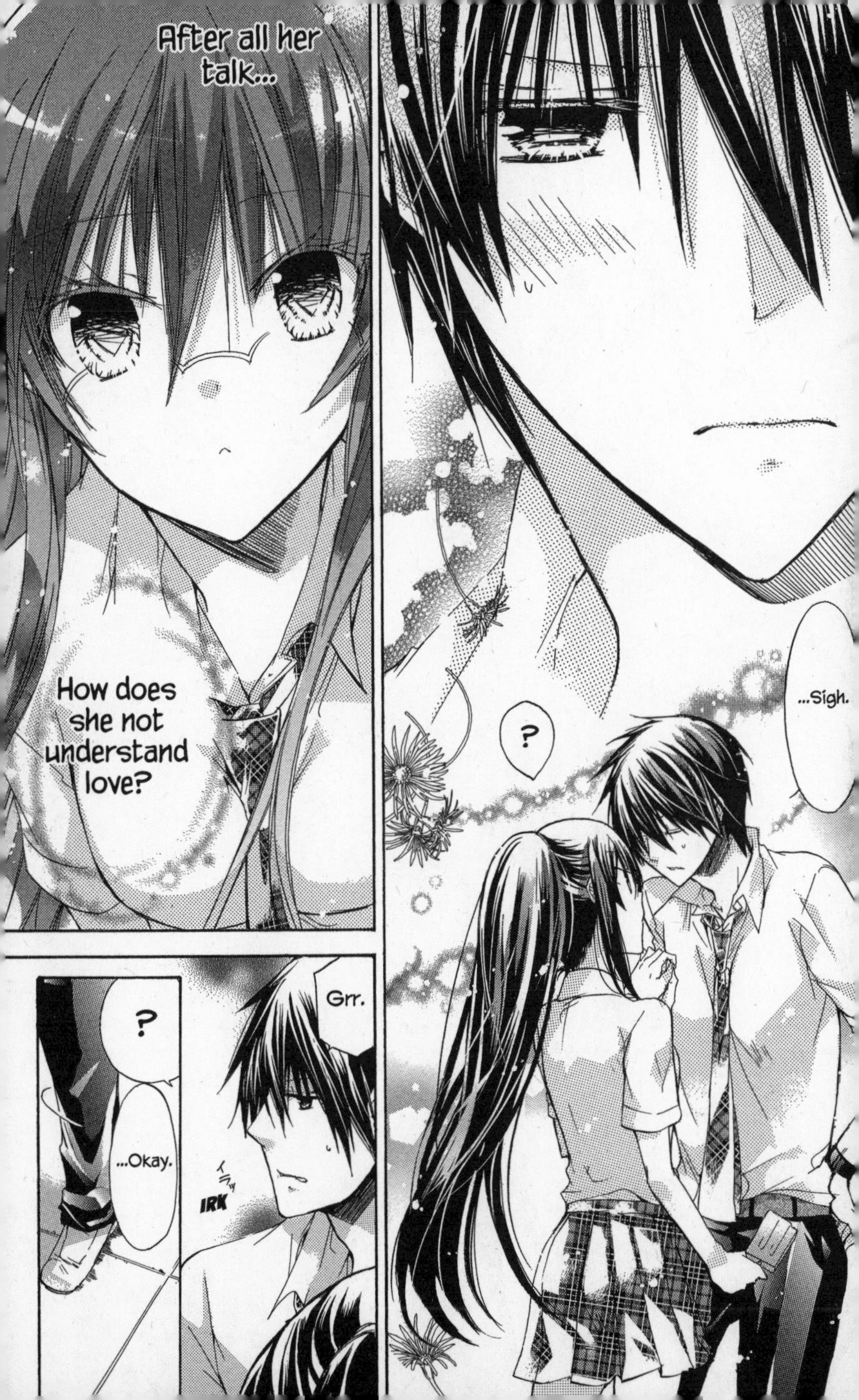
...Sigh.
?
After all her talk...
How does she not understand love?
Grr.
?
...Okay.
IRK

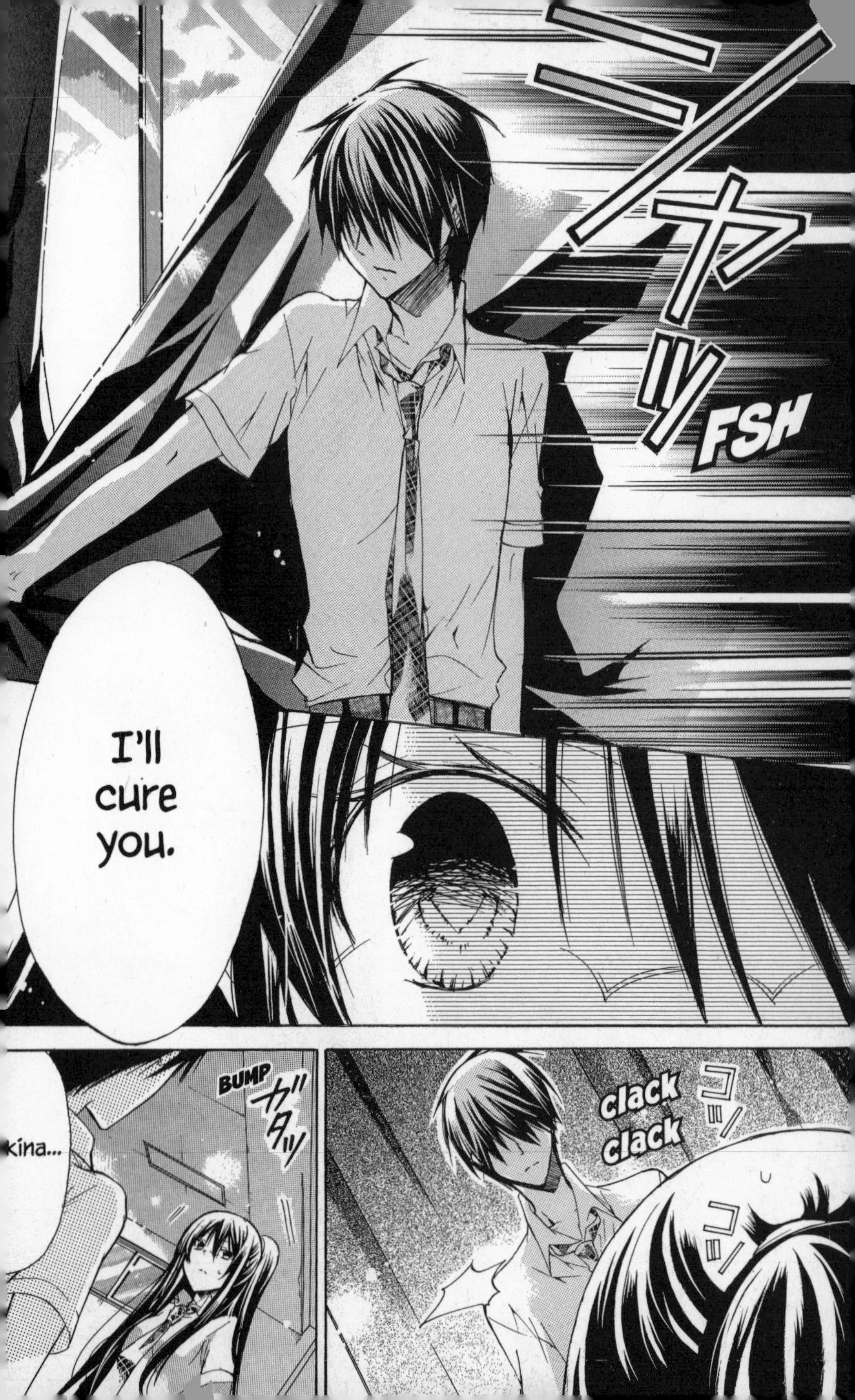
シャッ
FSH
I'll cure you.
clack clack
コン
コン
BUMP
ガタッ
kina...

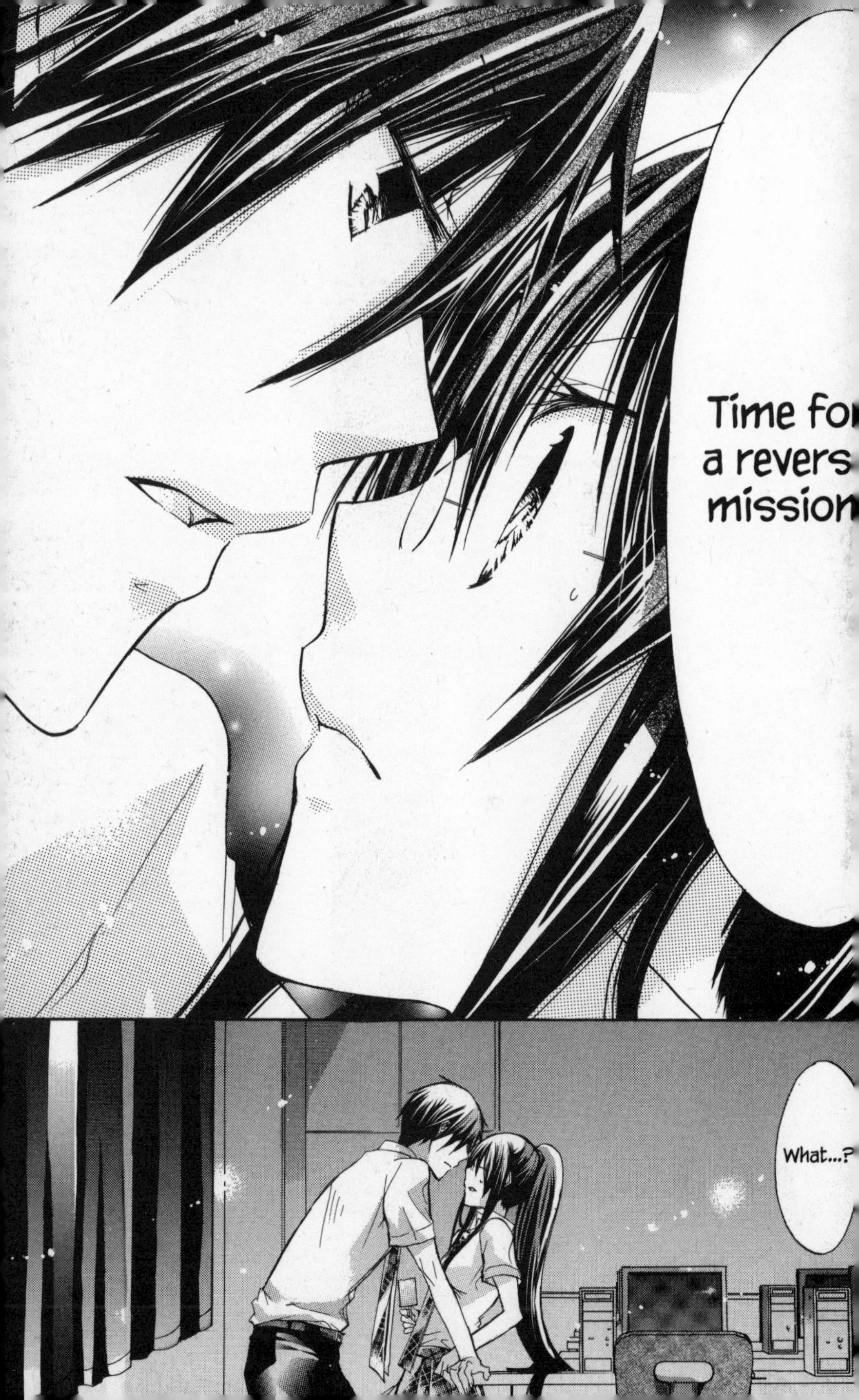
Time fo
a revers
mission
What...?

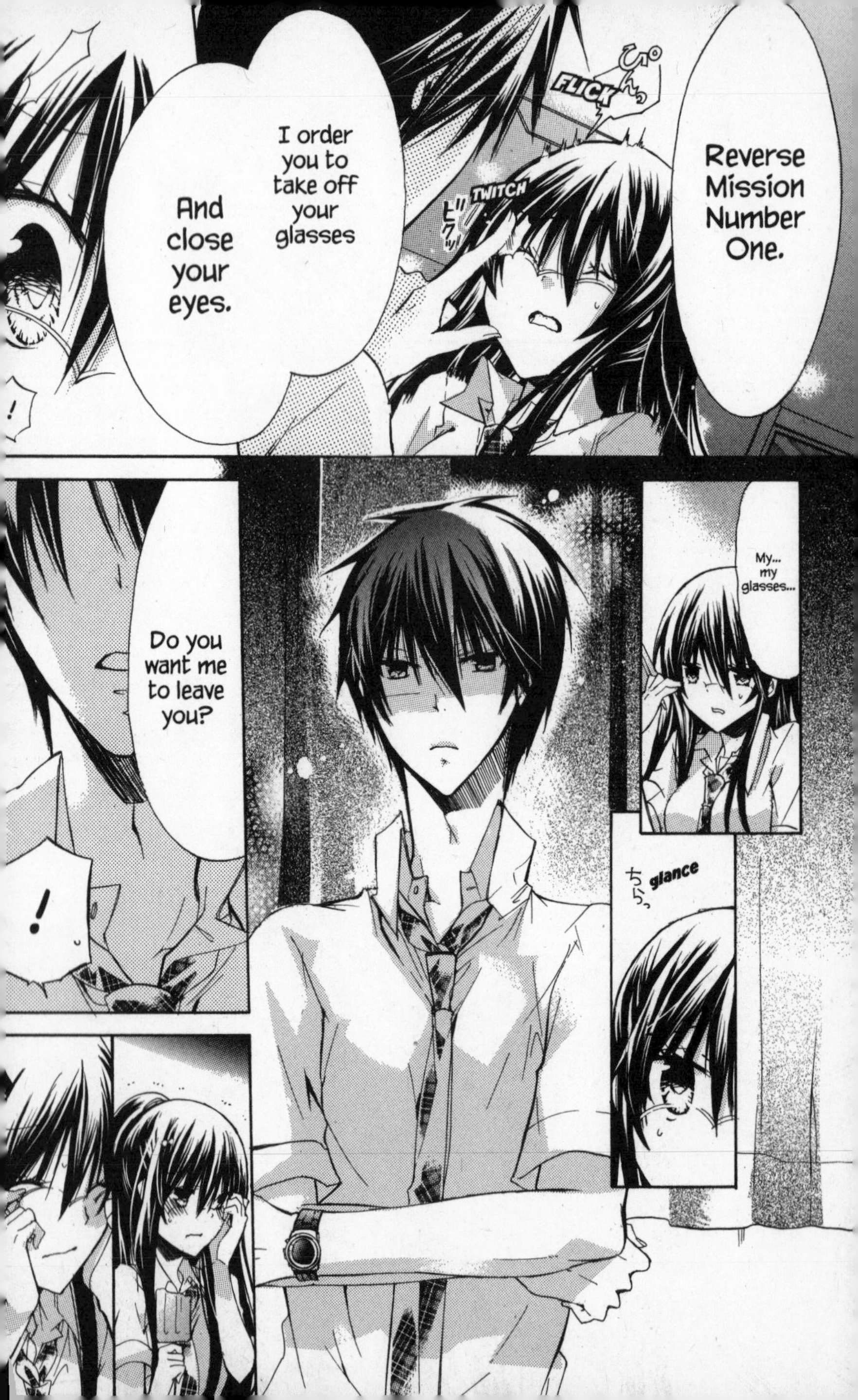
Reverse Mission Number One.
FLICK
ぴんっ
TWITCH
ビクッ
I order you to take off your glasses
And close your eyes.
!
My... my glasses...
glance
ちらっ
Do you want me to leave you?
!

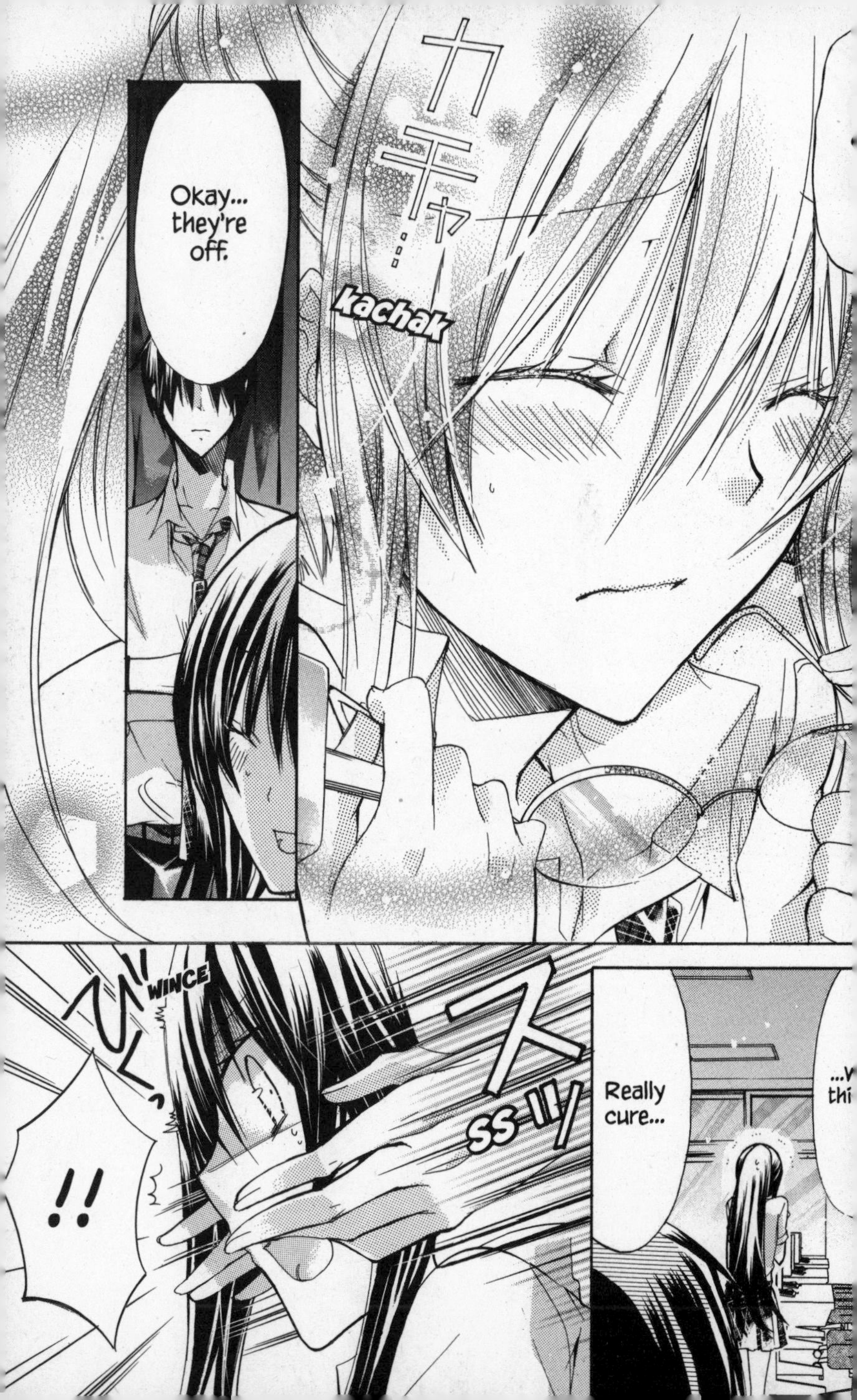
カチャ…
kachak
Okay... they're off.
Really cure...
スッ
ss
WINCE
!!

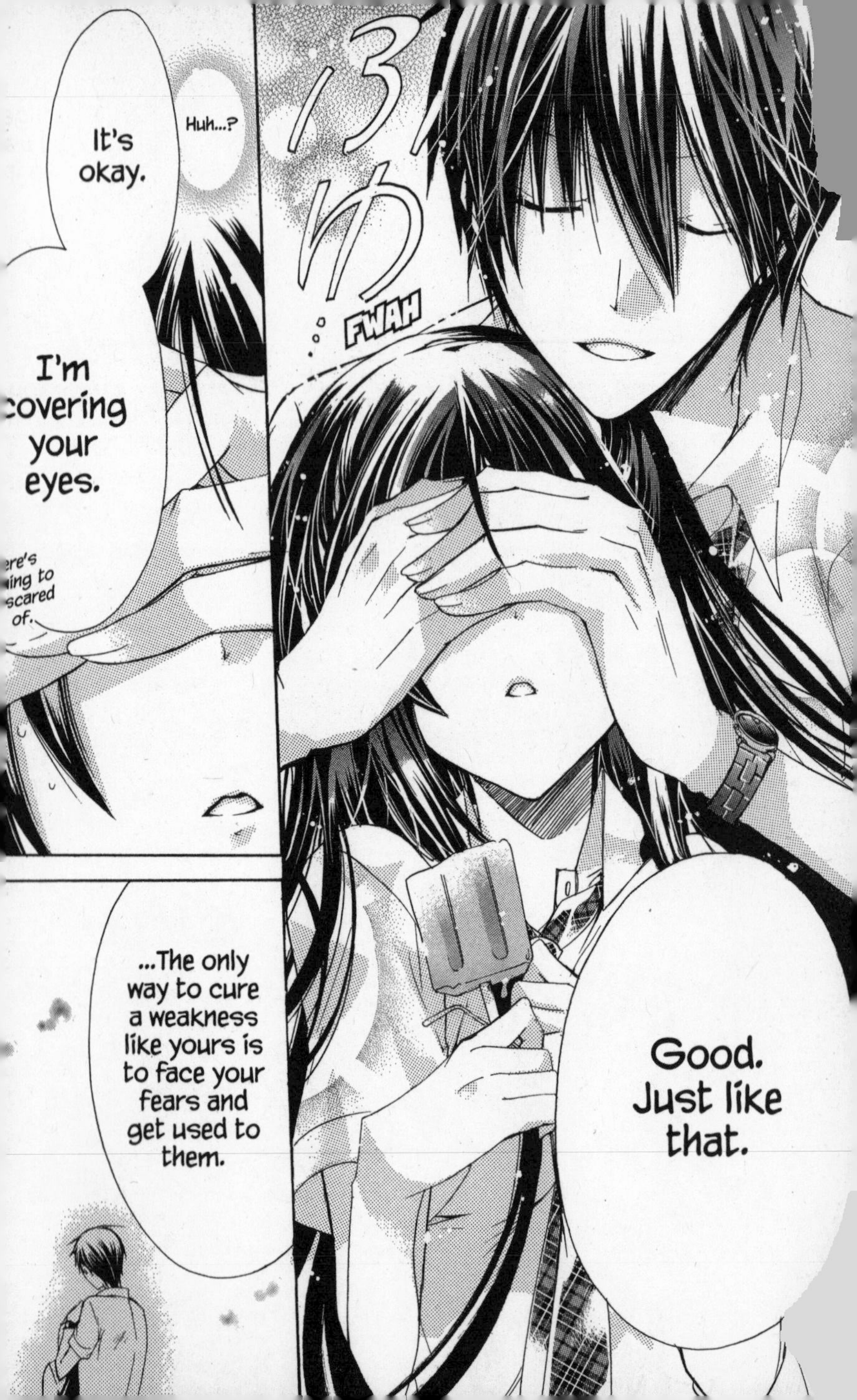
ふわ
FWAH
Good. Just like that.
Huh...?
It's okay.
I'm covering your eyes.
ere's ing to scared of.
...The only way to cure a weakness like yours is to face your fears and get used to them.

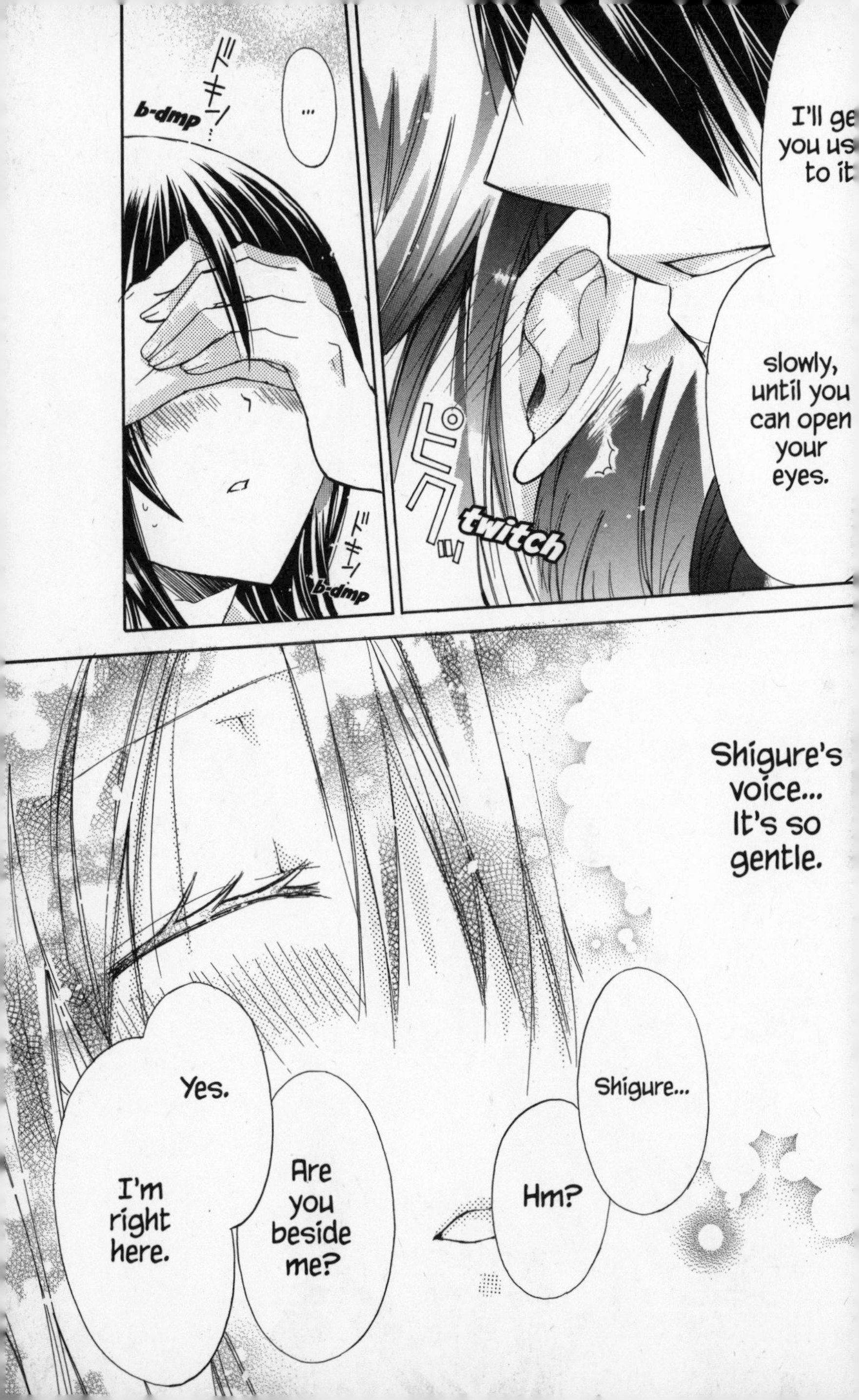
I'll ge you us to it
slowly, until you can open your eyes.
twitch
...
b-dmp
b-dmp
Shigure's voice... It's so gentle.
Shigure...
Hm?
Are you beside me?
Yes.
I'm right here.

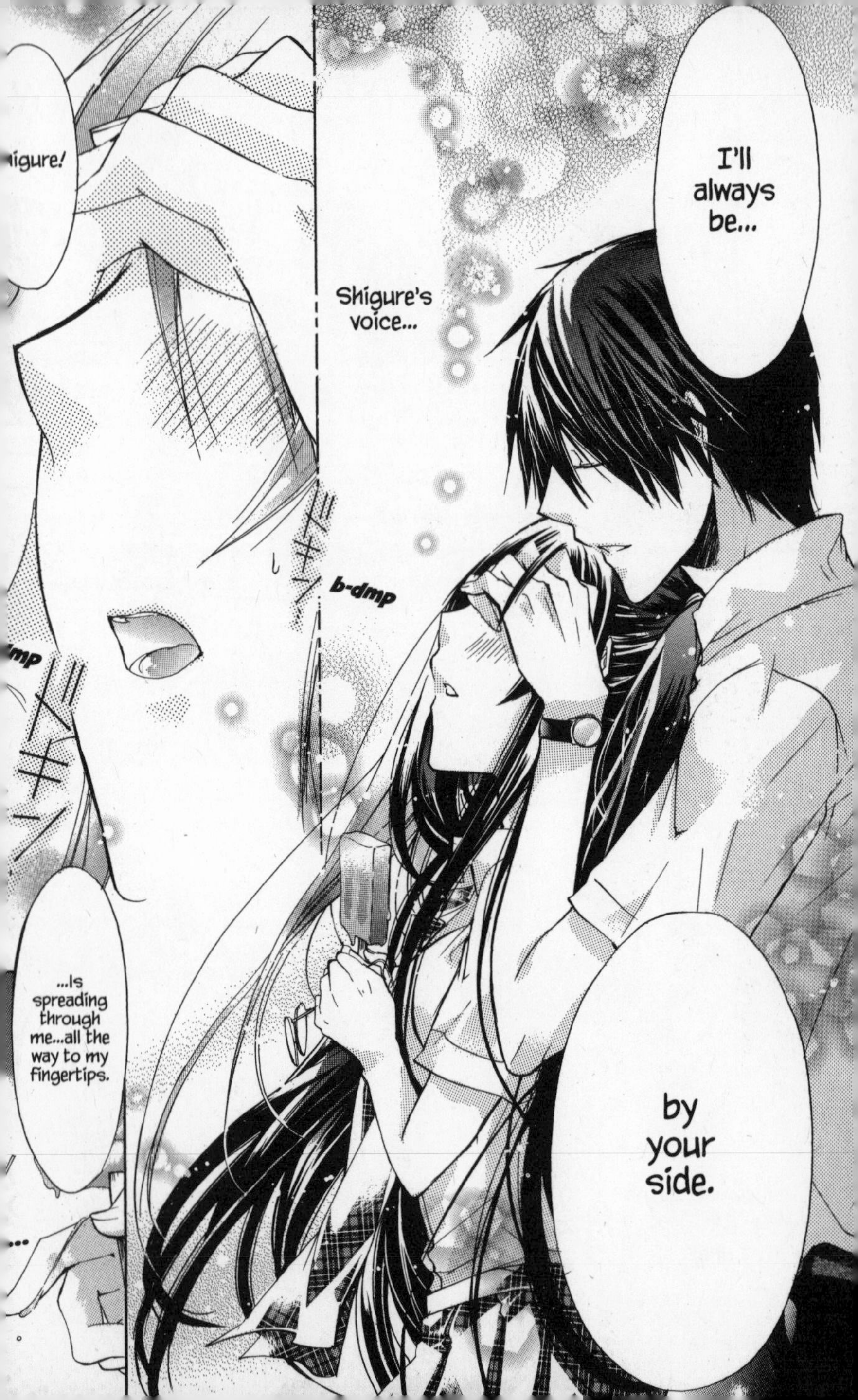
I'll always be...
Shigure's voice...
b-dmp
by your side.
higure!
dmp
...Is spreading through me...all the way to my fingertips.
...

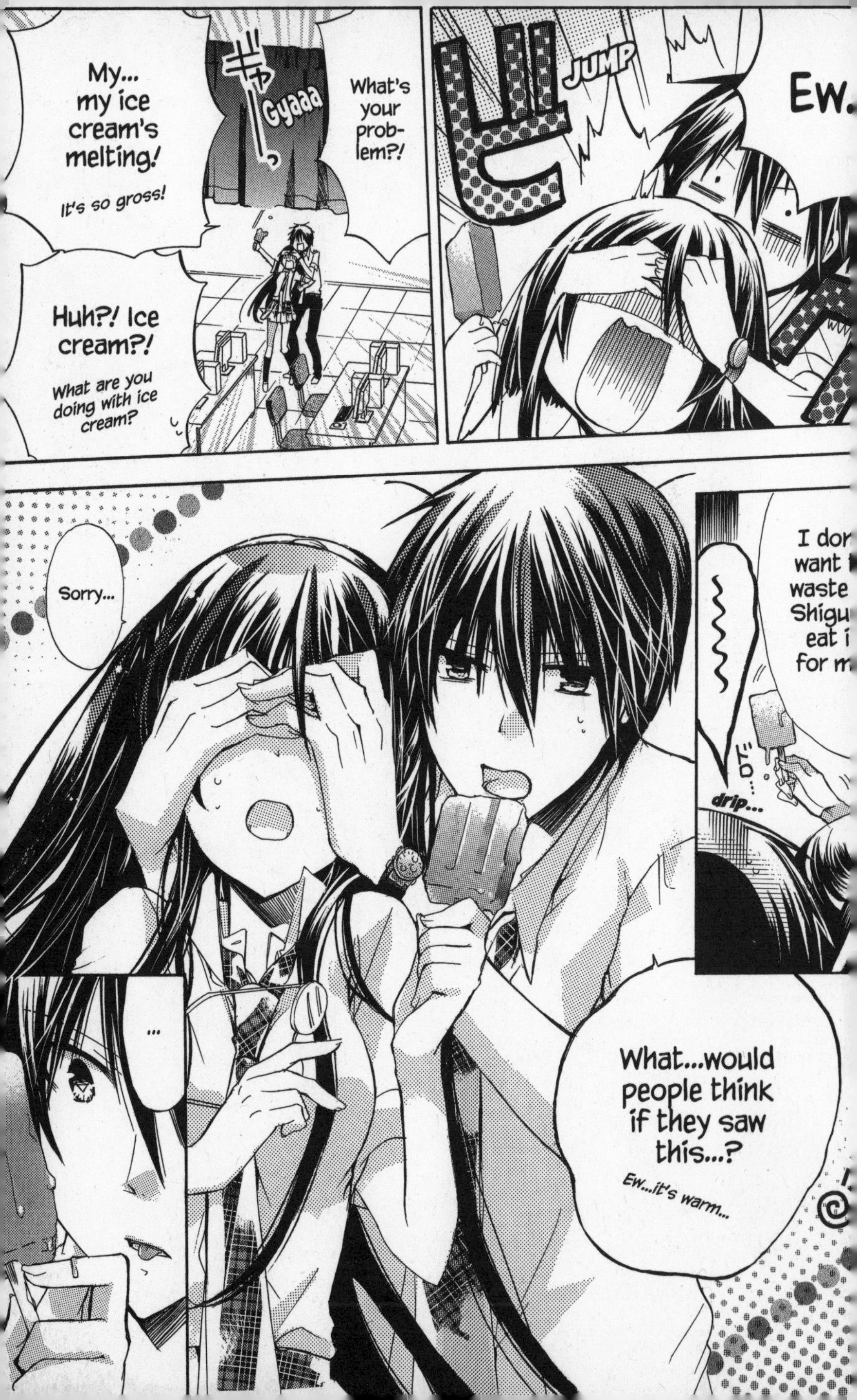

JUMP
Ew.
What's your prob-lem?!
Gyaaa
My... my ice cream's melting!
It's so gross!
Huh?! Ice cream?!
What are you doing with ice cream?
I dor want t waste Shigu eat i for m
drip...
Sorry...
What...would people think if they saw this...?
Ew...it's warm...
...

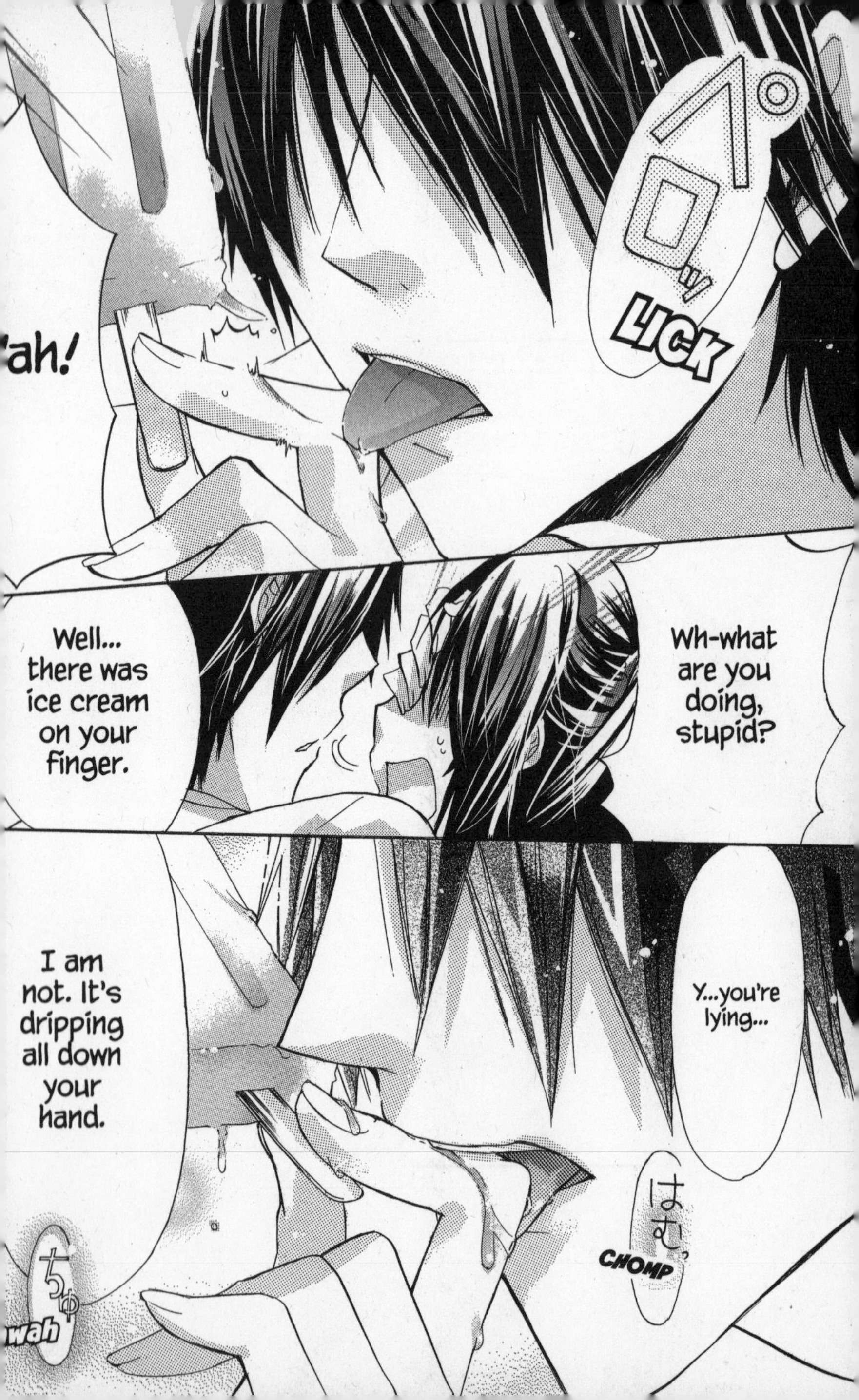
ペロ
LICK
ah!
Wh-what are you doing, stupid?
Well... there was ice cream on your finger.
Y...you're lying...
はむっ
CHOMP
I am not. It's dripping all down your hand.
ちゅ
wah

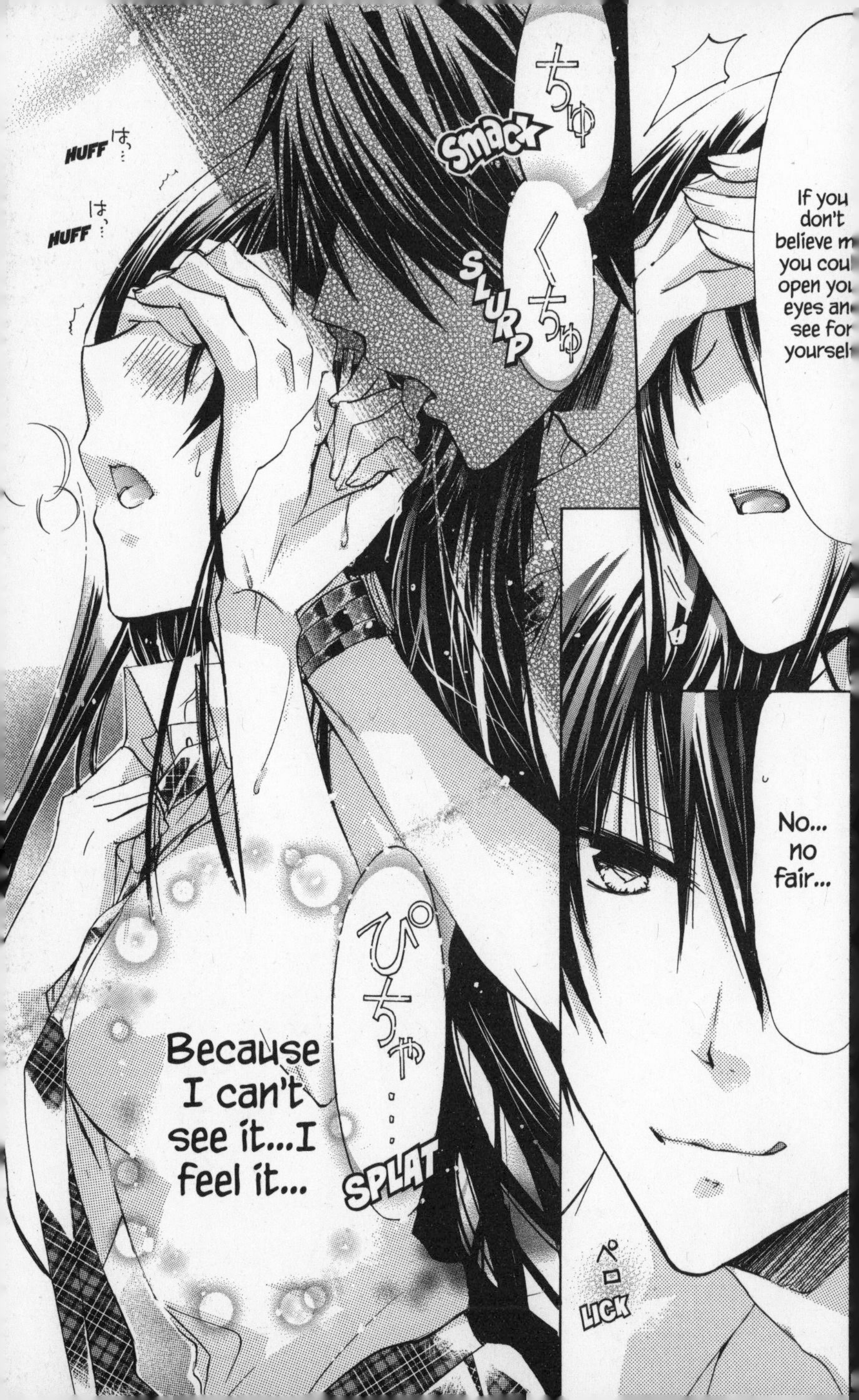

If you don't believe m you cou open you eyes an see for yoursel
No... no fair...
ペロ
LICK
ちゅ
SMACK
くちゅ
SLURP
HUFF はっ…
HUFF はっ…
ぴちゅ…
SPLAT
Because I can't see it...I feel it...

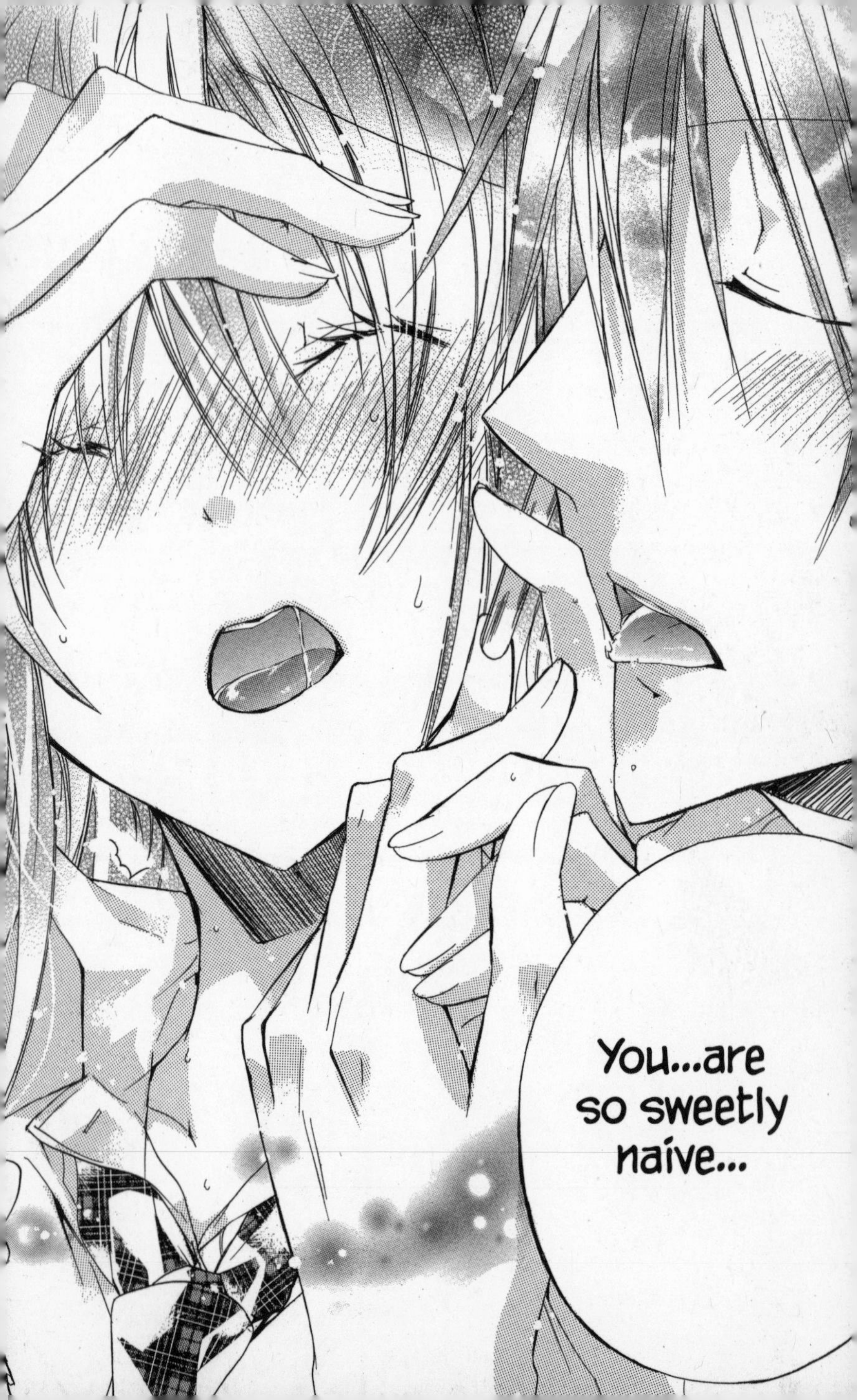
You...are so sweetly naive...

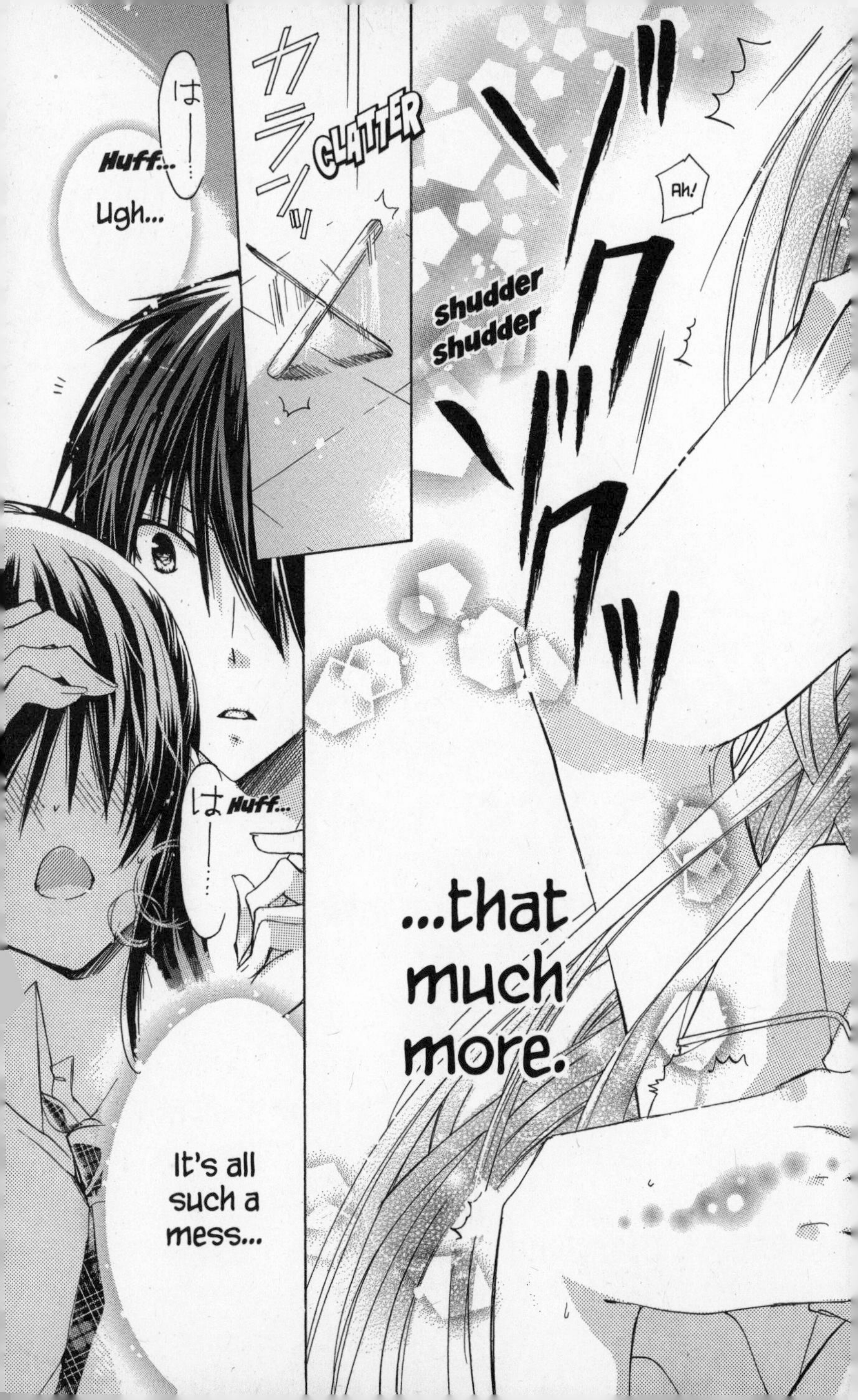

Ah!
Shudder shudder
...that much more.
CLATTER
Huff...
Ugh...
Huff...
It's all such a mess...

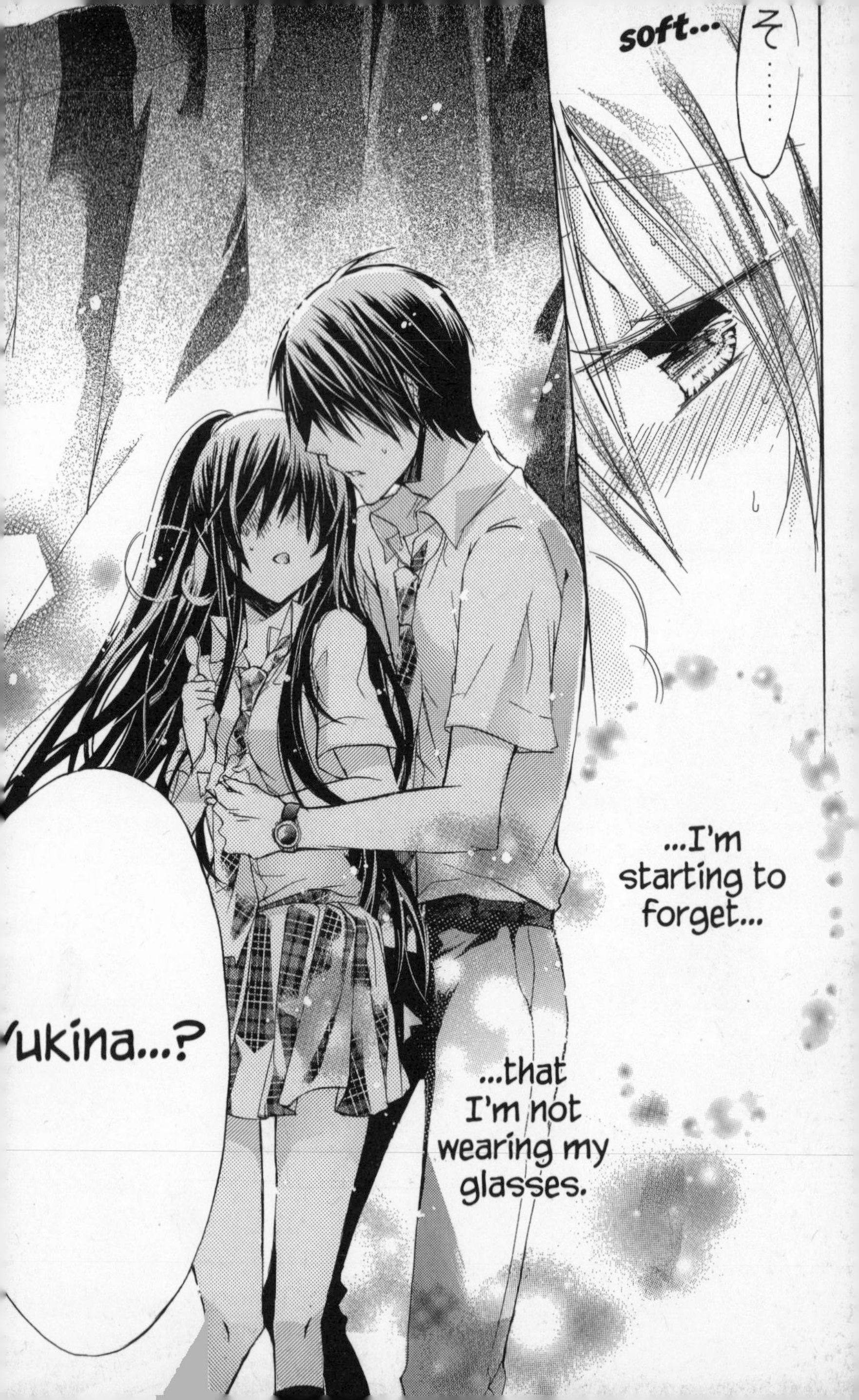
soft...
そ……
...I'm starting to forget...
...that I'm not wearing my glasses.
ukina...?

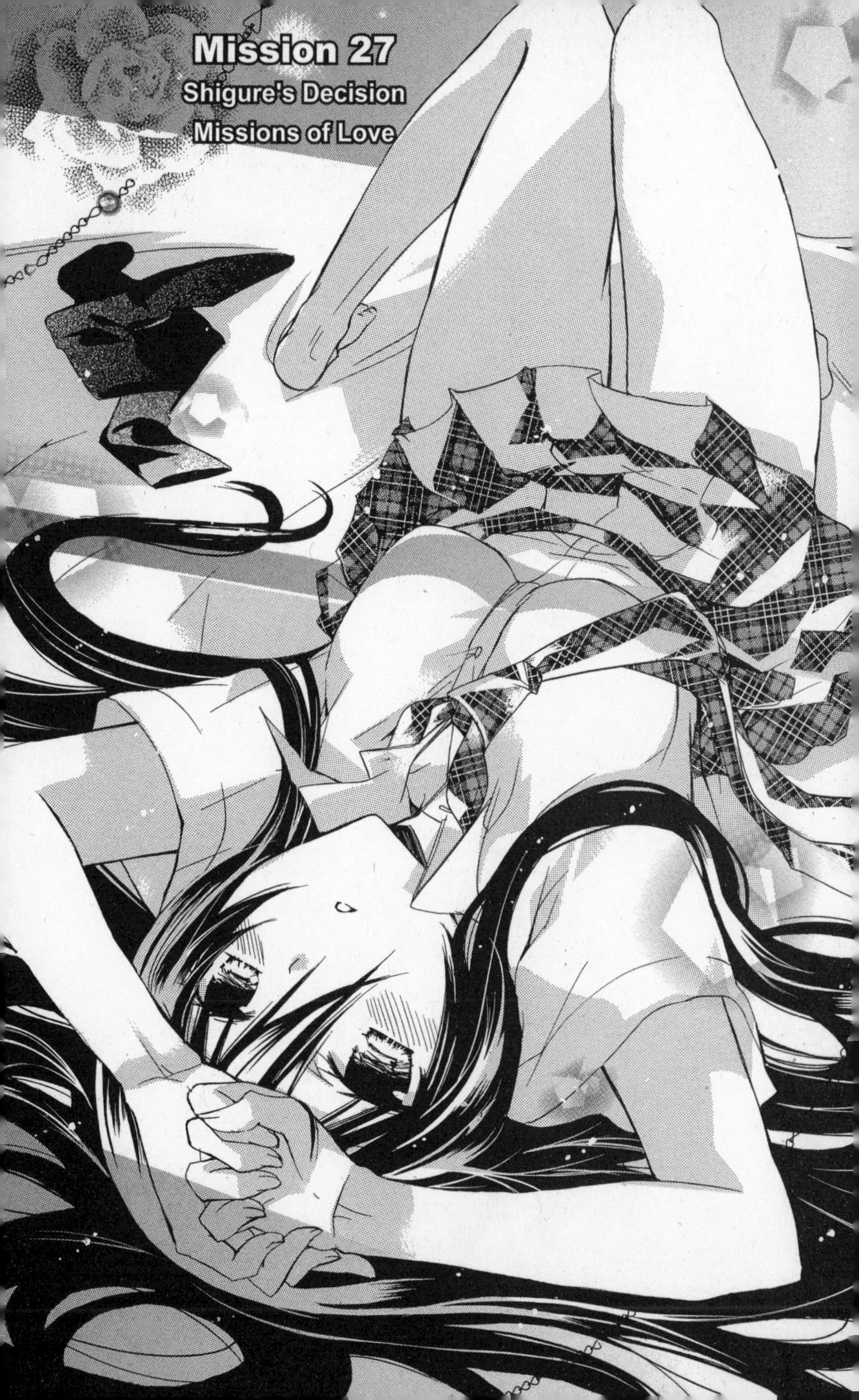
Mission 27
Shigure's Decision
Missions of Love

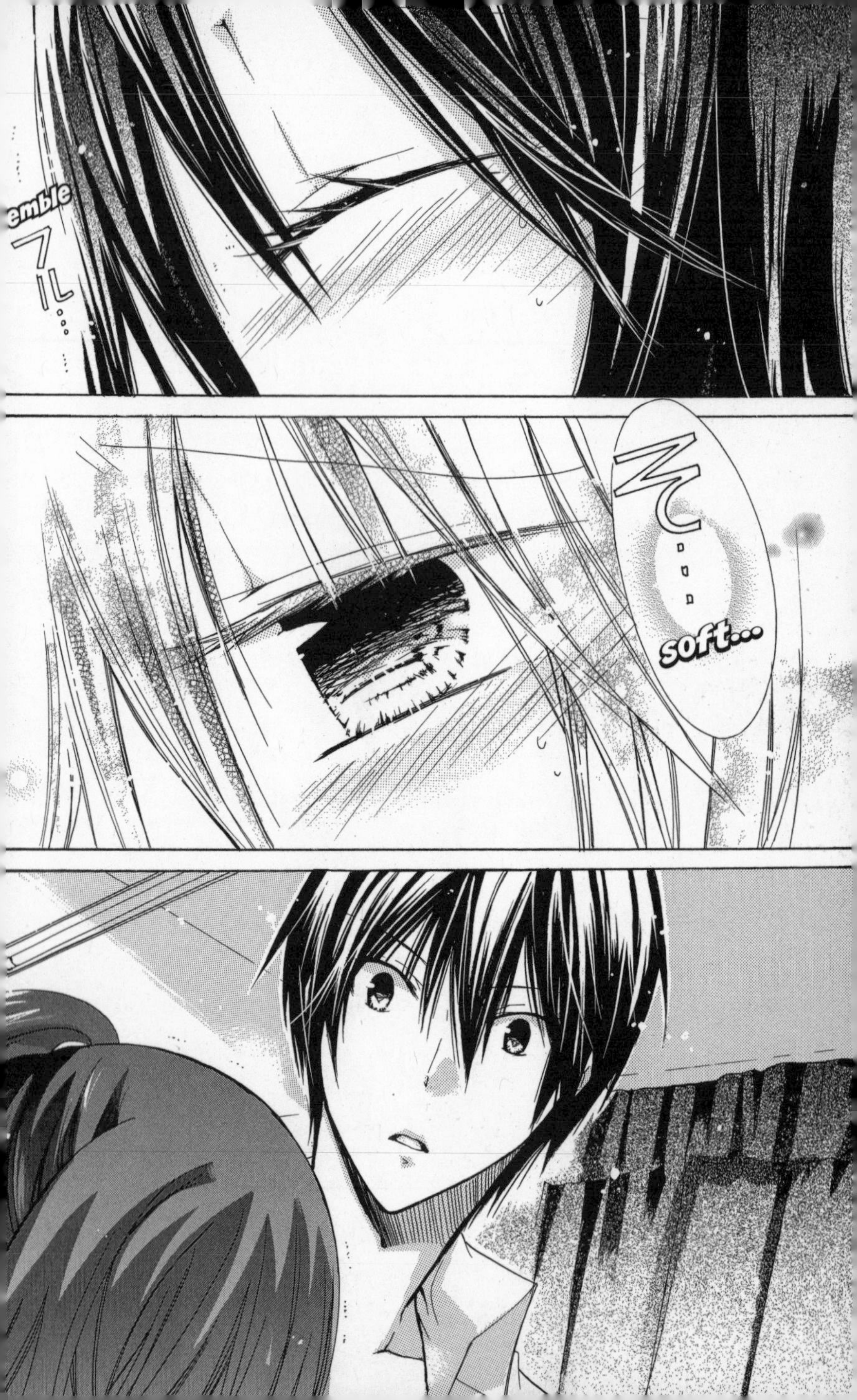

...tremble
フル...
...
ん...
soft...

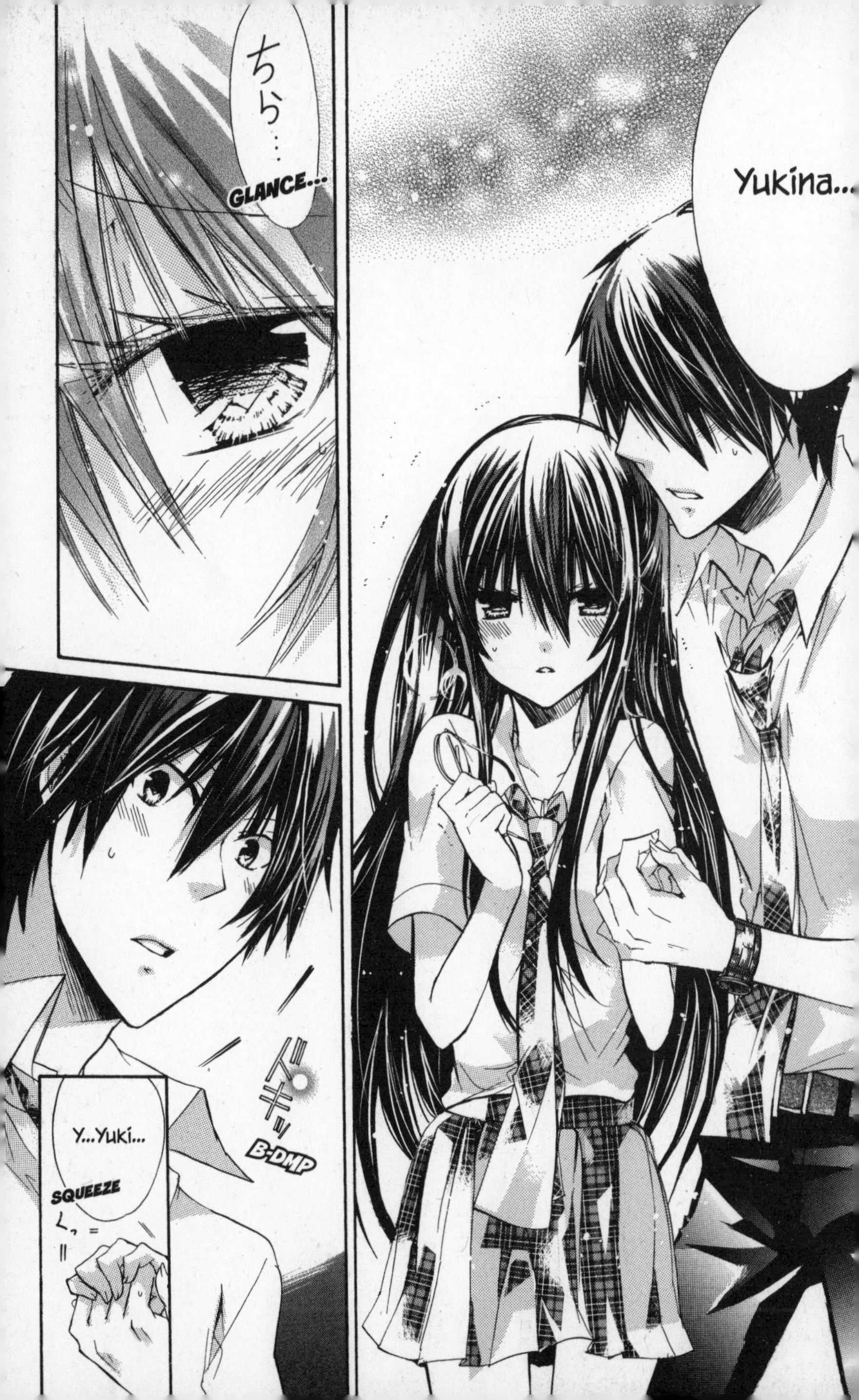

Yukina...
ちら…
GLANCE...
B-DMP
Y...Yuki...
SQUEEZE

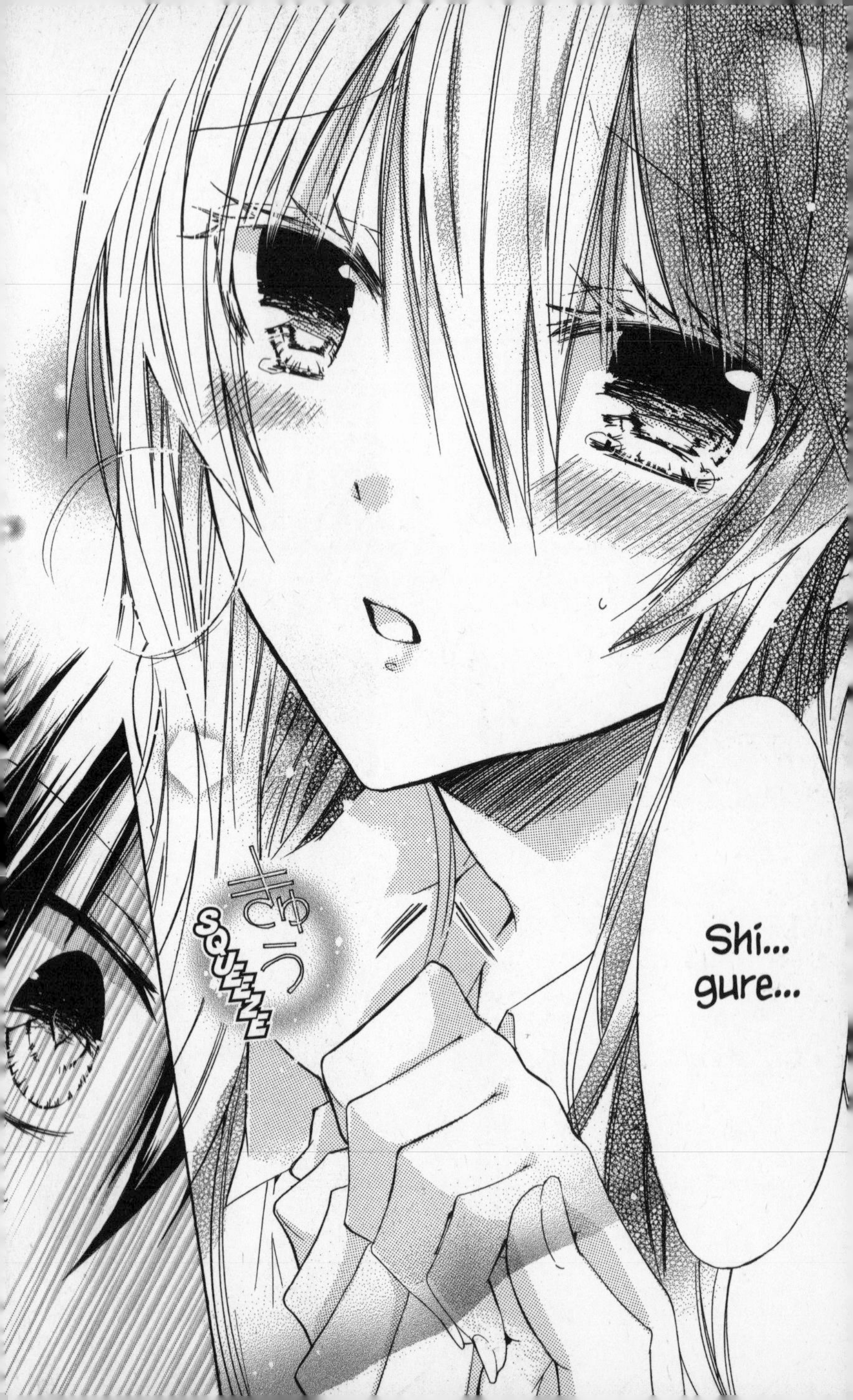
Shi... gure...
SQUEEZE

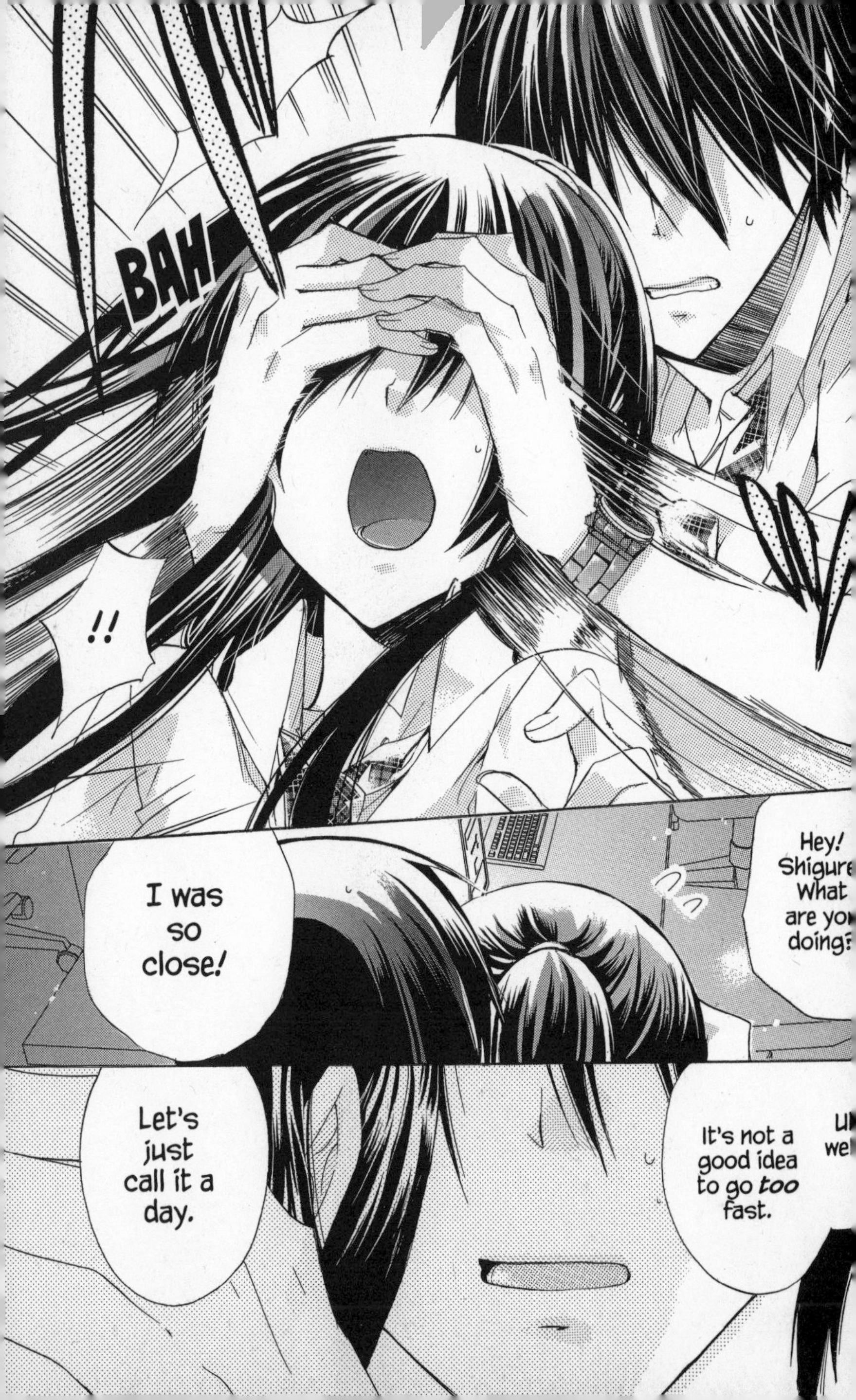
BAH
!!
Hey! Shigure What are yo doing?
I was so close!
It's not a good idea to go *too* fast.
Let's just call it a day.

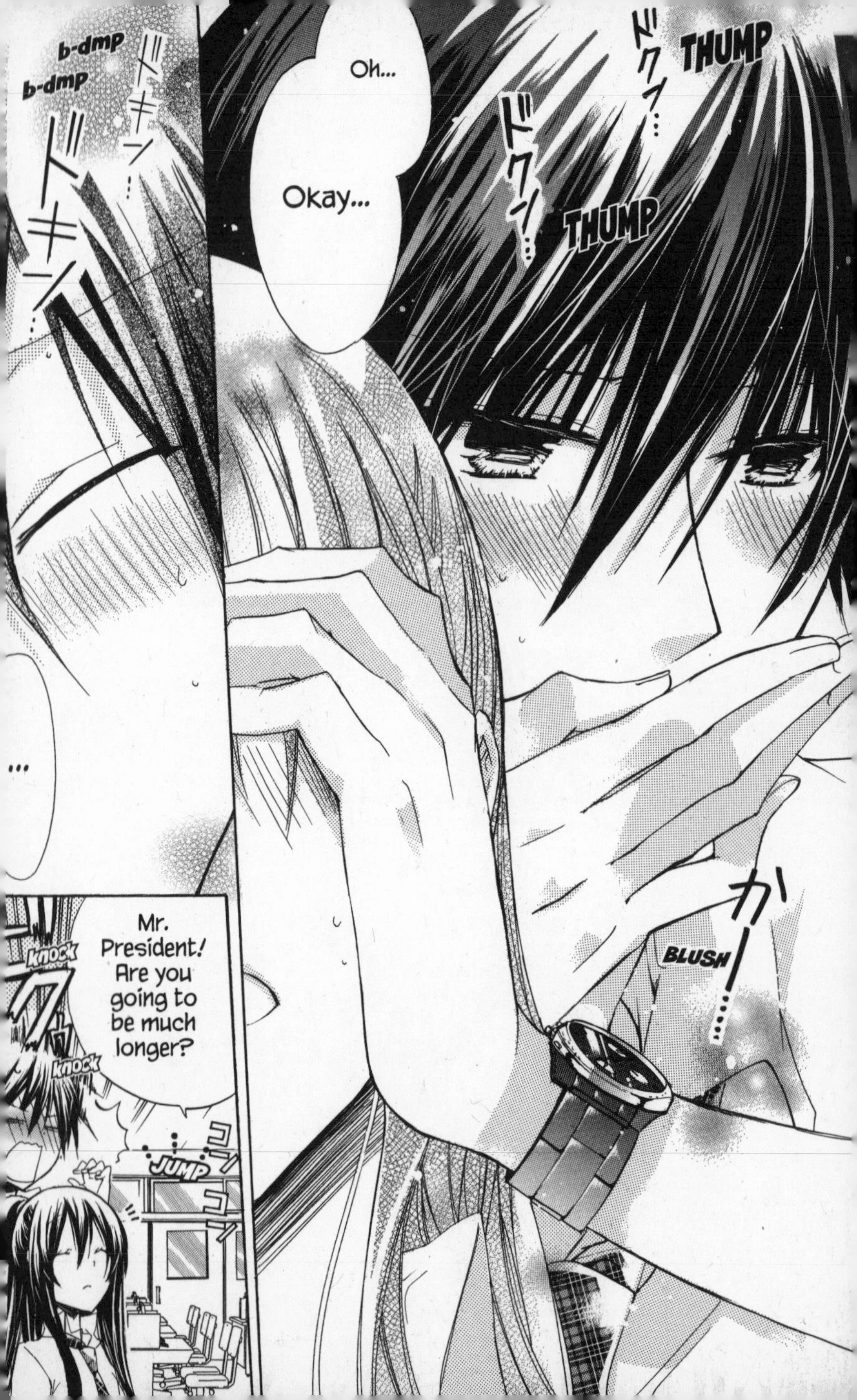

ドクン…
THUMP
ドクン…
THUMP
Oh...
Okay...
かーー…
BLUSH
ドキン…
b-dmp
ドキン…
b-dmp
...
コン
knock
コン
knock
Mr. President! Are you going to be much longer?
JUMP

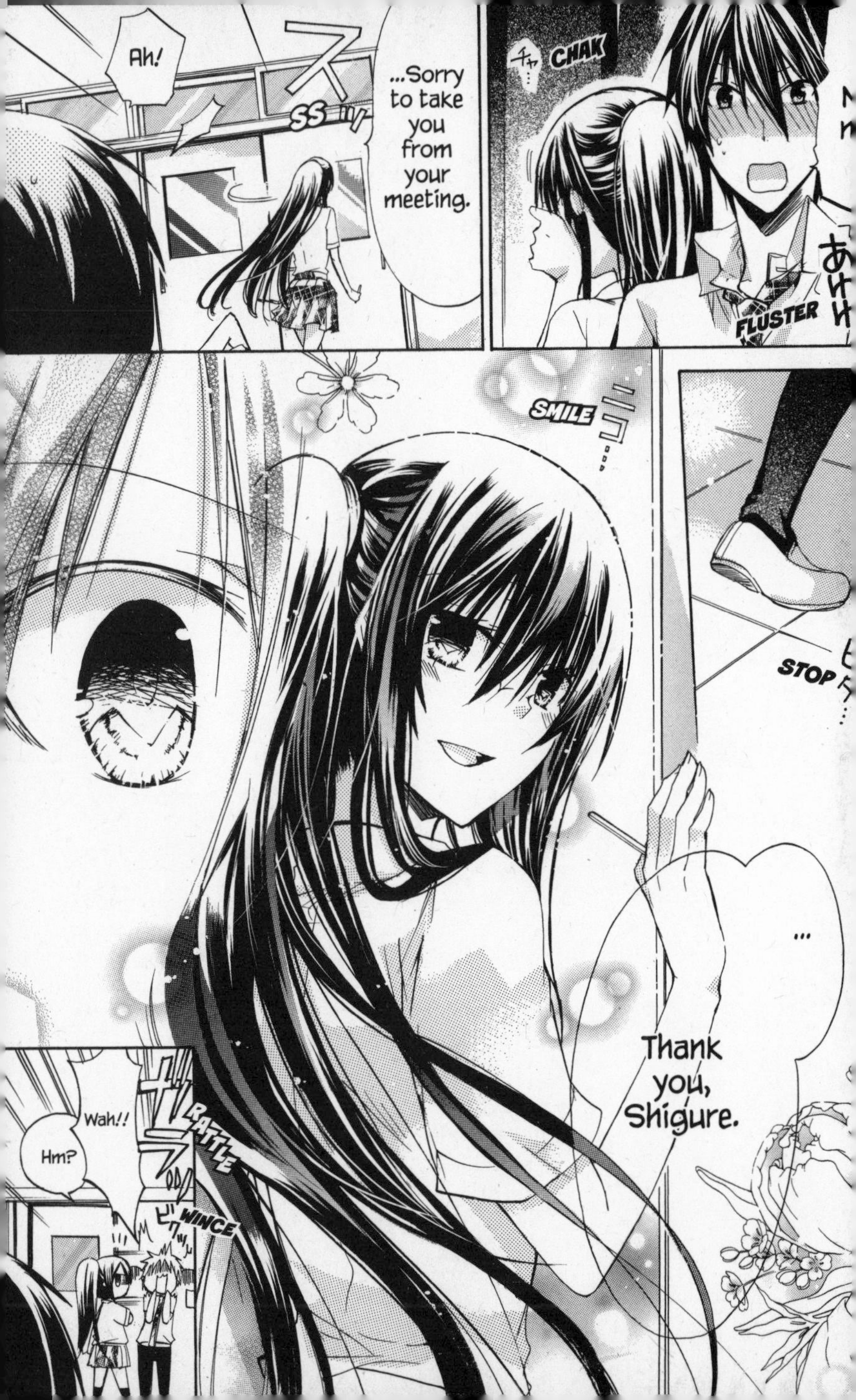

CHAK
FLUSTER
Ah!
...Sorry to take you from your meeting.
SS
STOP
SMILE
...
Thank you, Shigure.
Wah!!
Hm?
RATTLE
WINCE

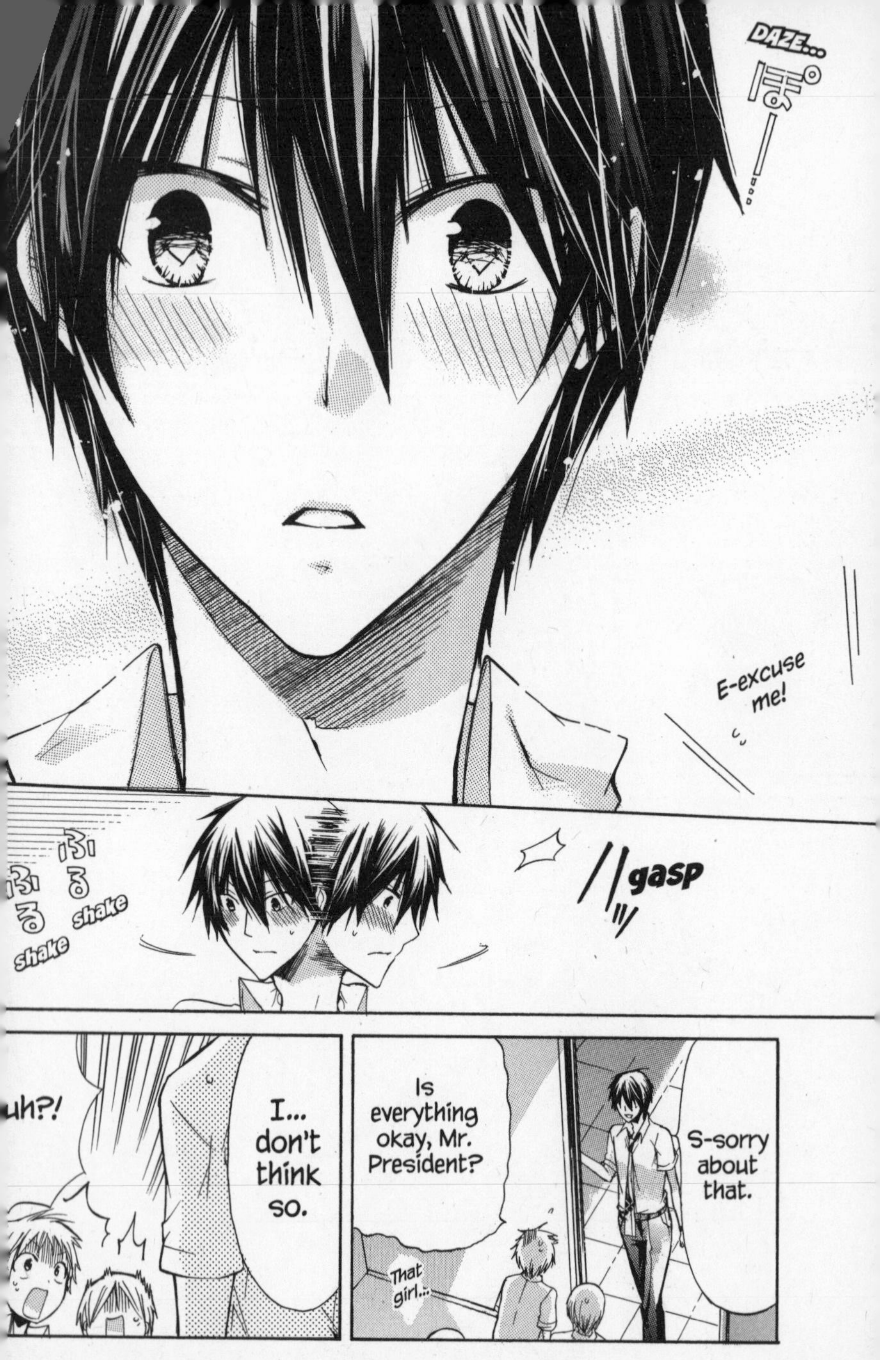
DAZE...
ぽーー…
E-excuse me!
gasp
ふるふる
shake
ふるふる
shake
S-sorry about that.
Is everything okay, Mr. President?
That girl...
I... don't think so.
uh?!

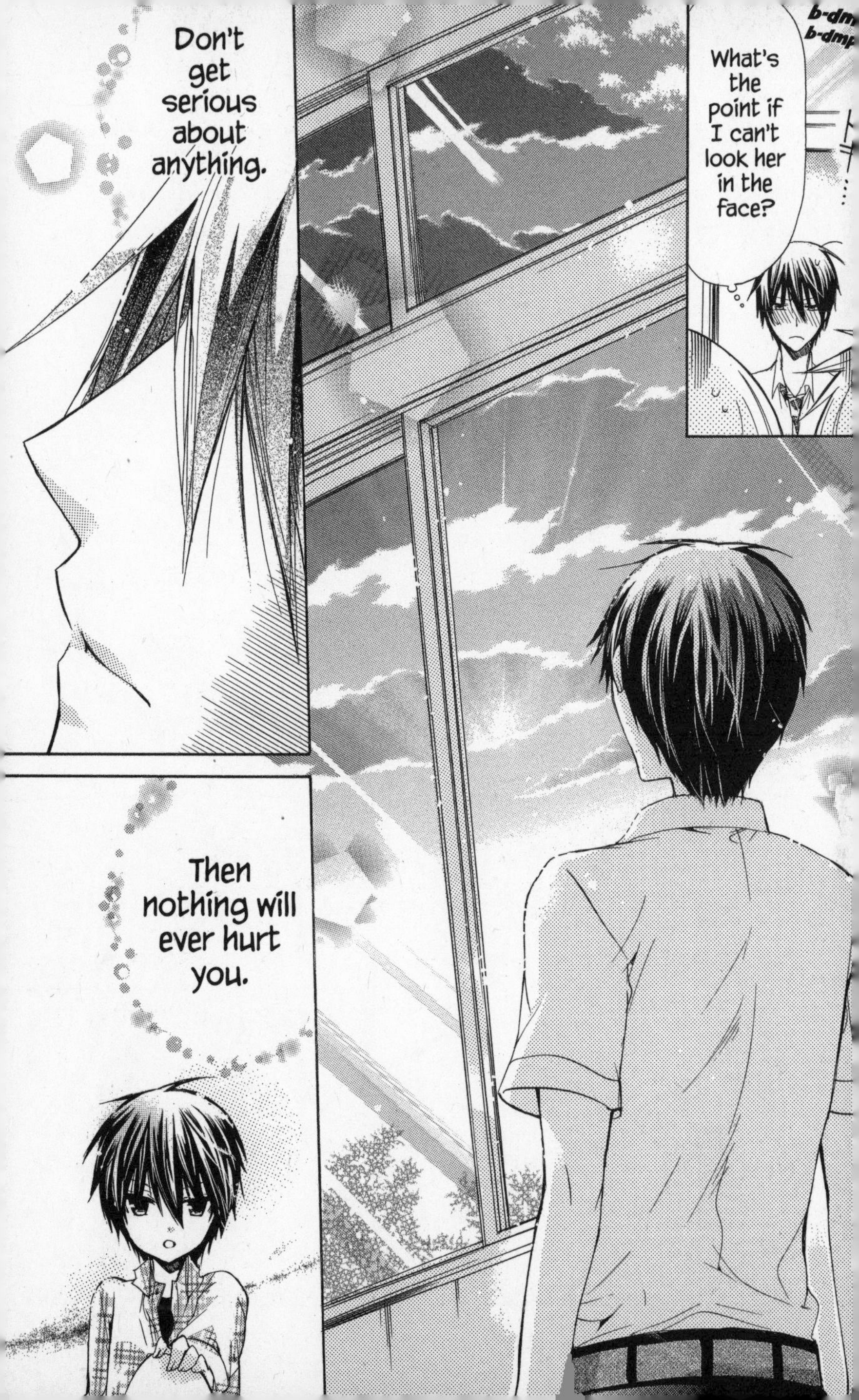
b-dm
b-dmp
What's the point if I can't look her in the face?
Don't get serious about anything.
Then nothing will ever hurt you.

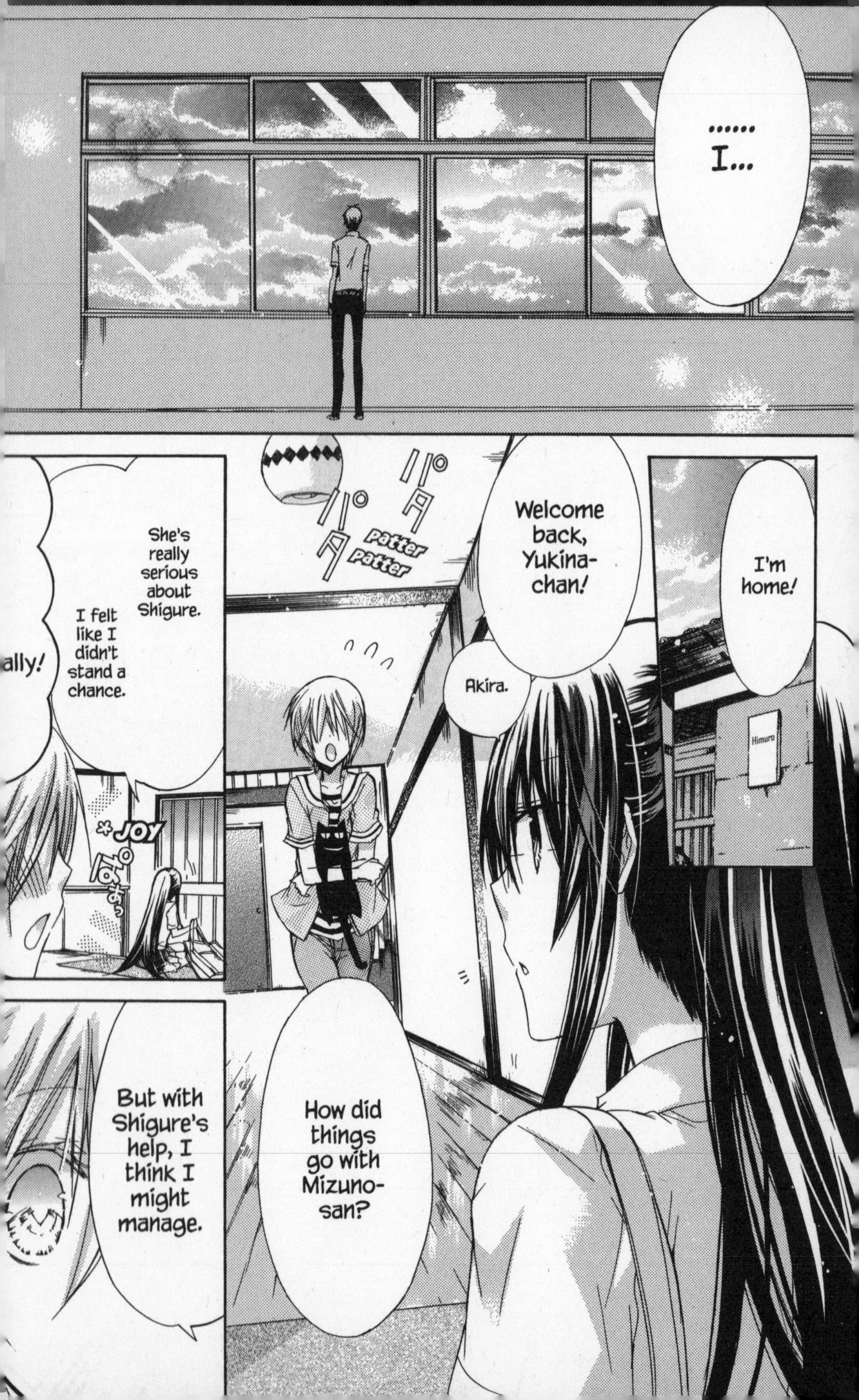

...... I...
I'm home!
Welcome back, Yukina-chan!
Akira.
パタ パタ
patter patter
How did things go with Mizuno-san?
She's really serious about Shigure.
I felt like I didn't stand a chance.
ally!
JOY
But with Shigure's help, I think I might manage.

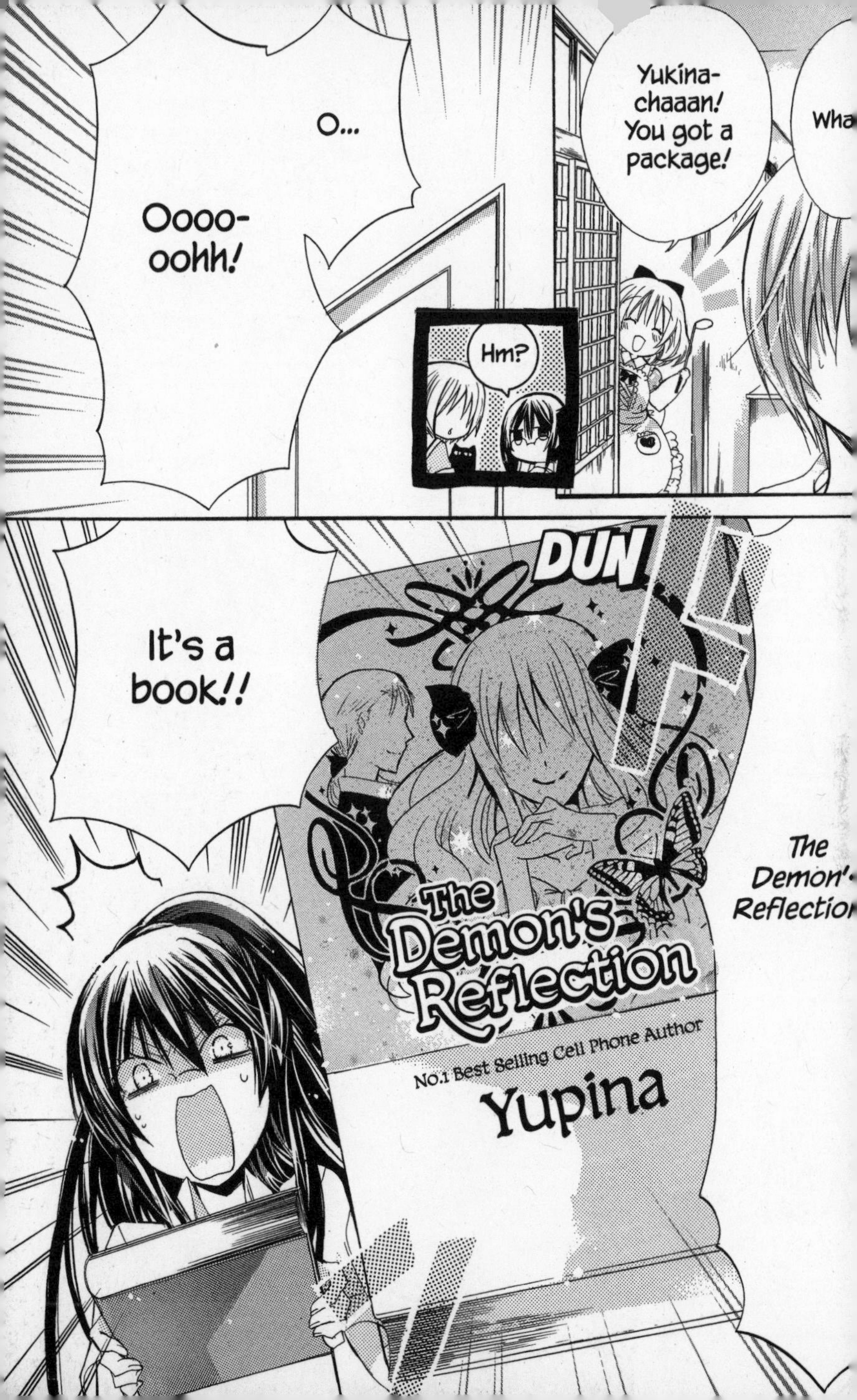
Wha
Yukina-chaaan! You got a package!
Hm?
O...
Oooo-oohh!
DUN
The Demon'
Reflectio
The Demon's Reflection
No.1 Best Selling Cell Phone Author
Yupina
It's a book!!

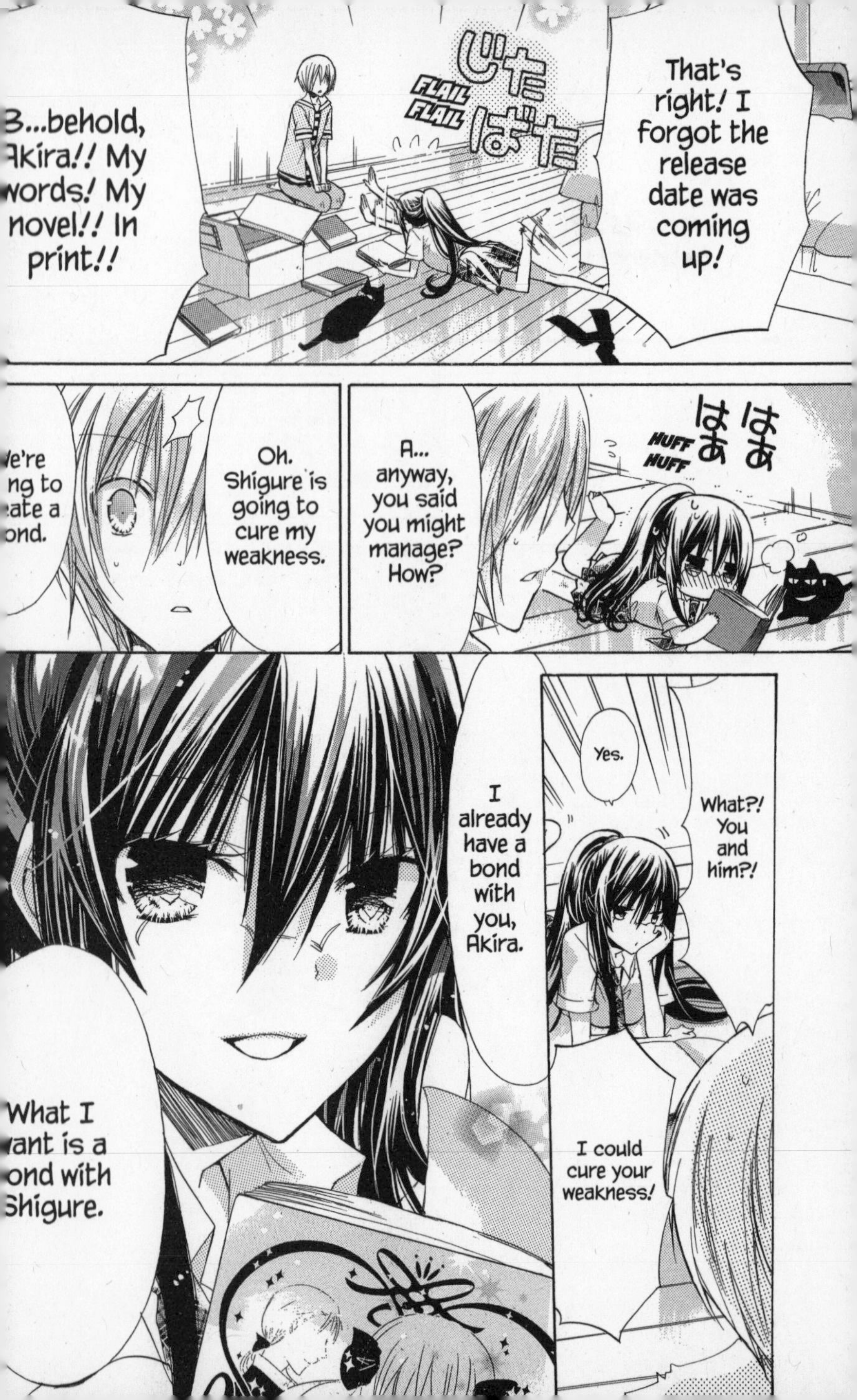
That's right! I forgot the release date was coming up!
じたばた
FLAIL FLAIL
B...behold, Akira!! My words! My novel!! In print!!
はぁはぁ
HUFF HUFF
A... anyway, you said you might manage? How?
Oh. Shigure is going to cure my weakness.
e're ng to ate a ond.
Yes.
What?! You and him?!
I could cure your weakness!
I already have a bond with you, Akira.
What I ant is a ond with higure.

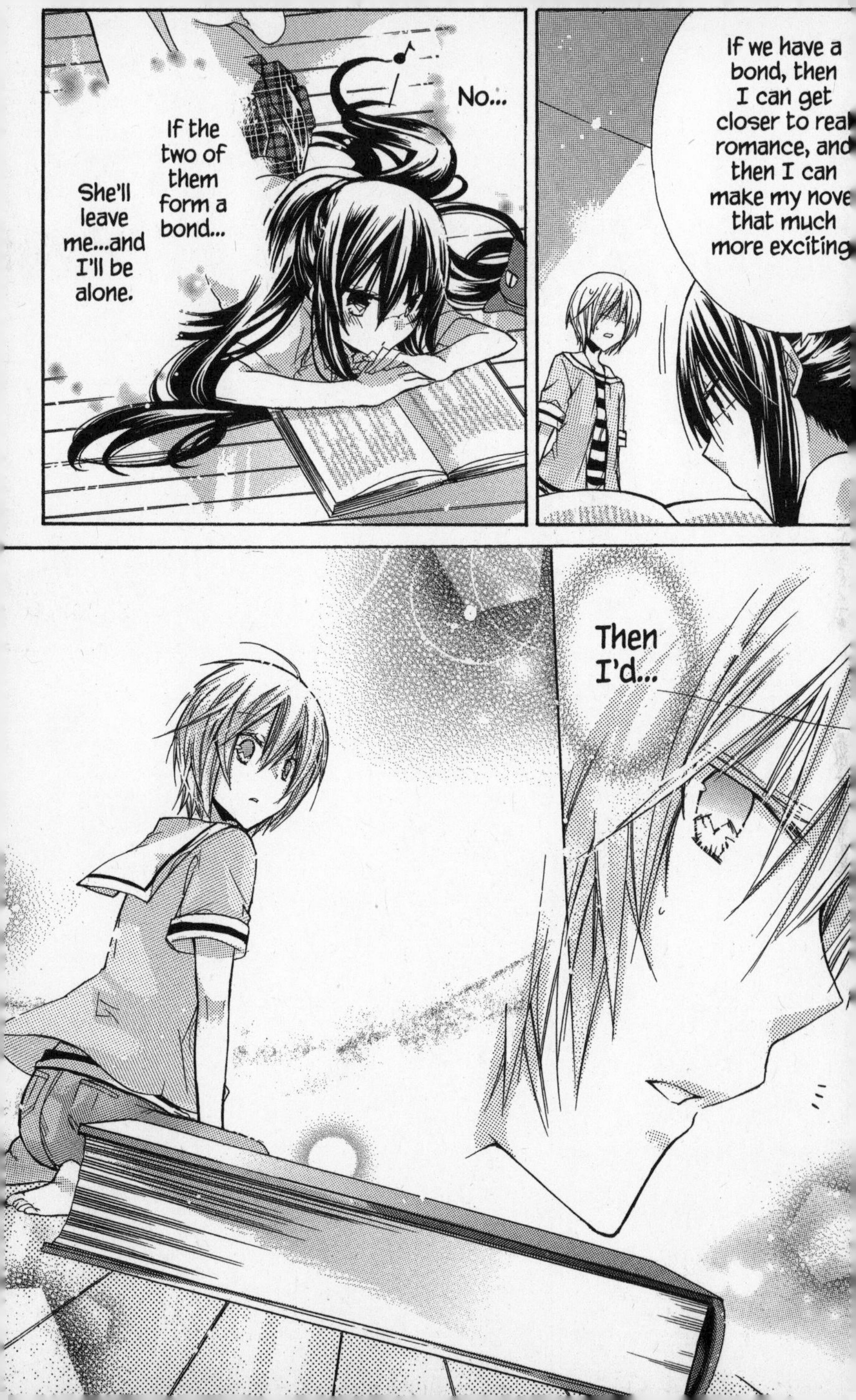
If we have a bond, then I can get closer to real romance, and then I can make my nove that much more exciting
No...
If the two of them form a bond...
She'll leave me...and I'll be alone.
Then I'd...

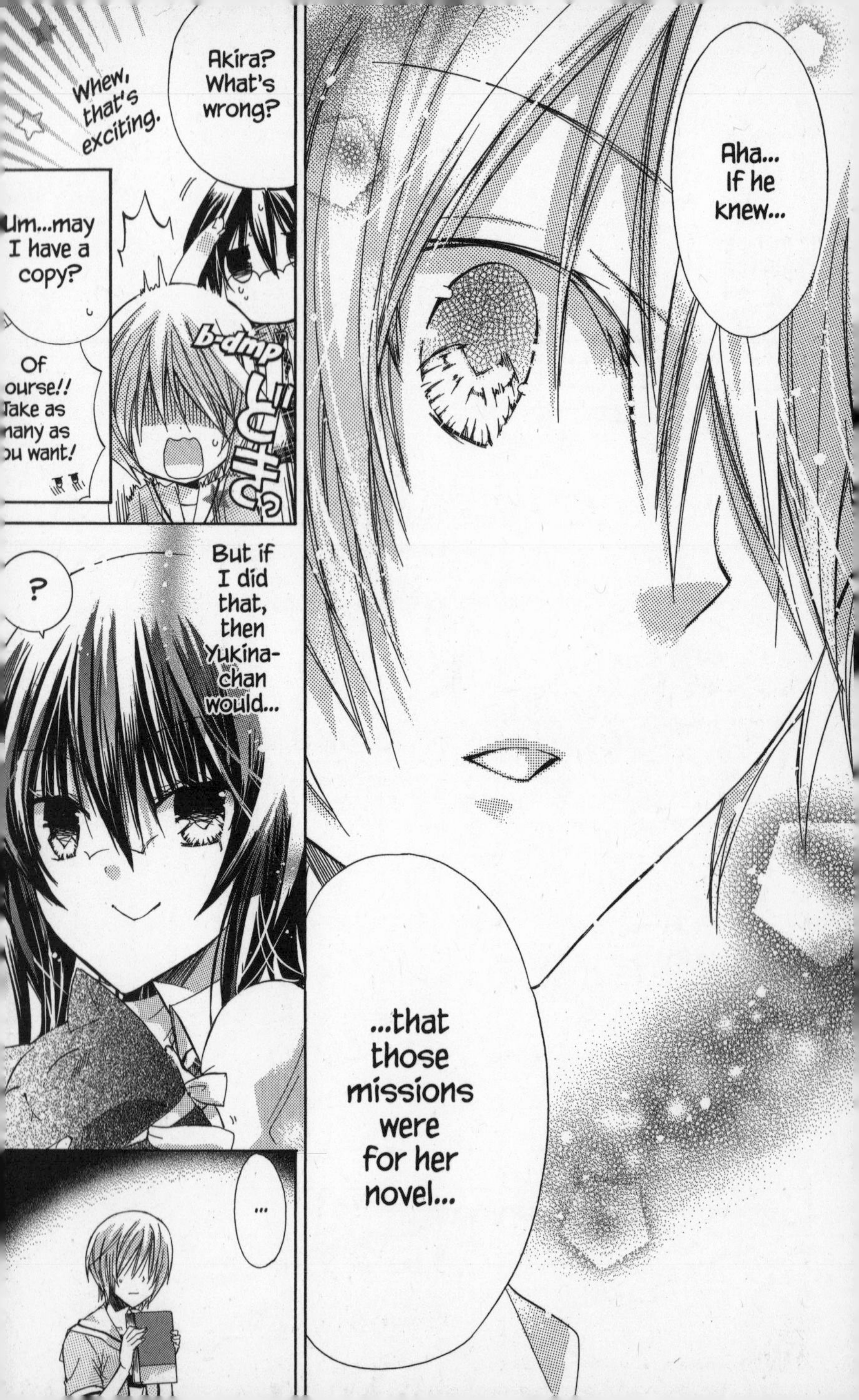
Aha... If he knew...
...that those missions were for her novel...
Akira? What's wrong?
Whew, that's exciting.
b-dmp
どきっ
Um...may I have a copy?
Of ourse!! Take as nany as ou want!
But if I did that, then Yukina-chan would...
?
...

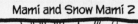

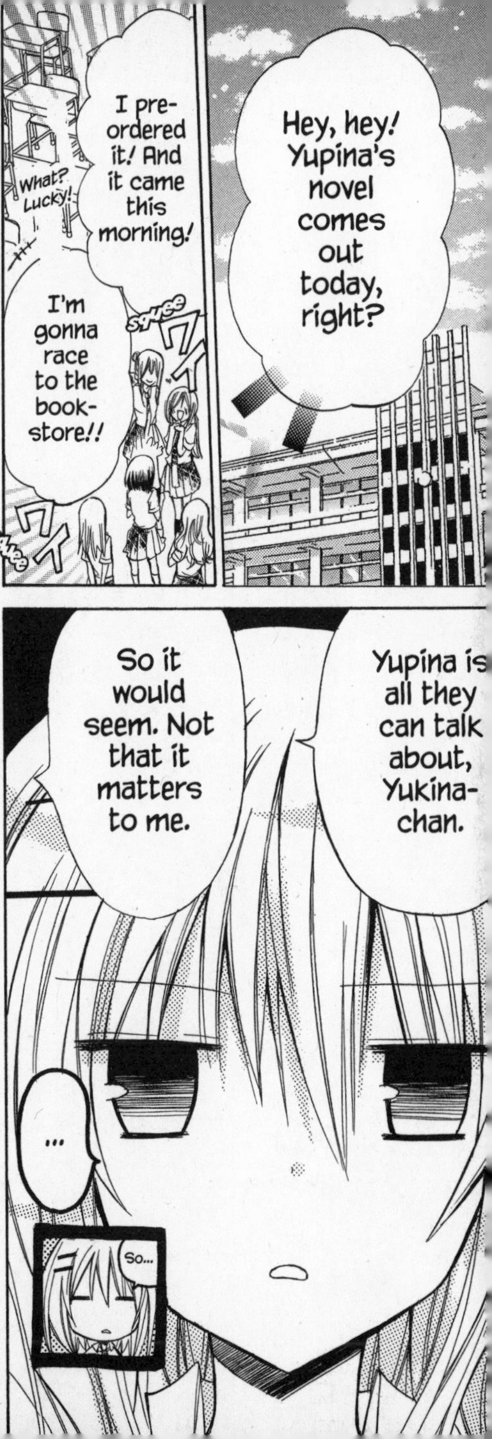
Hey, hey! Yupina's novel comes out today, right?
I pre-ordered it! And it came this morning!
What? Lucky!
squee
ワイ
I'm gonna race to the bookstore!!
ワイ
squee
Yupina is all they can talk about, Yukina-chan.
So it would seem. Not that it matters to me.
...
So...

Mami and Snow Mami 2

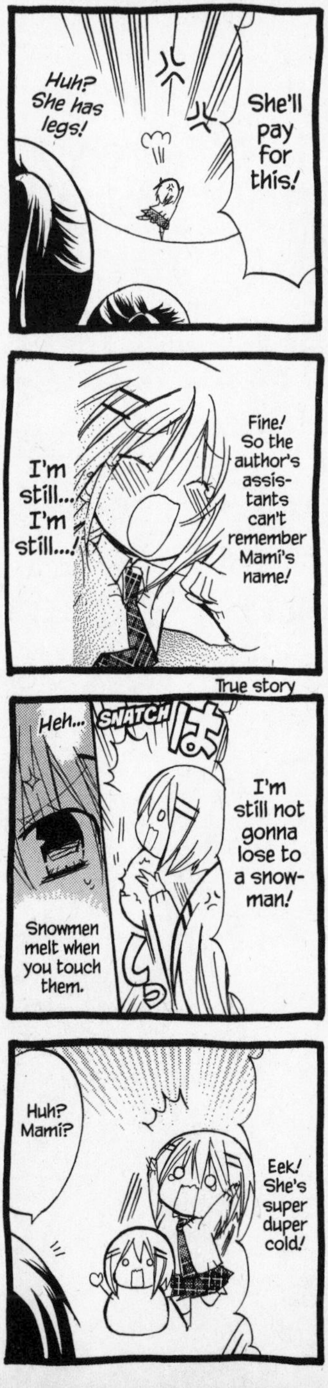
She'll pay for this!
Huh? She has legs!
Fine! So the author's assistants can't remember Mami's name!
I'm still... I'm still...!
True story
SNATCH
は
I'm still not gonna lose to a snowman!
Heh...
Snowmen melt when you touch them.
Eek! She's super duper cold!
Huh? Mami?

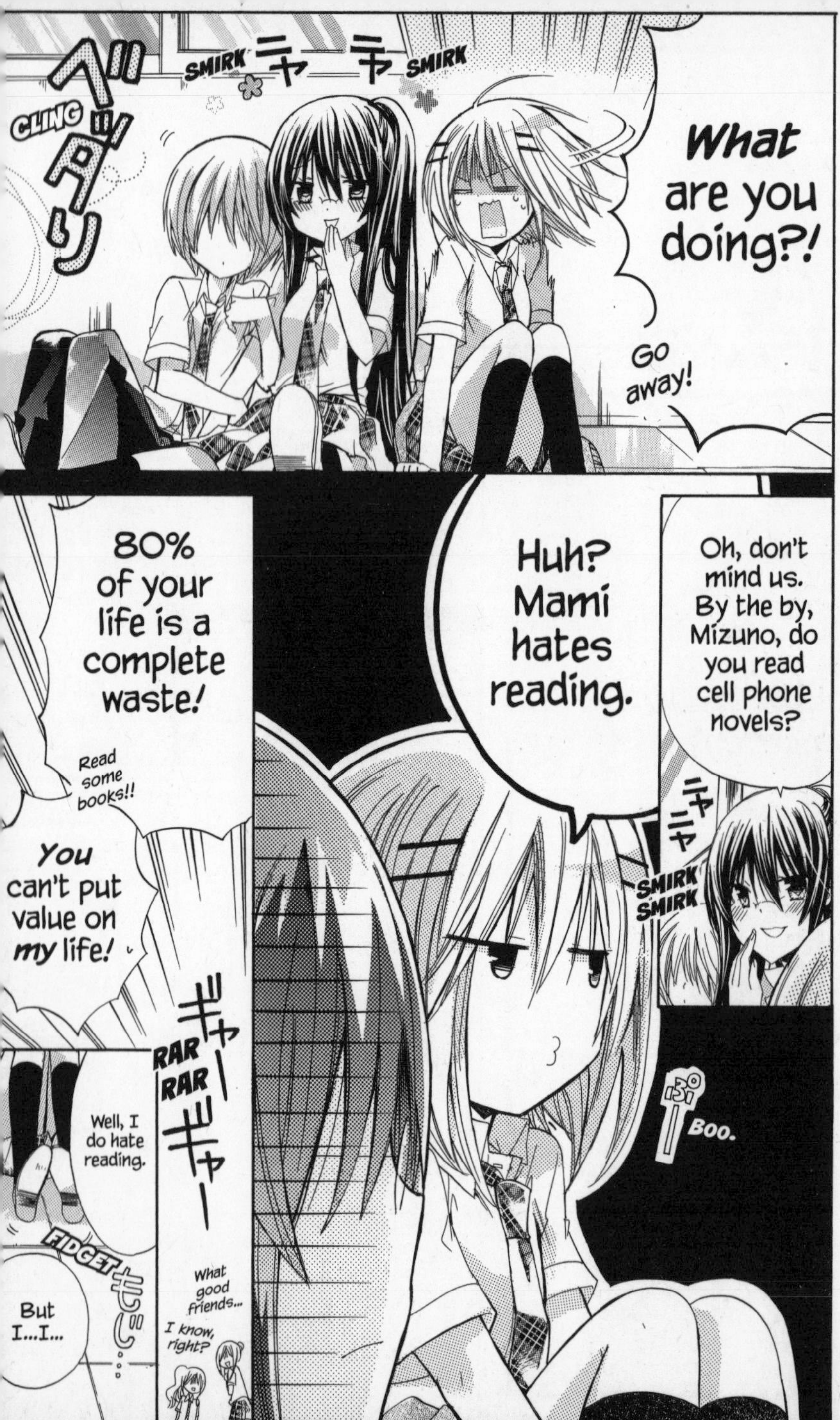
What are you doing?!
Go away!
SMIRK SMIRK
CLING
Oh, don't mind us. By the by, Mizuno, do you read cell phone novels?
SMIRK SMIRK
Huh? Mami hates reading.
BOO.
80% of your life is a complete waste!
Read some books!!
You can't put value on my life!
RAR RAR
Well, I do hate reading.
FIDGET
But I...I...
What good friends...
I know, right?

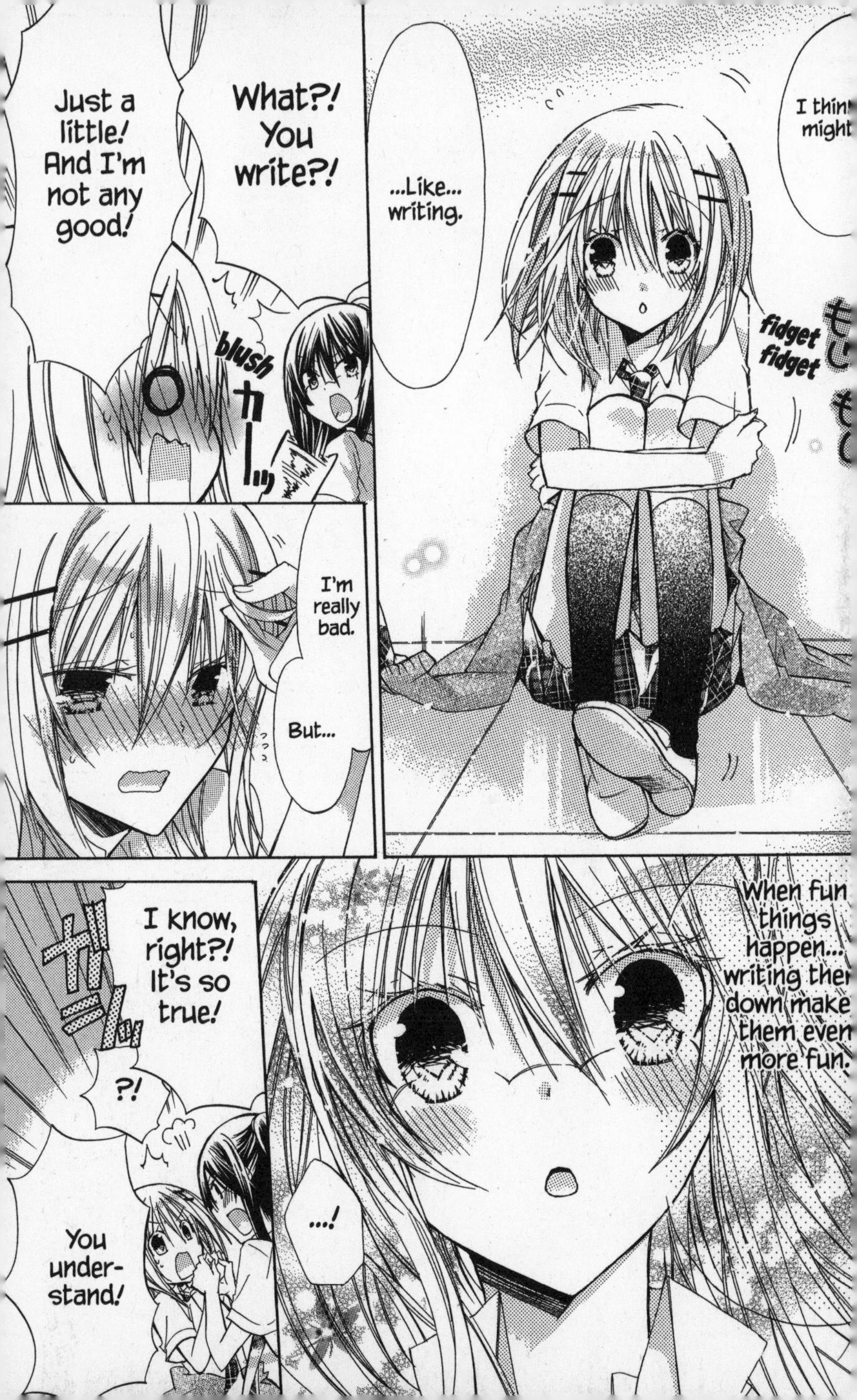
I thin
might
fidget fidget
...Like... writing.
What?! You write?!
blush
Just a little! And I'm not any good!
I'm really bad.
But...
When fun things happen... writing the down make them even more fun.
...!
I know, right?! It's so true!
?!
You under-stand!

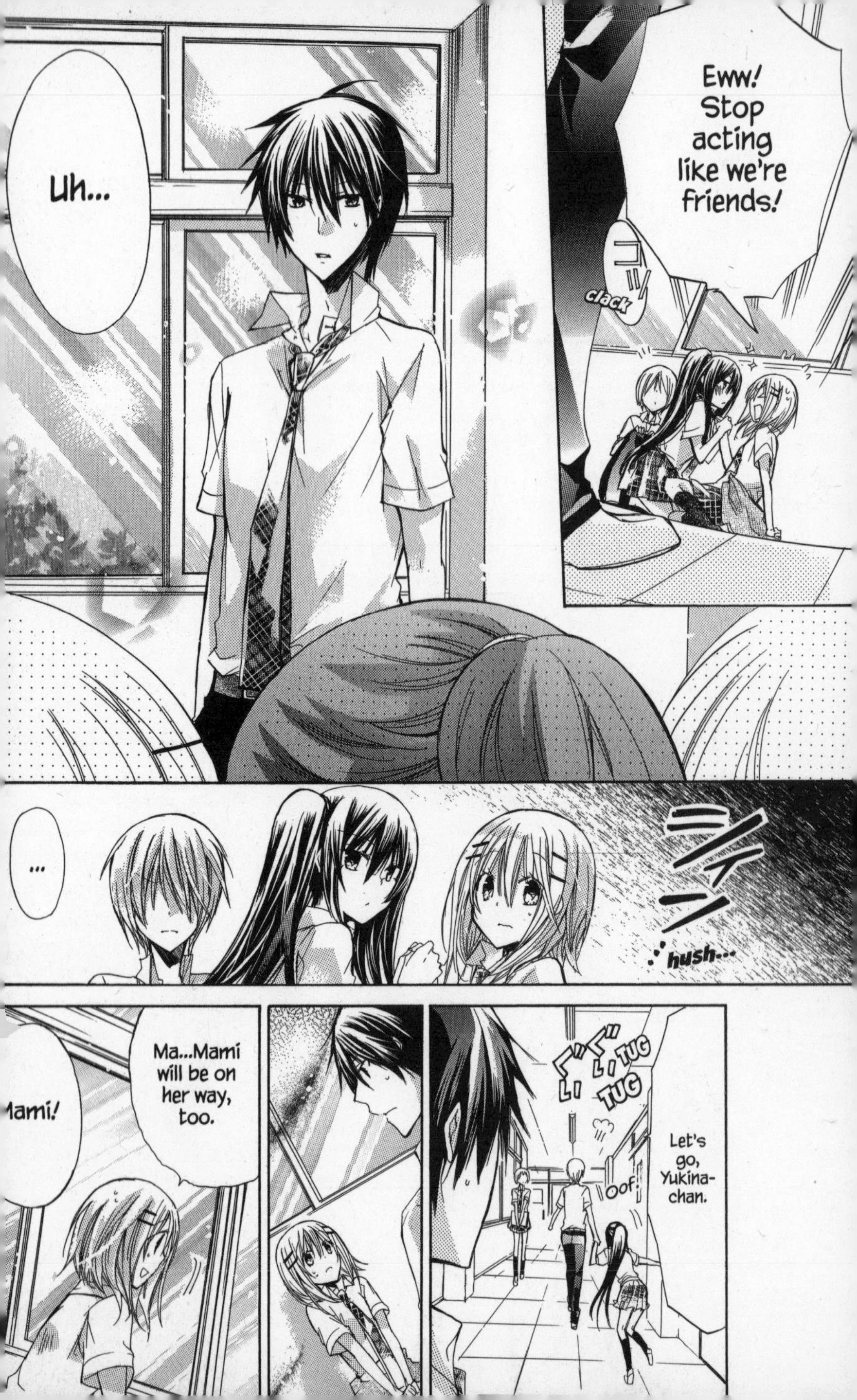
Eww! Stop acting like we're friends!
clack
Uh...
hush...
...
TUG TUG
Let's go, Yukina-chan.
Oof!
Ma...Mami will be on her way, too.
Mami!

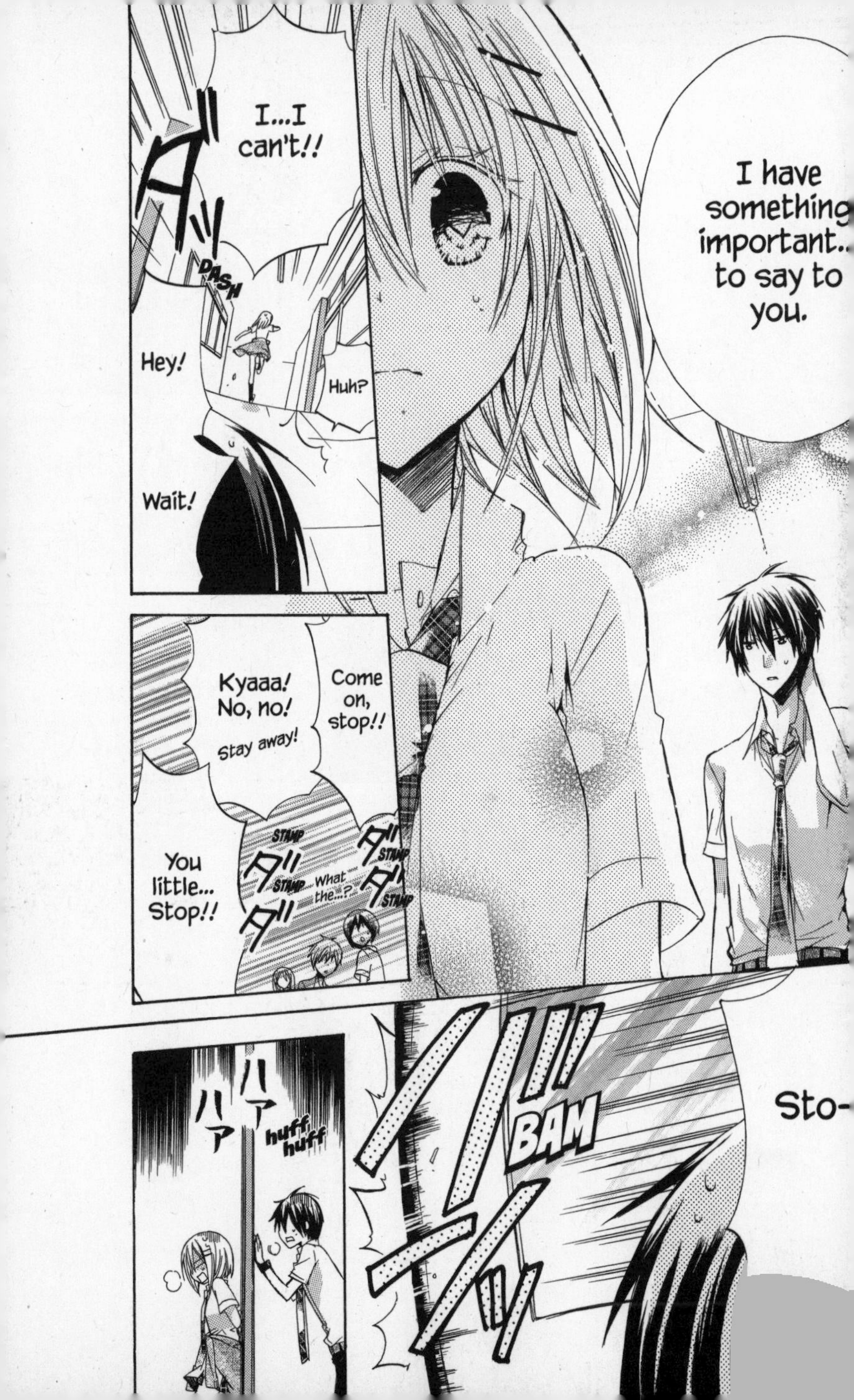
I have something important... to say to you.
I...I can't!!
DASH
Huh?
Hey!
Wait!
Come on, stop!!
Kyaaa! No, no! Stay away!
STAMP
STAMP
What the...?
STAMP
STAMP
You little... Stop!!
Sto-
BAM
ハァ ハァ
huff huff

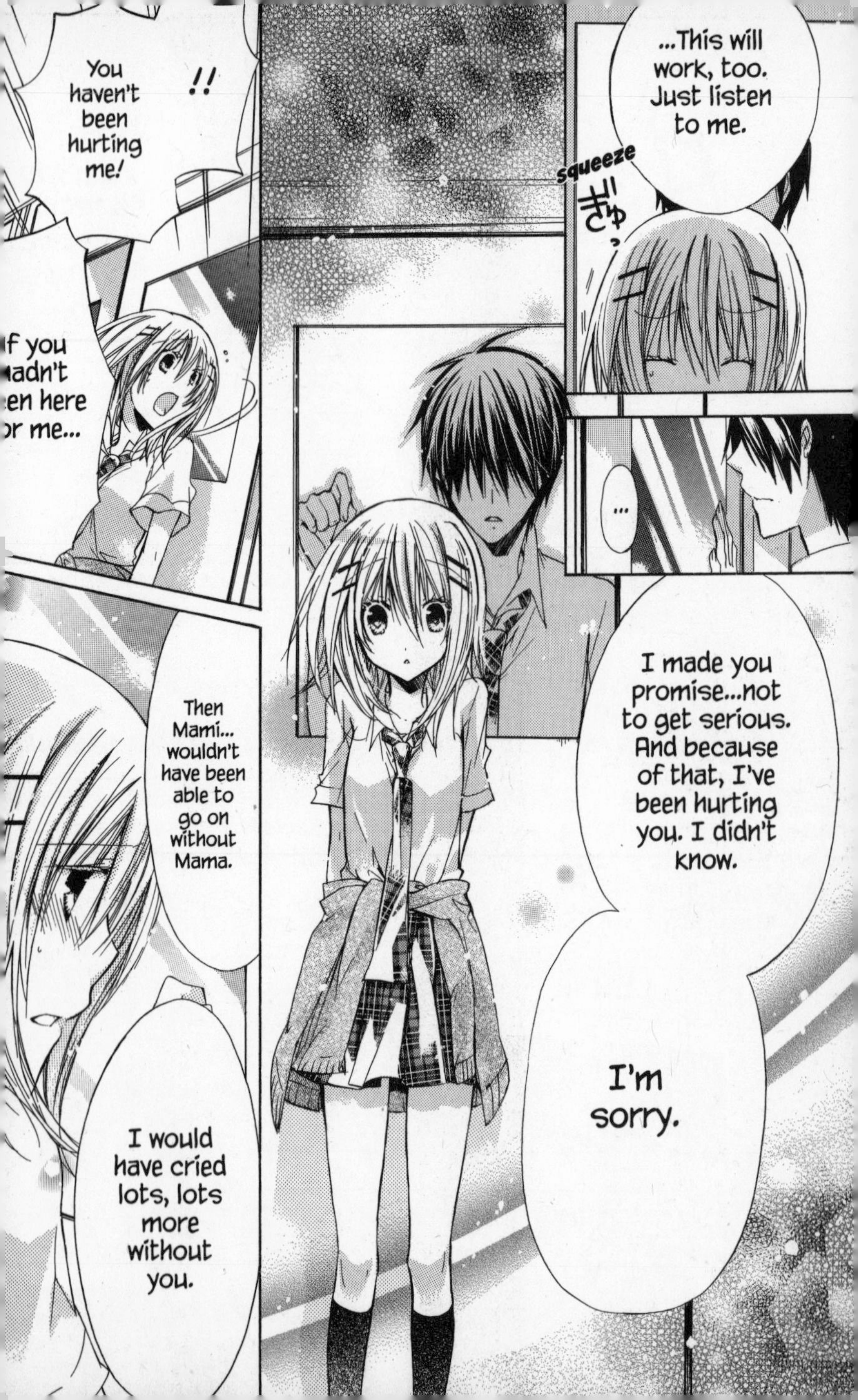
...This will work, too. Just listen to me.
squeeze
ぎゅ
...
I made you promise...not to get serious. And because of that, I've been hurting you. I didn't know.
I'm sorry.
You haven't been hurting me!
!!
f you adn't en here r me...
Then Mami... wouldn't have been able to go on without Mama.
I would have cried lots, lots more without you.

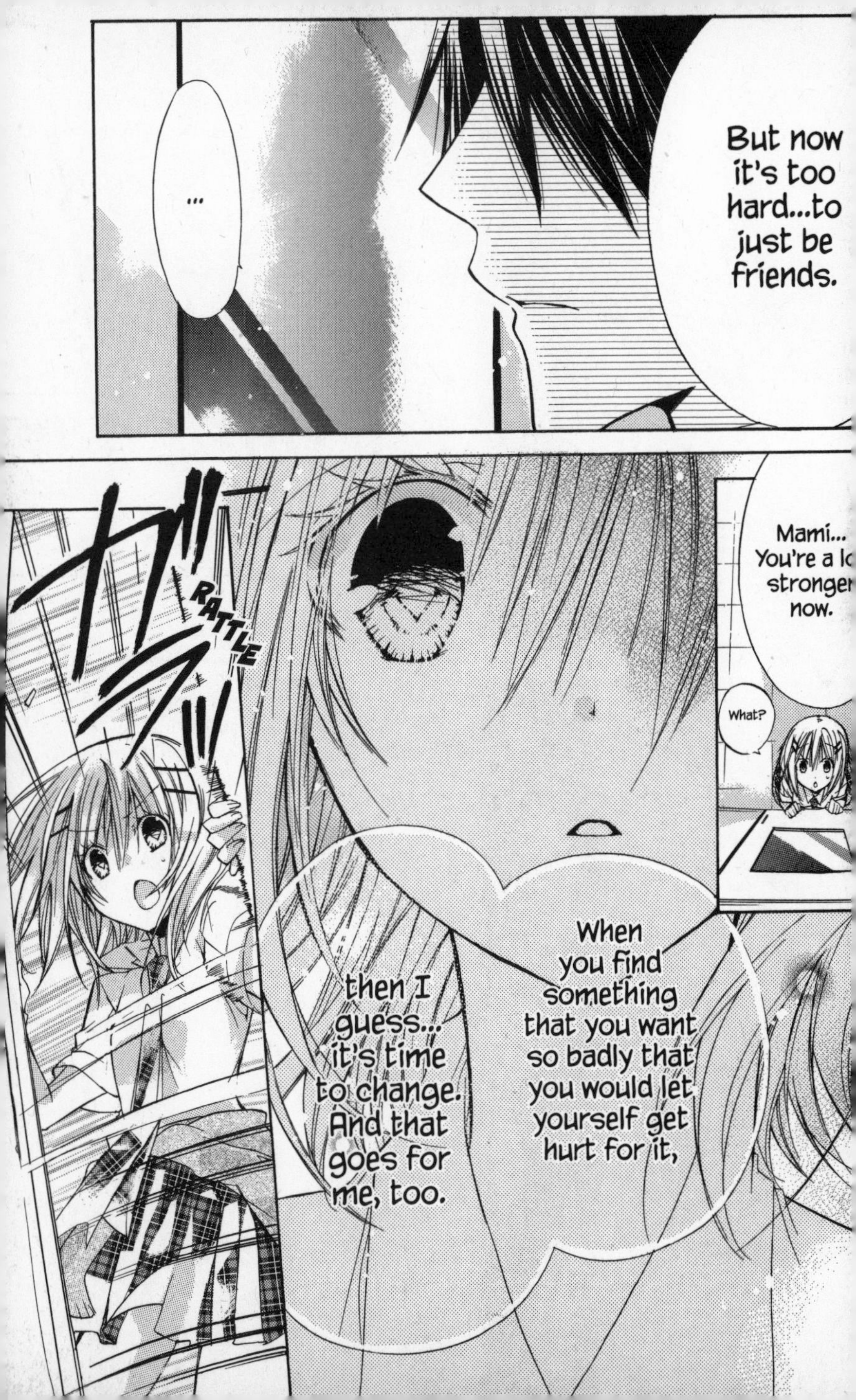
But now it's too hard...to just be friends.
...
Mami... You're a lo stronger now.
What?
When you find something that you want so badly that you would let yourself get hurt for it,
then I guess... it's time to change. And that goes for me, too.
RATTLE

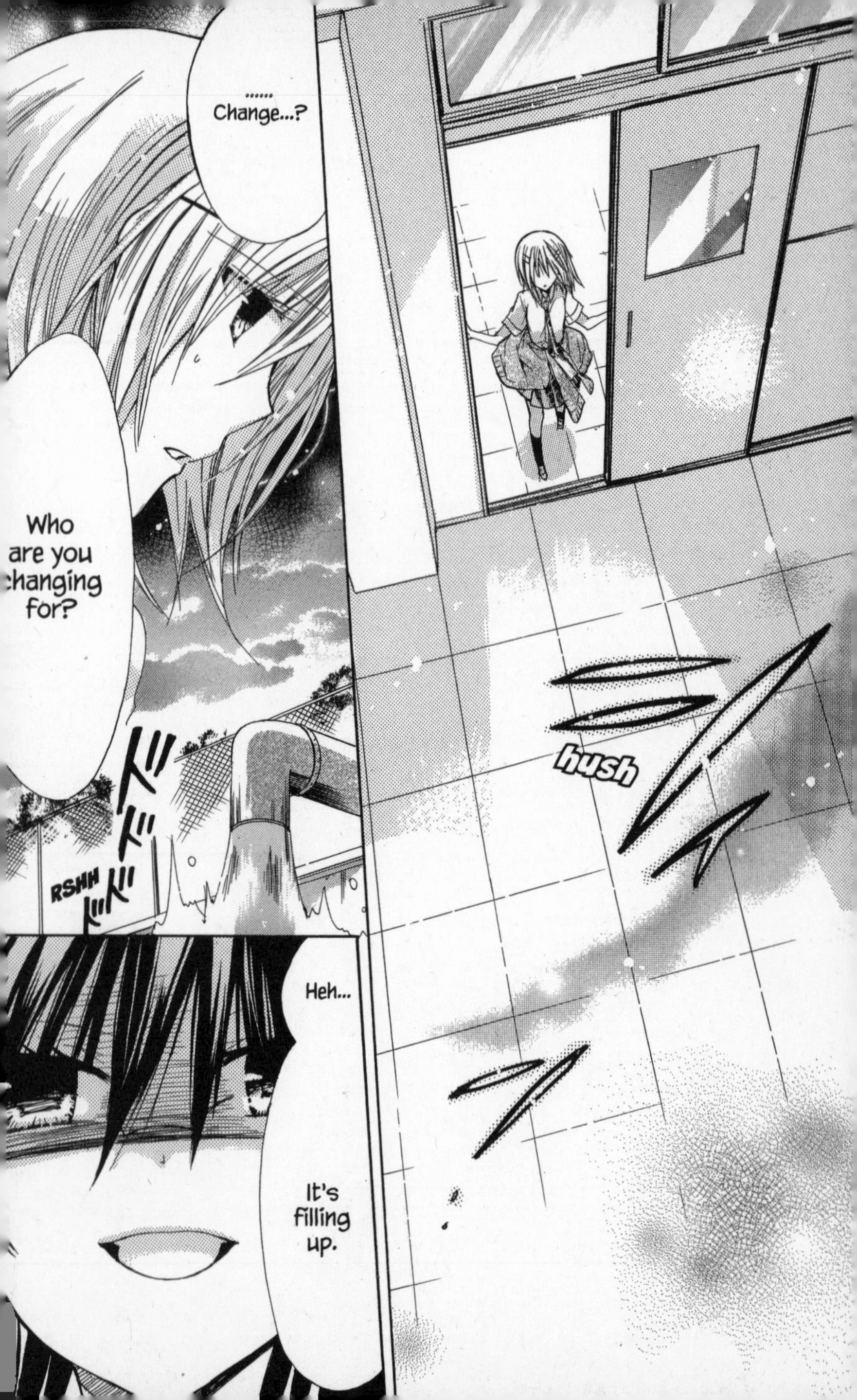
hush
...... Change...?
Who are you changing for?
RSHH
Heh...
It's filling up.

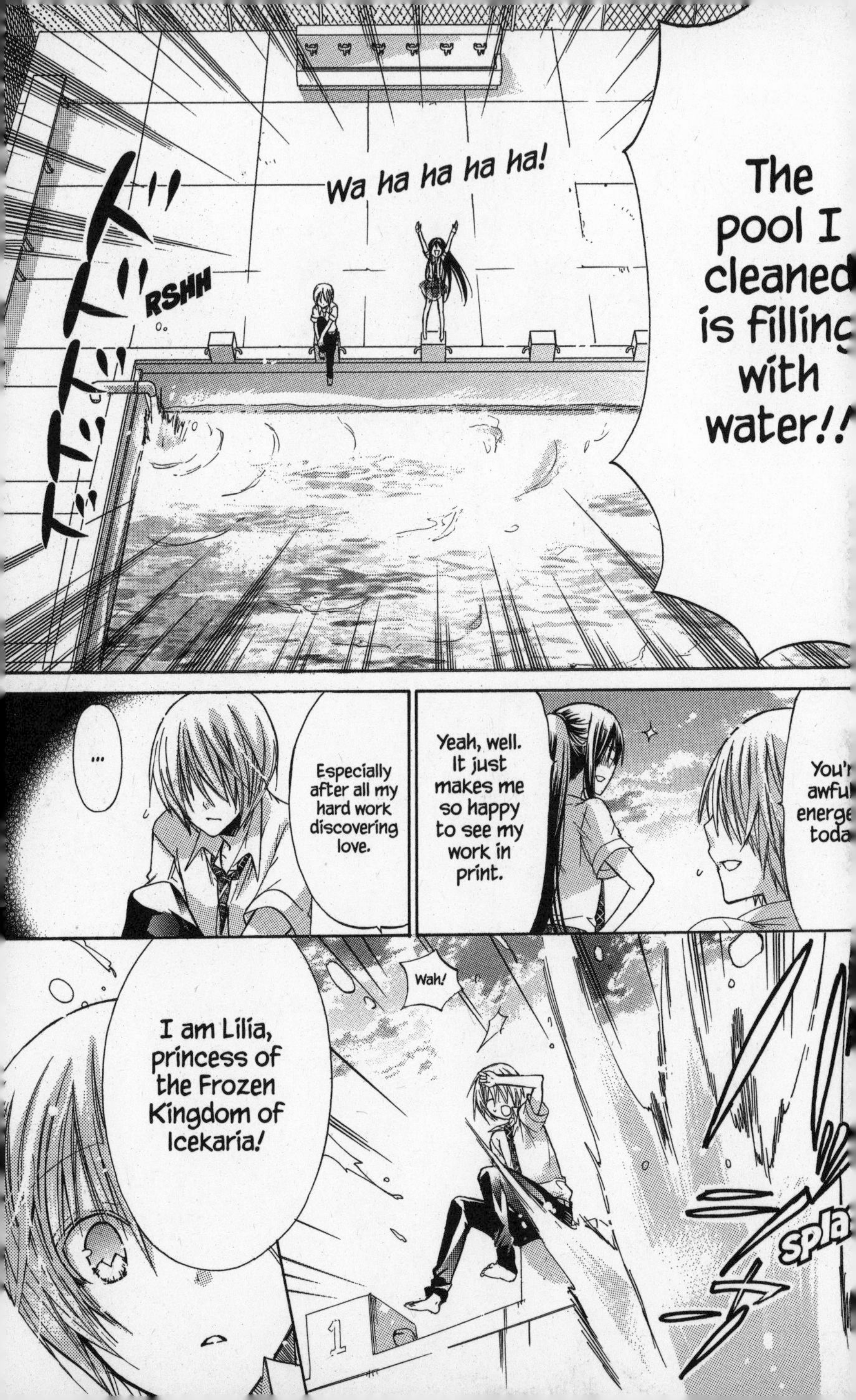
The pool I cleaned is filling with water!!
Wa ha ha ha ha!
RSHH
You'r awfu energe toda
Yeah, well. It just makes me so happy to see my work in print.
Especially after all my hard work discovering love.
...
Spla
Wah!
I am Lilia, princess of the Frozen Kingdom of Icekaria!

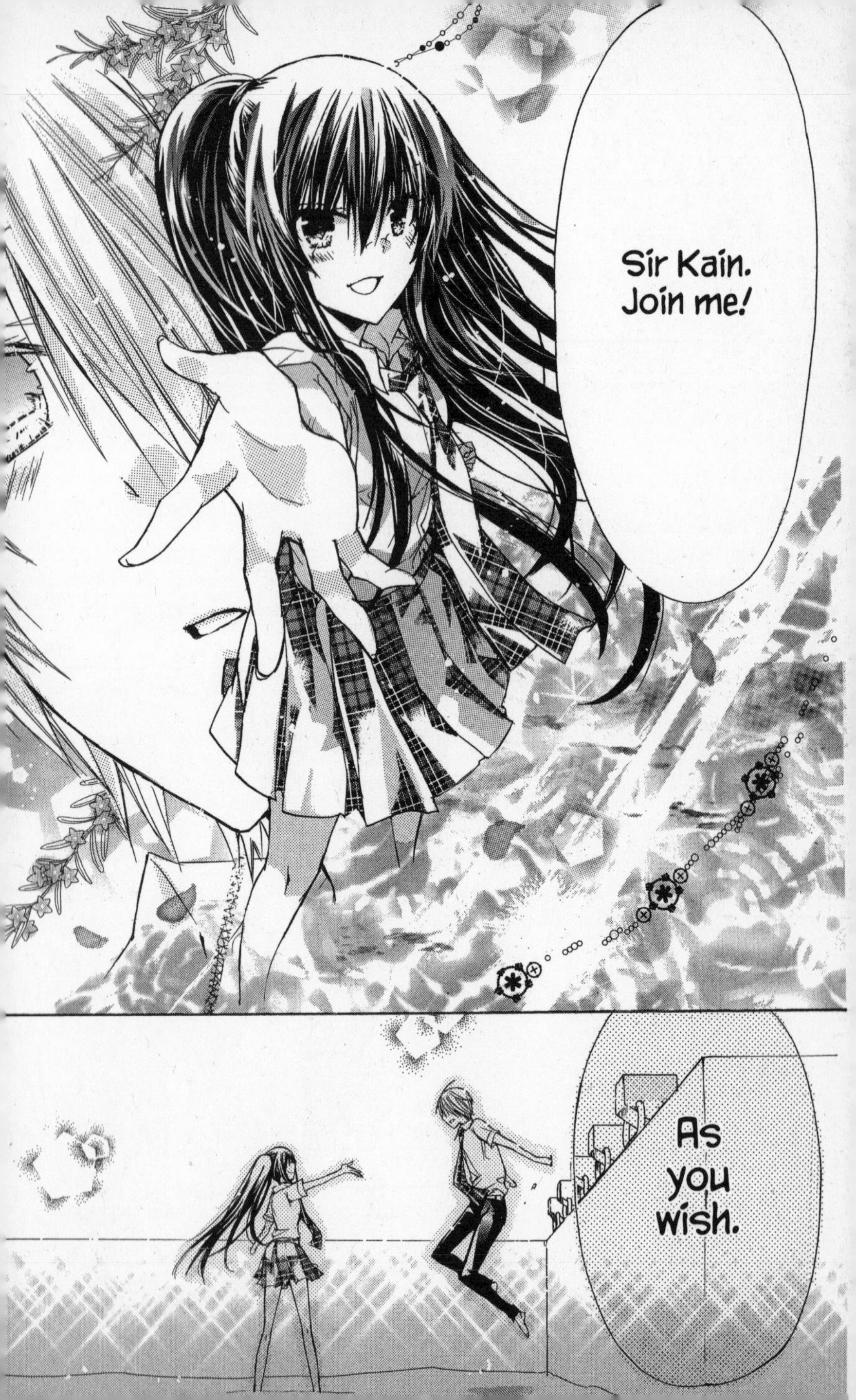
Sir Kain. Join me!
As you wish.

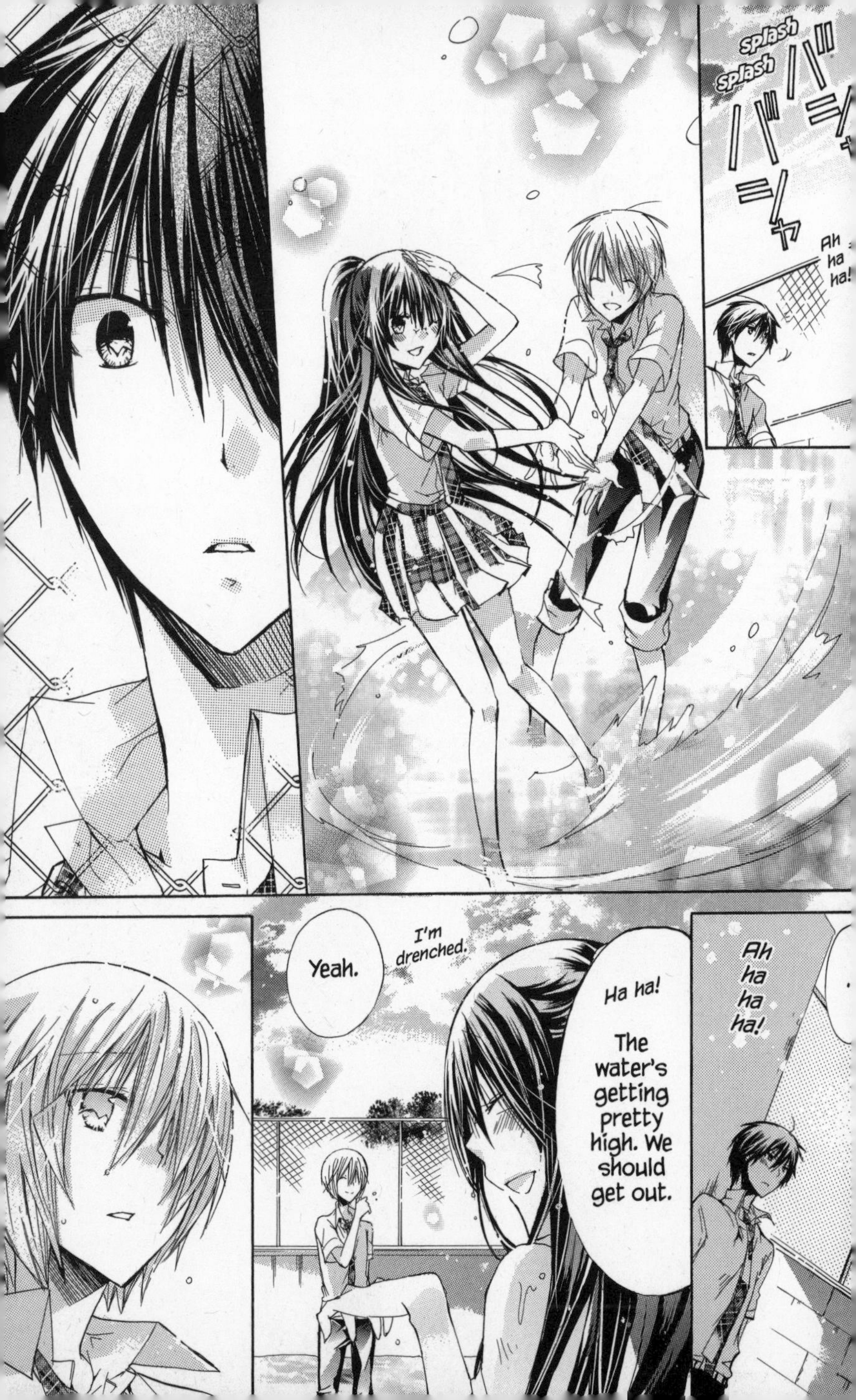
splash
splash
バシャバシャ
Ah ha ha!
Ah ha ha ha!
Ha ha!
The water's getting pretty high. We should get out.
I'm drenched.
Yeah.

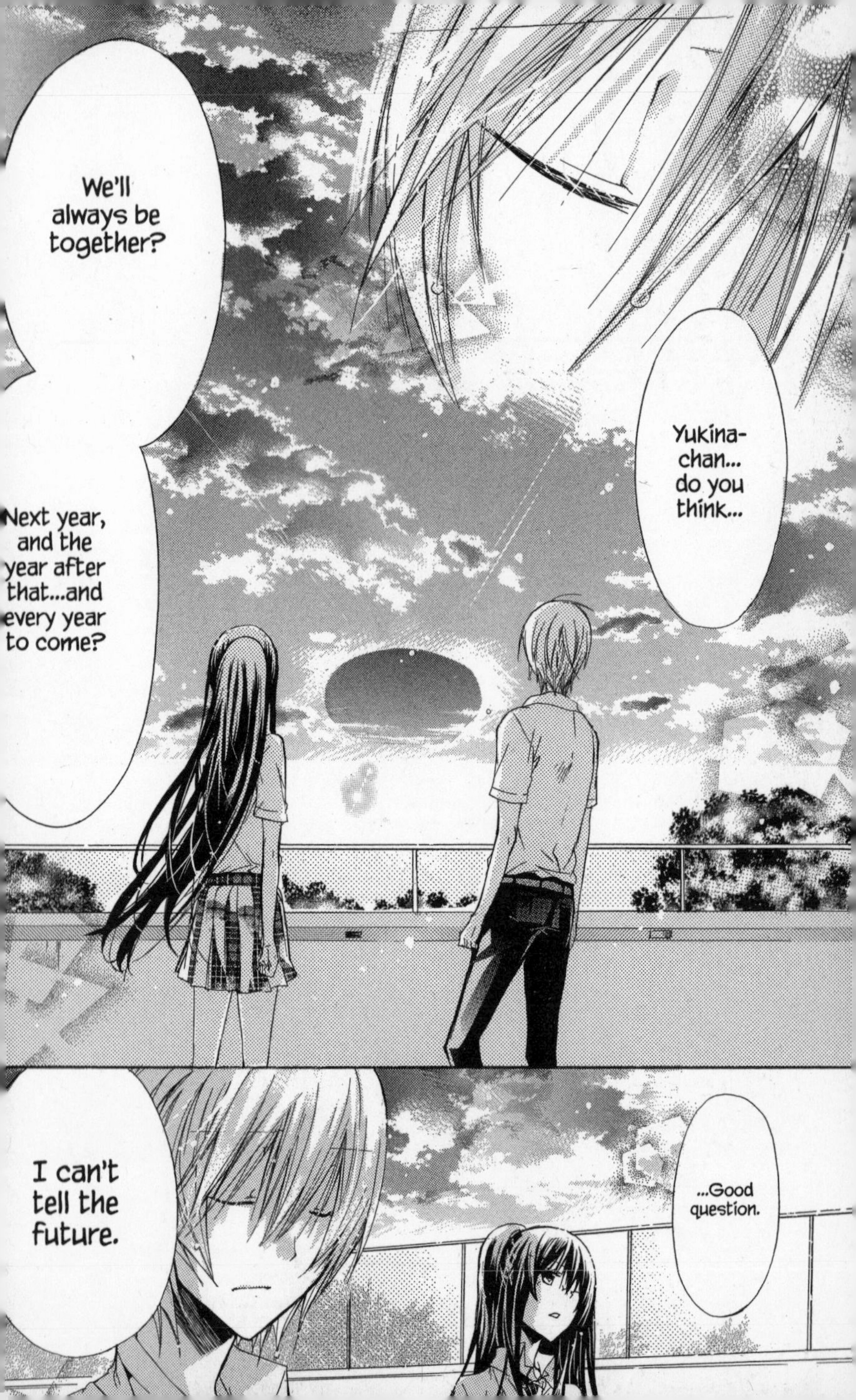
Yukina-chan... do you think...
We'll always be together?
Next year, and the year after that...and every year to come?
...Good question.
I can't tell the future.

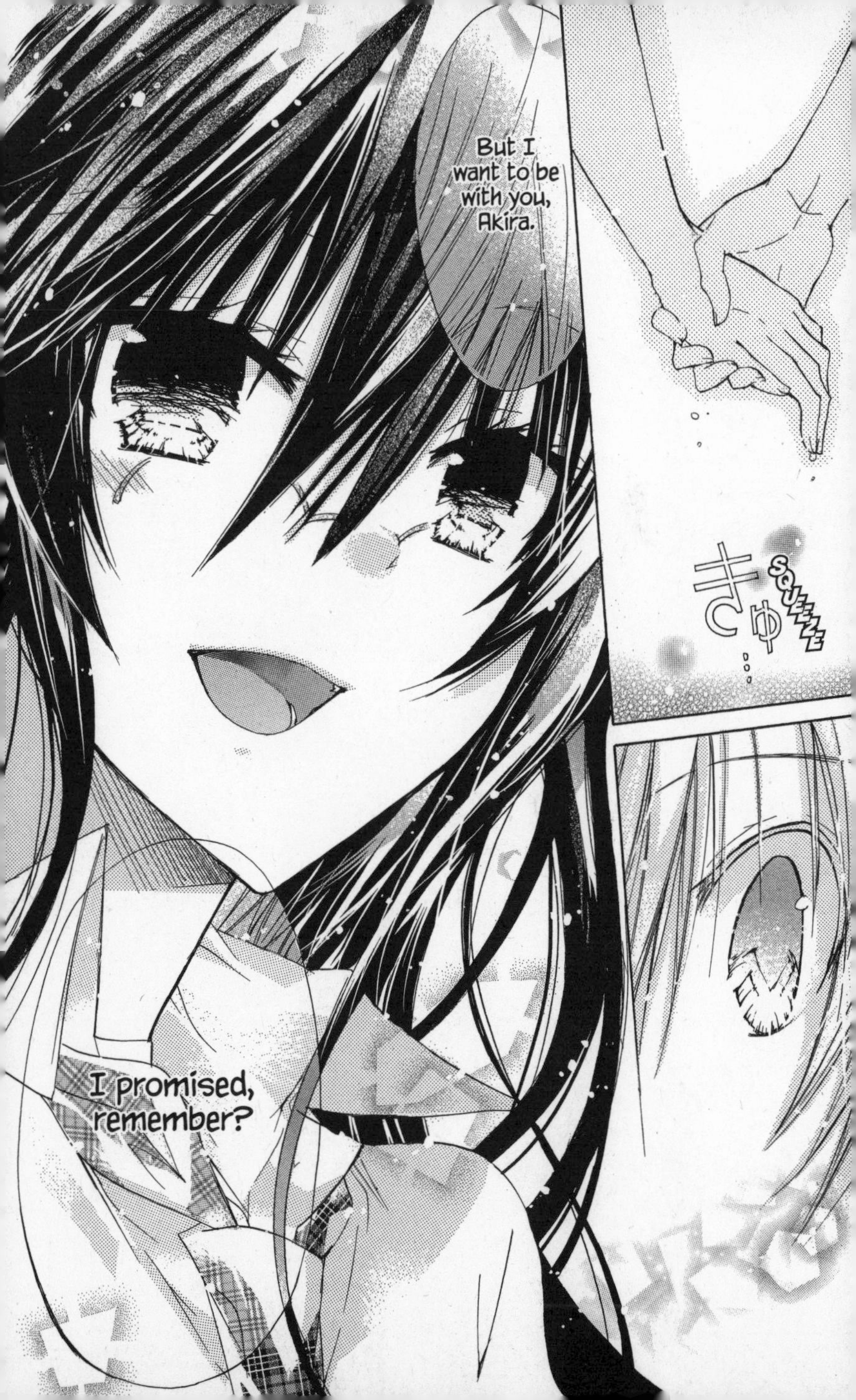
きゅ
SQUEEZE
But I want to be with you, Akira.
I promised, remember?

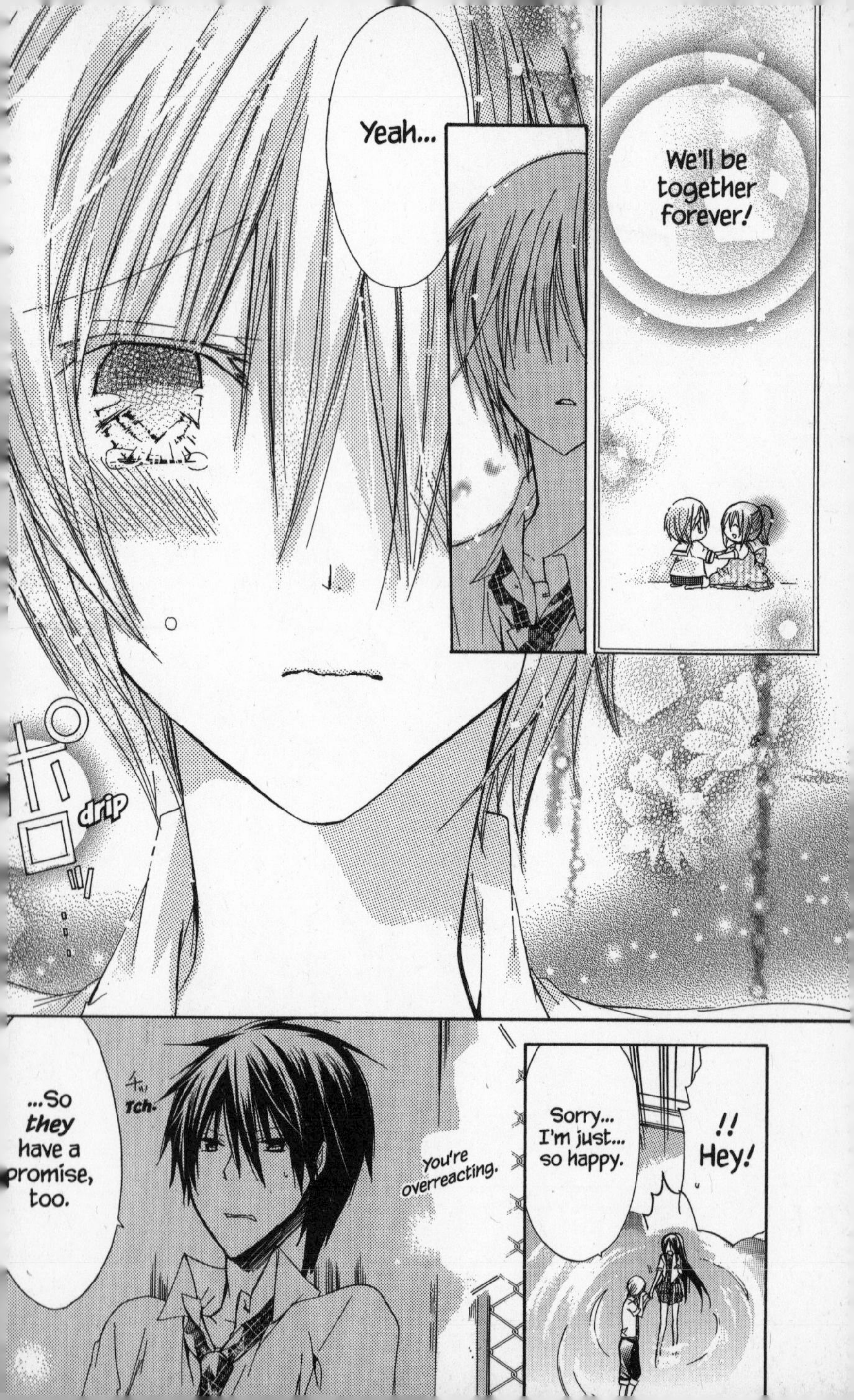
We'll be together forever!
Yeah...
drip
!! Hey!
Sorry... I'm just... so happy.
You're overreacting.
Tch.
...So they have a promise, too.

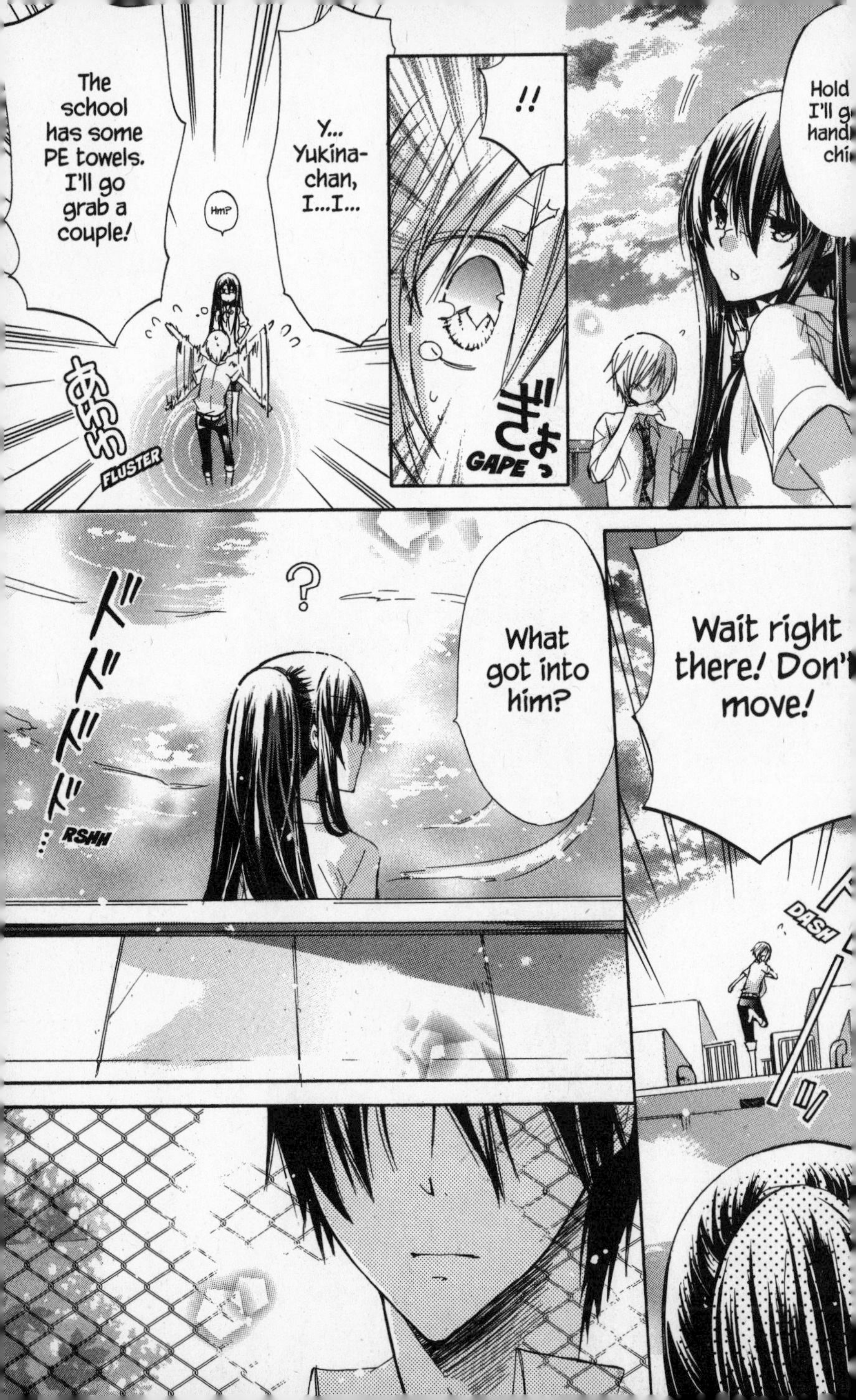
Hold
I'll g
hand
chi
!!
ぎょっ
GAPE
Y... Yukina-chan, I...I...
Hm?
The school has some PE towels. I'll go grab a couple!
あわわ
FLUSTER
Wait right there! Don'
move!
ドッ
DASH
What got into him?
?
ドドドドド...
RSHH

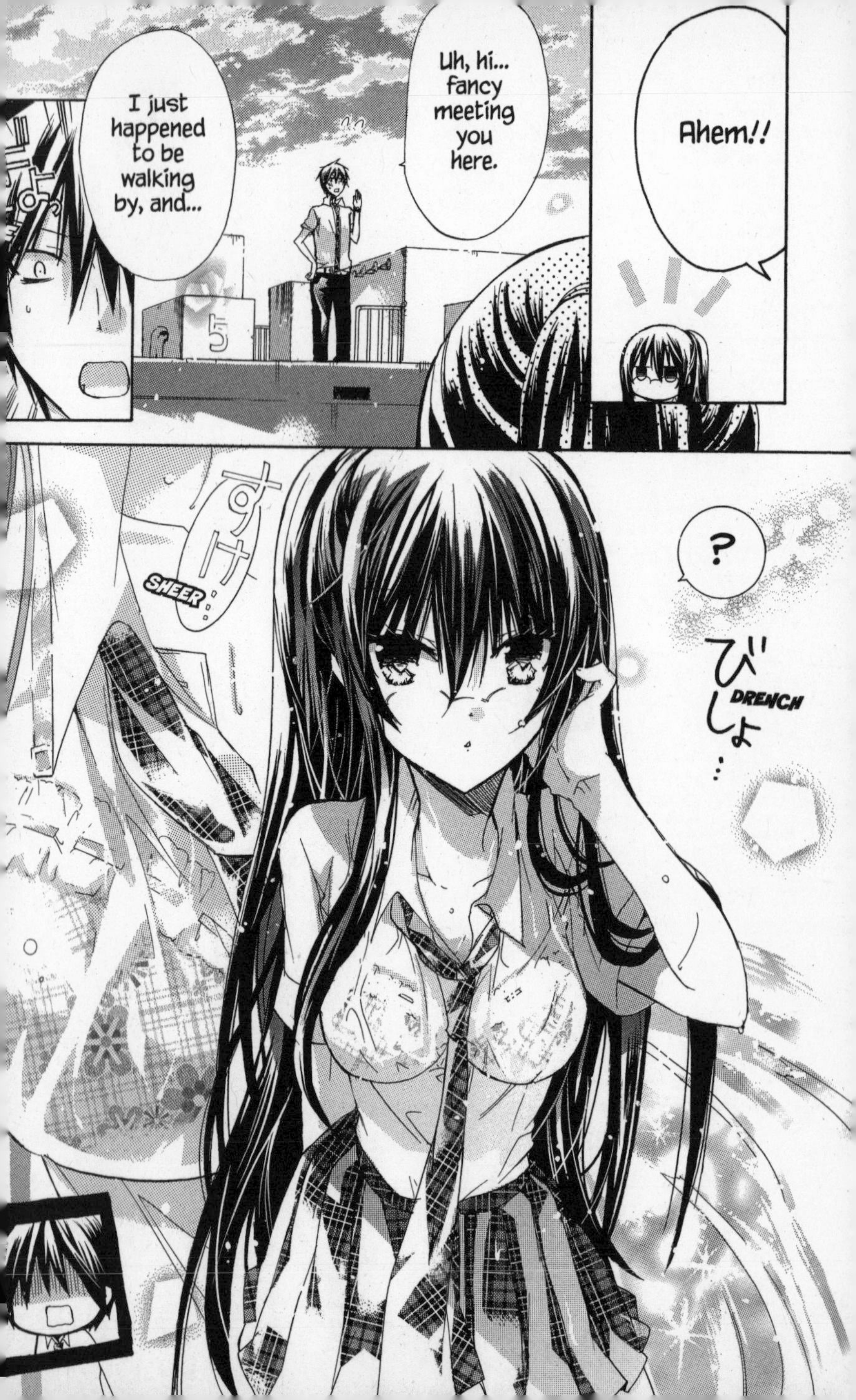
Ahem!!
Uh, hi... fancy meeting you here.
I just happened to be walking by, and...
?
びしょ…
DRENCH
すけ…
SHEER

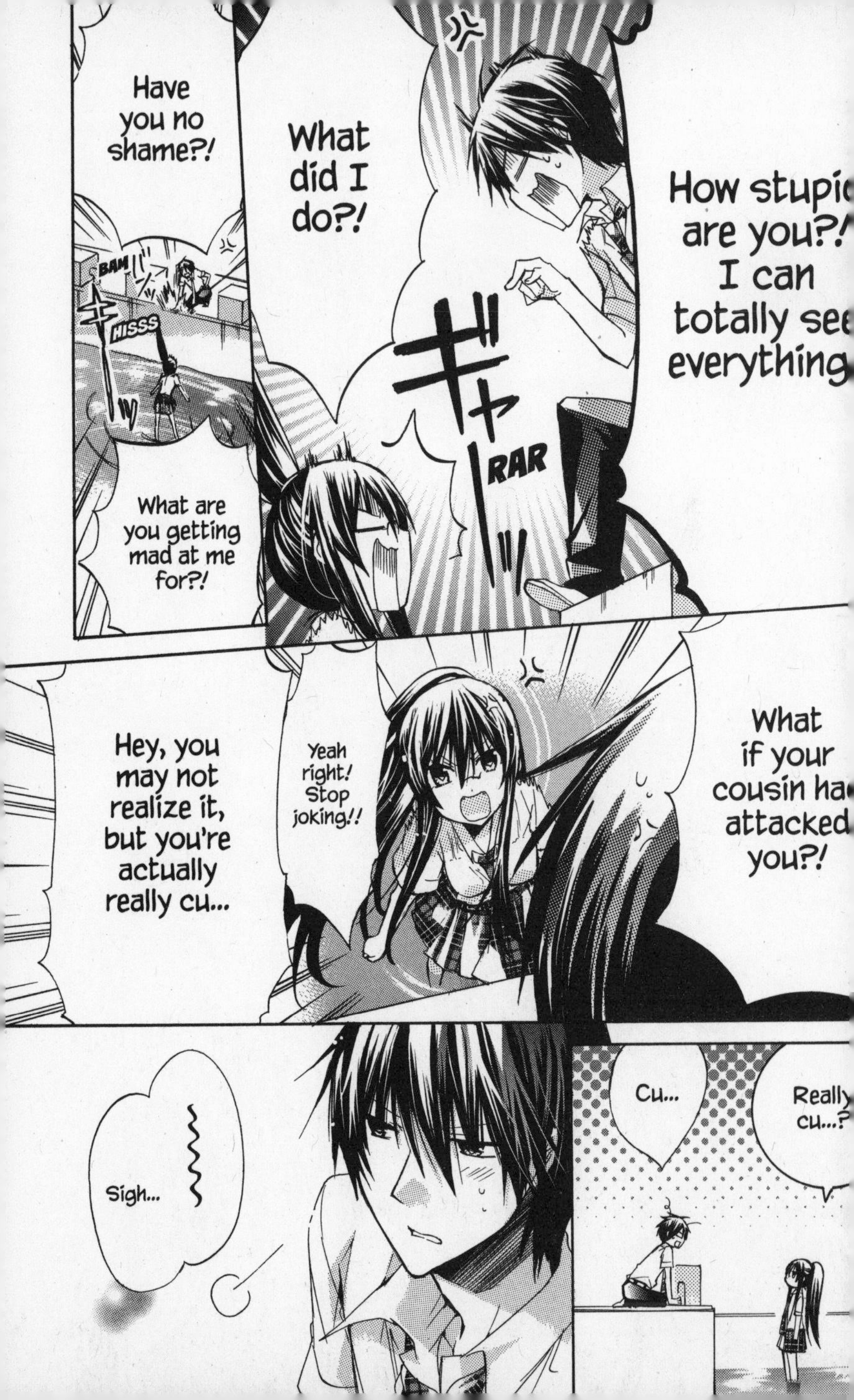
How stupi are you?! I can totally se everything
What did I do?!
RAR
What are you getting mad at me for?!
Have you no shame?!
BAM
HISSS
What if your cousin ha attacked you?!
Yeah right! Stop joking!!
Hey, you may not realize it, but you're actually really cu...
Really cu...?
Cu...
Sigh...

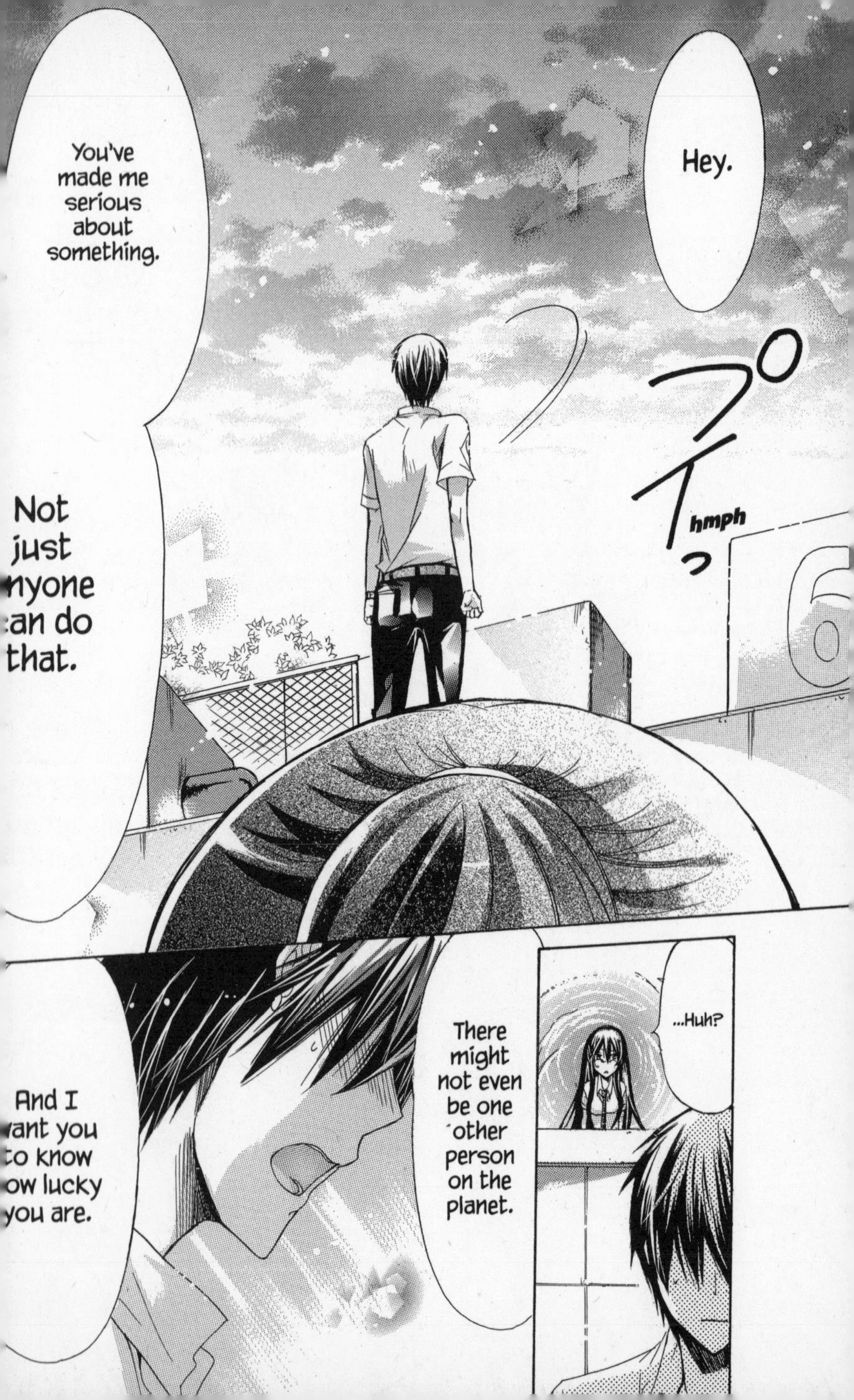
Hey.
プイッ
hmph
You've made me serious about something.
Not just nyone an do that.
...Huh?
There might not even be one other person on the planet.
And I vant you to know ow lucky you are.

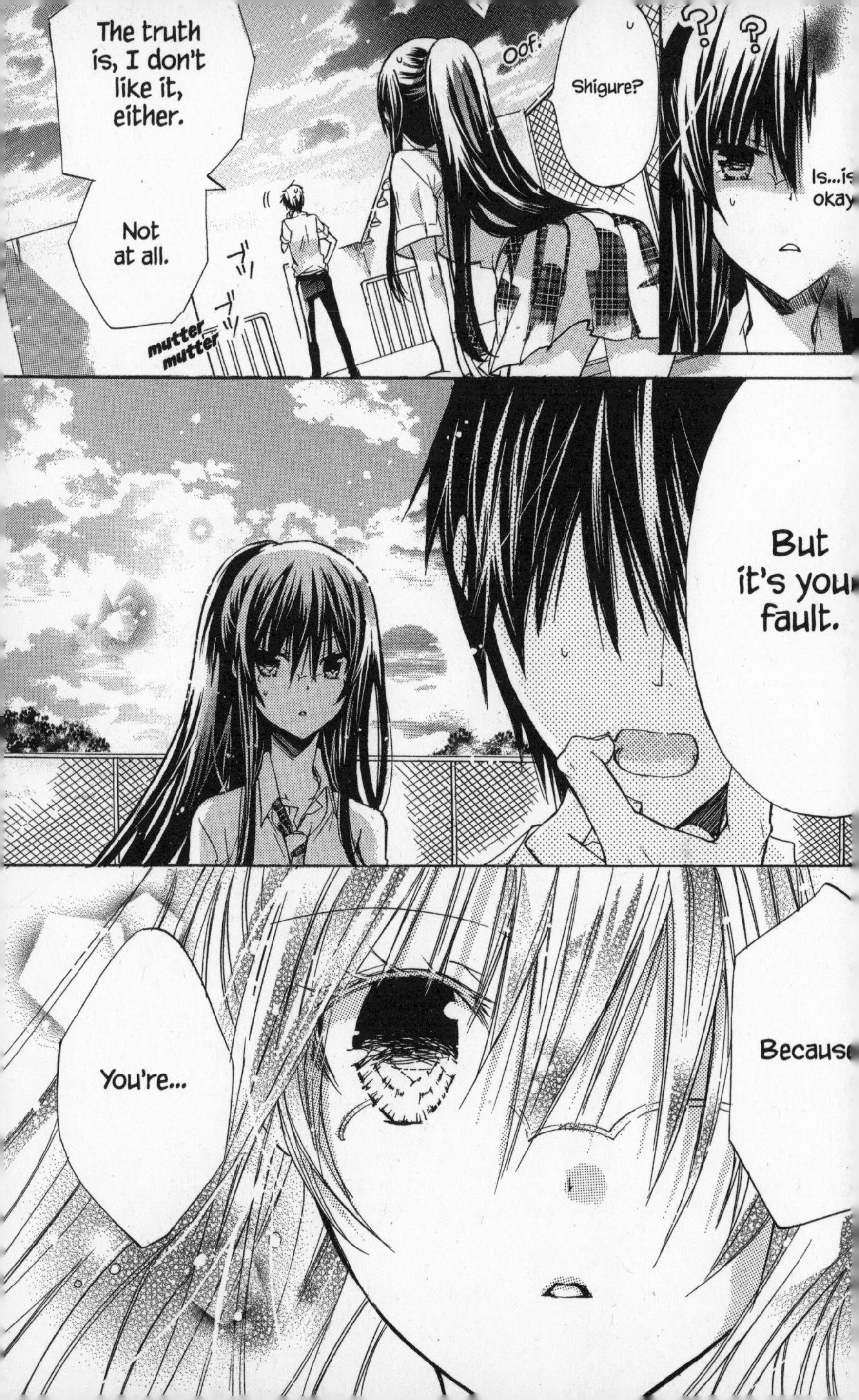
Is...is
okay
Oof.
Shigure?
The truth is, I don't like it, either.
Not at all.
ブツ ブツ
mutter mutter
But it's your fault.
Because
You're...

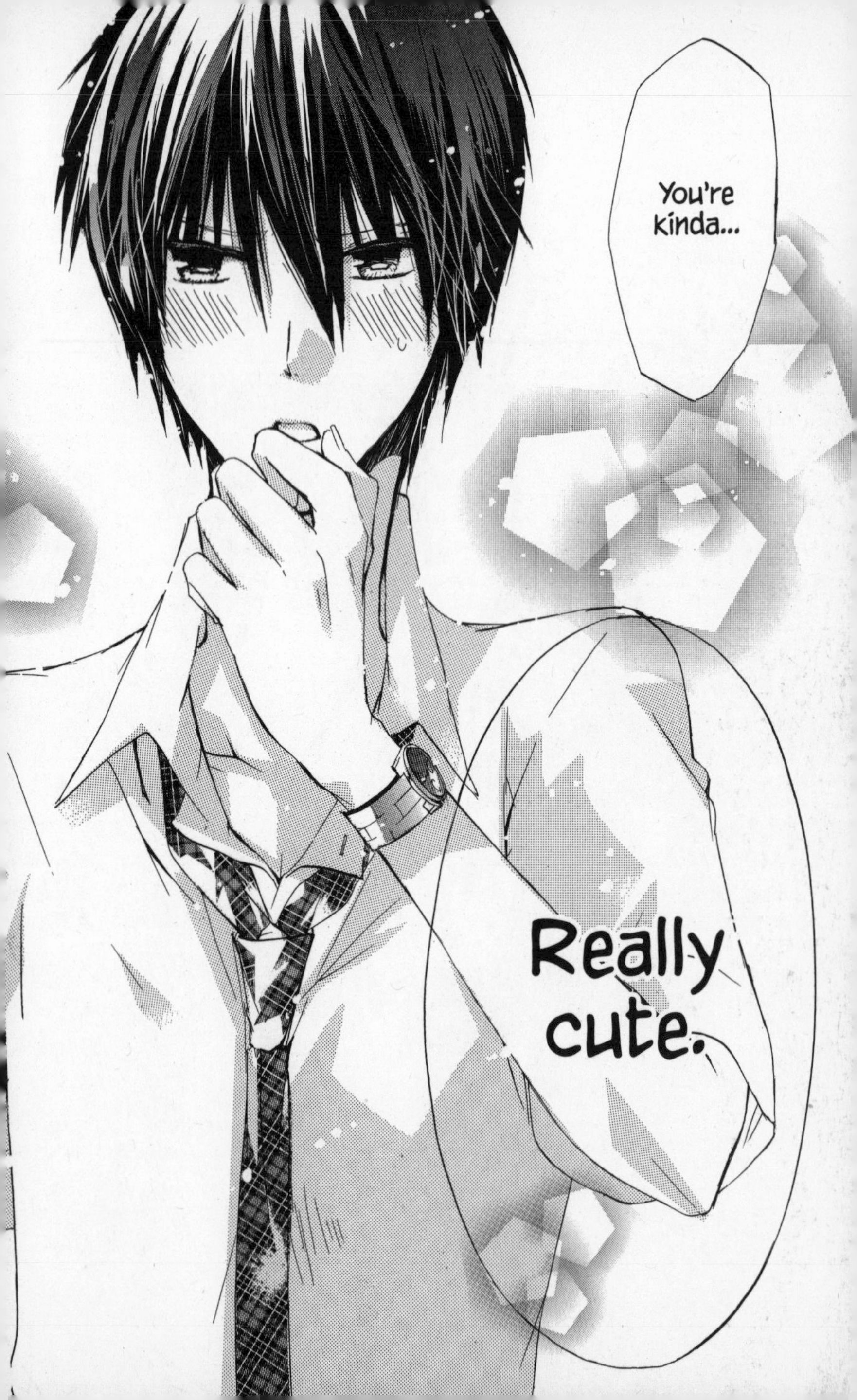
You're kinda...
Really cute.

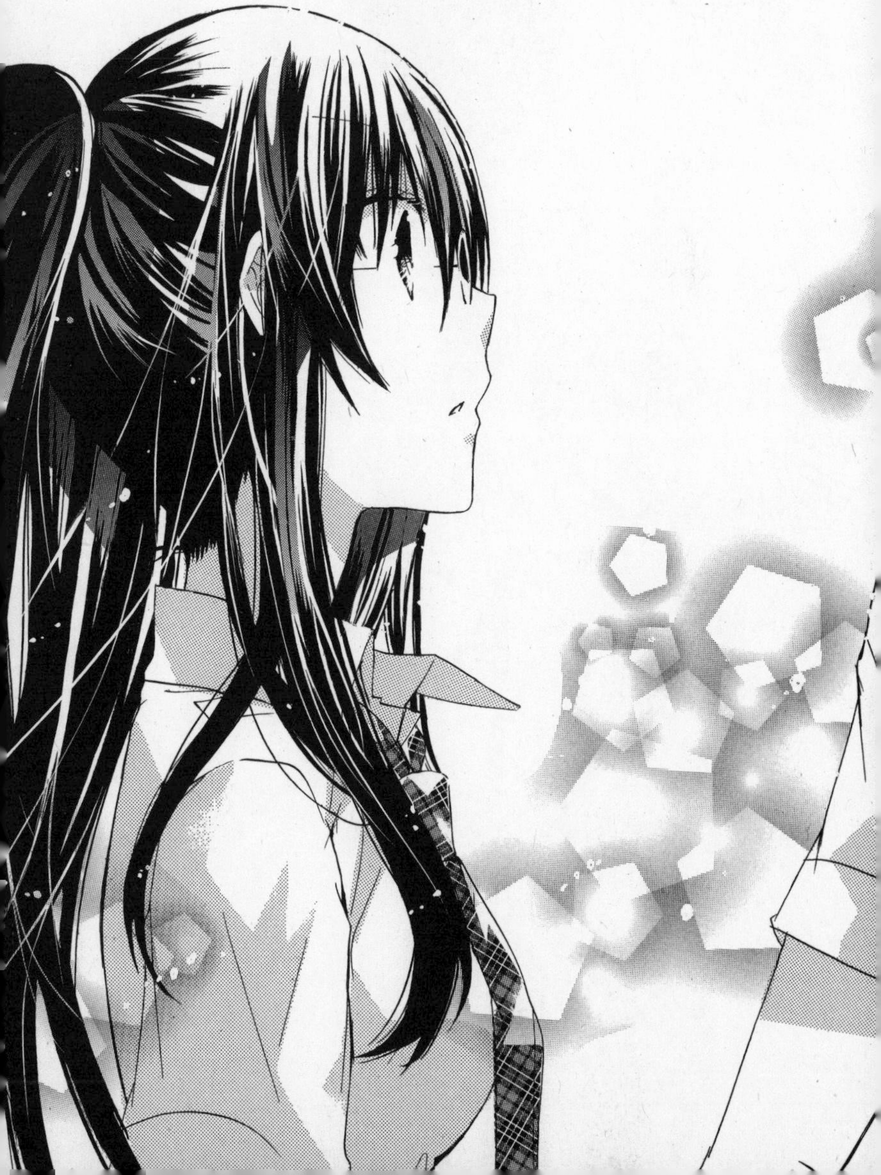

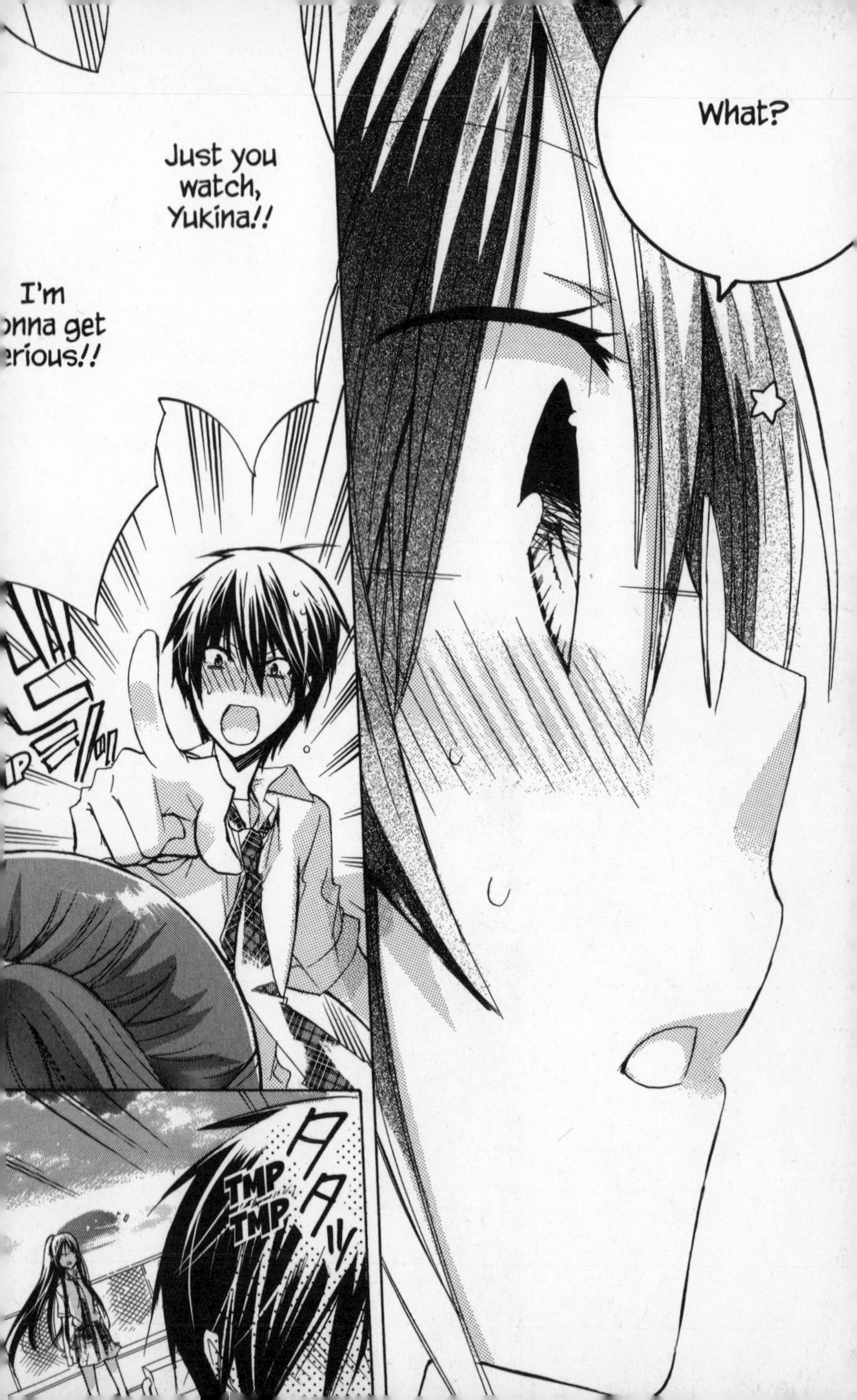
What?
Just you watch, Yukina!!
I'm onna get erious!!
TMP TMP

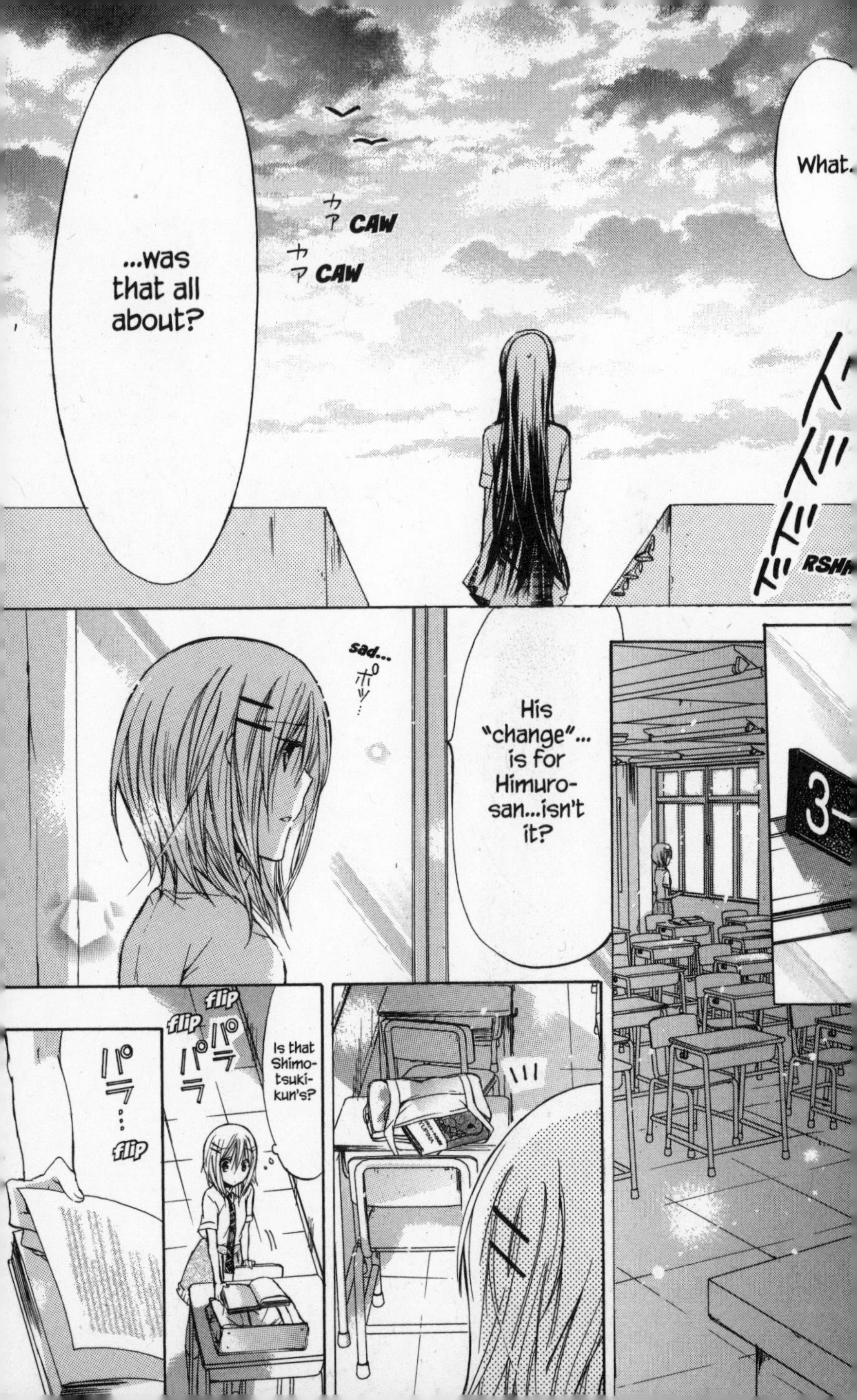

What.
RSHH
カア CAW
カア CAW
...was that all about?
3-
His "change"... is for Himuro-san...isn't it?
sad... ポツ…
Is that Shimotsuki-kun's?
flip
flip
パラ
パラ
パラ…
flip

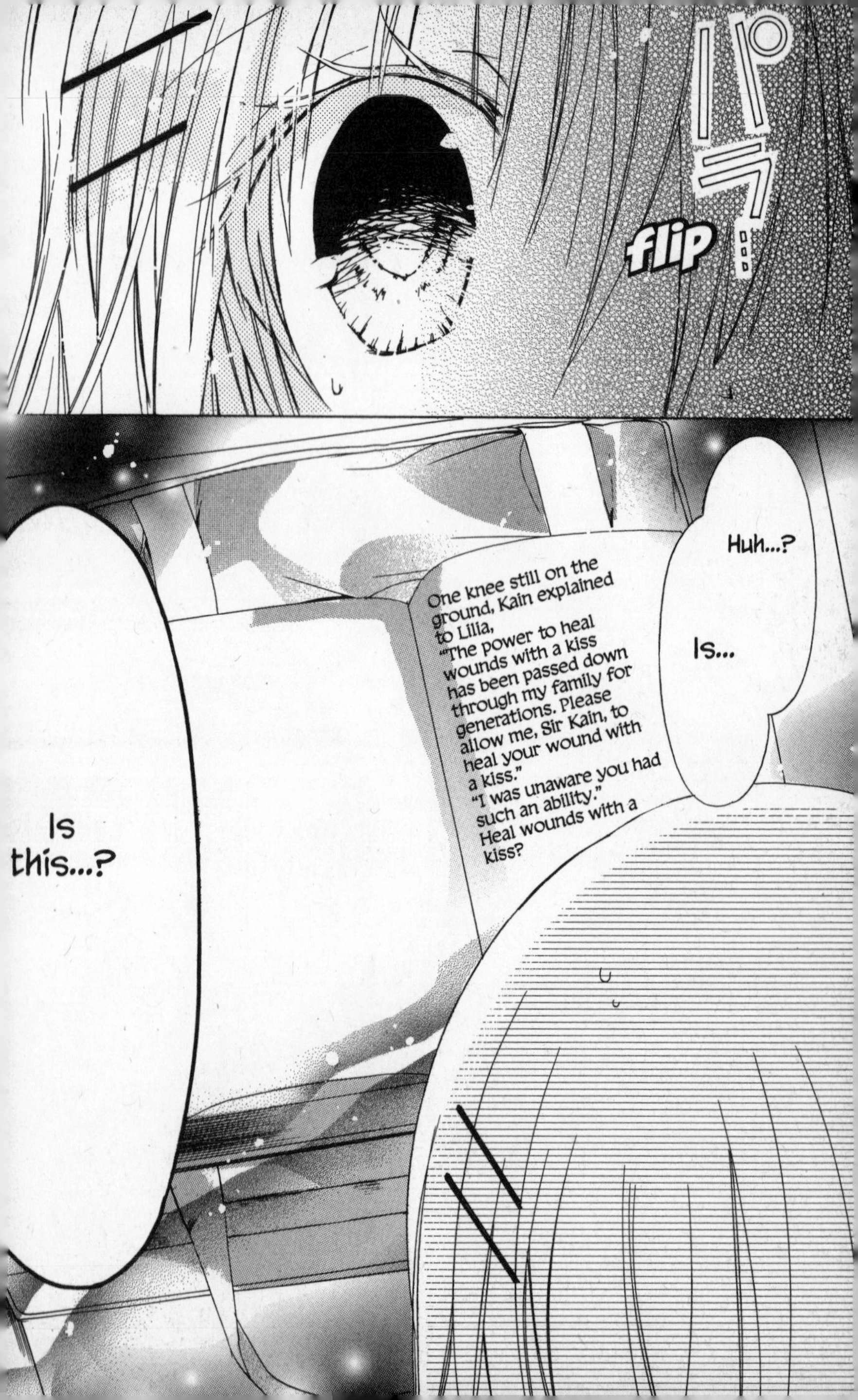
パラ…
flip
Huh...?
Is...
One knee still on the ground, Kain explained to Lilia, "The power to heal wounds with a kiss has been passed down through my family for generations. Please allow me, Sir Kain, to heal your wound with a kiss." "I was unaware you had such an ability." Heal wounds with a kiss?
Is this...?

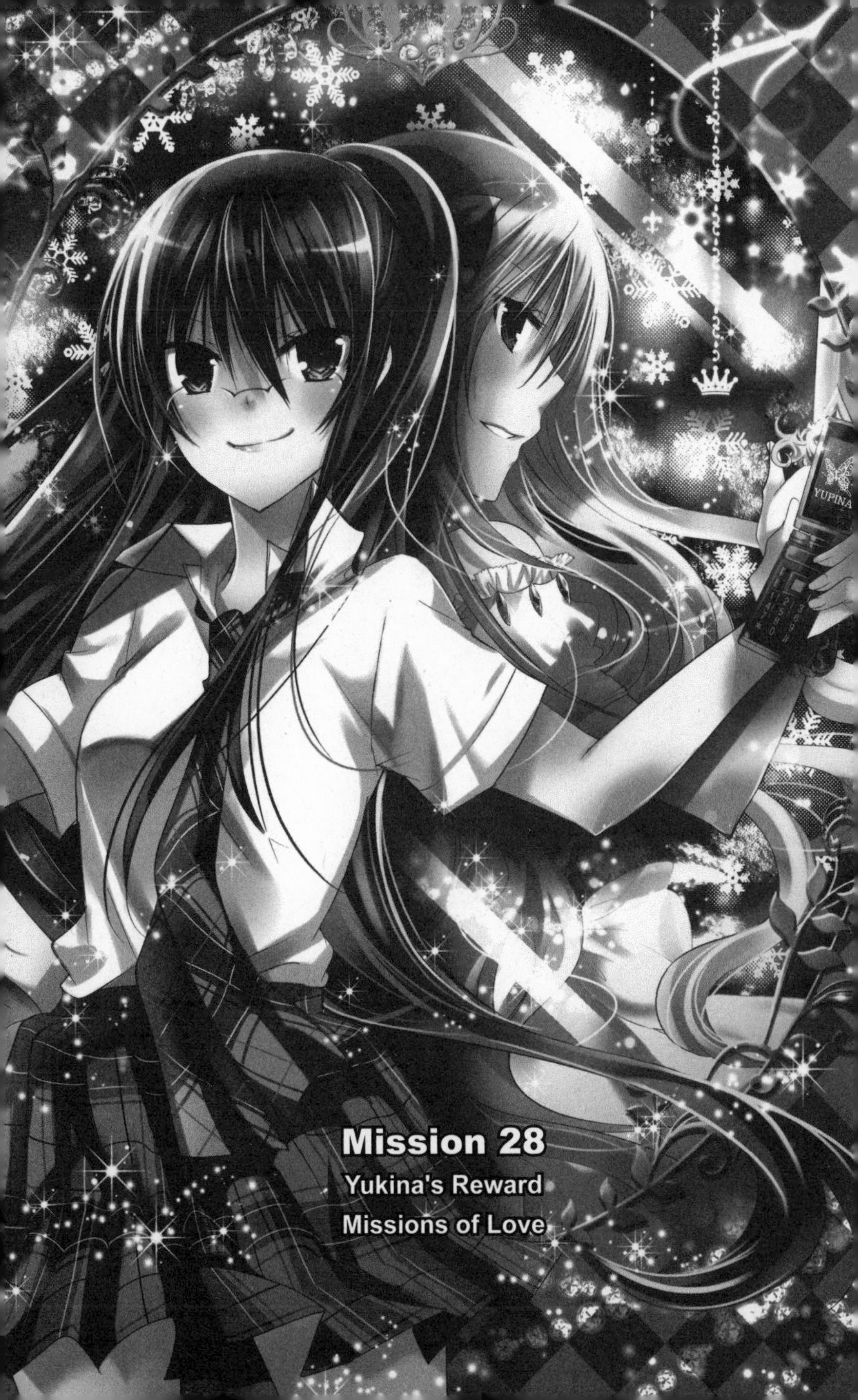
YUPINA
Mission 28
Yukina's Reward
Missions of Love

Missions of Love

It is time for love.
Secret cell phone novelist vs. the most popular boy in school.
A mission of love for absolute servitude.

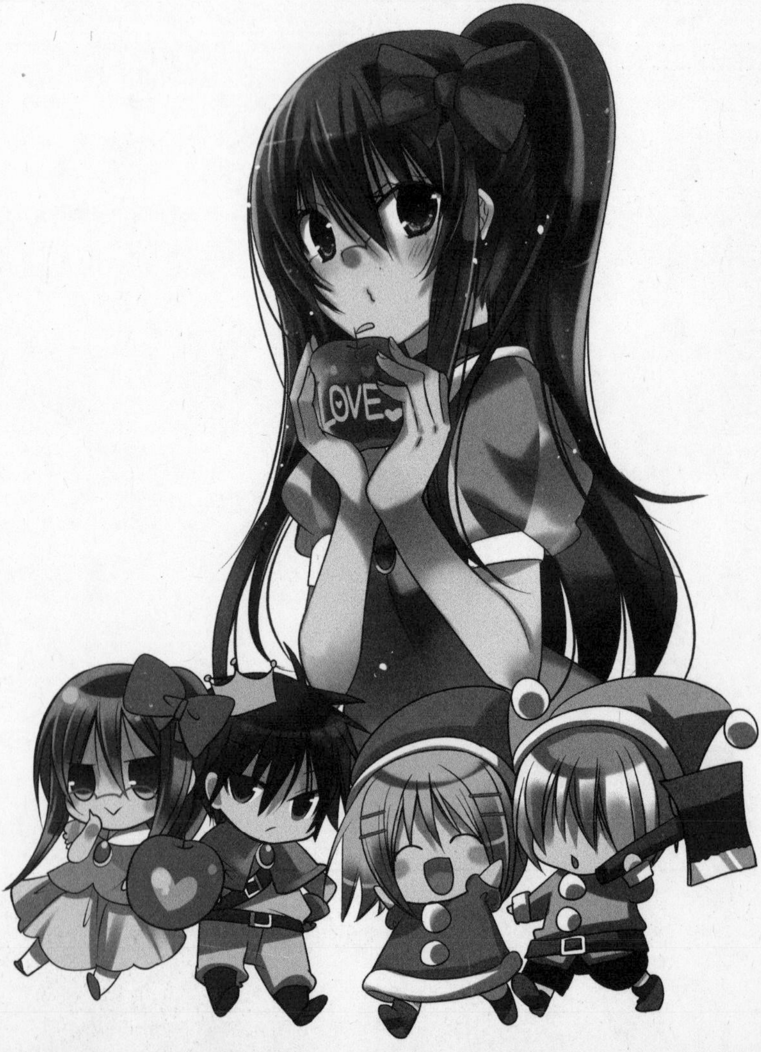
LOVE

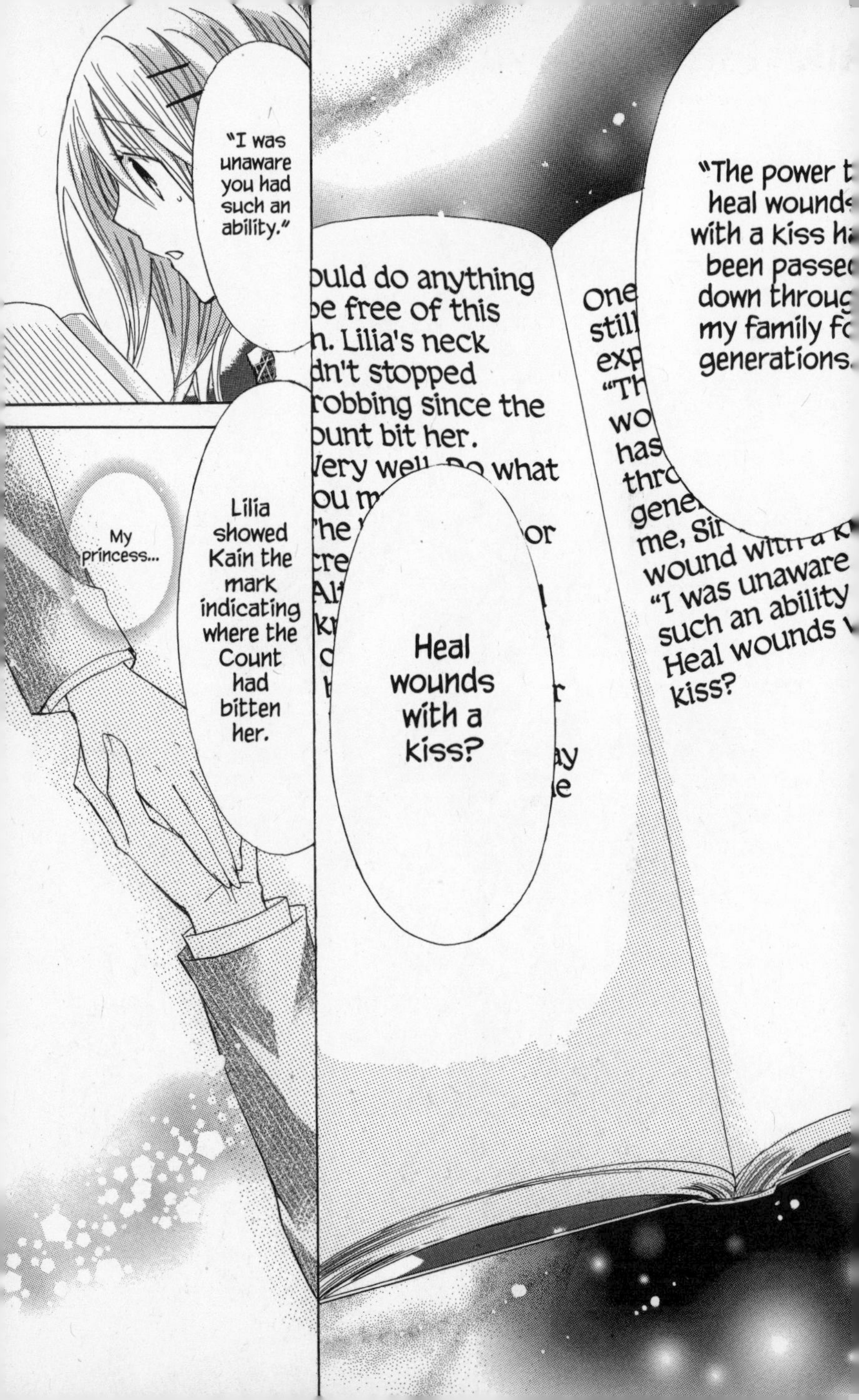
"The power t heal wounds with a kiss h been passe down throug my family fo generations.
Heal wounds with a kiss?
ould do anything
e free of this
n. Lilia's neck
dn't stopped
robbing since the
ount bit her.
One
still
wound with a k
"I was unaware
such an ability
Heal wounds w
kiss?
"I was unaware you had such an ability."
Lilia showed Kain the mark indicating where the Count had bitten her.
My princess...

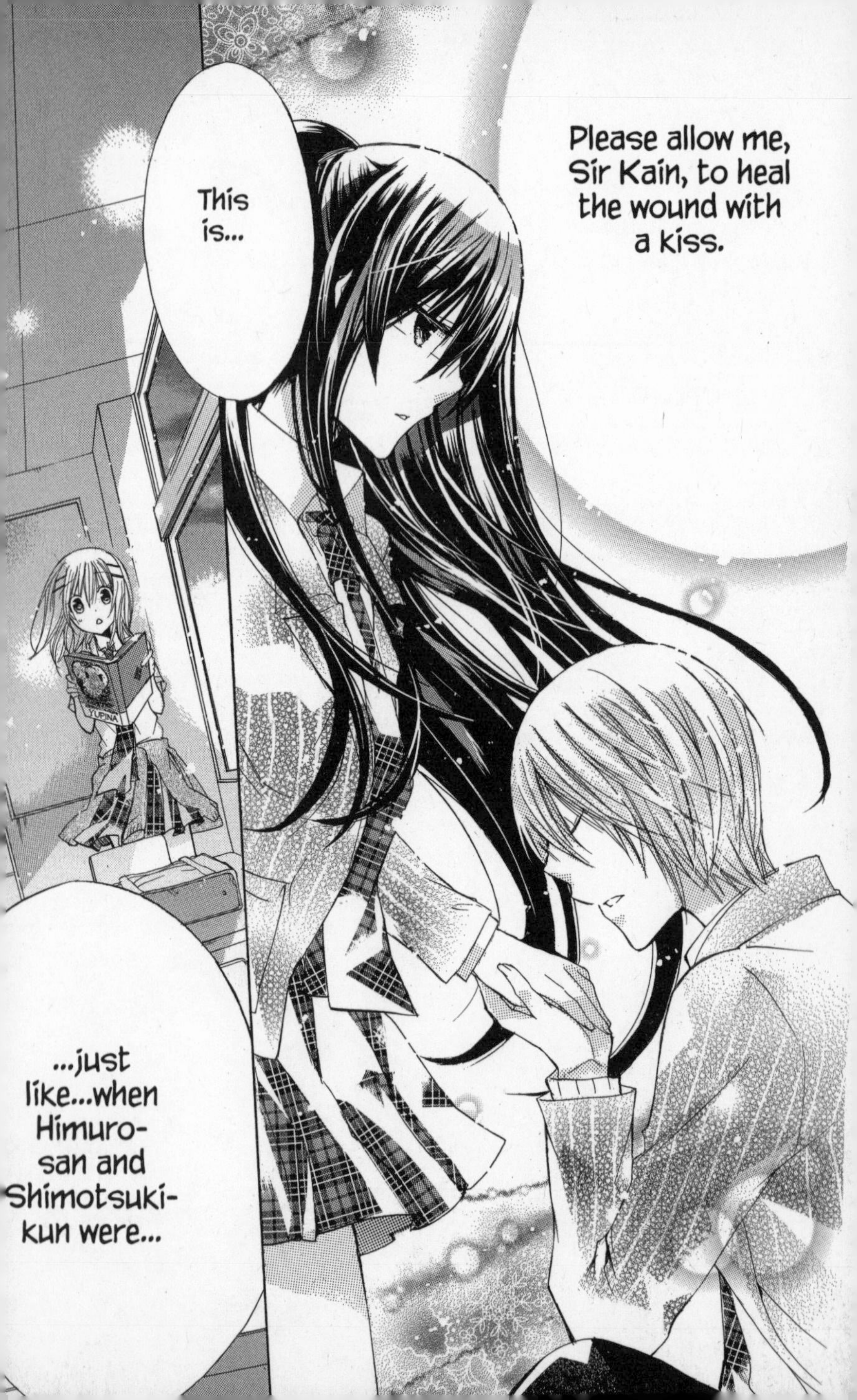
Please allow me, Sir Kain, to heal the wound with a kiss.
This is...
YUPINA
...just like...when Himuro-san and Shimotsuki-kun were...

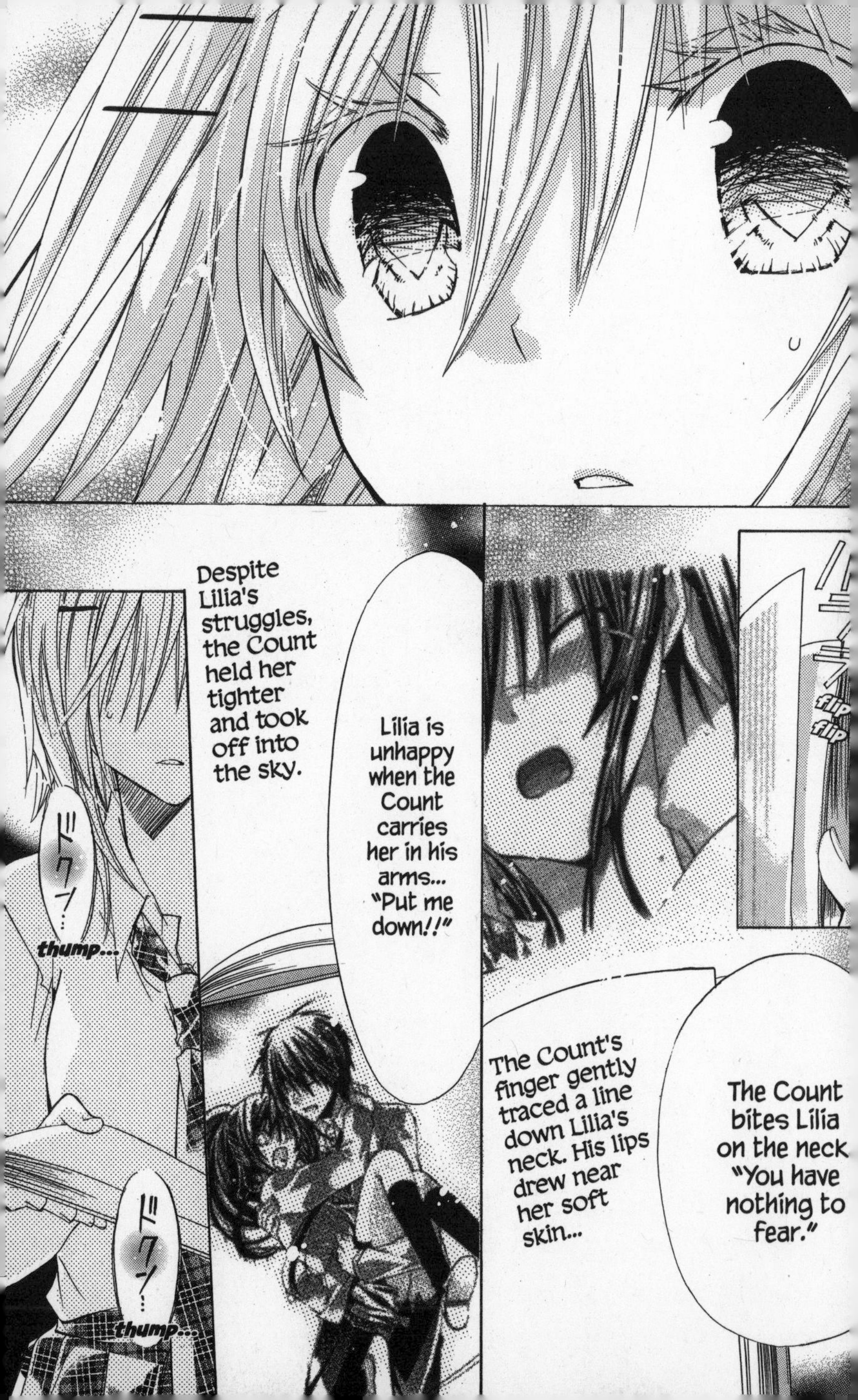
flip flip
The Count bites Lilia on the neck "You have nothing to fear."
The Count's finger gently traced a line down Lilia's neck. His lips drew near her soft skin...
Lilia is unhappy when the Count carries her in his arms... "Put me down!!"
Despite Lilia's struggles, the Count held her tighter and took off into the sky.
ドクン…
thump...
ドクン…
thump...

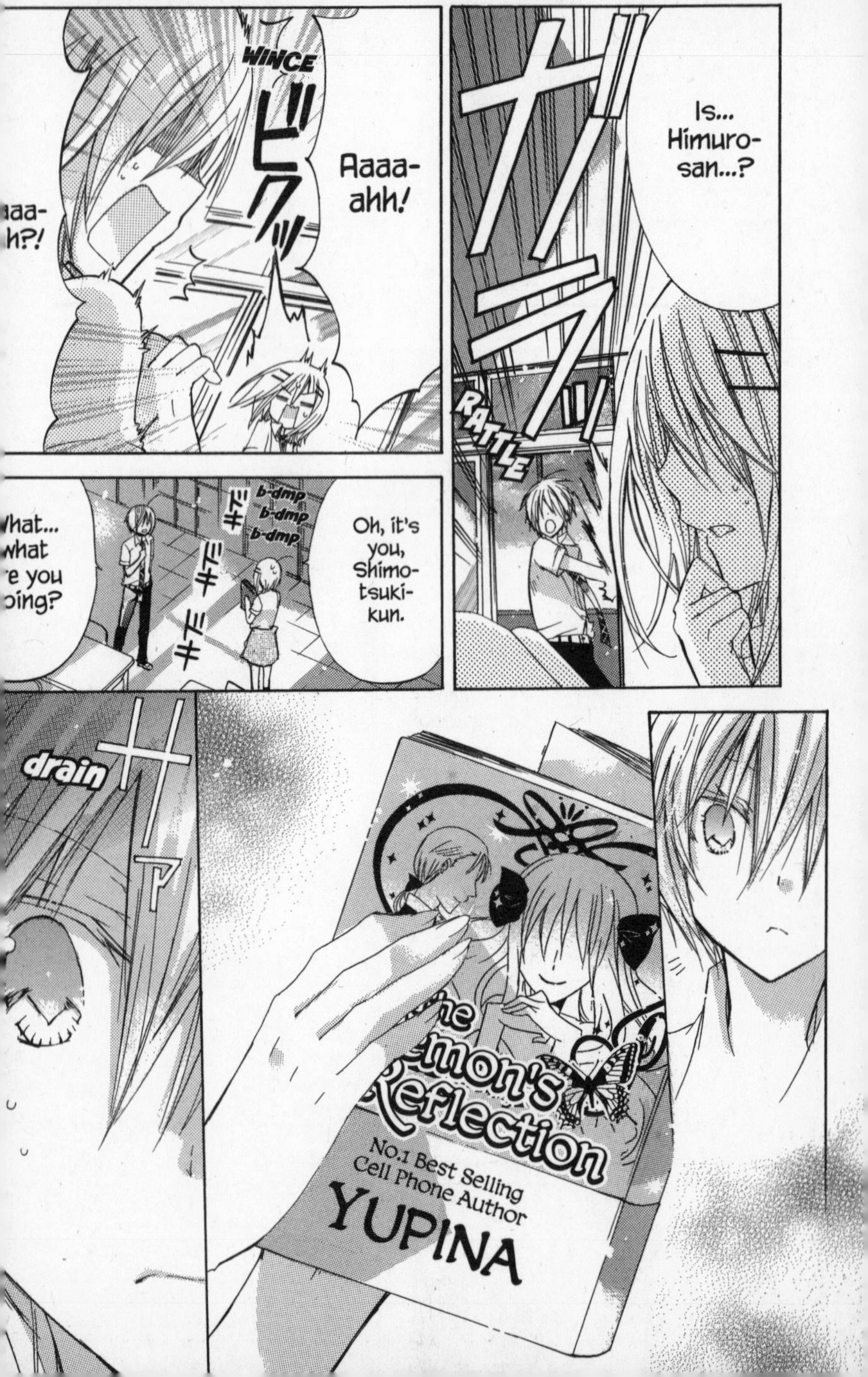
RATTLE
Is... Himuro-san...?
WINCE
Aaaa-ahh!
aaa-h?!
b-dmp b-dmp b-dmp
Oh, it's you, Shimotsuki-kun.
hat... what e you oing?
emon's Reflection
No.1 Best Selling Cell Phone Author
YUPINA
drain

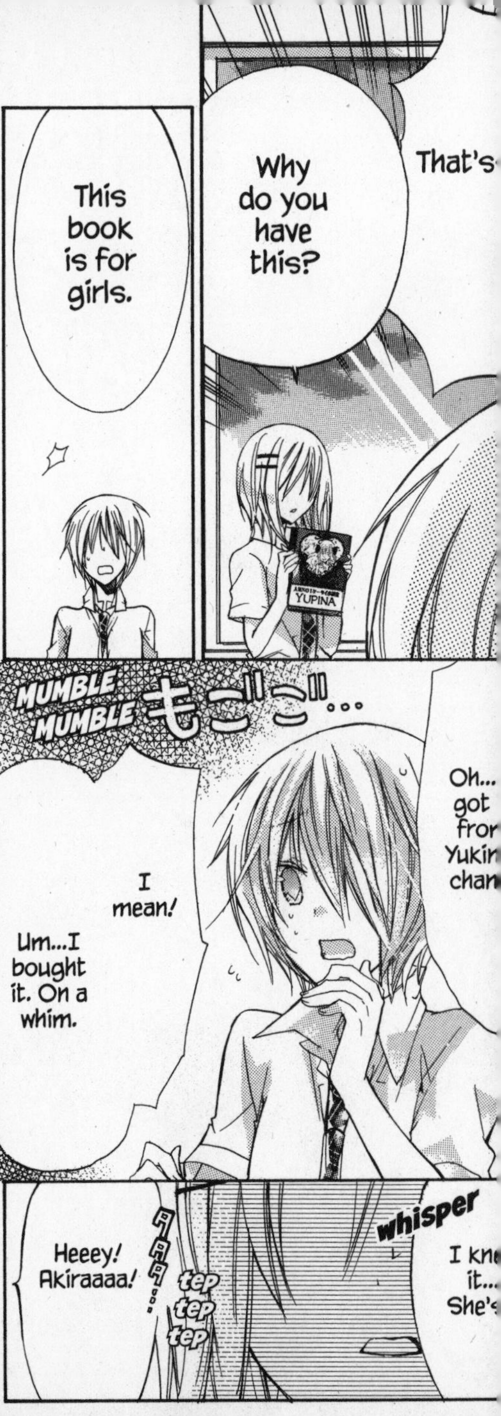
That's
Why do you have this?
This book is for girls.
YUPINA
Oh... got fror Yukin chan
MUMBLE MUMBLE もごもご...
I mean!
Um...I bought it. On a whim.
whisper
I kne it... She's
Heeey! Akiraaaa!
タタタ...
tep tep tep

Mami and Snow Mami 3

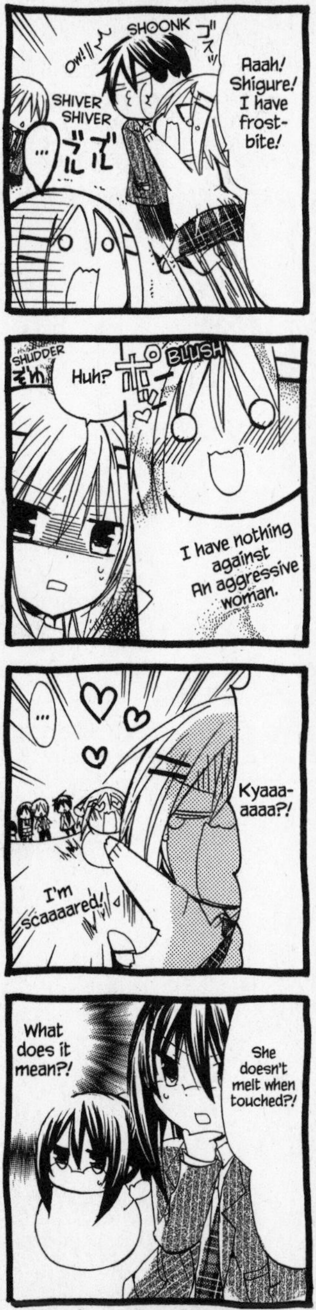
Aaah! Shigure! I have frost-bite!
SHOONK ゴスッ
OW!
SHIVER SHIVER ブルブル
...
BLUSH ポッ
Huh?
SHUDDER ぞわ
I have nothing against An aggressive woman.
Kyaaa-aaaa?!
...
I'm scaaaared!
She doesn't melt when touched?!
What does it mean?!

I'm dragging this out too long?! ...What will I do?!

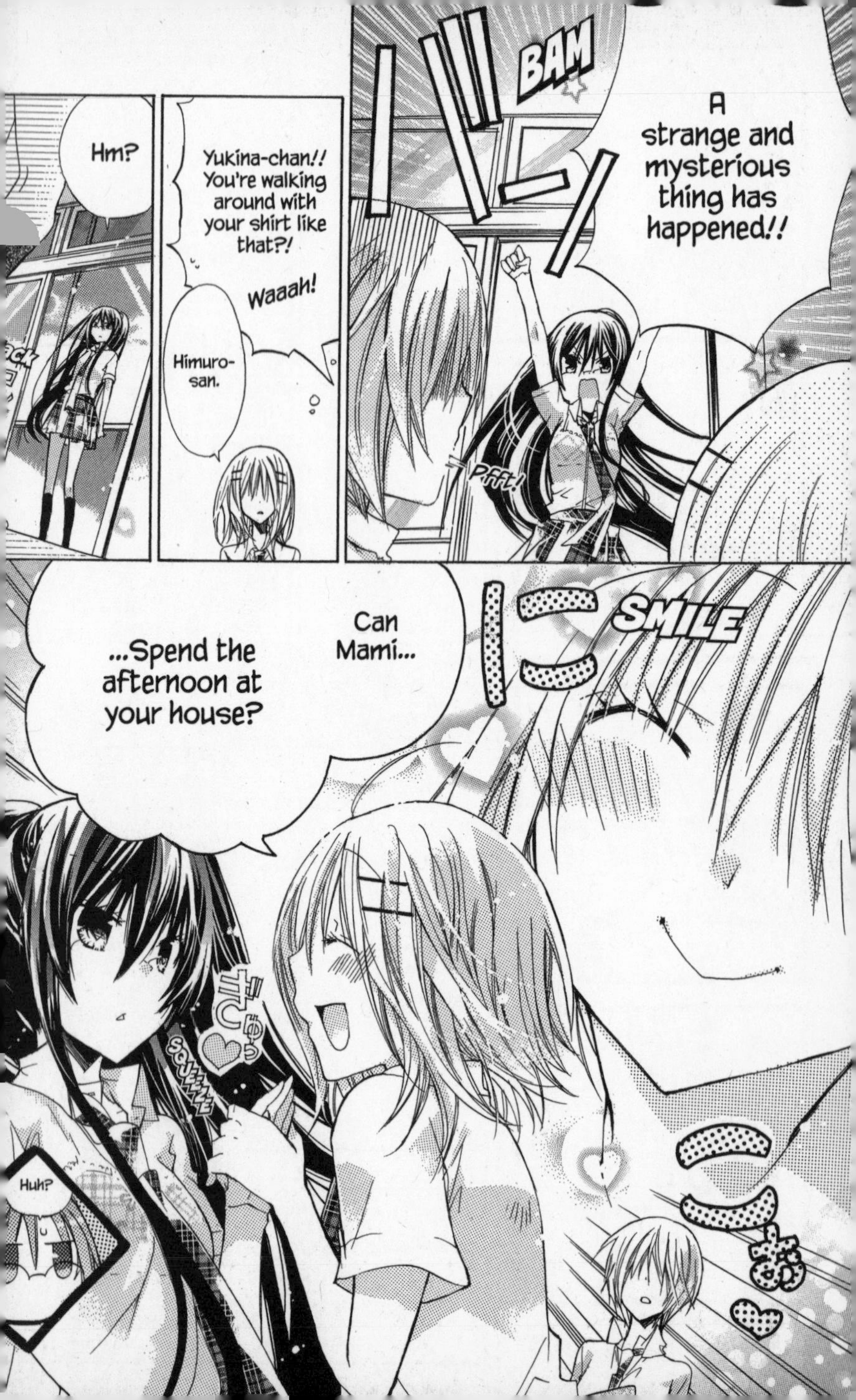
BAM
A strange and mysterious thing has happened!!
Pffft!
Yukina-chan!! You're walking around with your shirt like that?!
Waaah!
Himuro-san.
Hm?
SMILE
Can Mami...
...Spend the afternoon at your house?
SQUEEZE
Huh?

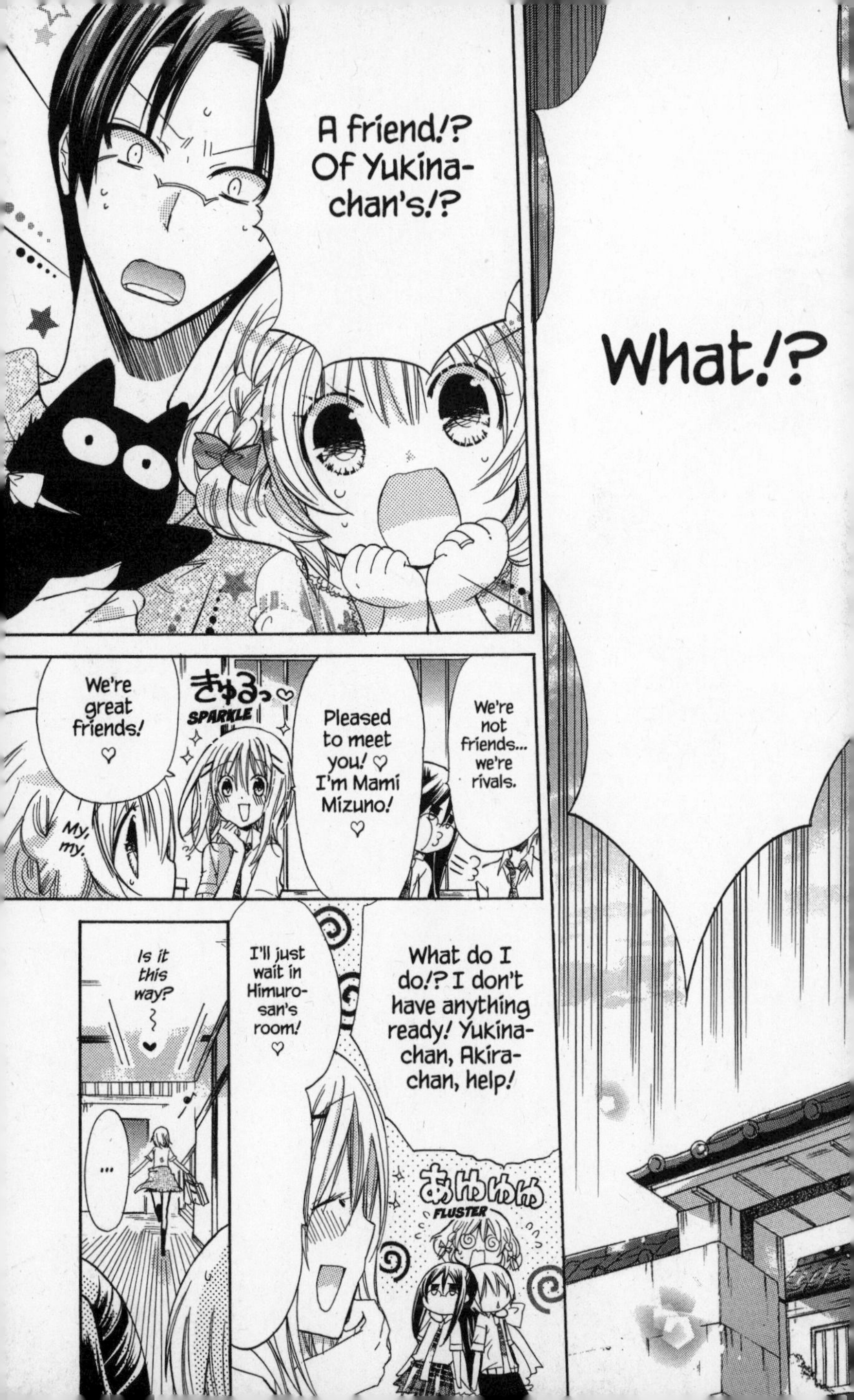
What!?
A friend!? Of Yukina-chan's!?
We're not friends... we're rivals.
Pleased to meet you! ♡ I'm Mami Mizuno! ♡
きゅるっ♡
SPARKLE
We're great friends! ♡
My, my.
What do I do!? I don't have anything ready! Yukina-chan, Akira-chan, help!
あゆゆゆ
FLUSTER
I'll just wait in Himuro-san's room! ♡
Is it this way? ♥
...

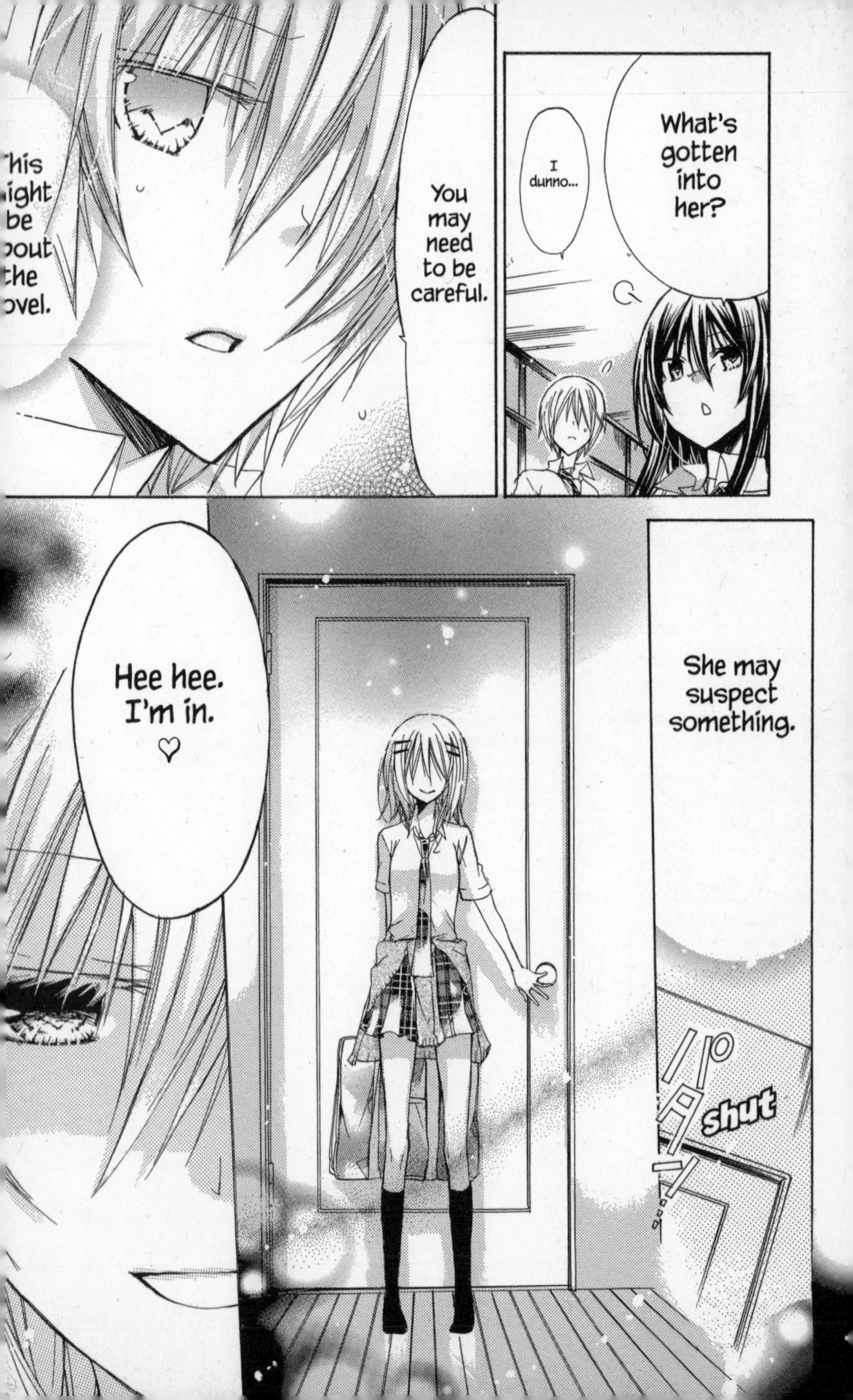
What's gotten into her?
I dunno...
You may need to be careful.
his ight be bout the ovel.
She may suspect something.
パタン
Shut
Hee hee. I'm in. ♡

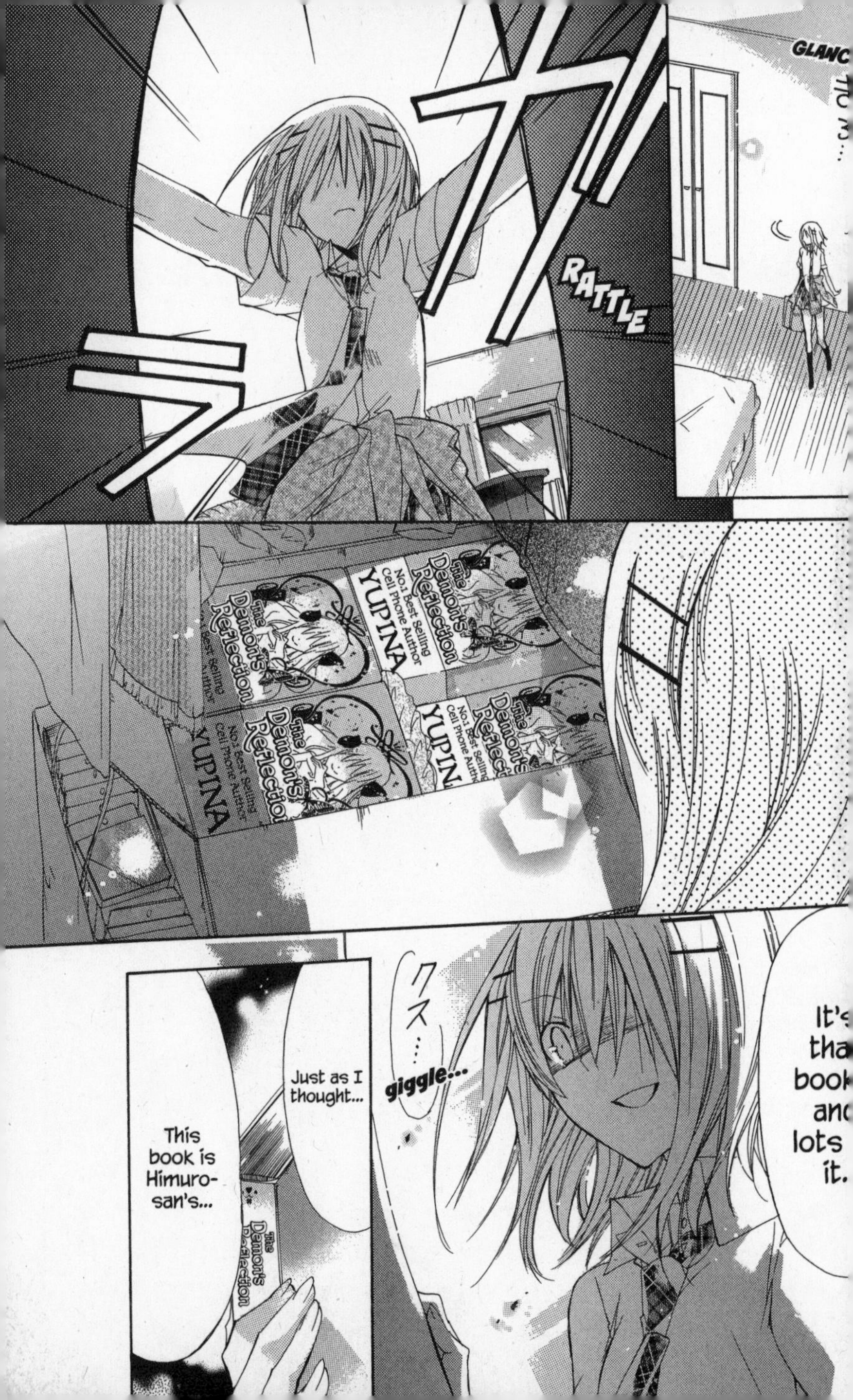

GLANC
RATTLE
The Demon's Reflection
No.1 Best Selling Cell Phone Author
YUPINA
It's tha book and lots it.
クス…
giggle...
Just as I thought...
This book is Himuro-san's...
The Demon's Reflection

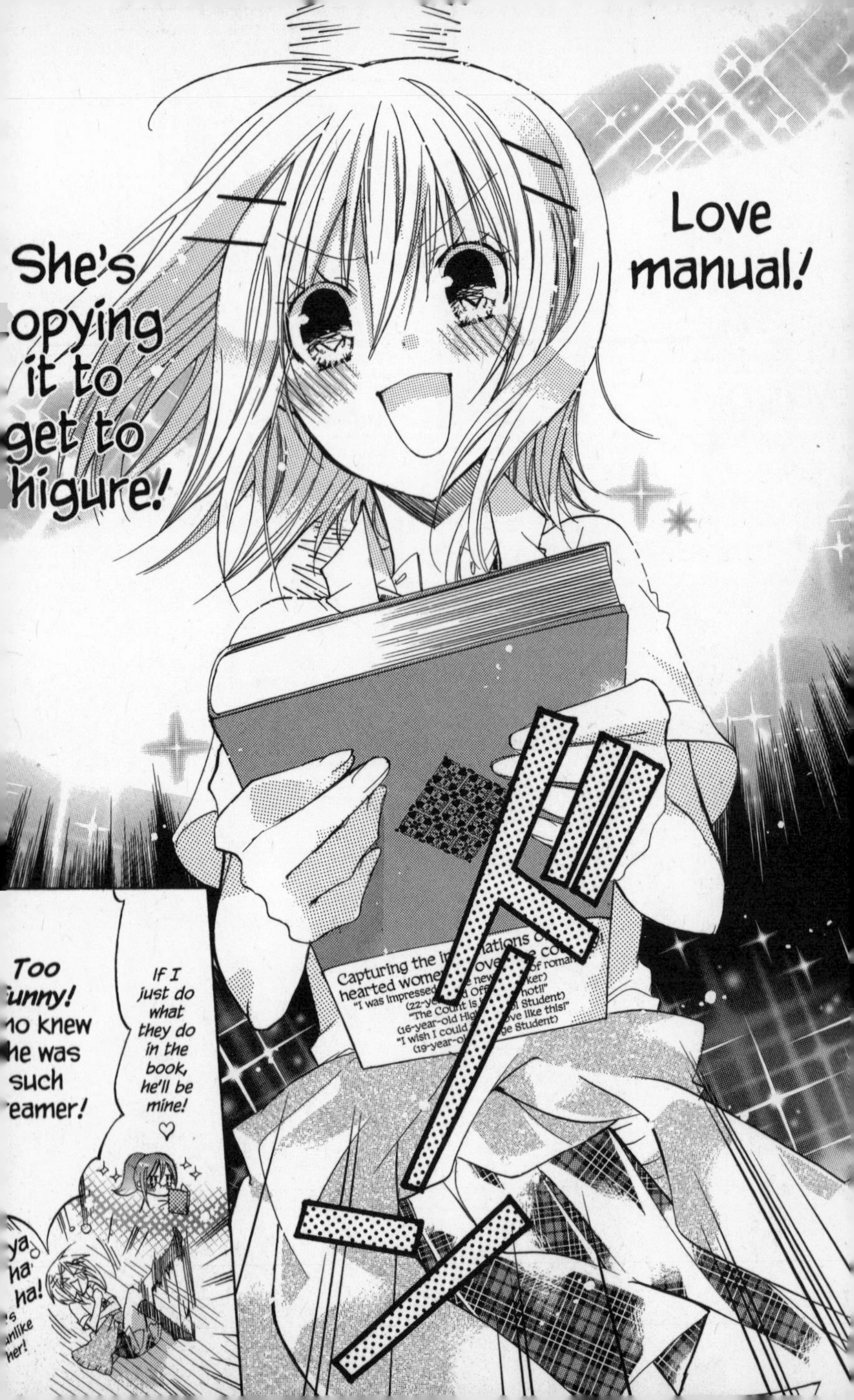
Love manual!
She's opying it to get to higure!
If I just do what they do in the book, he'll be mine! ♡
Too unny! no knew he was such eamer!
ya ha ha!
s unlike her!

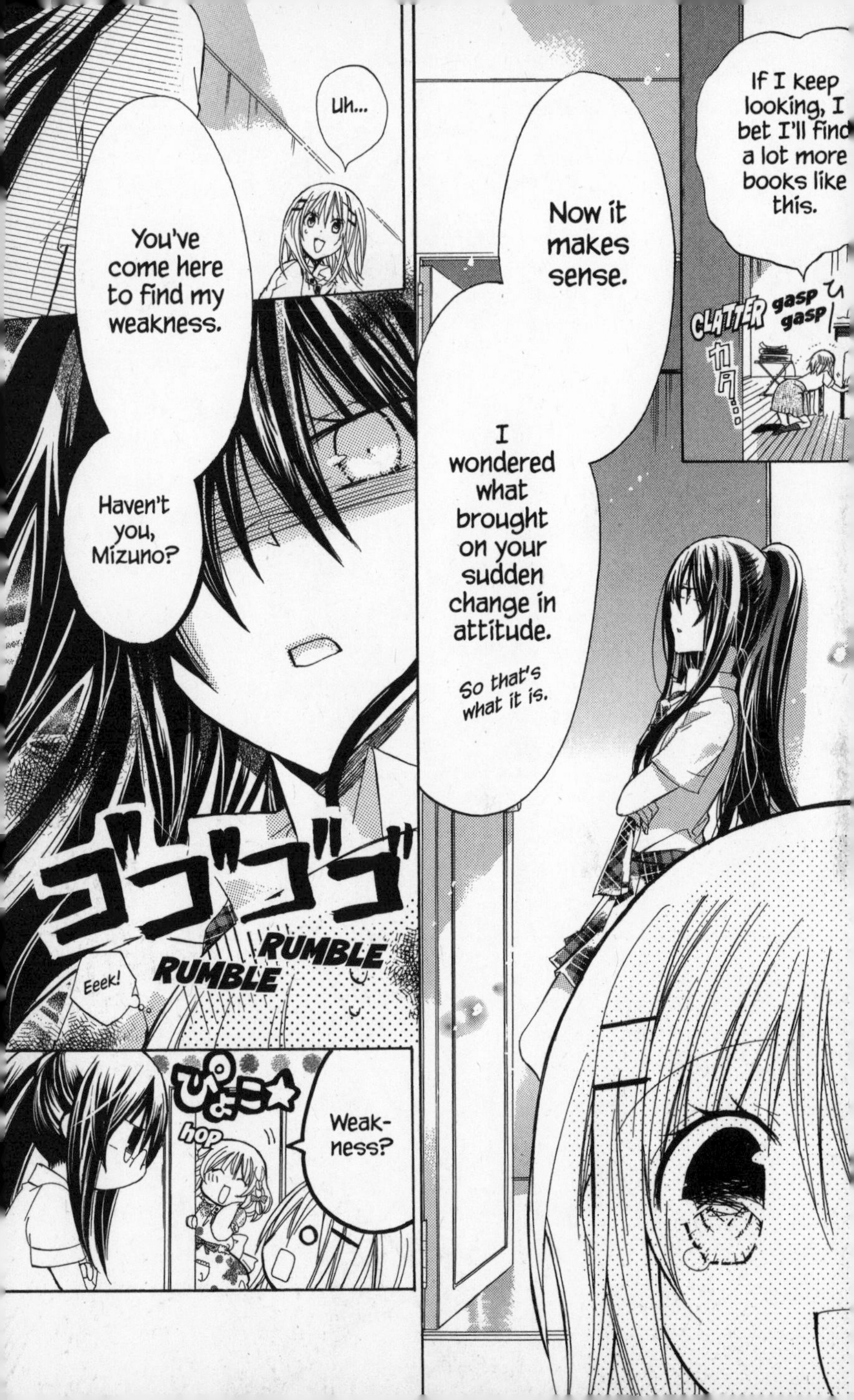

If I keep looking, I bet I'll find a lot more books like this.
CLATTER
カタ…
gasp gasp
Now it makes sense.
I wondered what brought on your sudden change in attitude.
So that's what it is.
Uh...
You've come here to find my weakness.
Haven't you, Mizuno?
ゴゴゴゴ
RUMBLE RUMBLE
Eeek!
ぴょこ☆
hop
Weak-ness?

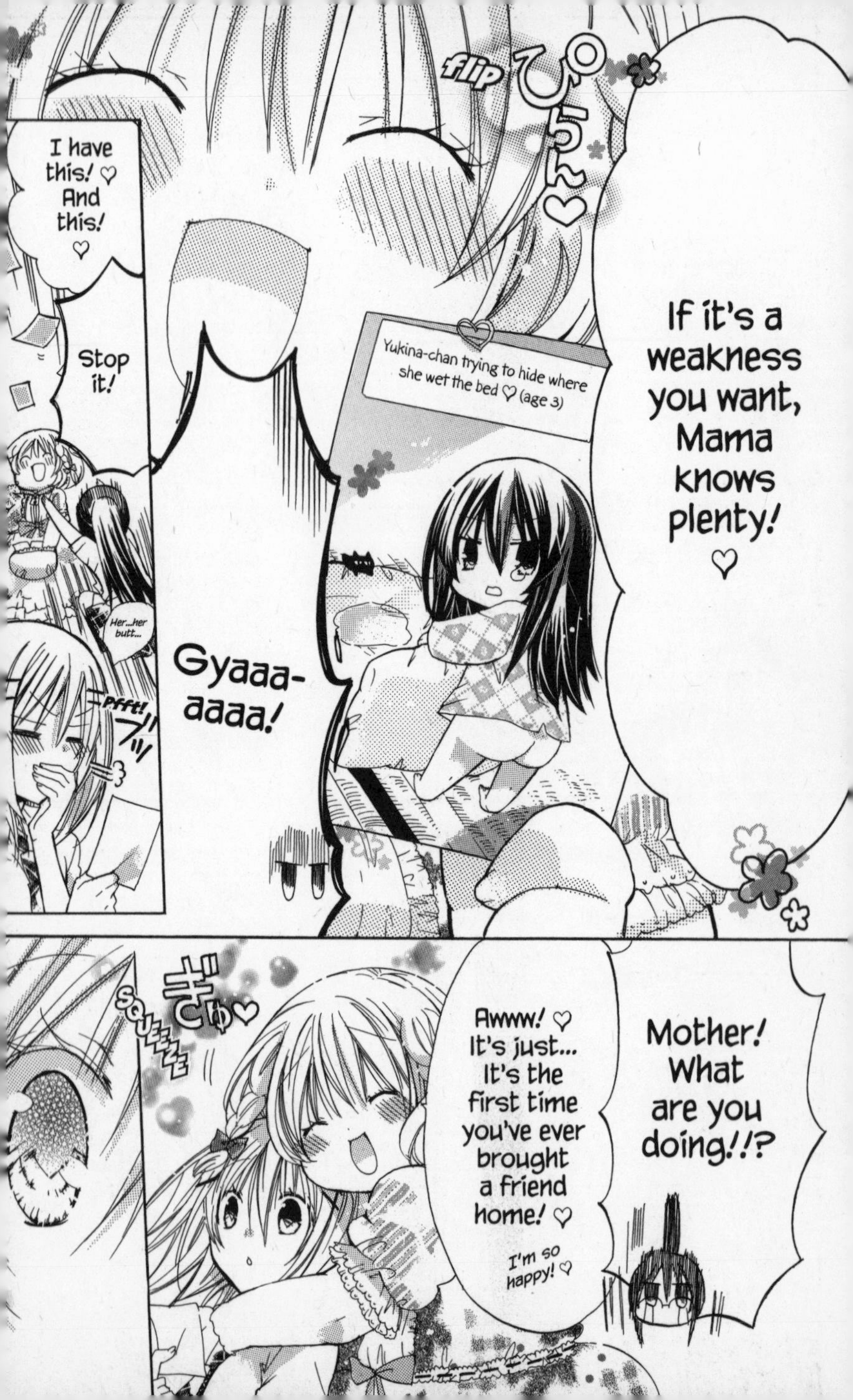
flip ぴらん♡
If it's a weakness you want, Mama knows plenty! ♡
Yukina-chan trying to hide where she wet the bed ♡ (age 3)
Gyaaa-aaaa!
I have this! ♡ And this! ♡
Stop it!
Her...her butt...
Pfft! ブッ
Mother! What are you doing!!?
Awww! ♡ It's just... It's the first time you've ever brought a friend home! ♡
I'm so happy! ♡
ぎゅ♡ SQUEEZE

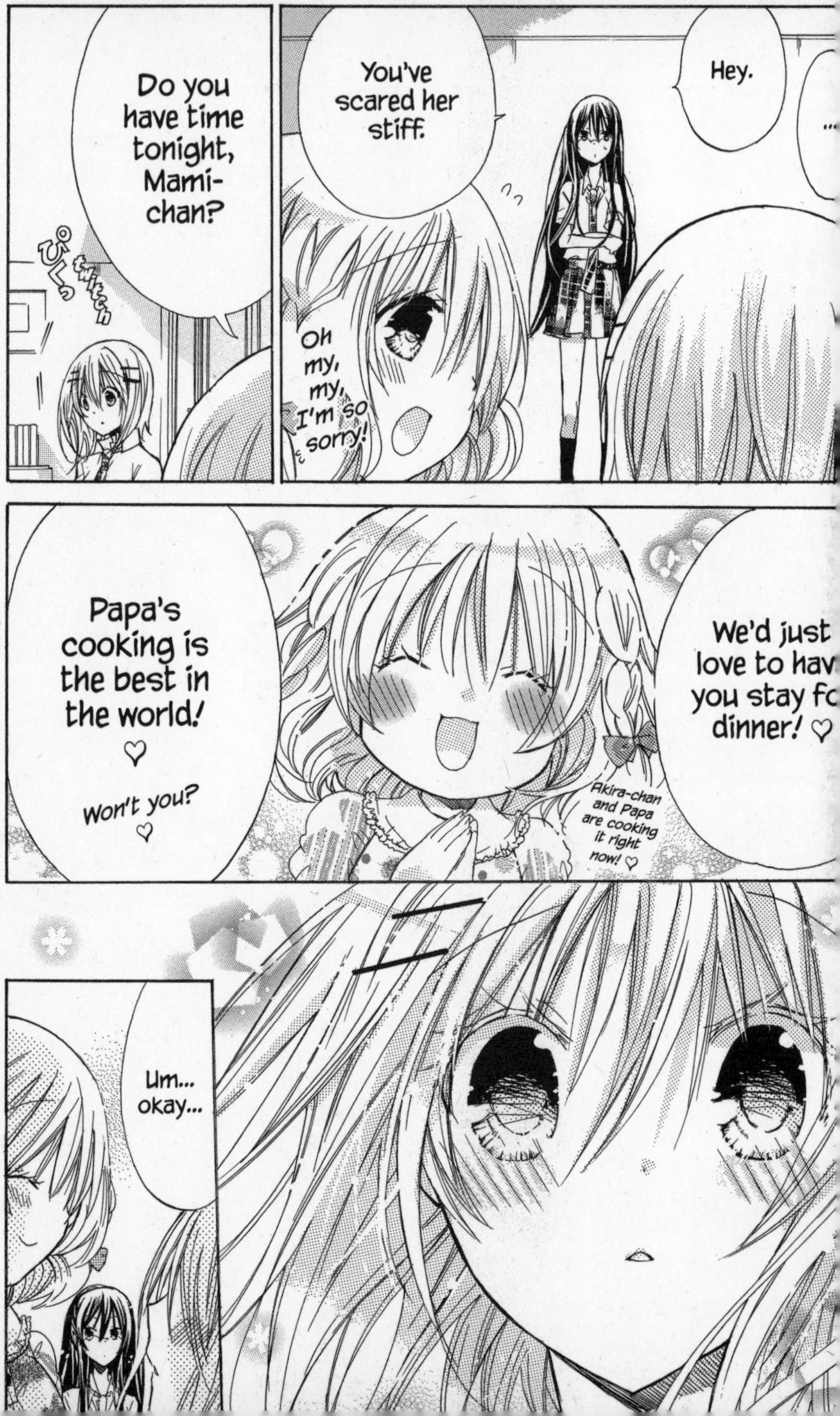
Hey.
...
You've scared her stiff.
Oh my, my, I'm so sorry!
Do you have time tonight, Mami-chan?
twitch
ぴくっ
We'd just love to hav you stay fo dinner! ♡
Akira-chan and Papa are cooking it right now! ♡
Papa's cooking is the best in the world! ♡
Won't you? ♡
Um... okay...

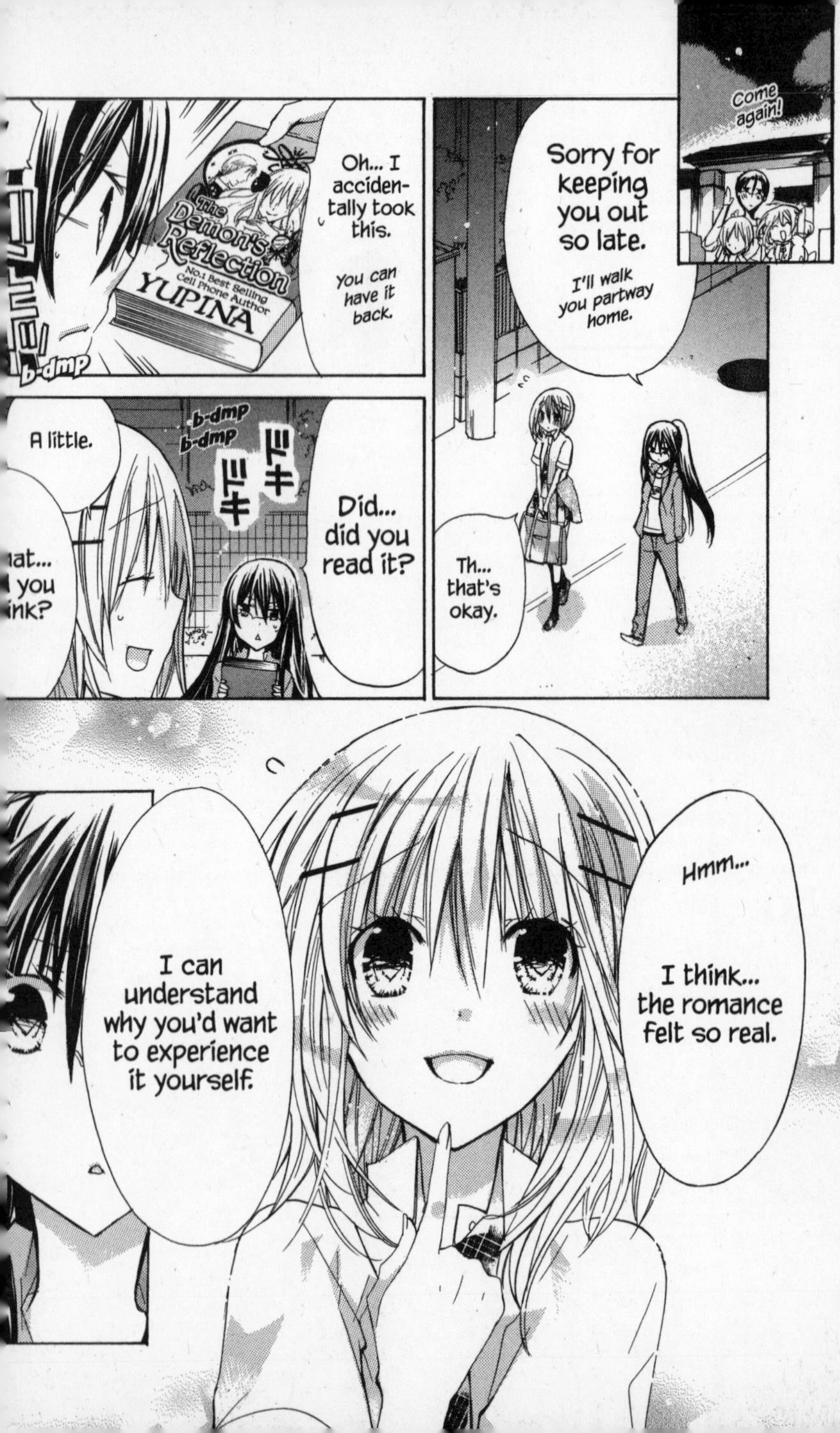
Come again!
Sorry for keeping you out so late.
I'll walk you partway home.
Th... that's okay.
Oh... I accidentally took this.
You can have it back.
The Demon's Reflection
No.1 Best Selling Cell Phone Author
YUPINA
b-dmp
Did... did you read it?
ドキ ドキ
b-dmp b-dmp
A little.
Hmm...
I think... the romance felt so real.
I can understand why you'd want to experience it yourself.

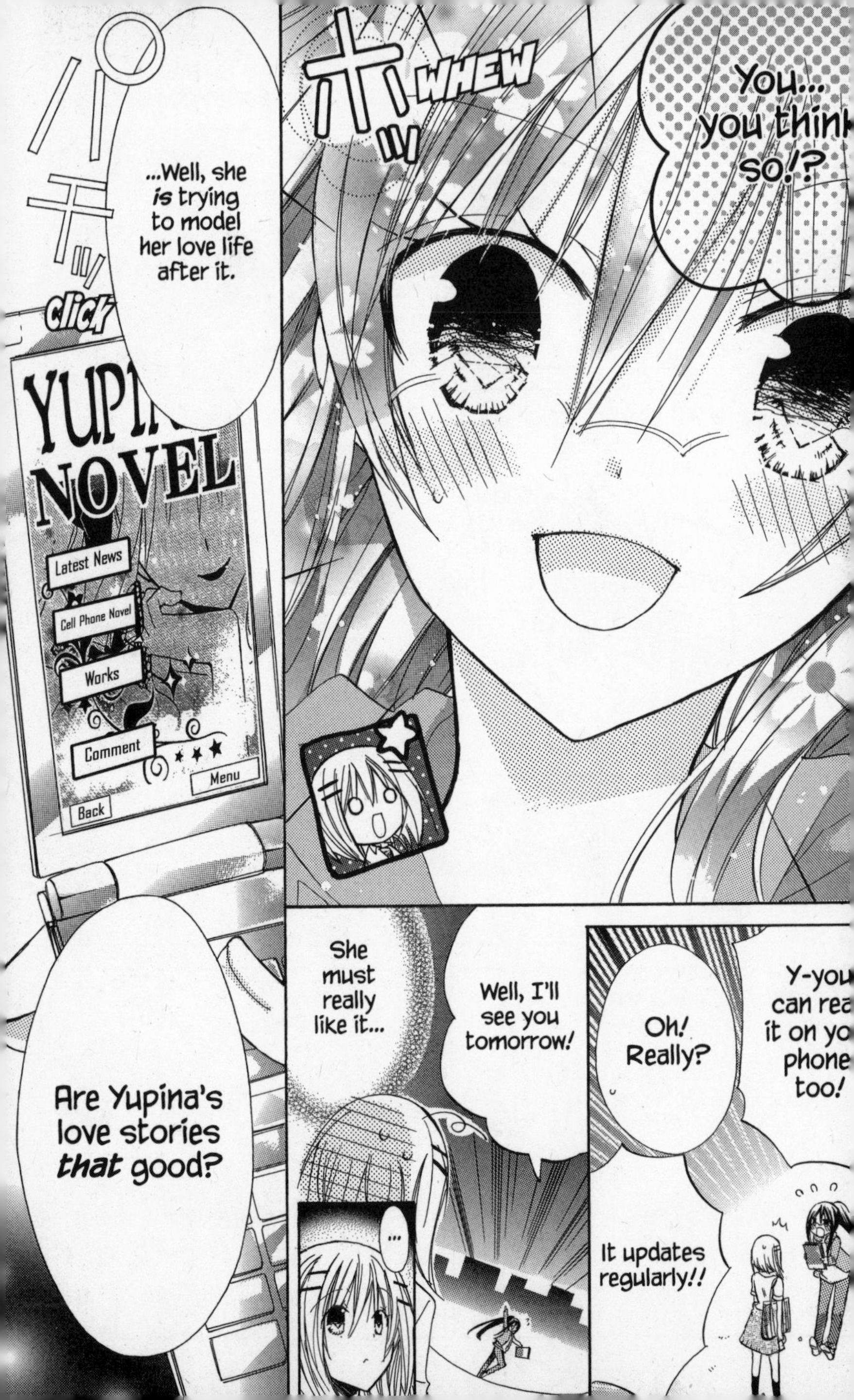

You... you think so!?
WHEW
Y-you can rea it on yo phone too!
Oh! Really?
It updates regularly!!
Well, I'll see you tomorrow!
She must really like it...
...
click
...Well, she *is* trying to model her love life after it.
YUPI
NOVEL
Latest News
Cell Phone Novel
Works
Comment
Menu
Back
Are Yupina's love stories *that* good?

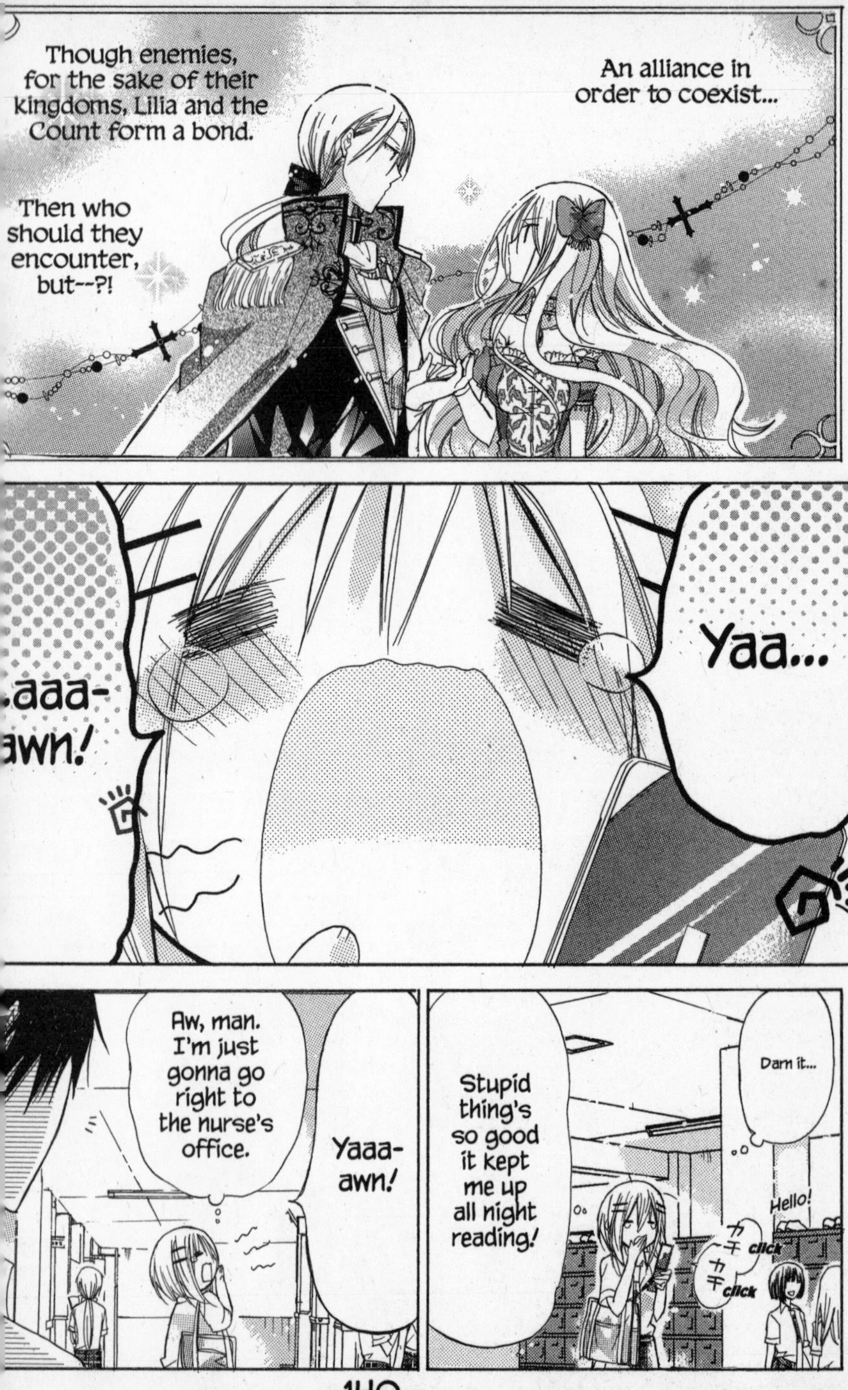
An alliance in order to coexist...
Though enemies, for the sake of their kingdoms, Lilia and the Count form a bond.
Then who should they encounter, but--?!
Yaa...
.aaa-awn!
Darn it...
Hello!
カチ click
カチ click
Stupid thing's so good it kept me up all night reading!
Yaaa-awn!
Aw, man. I'm just gonna go right to the nurse's office.

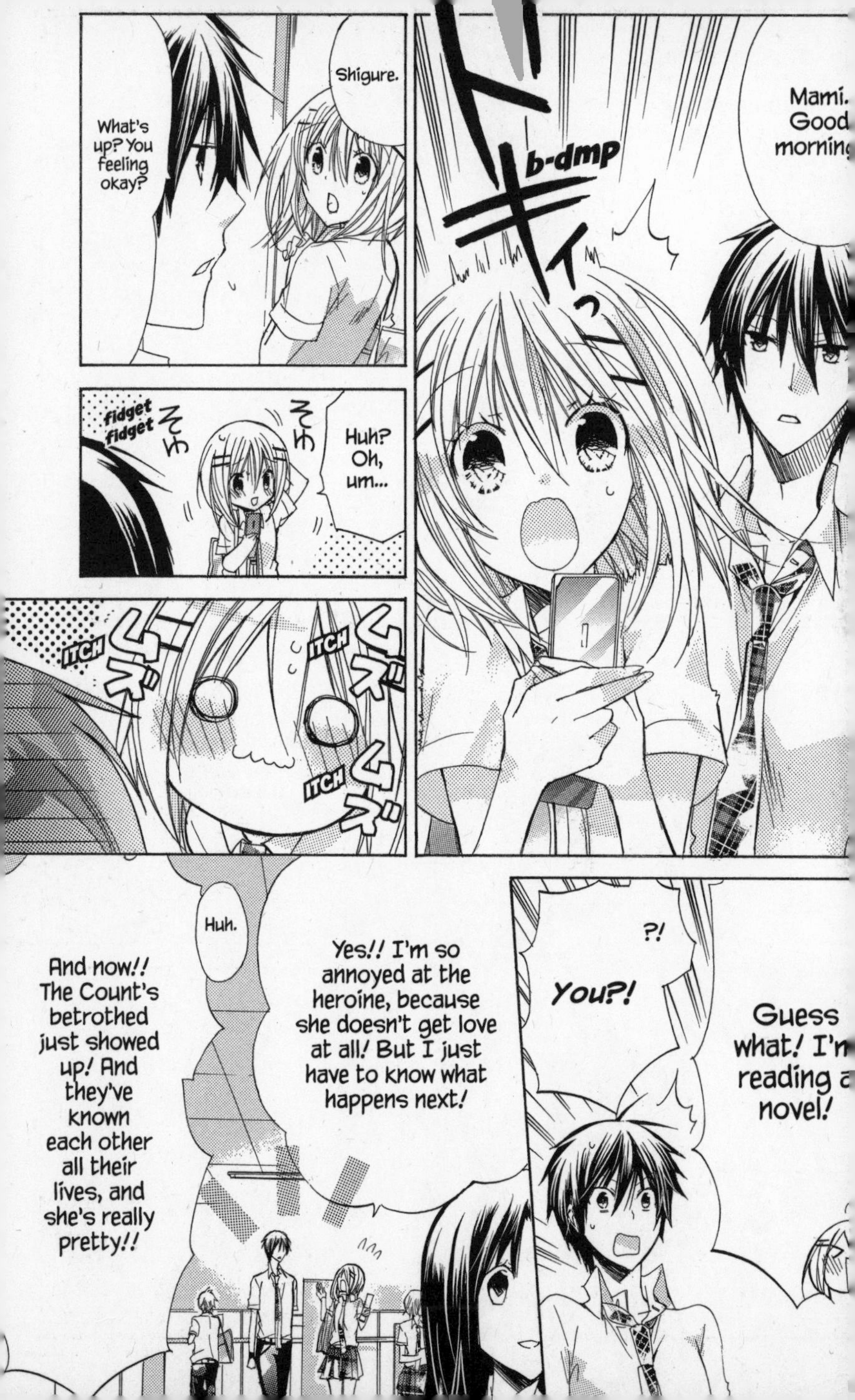
Mami. Good mornin
b-dmp
Shigure.
What's up? You feeling okay?
Huh? Oh, um...
fidget fidget
ITCH
ITCH
ITCH
Guess what! I'm reading a novel!
You?!
?!
Yes!! I'm so annoyed at the heroine, because she doesn't get love at all! But I just have to know what happens next!
Huh.
And now!! The Count's betrothed just showed up! And they've known each other all their lives, and she's really pretty!!

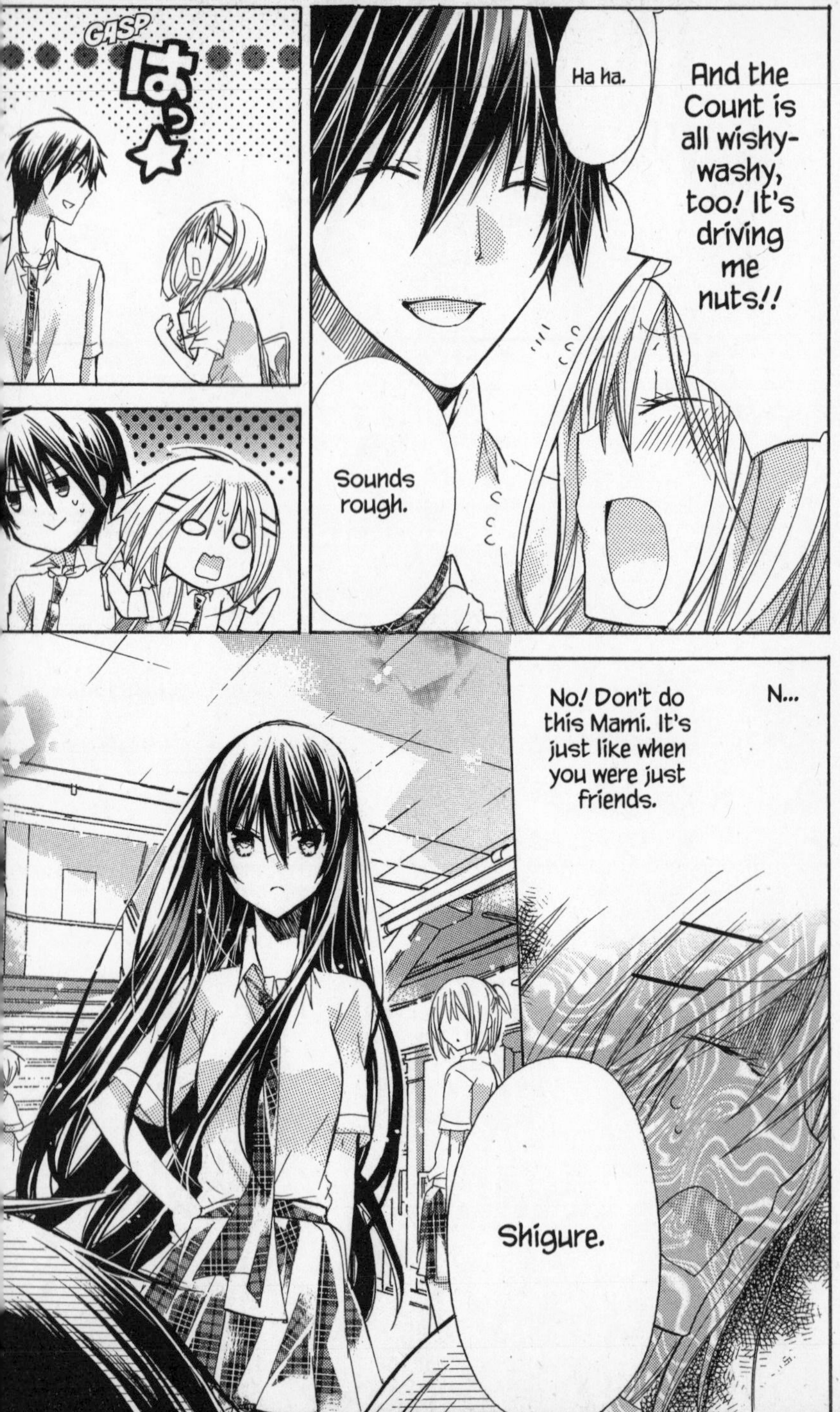
And the Count is all wishy-washy, too! It's driving me nuts!!
Ha ha.
Sounds rough.
GASP
はっ
N...
No! Don't do this Mami. It's just like when you were just friends.
Shigure.

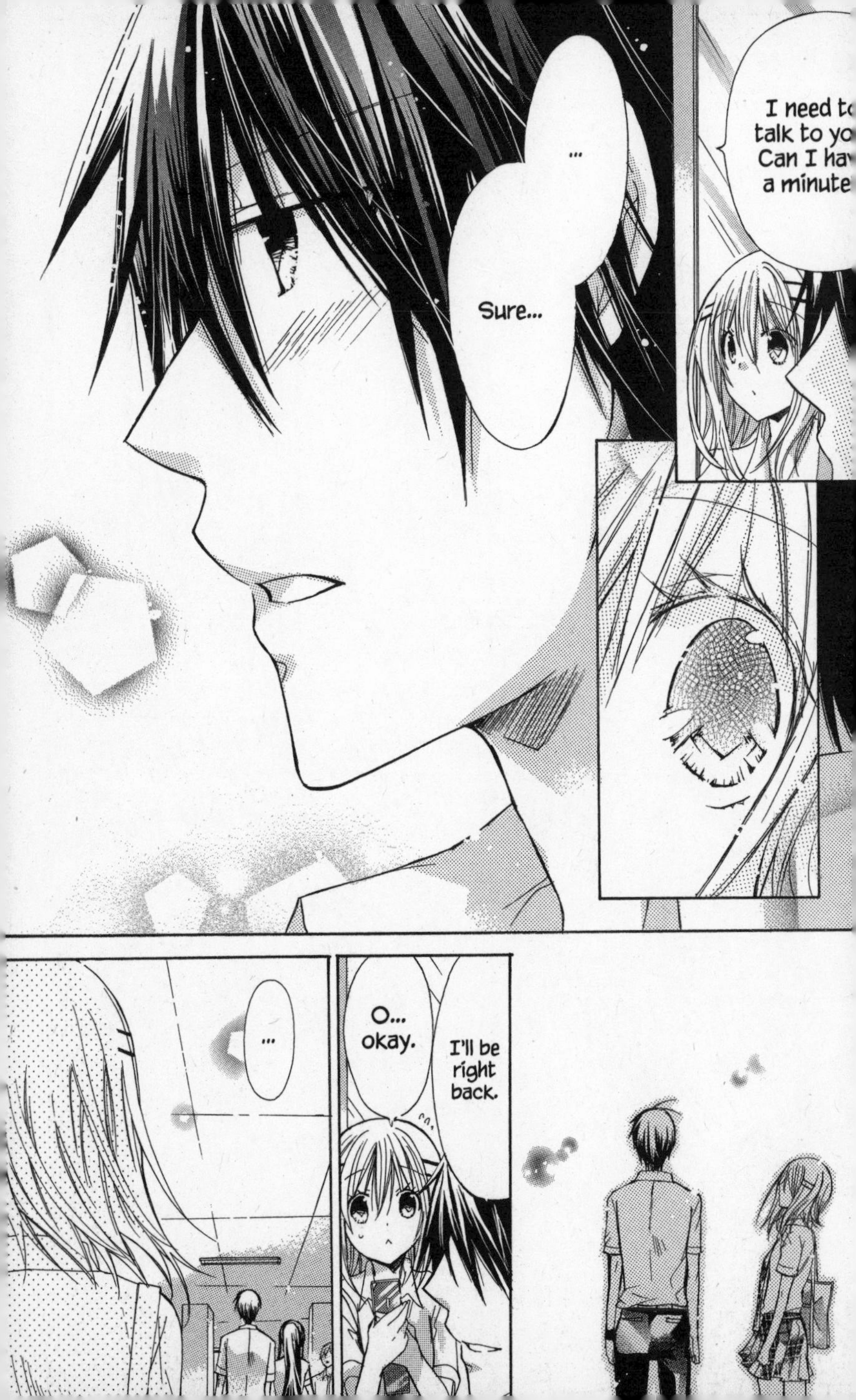
I need t
talk to yo
Can I hav
a minute
...
Sure...
I'll be right back.
O... okay.
...

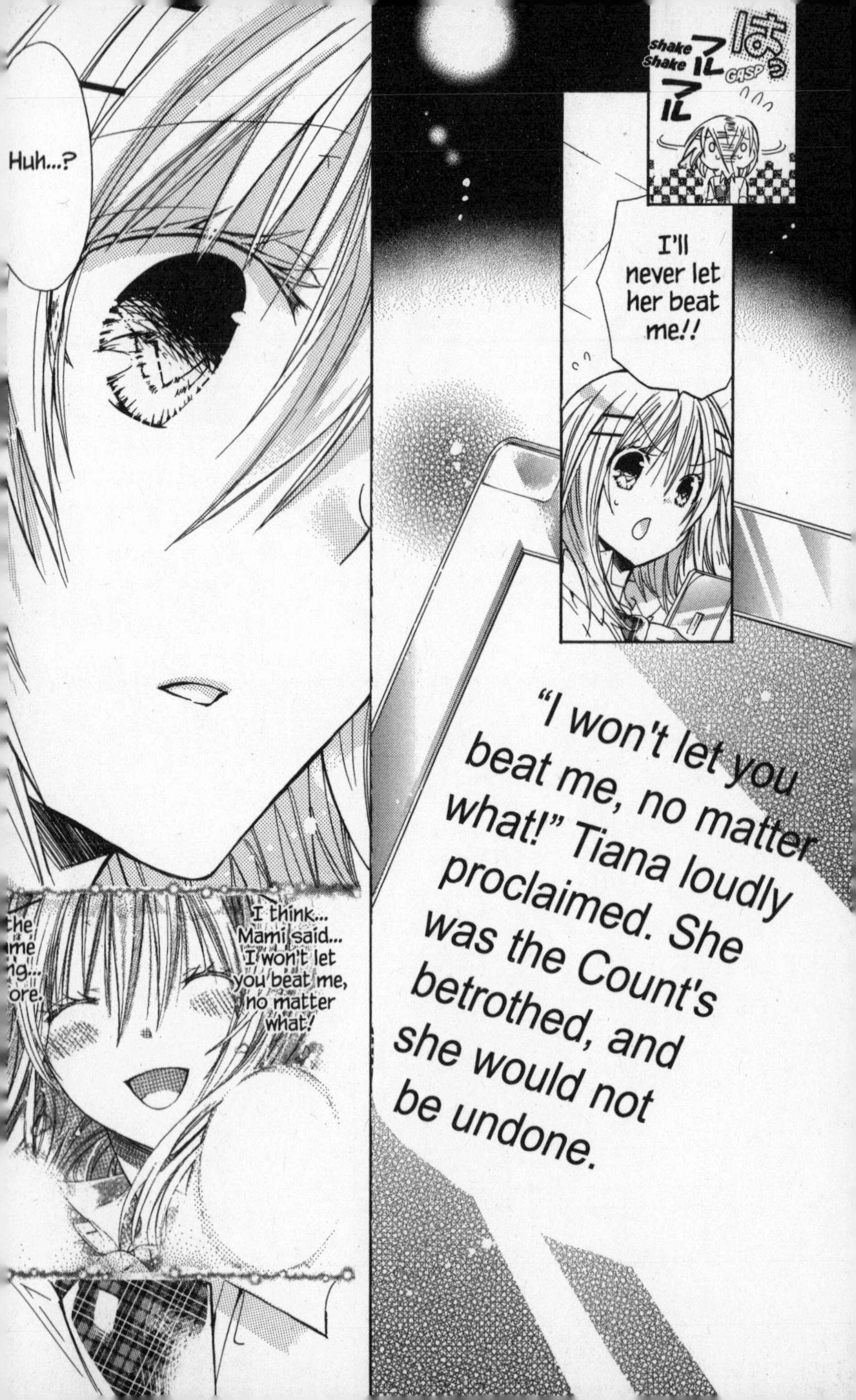
shake shake
GASP
I'll never let her beat me!!
"I won't let you beat me, no matter what!" Tiana loudly proclaimed. She was the Count's betrothed, and she would not be undone.
Huh...?
I think... Mami said... I won't let you beat me, no matter what!

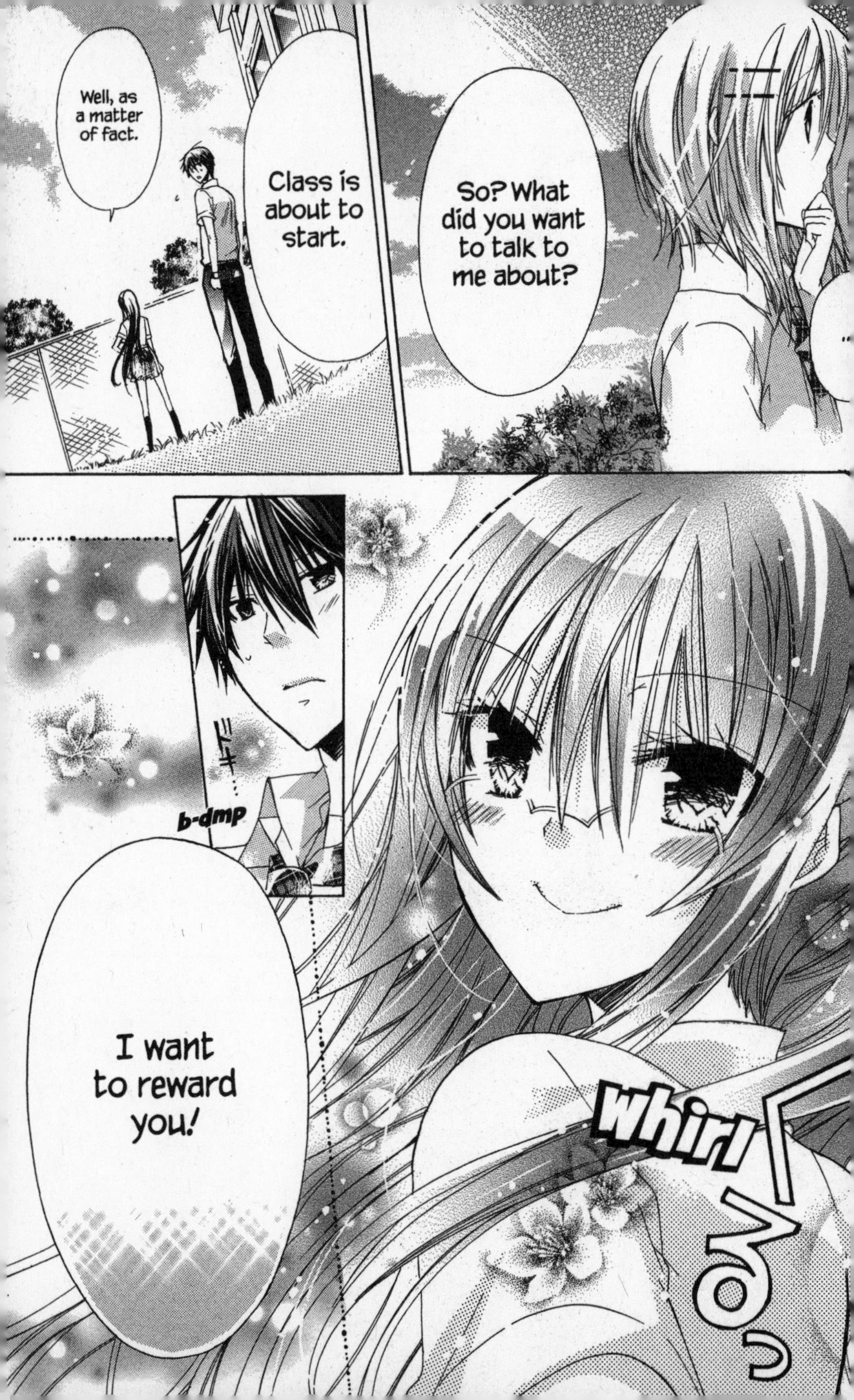
So? What did you want to talk to me about?
Class is about to start.
Well, as a matter of fact.
ドキ…
b-dmp
whirl
くるっ
I want to reward you!

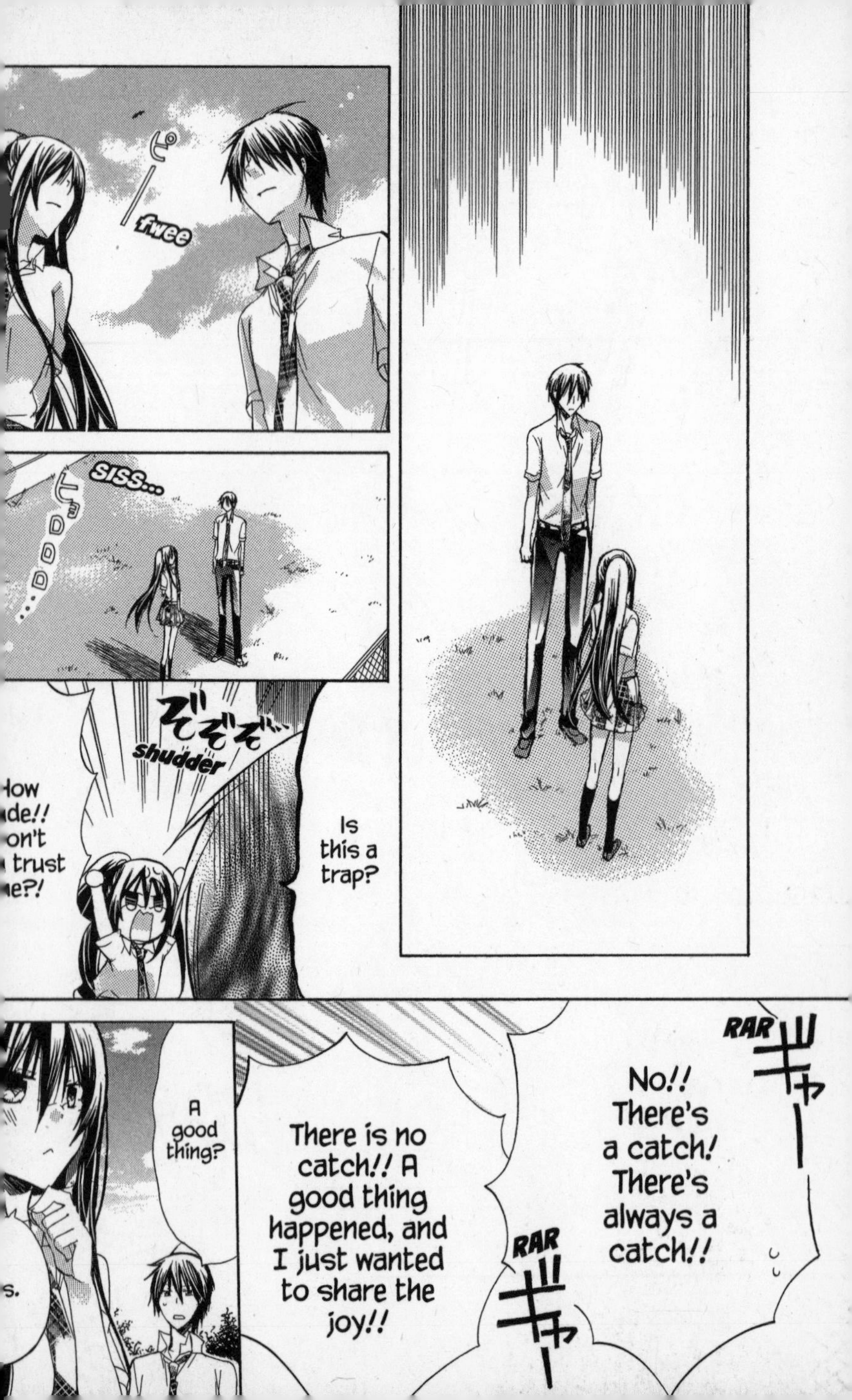
fwee
SISS...
ぞぞぞ
shudder
Is this a trap?
How
de!!
on't
trust
e?!
RAR
ギャー
No!! There's a catch! There's always a catch!!
RAR
ギャー
There is no catch!! A good thing happened, and I just wanted to share the joy!!
A good thing?
s.

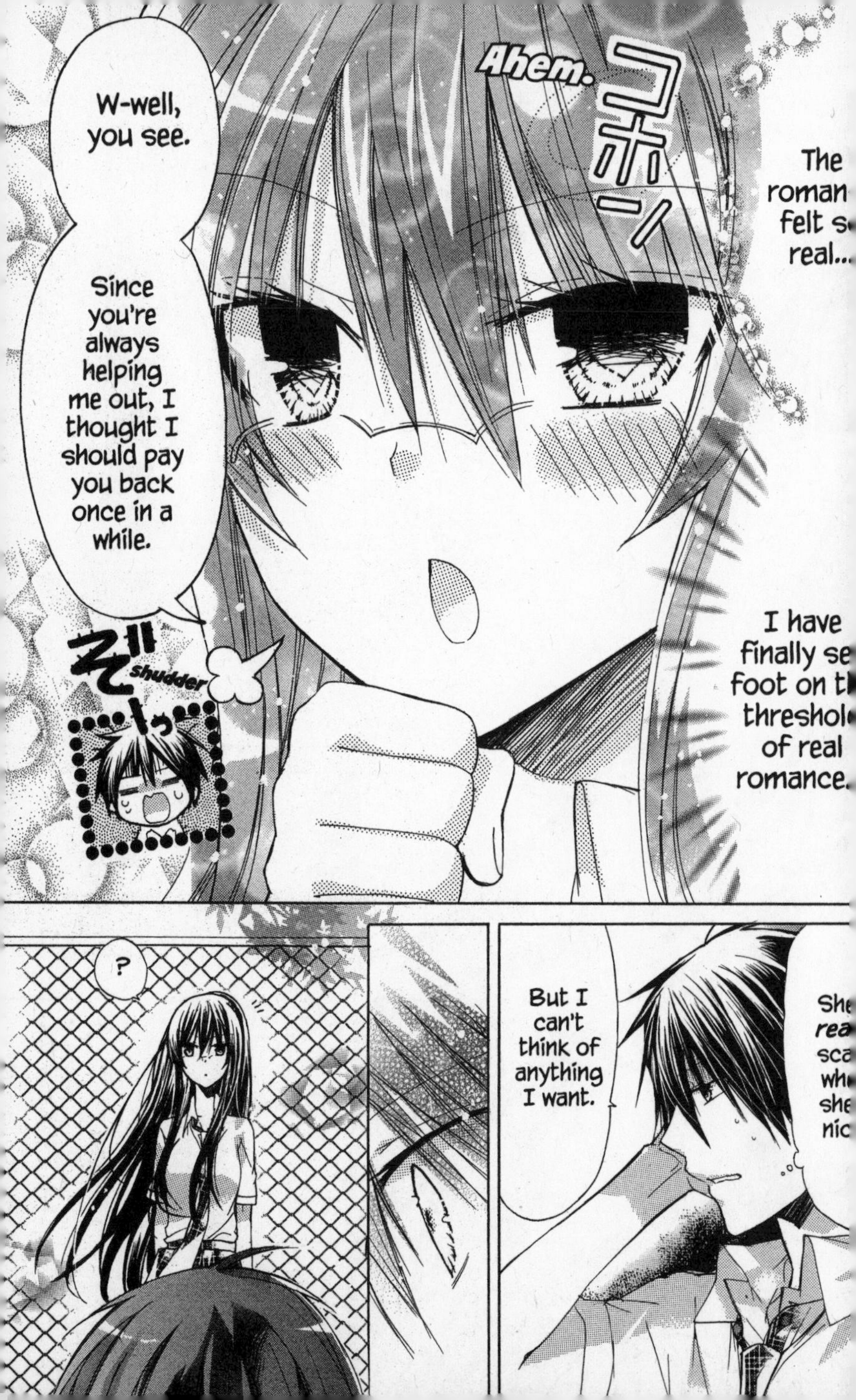

The roman felt s real...
Ahem.
コホーン
W-well, you see.
I have finally se foot on t thresho of real romance.
Since you're always helping me out, I thought I should pay you back once in a while.
shudder
She rea sca wh she nic
But I can't think of anything I want.
?

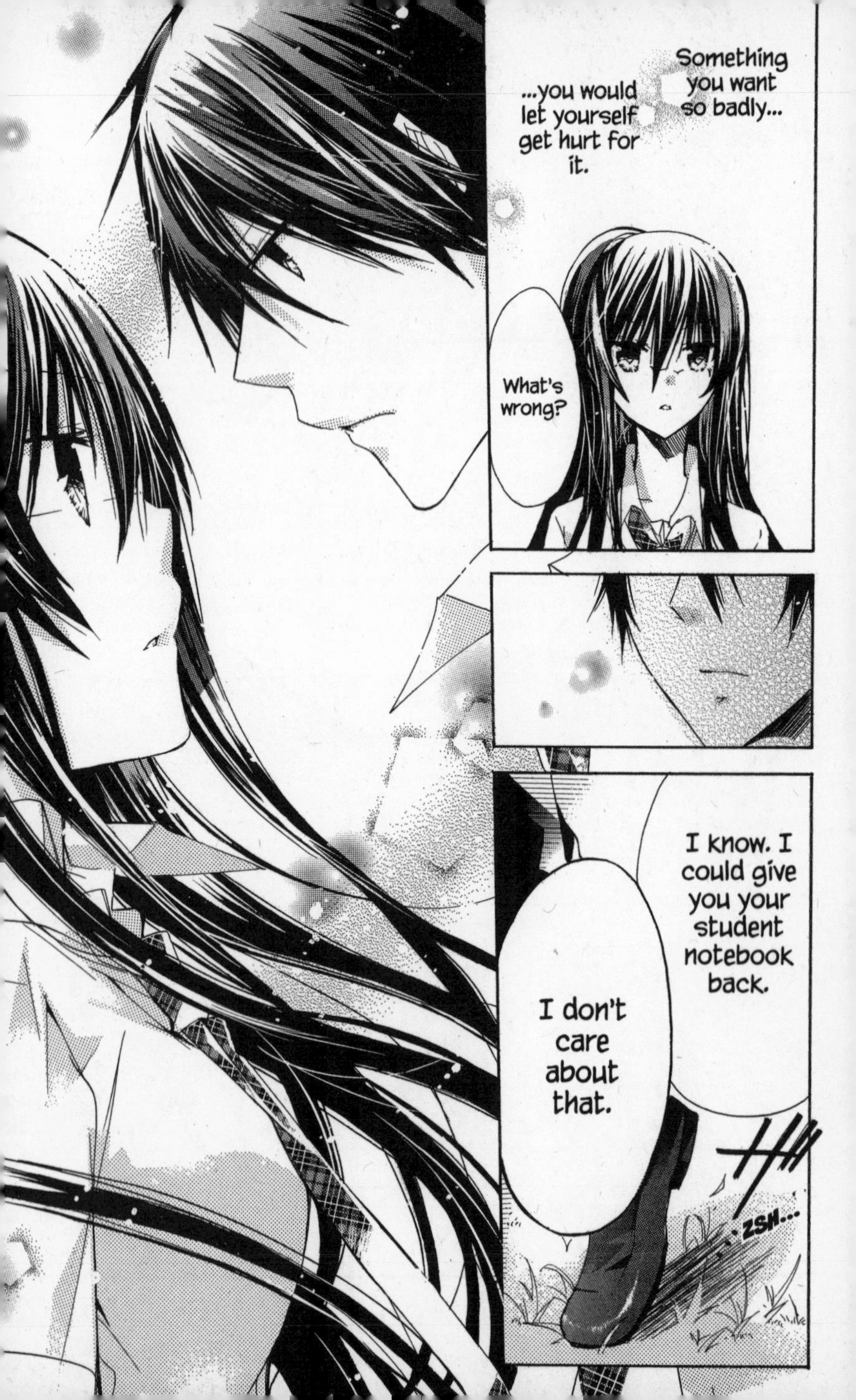
Something you want so badly...
...you would let yourself get hurt for it.
What's wrong?
I know. I could give you your student notebook back.
I don't care about that.
ZSH...

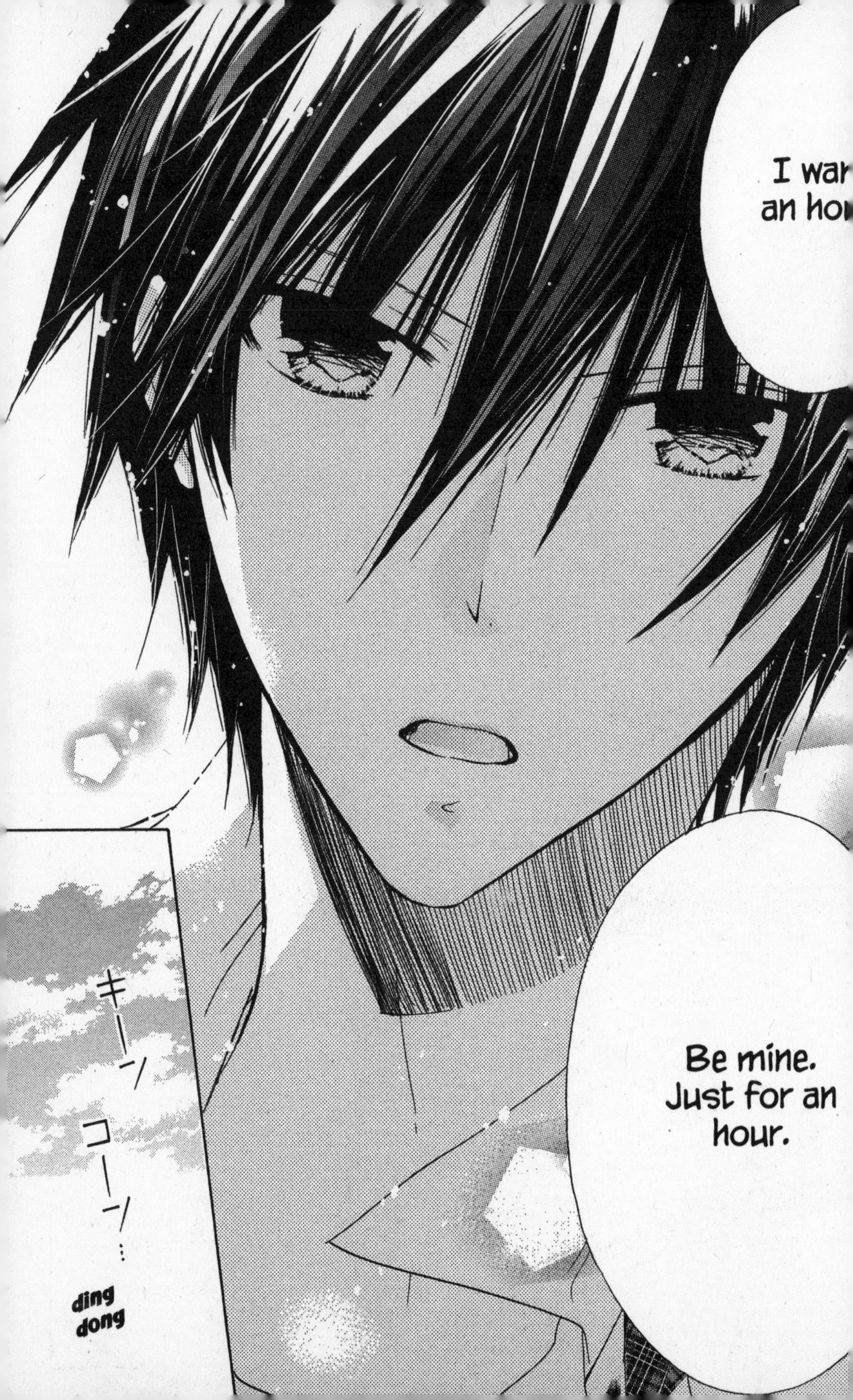
I wan
an ho
Be mine. Just for an hour.
キーンコーン…
ding dong

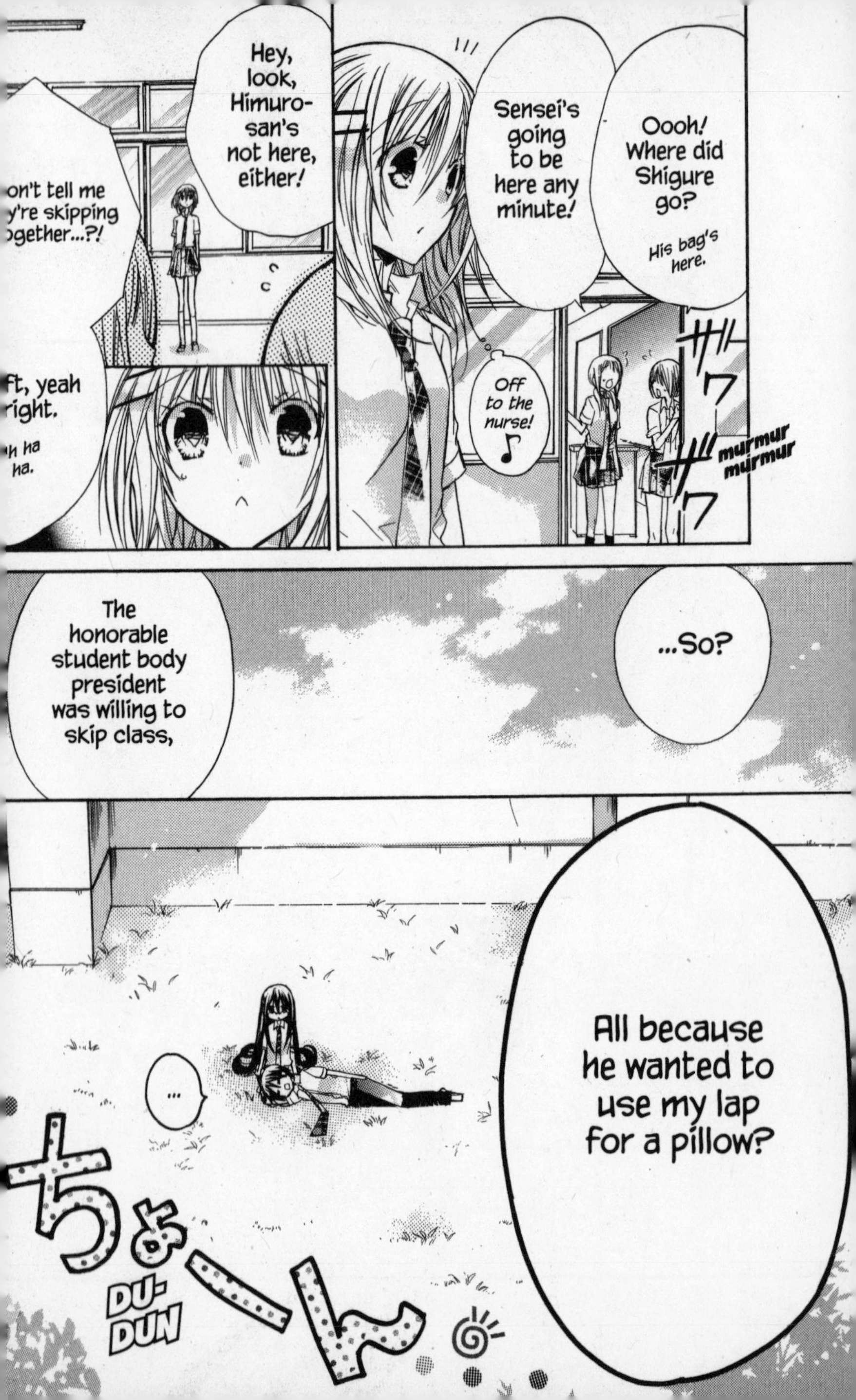
Oooh! Where did Shigure go?
His bag's here.
Sensei's going to be here any minute!
Off to the nurse! ♪
ザワザワ
murmur murmur
Hey, look, Himuro-san's not here, either!
on't tell me y're skipping ogether...?!
ft, yeah right.
h ha ha.
...So?
The honorable student body president was willing to skip class,
All because he wanted to use my lap for a pillow?
...
ちょーん
DU-DUN

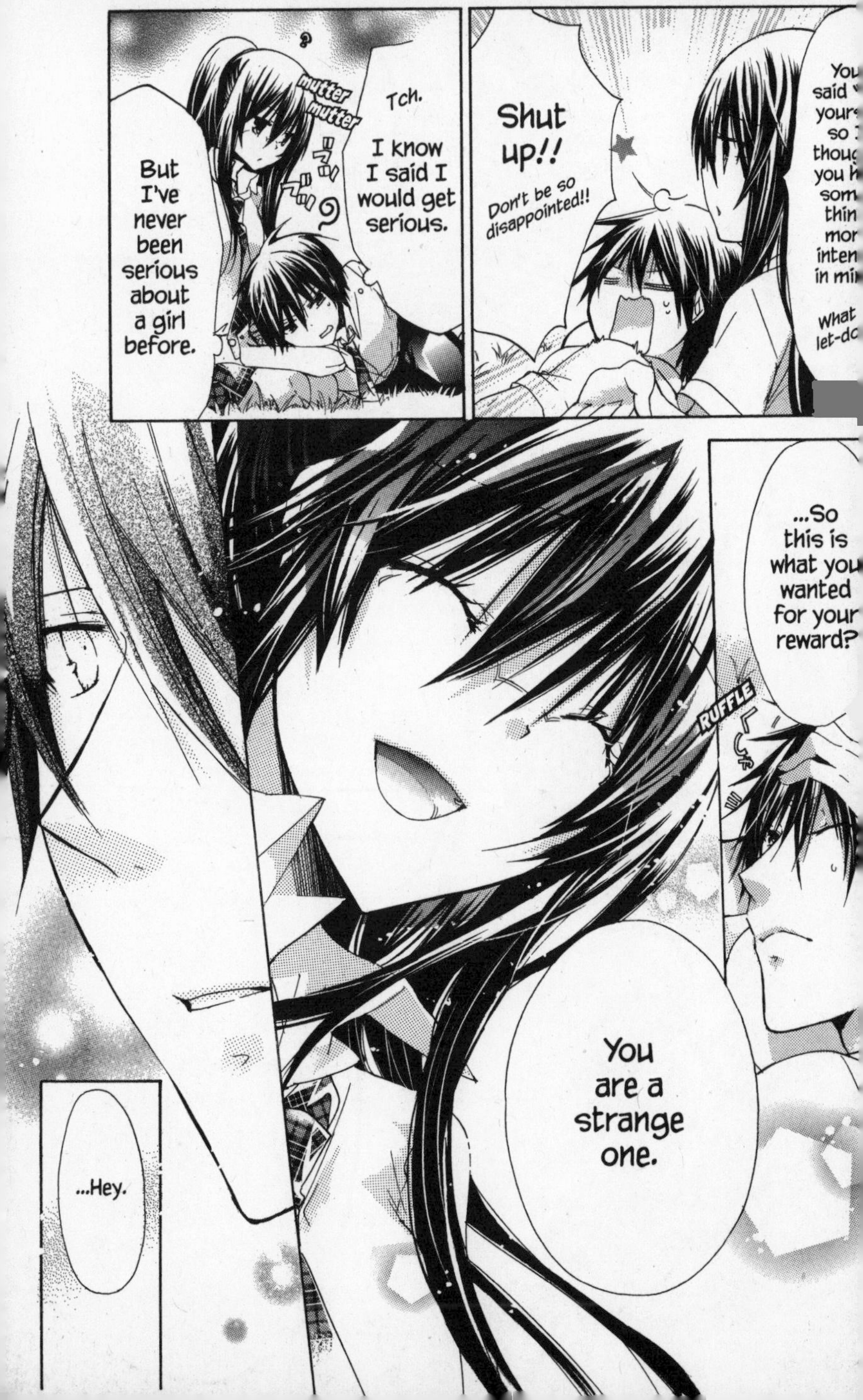
You said yours so I thoug you h som thin mor inten in mi
What let-do
Shut up!!
Don't be so disappointed!!
Tch.
I know I said I would get serious.
mutter mutter
But I've never been serious about a girl before.
...So this is what you wanted for your reward?
RUFFLE
You are a strange one.
...Hey.

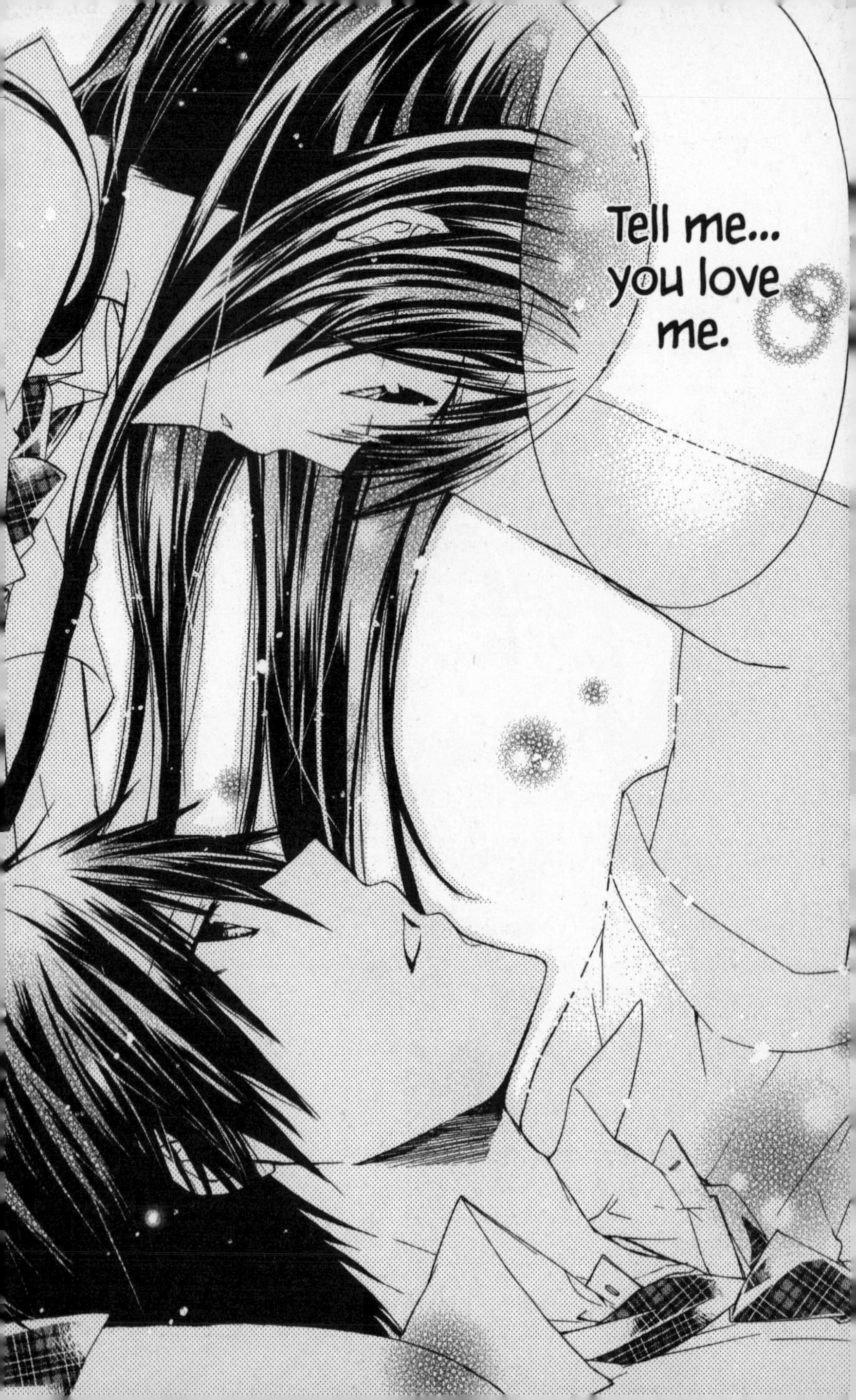
Tell me...
you love
me.

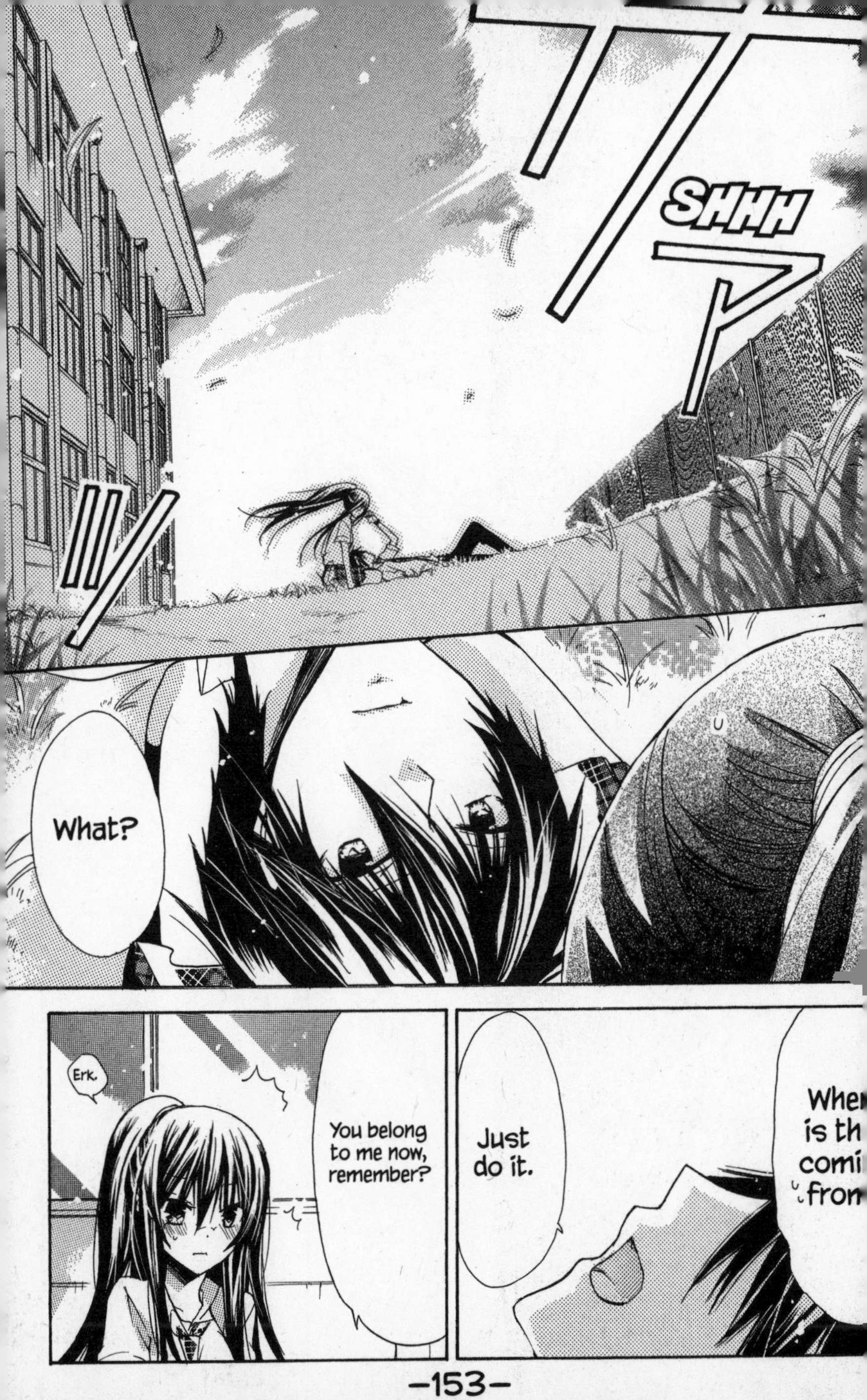
SHHH
What?
Wher is th comi from
Just do it.
You belong to me now, remember?
Erk.

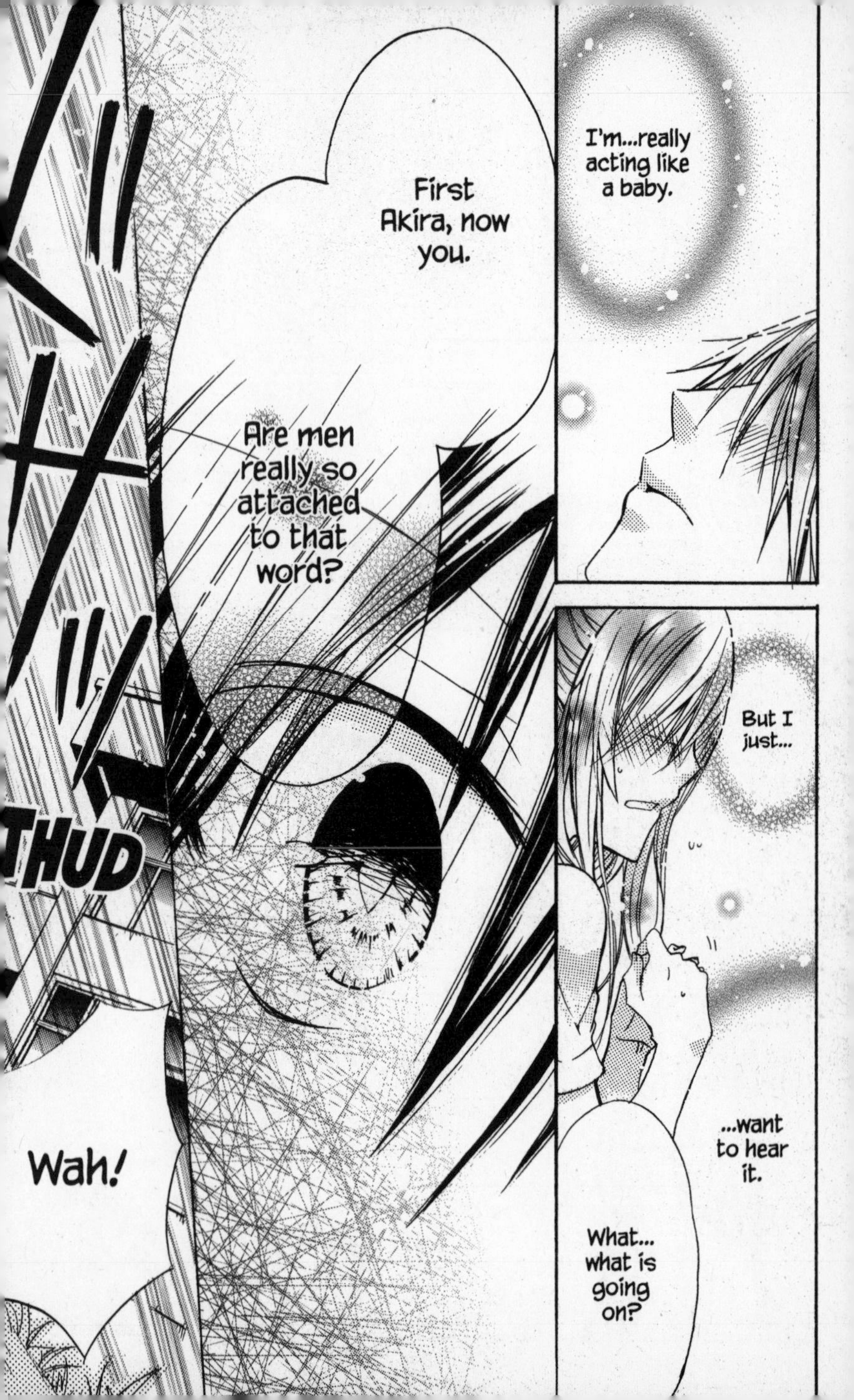
I'm...really acting like a baby.
But I just...
...want to hear it.
What... what is going on?
First Akira, now you.
Are men really so attached to that word?
THUD
Wah!

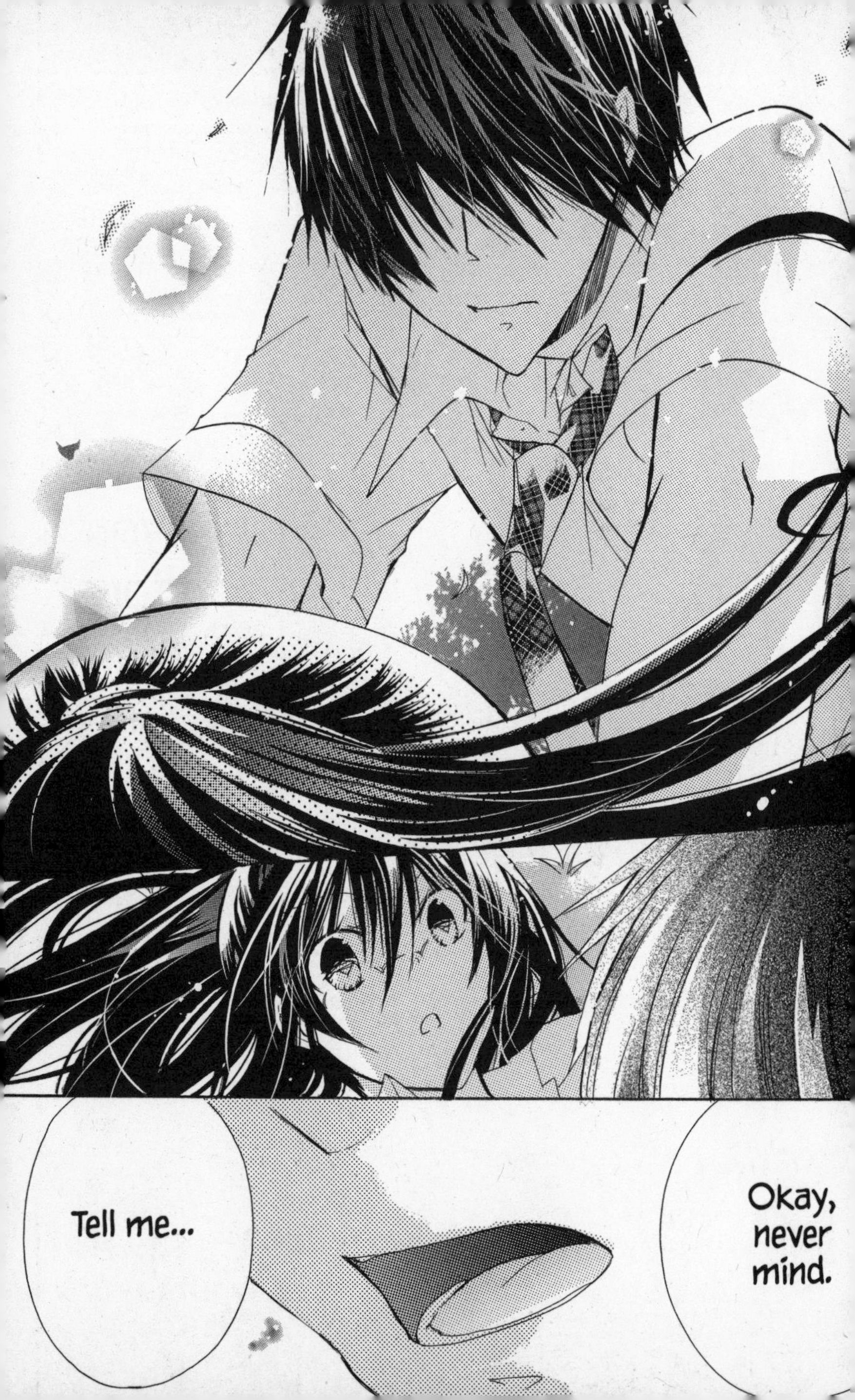
Okay, never mind.
Tell me...

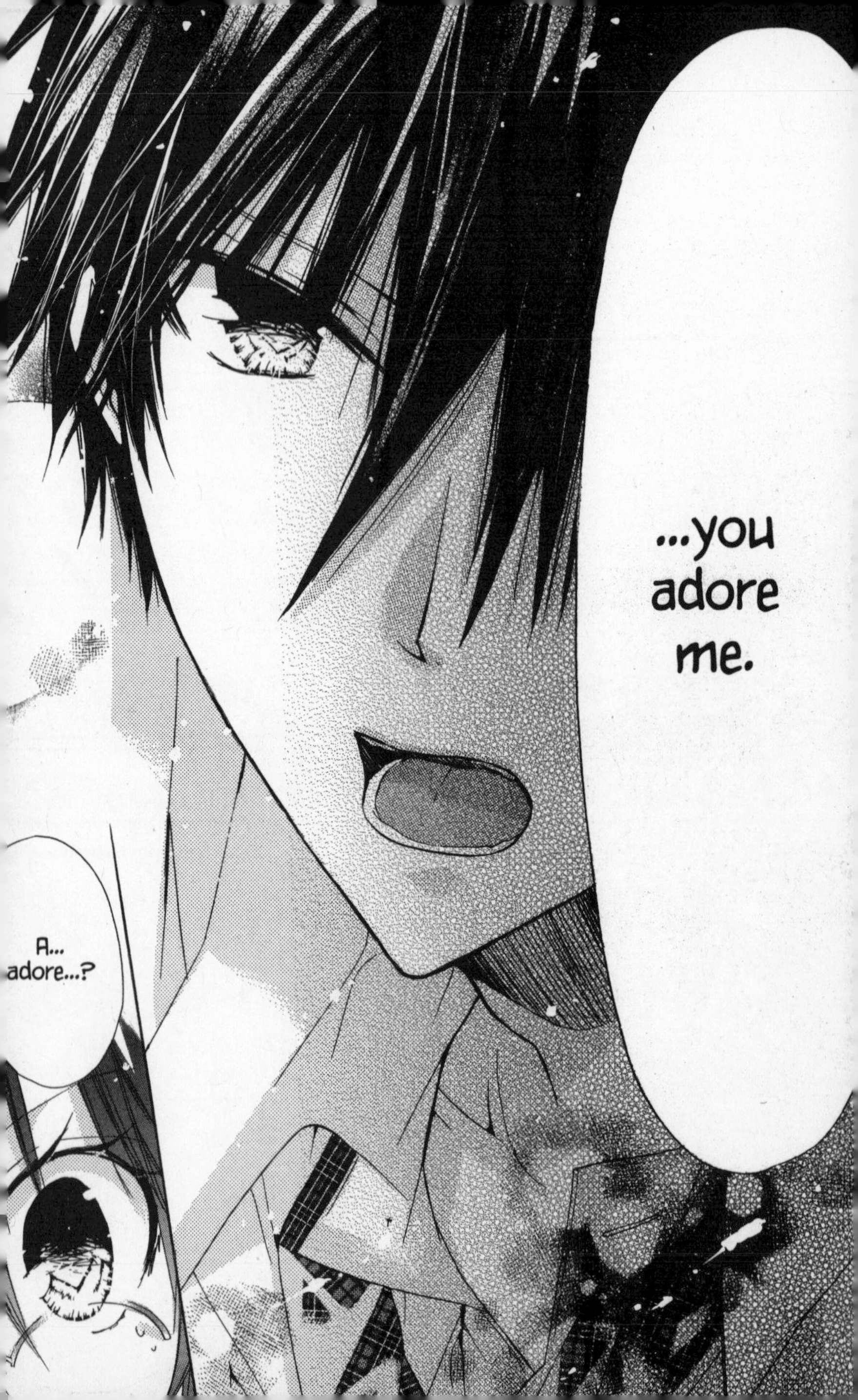
...you adore me.
A... adore...?

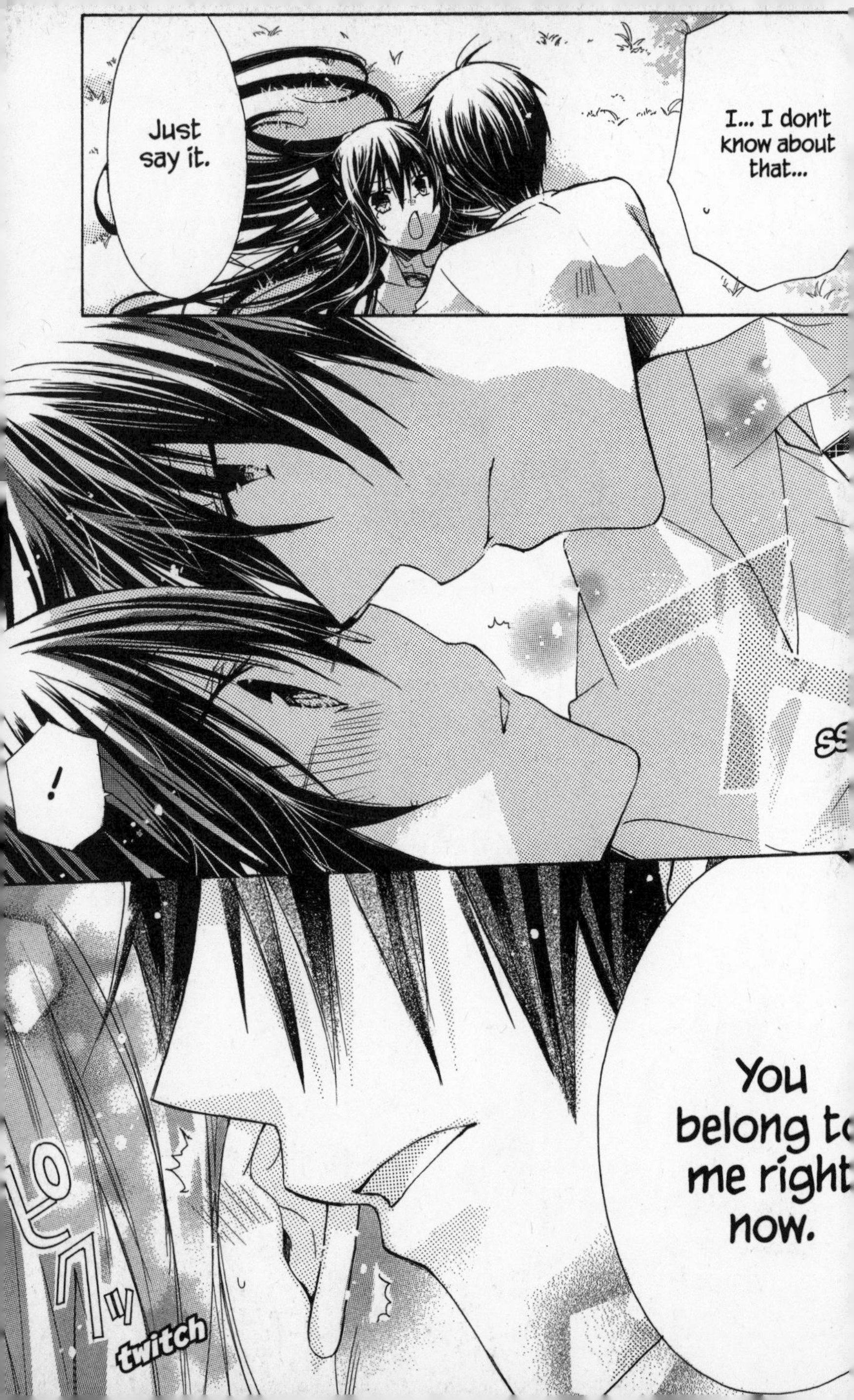
I... I don't know about that...
Just say it.
SS
!
You belong t
me right
now.
twitch

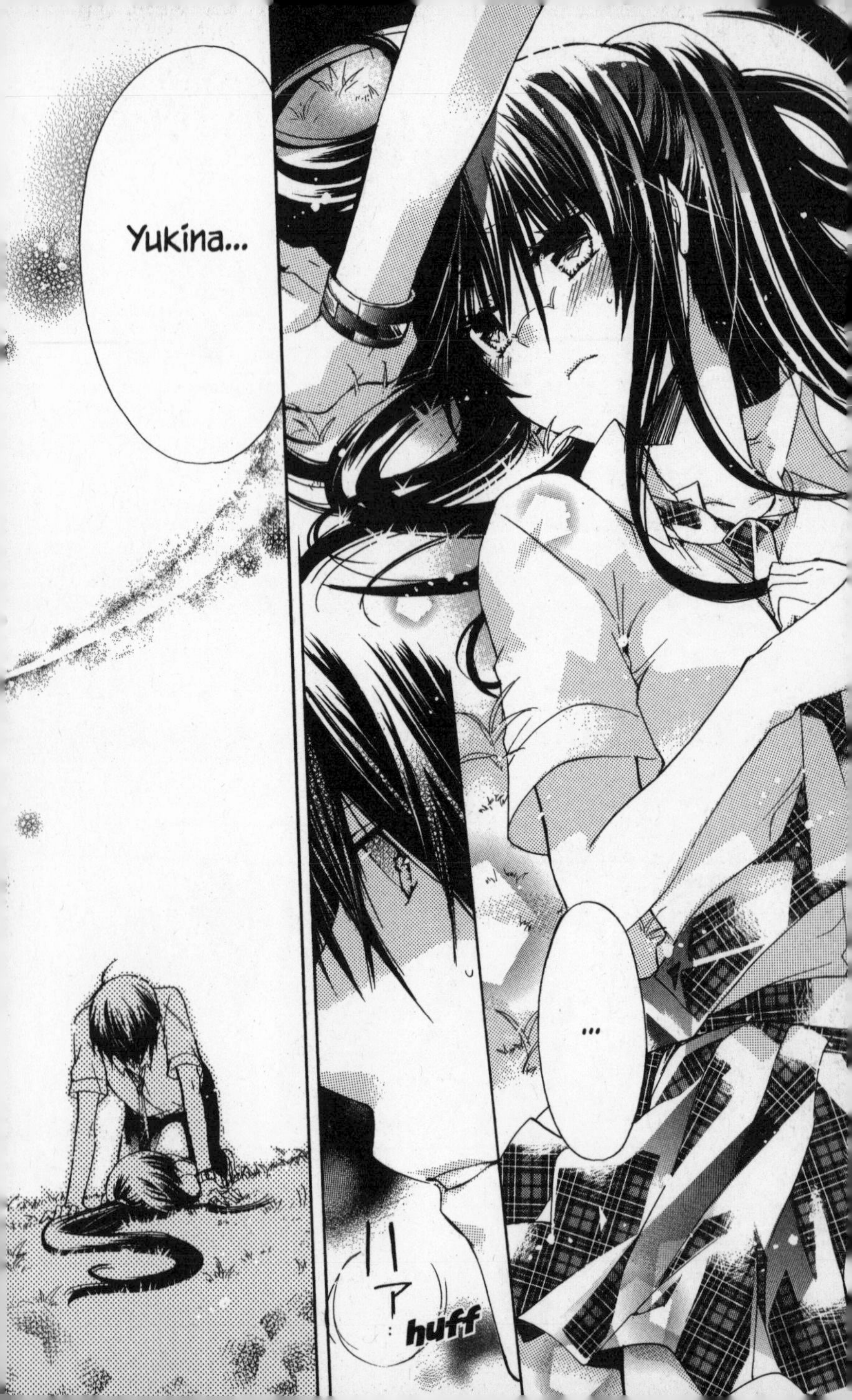
...
ハァ…
huff
Yukina...

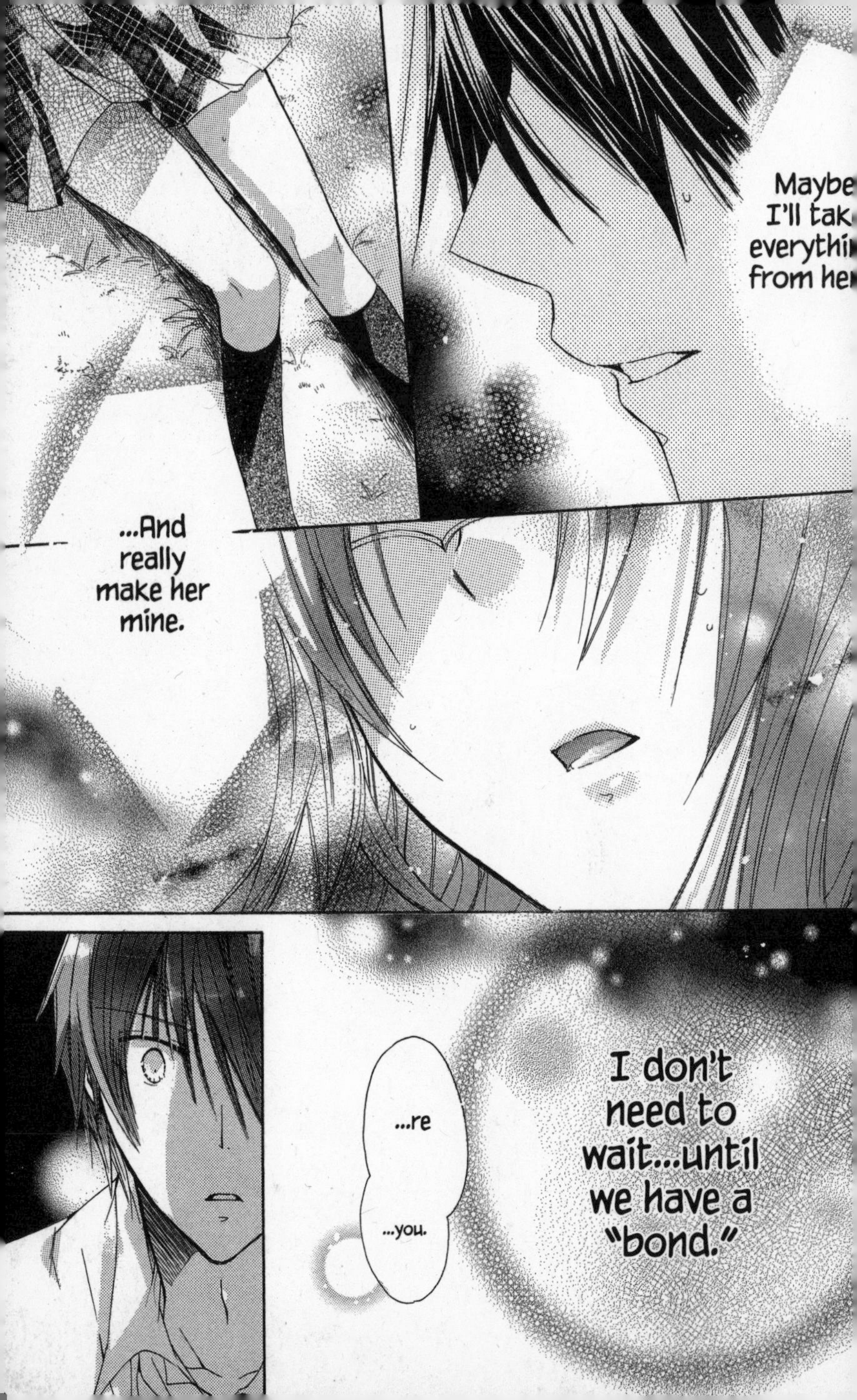
Maybe I'll tak everythi from he
...And really make her mine.
I don't need to wait...until we have a "bond."
...re
...you.

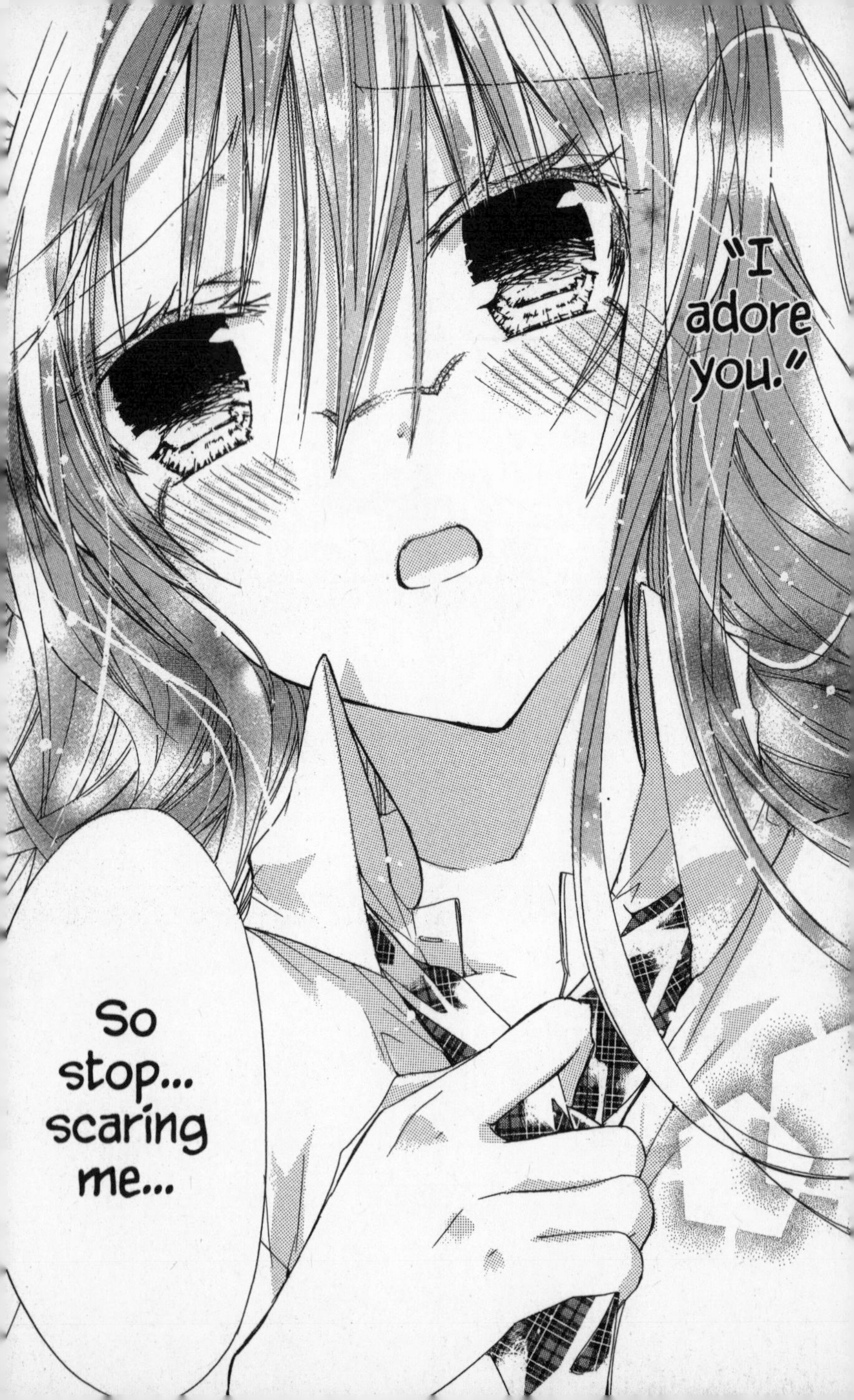
"I adore you."
So stop... scaring me...

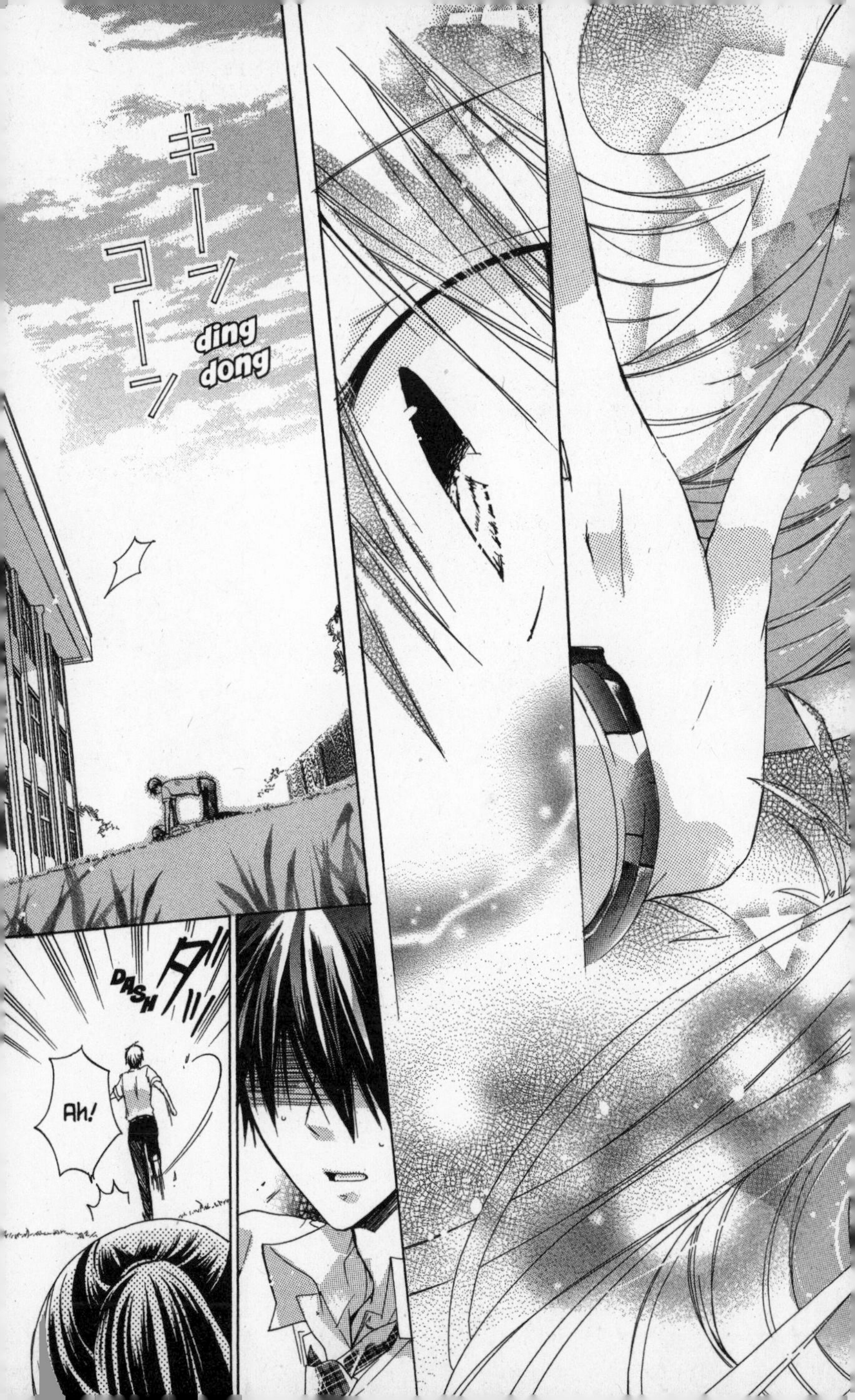
キーン
コーン
ding dong
DASH
Ah!

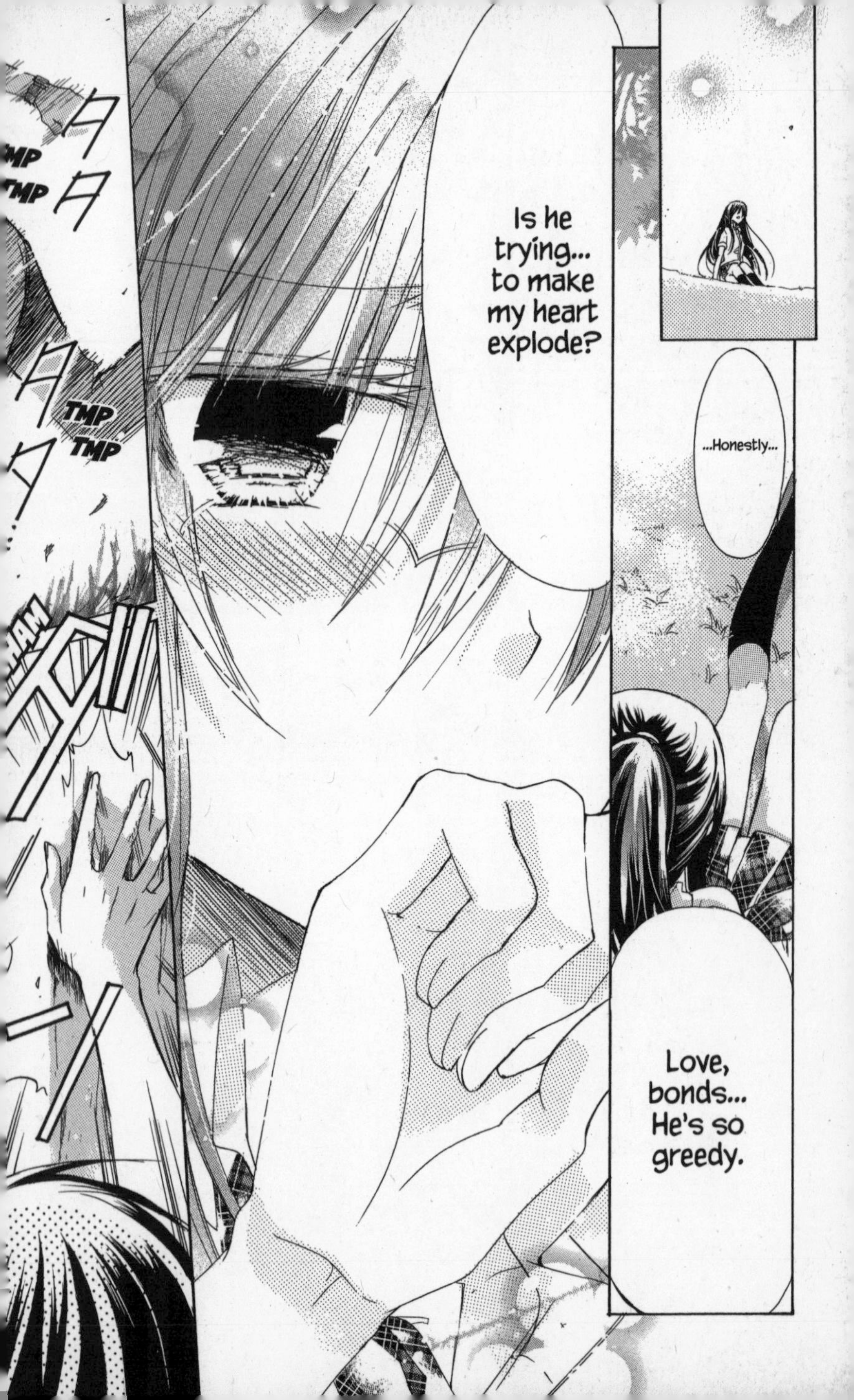
...Honestly...
Love, bonds... He's so greedy.
Is he trying... to make my heart explode?
TMP
TMP
TMP
TMP

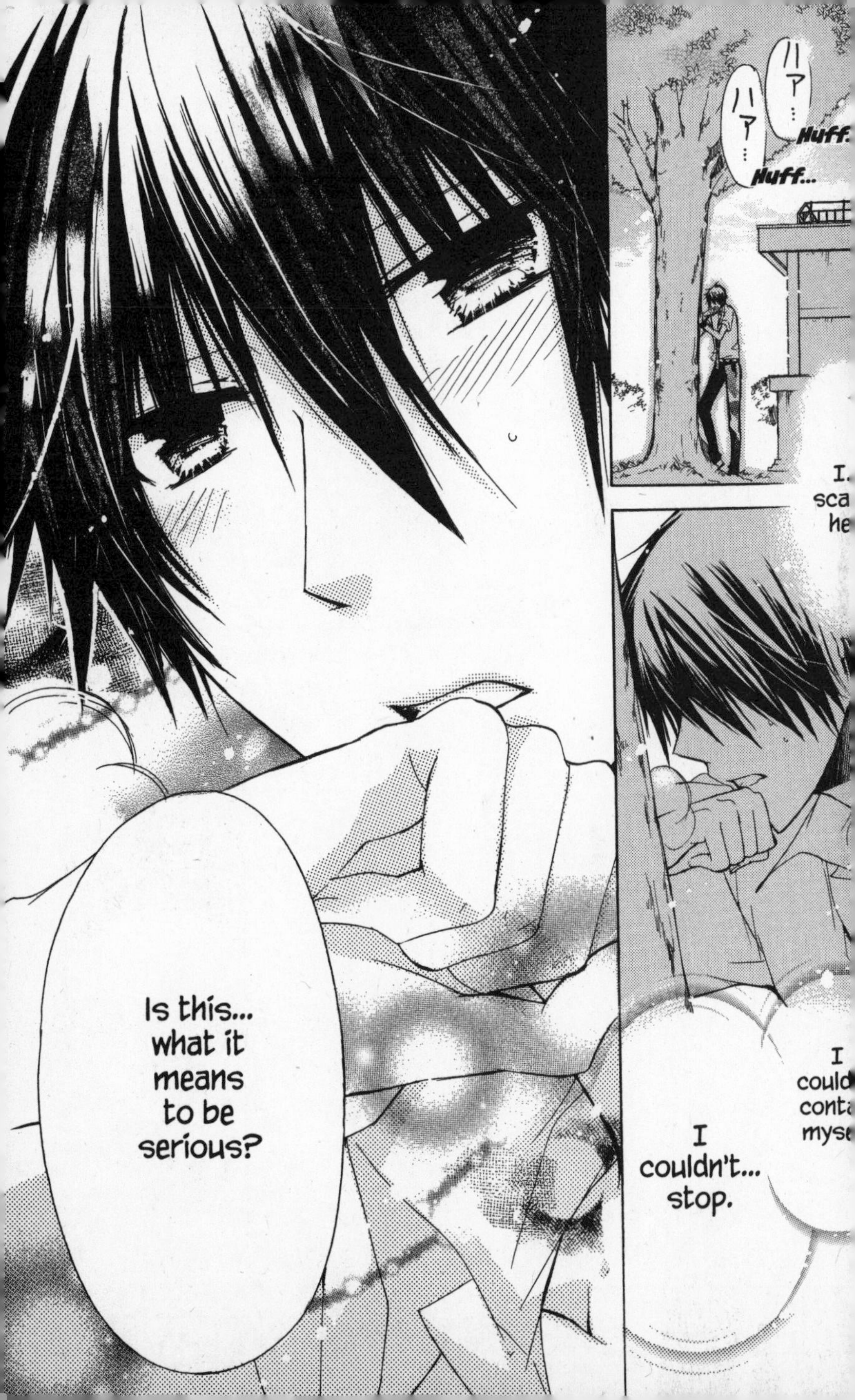
ハア…
ハア…
Huff...
Huff...
I couldn't... stop.
Is this... what it means to be serious?

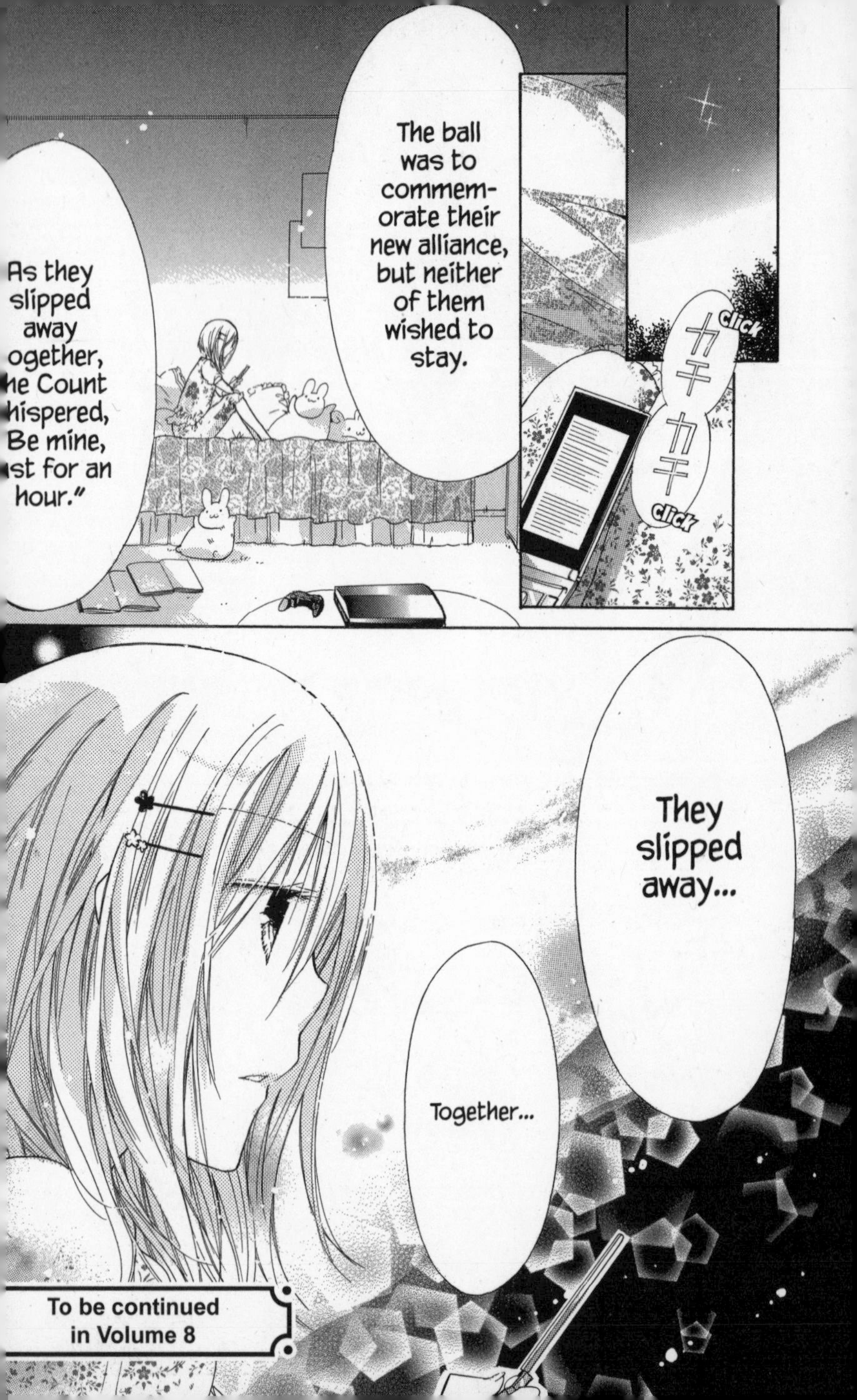
Click
カチ
カチ
Click
The ball was to commemorate their new alliance, but neither of them wished to stay.
As they slipped away ogether, he Count hispered, Be mine, st for an hour."
They slipped away...
Together...
To be continued in Volume 8

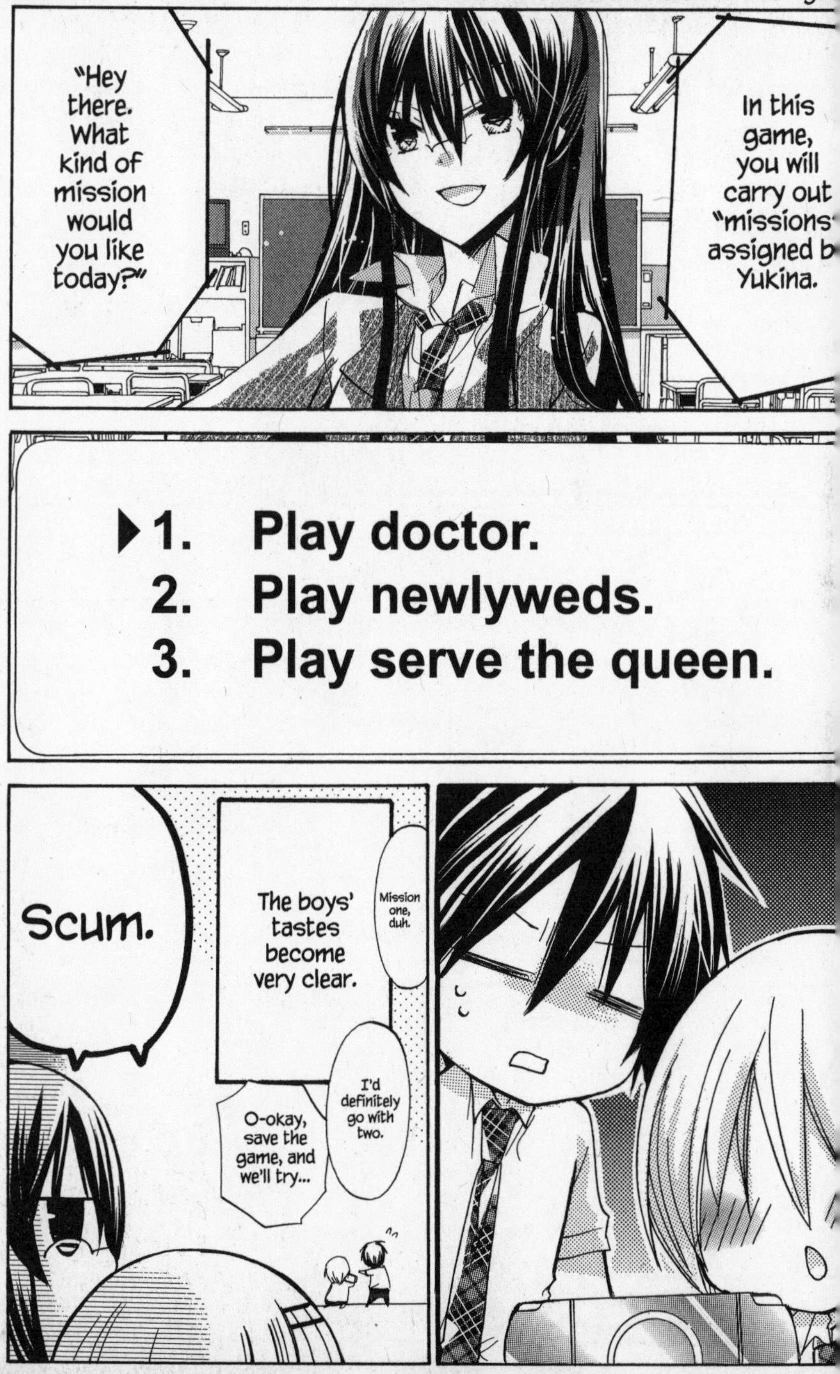
In this game, you will carry out "missions assigned b Yukina.
"Hey there. What kind of mission would you like today?"
1. Play doctor.
2. Play newlyweds.
3. Play serve the queen.
Mission one, duh.
The boys' tastes become very clear.
Scum.
I'd definitely go with two.
O-okay, save the game, and we'll try...

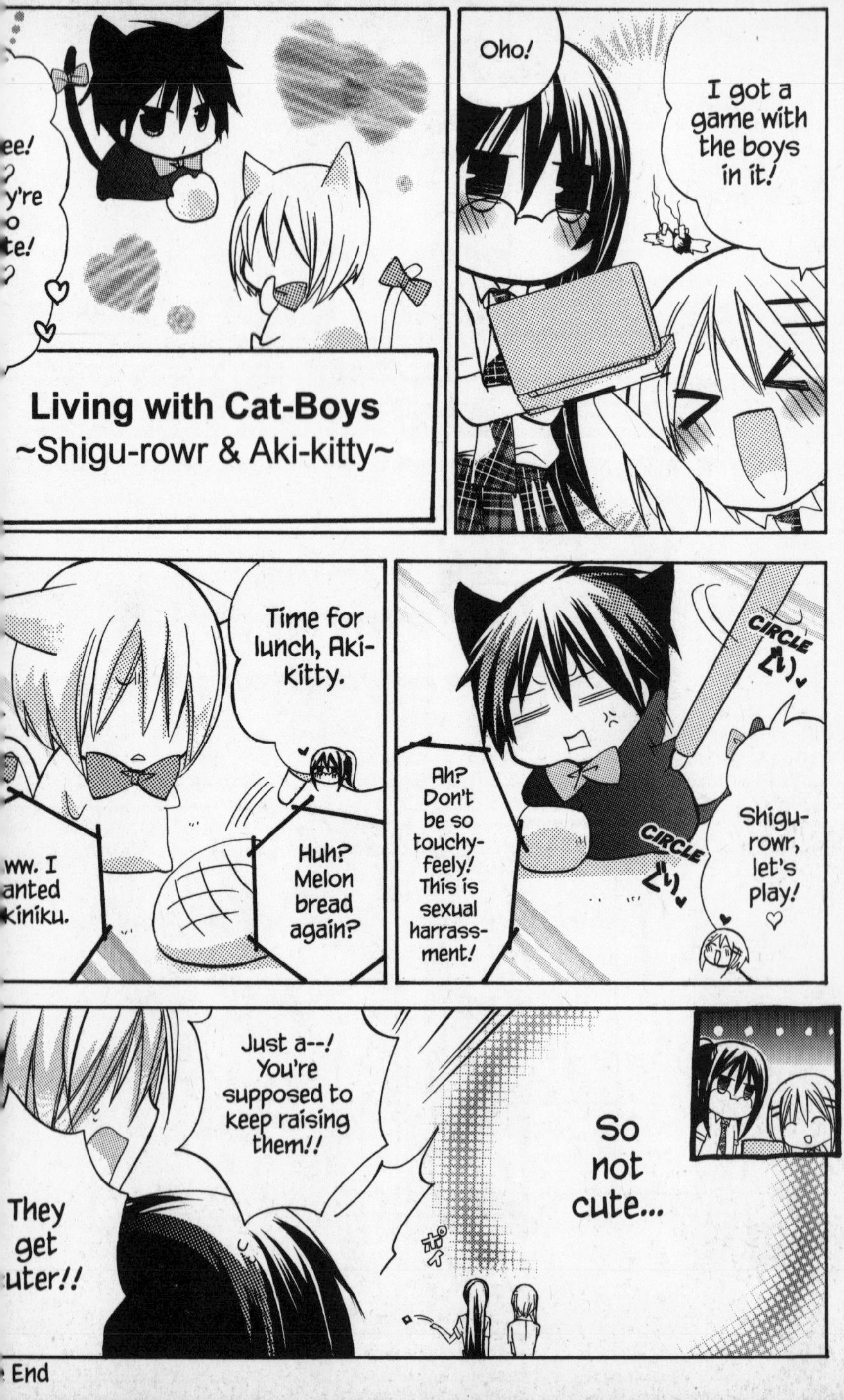
Oho!
I got a game with the boys in it!
ee!
y're
o
te!
Living with Cat-Boys
~Shigu-rowr & Aki-kitty~
Shigu-rowr, let's play!
CIRCLE
CIRCLE
Ah? Don't be so touchy-feely! This is sexual harrass-ment!
Time for lunch, Aki-kitty.
Huh? Melon bread again?
ww. I anted kiniku.
So not cute...
Just a--! You're supposed to keep raising them!!
They get uter!!
End

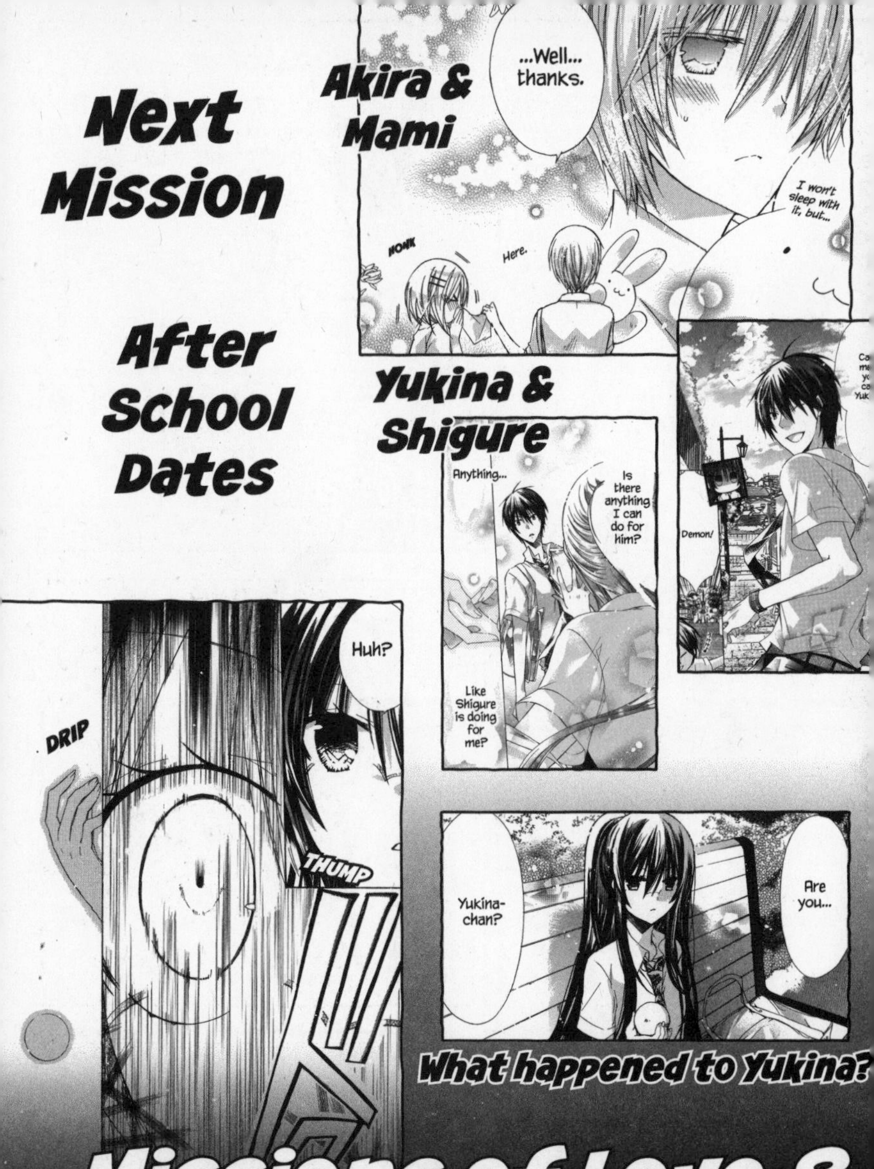
Next Mission
After School Dates
Akira & Mami
...Well... thanks.
I won't sleep with it, but...
Here.
HONK
Yukina & Shigure
Demon!
Is there anything I can do for him?
Anything...
Like Shigure is doing for me?
Are you...
Yukina-chan?
Huh?
THUMP
DRIP
What happened to Yukina?

Missions of Love 8 Coming soon!

And...
Limited Edition with Drama CD!! (Japan only)

①

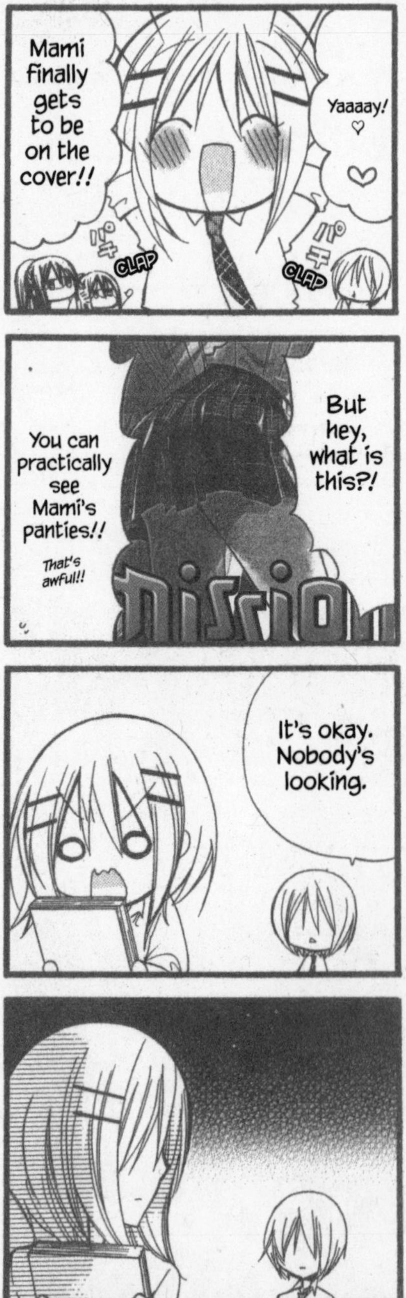

Mami finally gets to be on the cover!!
Yaaaay! ♡
CLAP
CLAP
But hey, what is this?!
You can practically see Mami's panties!!
That's awful!!
It's okay. Nobody's looking.

②

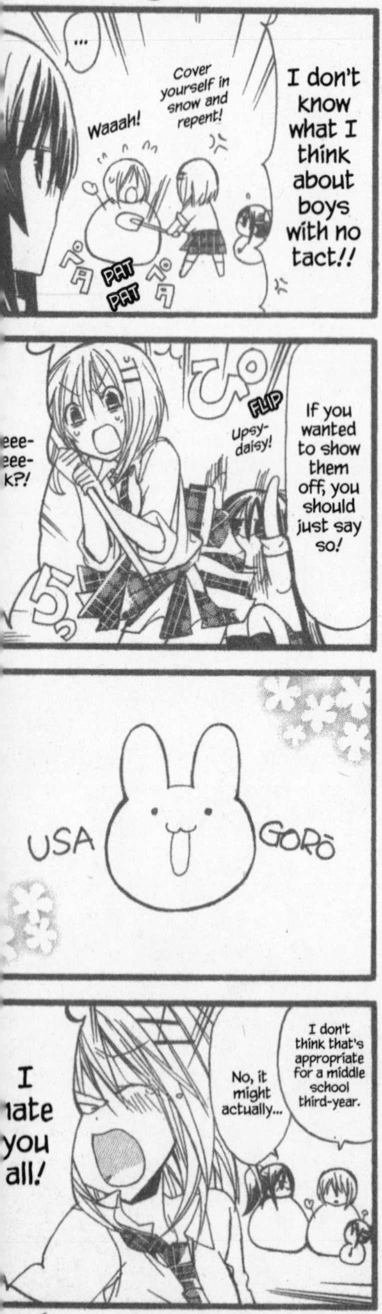

I don't know what I think about boys with no tact!!
Cover yourself in snow and repent!
Waaah!
...
PAT PAT
If you wanted to show them off, you should just say so!
FLIP
Upsy-daisy!
eee-eee-k?!
USA GORŌ
I don't think that's appropriate for a middle school third-year.
No, it might actually...
I hate you all!

I'm not even in this bit.

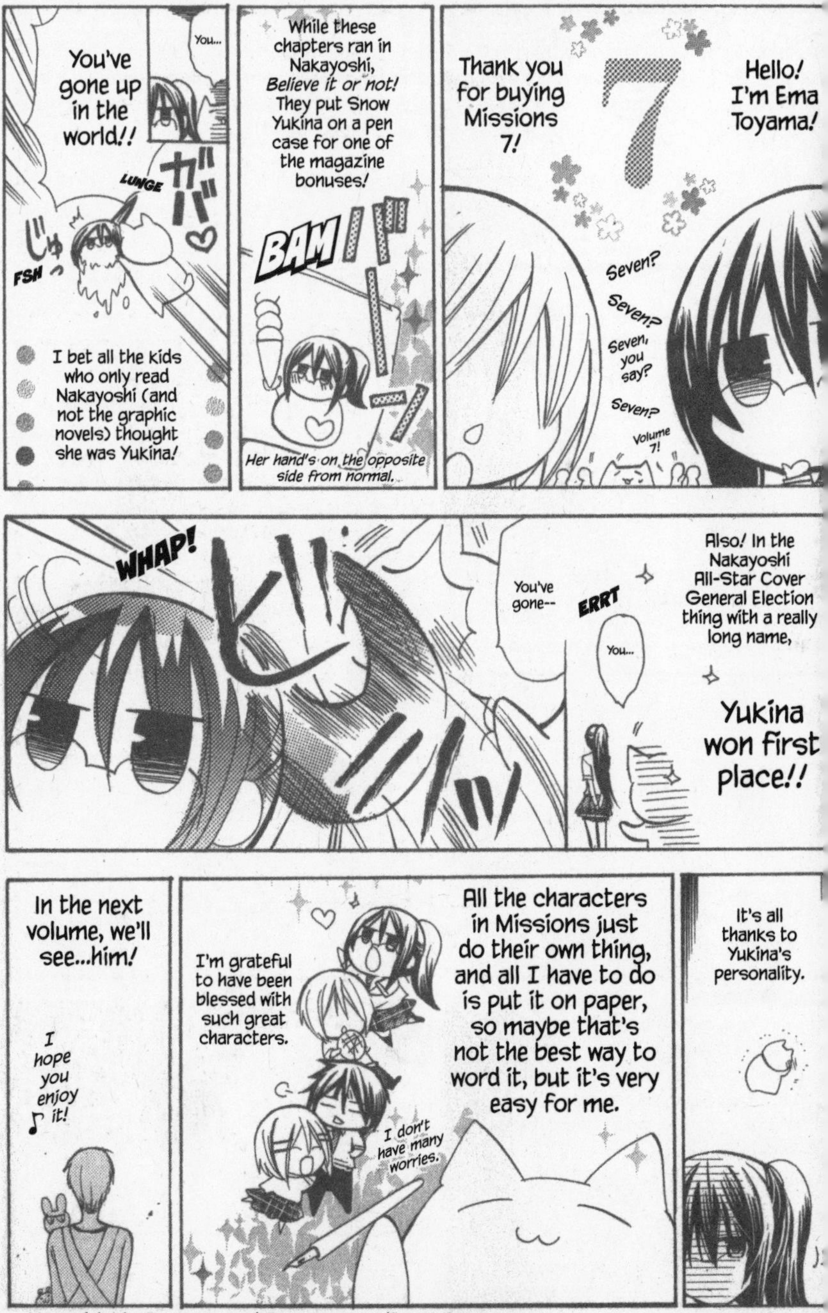
Hello! I'm Ema Toyama!
Thank you for buying Missions 7!
7
Seven?
Seven?
Seven, you say?
Seven?
Volume 7!
While these chapters ran in Nakayoshi, *Believe it or not!* They put Snow Yukina on a pen case for one of the magazine bonuses!
BAM
Her hand's on the opposite side from normal.
You've gone up in the world!!
You...
LUNGE
FSH
I bet all the kids who only read Nakayoshi (and not the graphic novels) thought she was Yukina!
Also! In the Nakayoshi All-Star Cover General Election thing with a really long name,
Yukina won first place!!
You...
ERRT
You've gone--
WHAP!
It's all thanks to Yukina's personality.
All the characters in Missions just do their own thing, and all I have to do is put it on paper, so maybe that's not the best way to word it, but it's very easy for me.
I'm grateful to have been blessed with such great characters.
I don't have many worries.
In the next volume, we'll see...him!
I hope you enjoy it! ♪

My assistants Ryo-sama and Zo-sama, my editor N-jima-sama

Translation Notes

apanese is a tricky language for most Westerners, and translation is often more art than cience. For your edification and reading pleasure, here are notes on some of the places here we could have gone in a different direction with our translation of the work, or where a Japanese cultural reference is used.

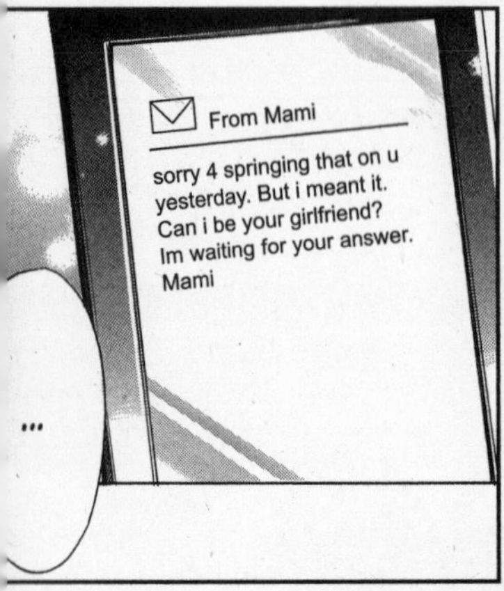
From Mami
sorry 4 springing that on u yesterday. But i meant it. Can i be your girlfriend? Im waiting for your answer. Mami
...

Can I be your girlfriend?, page 24
[24.4]
Japanese is a language known for its vagueness, always implying things without saying them. Technically, Mami didn't come out and ask if she could be Shigure's girlfriend—she only said, "I like you, and I want an answer." But without a question, it might come across as very odd in English to have them talking about answers. Confessing one's love in Japan, or at least in manga, is often the same as asking someone out for the first time: "I like you, so let's go out and see how it works." And so the phrase "I like you" is pretty much the same as asking the question, "Can I be your girlfriend?"

sagoro, page 53
3.3]
e character Usagoro's name is a le less original than it may seem. In panese, the word for rabbit is usagi, d Goro is a fairly common boy's name. ombine them and you have a great, if mewhat obvious, name for a rabbit. cidentally, the Japanese name for kina's favorite character—the snow nny—is yuki-usagi.

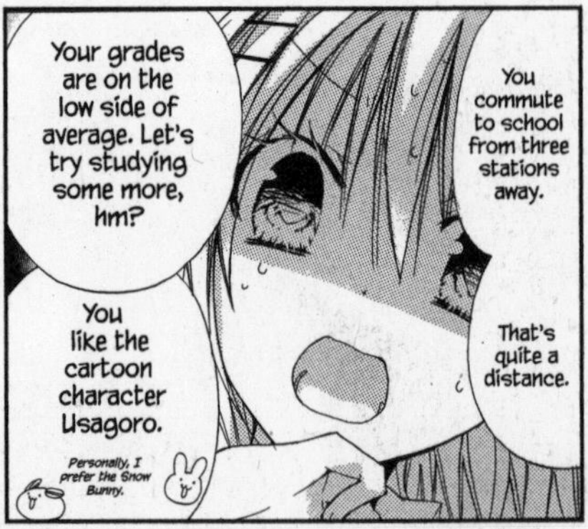
You commute to school from three stations away.
Your grades are on the low side of average. Let's try studying some more, hm?
That's quite a distance.
You like the cartoon character Usagoro.
Personally, I prefer the Snow Bunny.

Say I Love You.

KC KODANSH COMICS

Mei Tachibana has no friends — and says she doesn't need them!

But everything changes when she accidentally roundhouse kicks the most popular boy in school! However, Yamato Kurosawa isn't angry in the slightest— in fact, he thinks his ordinary life could use an unusual girl like Mei. But winning Mei's trust will be a tough task. How long will she refuse to say, "I love you"?

My Little Monster

OPPOSITES ATTRACT...MAYBE?

aru Yoshida is feared as an unstable and violent "monster."
izutani Shizuku is a grade-obsessed student with no friends.
ate brings these two together to form the most unlikely pair. Haru
rmly believes he's in love with Mizutani and she firmly believes
e's insane.

KC
KODANSHA
COMICS

SHERLOCK BONES

DEDUCTIVE DOG DETECTIVE

When Takeru adopts a new pet, he's in for a surprise—the dog is none other than the reincarnation of Sherlock Holmes. With no one else able to communicate with Holmes, Takeru is roped into becoming Sherdog's assistant, John Watson. Using his sleuthing skills, Holmes uncovers clues to solve the trickiest crimes.

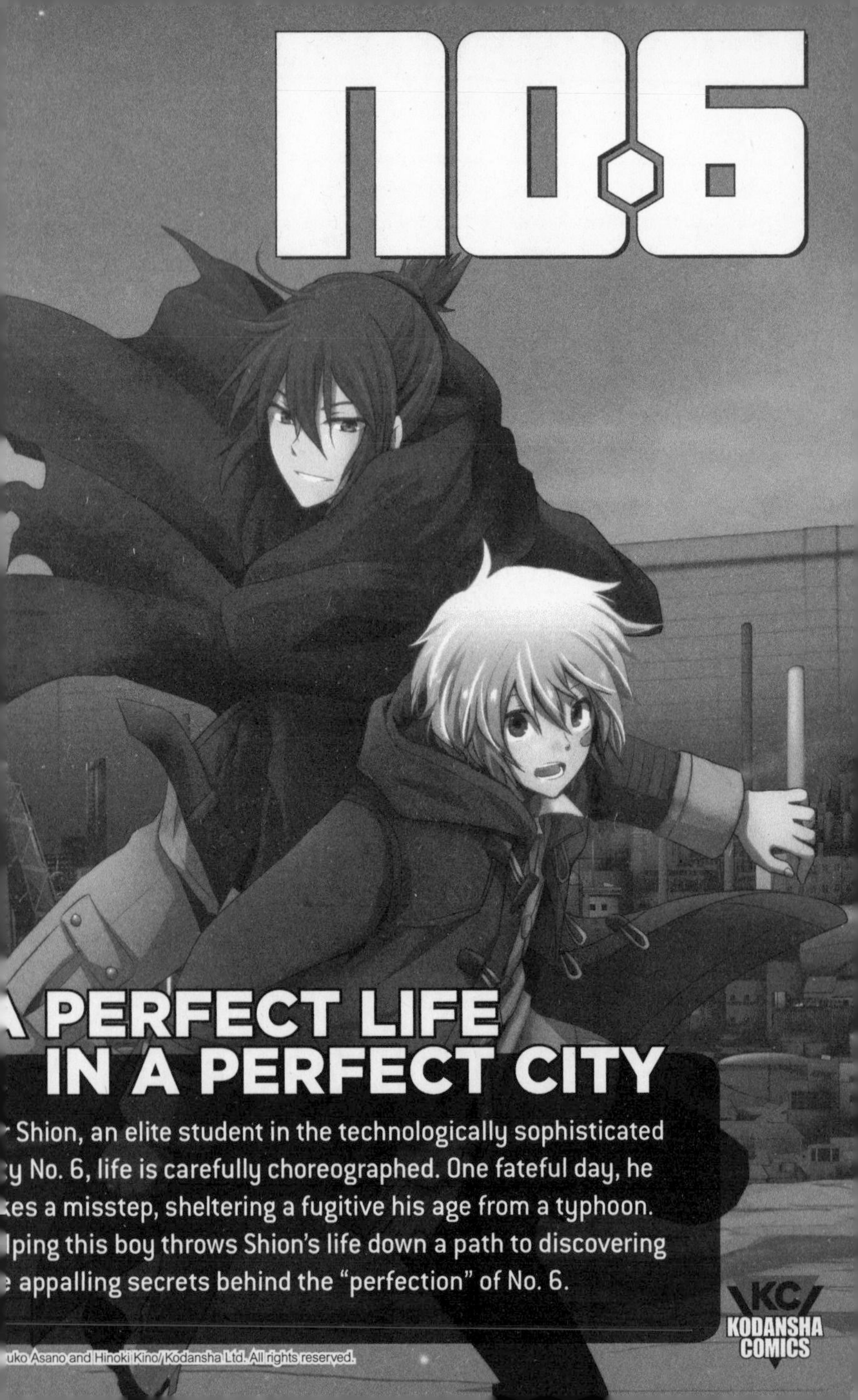
NO.6
A PERFECT LIFE
IN A PERFECT CITY
Shion, an elite student in the technologically sophisticated
y No. 6, life is carefully choreographed. One fateful day, he
kes a misstep, sheltering a fugitive his age from a typhoon.
lping this boy throws Shion's life down a path to discovering
e appalling secrets behind the "perfection" of No. 6.
KC
KODANSHA COMICS
uko Asano and Hinoki Kino/ Kodansha Ltd. All rights reserved.

Missions of Love volume 7 is a work of fiction. Names, characters, places, and incidents are the products of the author's imagination or are used fictitiously. Any resemblance to actual events, locales, or persons, living or dead, is entirely coincidental.

A Kodansha Comics Trade Paperback Original.

Published in the United States by Kodansha Comics, an imprint of Kodansha USA Publishing, LLC, New York.

Publication rights for this English edition arranged through Kodansha Ltd., Tokyo.

First published in Japan in 2011 by Kodansha Ltd., Tokyo, as *Watashi ni xx shinasai!*, volume 7.

ISBN 978-1-61262-289-7

Printed in the United States of America.

www.kodanshacomics.com

9 8 7 6 5 4 3 2 1

Translator: Alethea Nibley and Athena Nibley
Lettering: Paige Pumphrey

Mission 0:
Go Right to Left.

Japanese manga is written and drawn from right to left, which is opposite the way American graphic novels are composed. To preserve the original orientation of the art, and maintain the proper storytelling flow, this book has retained the right to left structure. Please go to what would normally be the last page and begin reading, right to left, top to bottom.